MODERN SPANISH SYNTAX

MODERN SPANISH SYNTAX

A Study in Contrast

YOLANDA R. SOLÉ / CARLOS A. SOLÉ

The University of Texas at Austin

D. C. HEATH AND COMPANY   Lexington, Massachusetts   Toronto

*To Carlitos, whose patience and
ability to entertain himself
made in part this book possible.*

PREFACE

Modern Spanish Syntax: A Study in Contrast is not a review grammar in the strict sense of the word. To review implies to go over what one already knows or is familiar with. The aim of this book is broader. It is an attempt to offer both the advanced student and the prospective and the current teacher a grammar which, while giving them the opportunity to test or synthesize their hypotheses about Spanish, will further their understanding of the language by bringing to their conscious awareness the contrasts that govern it.

We all know that people within a given speech community interact verbally, not in direct imitation of each other, but by learning to make the set of phonological and grammatical contrasts observed by other speakers. Although the significance of this axiom that language is a *system of contrasts* has not been overlooked throughout the years of foreign-language teaching, neither has it been specifically nor systematically emphasized within this sphere.

The notion of contrast within pedagogical contexts has been primarily associated with contrastive approaches *between* the target and source languages, rather than with the applicability of this notion *within* the target language itself. While we are far from disclaiming the actual and potential usefulness such contrastive approaches have, we nevertheless believe that concept attainment of the contrasts existent within the target language itself is far more essential and productive. A solely contrastive approach between source and target language, which for reasons of brevity and simplicity must always sacrifice some of the self-contained cohesiveness of each linguistic system, is far less likely to lead to a vision of the target language in its totality. We believe that it is only when the focus is on the contrasts within the target language itself, when the foreign-language learner can see the relationship of a part to the whole, that he will cease to perceive the grammatical rules of the foreign language as a collection of arbitrary statements, or arbitrary departures from his dominant or mother-tongue language. This is not a denial of the fact that the second-language learner brings to the learning situation a well-established set of rules, which at times enhances, and at others hinders, the learning of a different set of new linguistic rules. We acknowledge that an awareness of the contrasts that exist between Spanish and English will facilitate the learning task, and that some provision for these contrasts must also be made. Consequently, we incorporate within this book those contrasts between Spanish and English that theory and classroom practice have taught us to be useful in mastering Spanish.

Our emphasis, which is on the contrasts that exist within Spanish itself, and the awareness of the differences that exist between Spanish and English, accounts for the somewhat different order of presentation of certain grammatical topics as compared to that of other Spanish grammars. For example, Chapter 4 on Progressive Constructions precedes Chapter 5, which deals with The Simple Tenses of the Indicative: Preterit and Imperfect. Chapter 8 on Relative Pronouns precedes Chapter 12, which treats The Subjunctive and Indicative in Relative Clauses. Chapter 15, on **Ser** and **Estar**, follows Chapters 13 and 14, which deal with Nouns and Nominalizations and Adjectives, respectively. And since the most problematic areas for the English-speaker who studies Spanish center around those of the verbal and pronominal categories, these are presented in the first half of the book.

We have aimed at making this book a reasonably comprehensive study of Spanish syntax. Thus, we have not dealt only with those structures that are most productive in daily communication situations, but also with those items found in writings, which the advanced student of Spanish must know passively, if not actively, in order to handle literary and journalistic prose. To illustrate the grammatical explanations given, every effort has been made to offer culturally viable and vivid examples of current idiomatic and formal usage which occur in both oral and written language.

We hope that this book will be both appealing and meaningful to prospective and current language teachers, to advanced students of language and literature, and to American students of Spanish origin. Both teacher and student alike may wish or need to formulate certain generalizations about Spanish syntax, in order to self-regulate their speech or writing, or to regulate that of others. We also hope that it may prove useful for those students of literary texts who may find it necessary to differentiate—and to be able to verbalize the differences—between what is most habitual and what responds to a special sort of choice in a given writer's style.

Our own students in language courses, and in courses of Spanish syntax and style, have convinced us of the need for a book along the lines we have developed. We thank them for the inspiration they have provided us. We also wish to express our debt to our colleagues Lee Fontanella and Vicente Cantarino, who were always willing to answer endless questions regarding our hypotheses about English and Spanish respectively; and to all the linguists who as teachers or writers have sharpened our insights. Finally, we would like to acknowledge our appreciation to the staff of the Modern Language Department of D. C. Heath and Company for their valuable cooperation in bringing this work to fruition.

Y. R. S.
C. A. S.

CONTENTS

Chapter 3   **Pronouns: Personal, Object, Prepositional, and Neuter**

Chapter 4   **Progressive Constructions**

Chapter 7   **The Infinitive, the Gerund and the Past Participle**

Chapter 11   **Subjunctive and Indicative in Nominal Clauses**

Chapter 12   **Subjunctive and Indicative in Conditional, Relative, and Independent Clauses**

Chapter 13   **Nouns and Nominalization**

MODERN SPANISH SYNTAX

1

SIMPLE TENSES OF THE INDICATIVE: PRESENT, FUTURE, AND CONDITIONAL

The Present Tense

The notion of grammatical present does not refer only to the time co-existent with the moment of utterance, the actual here and now. The present tense is also used to express a time of indefinite duration which, in relation to the act of speech, may include present, past, and future dimensions and which may be considered an extended present. For these reasons, the present tense may be used in Spanish to describe (1) ongoing events at the moment of utterance; (2) repeated or continued events; (3) the existence of states and conditions, of a short or lasting duration; (4) future time or intent; and (5) actions begun in a prior dimension which are ongoing within the present. Whether the present describes an ongoing event, habitual actions not necessarily in progress at the time in question, future events, or actions begun in the past which are still in progress, depends largely upon the manner of the action, that is, the intrinsic nature of the event itself and/or its total context.

Although the present tenses of both Spanish and English have, by and large, equivalent functions, there are also important differences. The use of the English present is more limited as compared to Spanish. As a rule, the English present does not express a definite reference to simultaneity with now or this very moment; it does not express a future perspective in the sense of being able to refer to subsequent events; and it is not used for events begun in the past which are still in progress at present. Therefore, depending on the context, the Spanish simple present can correspond to the English present, present progressive, future, present perfect, or present perfect progressive tense.

SPANISH   ENGLISH

Present Tense

ONGOING EVENTS AT TIME
OF UTTERANCE

Present Progressive

Socorro, que se ahoga Cecilia.   *Help, Cecilia is drowning.*
La vida se le escapa.   *His life is slipping away.*

REPEATED OR CONTINUED ACTIONS

Present

Se ven a diario.   *They see each other daily.*
Estudian mucho.   *They study very hard.*

STATES OF BEING AND CONDITIONS,
SHORT OR LASTING

Present

No está en casa.   *He is not home.*
El Perú está situado en el hemisferio   *Peru is located in the Southern*
   sur.   *Hemisphere.*

FUTURE TIME OR INTENT

Future or Present Progressive

Vengo a las siete. $\begin{cases} \textit{I will come at seven.} \\ \textit{I am coming at seven.} \end{cases}$

Te llamo más tarde. $\begin{cases} \textit{I will call you later.} \\ \textit{I will be calling you later.} \end{cases}$

EVENTS BEGUN IN A PRIOR DIMENSION
AND STILL IN PROGRESS

Present Perfect/
Present Perfect Progressive

La conoce desde hace años.   *He has known her for years.*
Lo sabe desde la semana pasada.   *He has known it since last week.*
Trabaja allí desde enero.   *He has been working there since January.*

ACTUAL AND EXTENDED PRESENT CONTRASTED

The present may describe an action which is in progress at the time of the utterance coinciding with now or this very moment. It may describe habitual or subsequent events. In most instances the meaning being conveyed depends upon the nature of the event itself, the actual speech situation, and/or the linguistic context.

1. When the meaning of the verb refers to a conclusive event—one that must be terminated in order to be completed—ongoingness, subsequence, or habitual repetition can be conveyed. The speech situation or total context indicates which reading applies.

Ongoingness	*Habitual Repetition*	*Subsequence*
¿A dónde vas? *Where are you going?*	Va al cine todos los días. *He goes to the movies every day.*	Voy más tarde. *I will go later.*
Veo que llega solo. *I see that he is coming alone.*	Siempre llega tarde. *He always arrives late.*	Llega mañana. *He will arrive (is arriving) tomorrow.*
Calla porque viene Pedro. *Be quiet because Pedro is coming.*	Viene todas las tardes. *He comes every afternoon.*	Viene hoy a las cuatro. *He will come (is coming) today at four.*

2. When the meaning of the verb refers to a non-conclusive event, one that is durative in itself, either ongoingness or a habitually continued process may be described, depending upon the context. Subsequence or future time is less often expressed with these verbs.

Ongoingness	*Habituality*
(On the phone) ¿Con quién hablo? *With whom am I talking?*	Siempre le habla en español al niño. *She always talks to the child in Spanish.*
No quiero molestarlo porque ahora duerme. *I don't want to bother him because he is sleeping now.*	No quiero molestarlo cuando duerme. *I don't want to bother him when he sleeps.*
¿Qué sucede ahora, por qué lloras? *What is happening now, why are you crying?*	Nunca llora cuando algo le sucede. *He never cries when something happens to him.*
Trato de entender lo que me dices pero no puedo. *I am trying to understand what you are saying, but I cannot.*	Trato de entender cuando me hablas, pero no puedo. *I try to understand when you talk to me, but I cannot.*

OTHER USES OF THE EXTENDED PRESENT

In addition to the habitual present, which in Spanish is signaled by the context and/or adverbials of repetition and manner:

Se ven diariamente.	*They see each other daily.*
No se cansa nunca.	*He never tires.*
Se expresa muy bien.	*He expresses himself very well.*

other uses of the extended present exist which may or may not coincide with English usage.

1. Atemporal present

The temporal present describes states and conditions of a temporary or durative nature and current truths which have had indefinite extension in time.

Está enfermo.	*He is sick.*
La tierra está rodeada de mares.	*The earth is surrounded by seas.*
El hombre es mortal.	*Man is mortal.*
La poesía, dice Aristóteles, se basa en dos instintos del hombre: el instinto de imitación y el instinto de armonía.	*Poetry, says Aristotle, rests upon two instincts in man: the instinct of imitation and the instinct of harmony.*
De acuerdo a Freud, una obra de arte exterioriza la realidad inconsciente e interna de su autor.	*According to Freud, a work of art exteriorizes the unconscious inner reality of its author.*

2. Narrative present

The narrative present, used in literary writings, recreates in the here and now past or habitually-repeated events. It also describes ongoing actions. While the narrative present recreating past or habitual events is equally common in Spanish and English epics and poetry, the usage of the present to describe ongoing events, particularly in contemporary fiction, is by far more common in Spanish than in English narratives.

«¡Quién viene por la tarde tañendo su laúd sobre las nubes, como dentro de su morada!»	*Who is advancing through the evening playing his lute upon the clouds, as if in his own dwelling place?*
«¡Quién lo taña que vuelve las hojas de los árboles!»	*Who is playing til he turns the leaves over the trees?*
Molinari, *Oda*	
«¿... Qué dicen? Un silencio con hedores reposa...»	*What are they saying? A stenching silence settles down ...*
«...¿Quién arruga el sudario? ¡No es verdad lo que dice!»	*Who is creasing the shroud? What he is saying is not true!*

«Aquí no canta nadie, ni llora en el rincón, ni pica las espuelas, ni espanta la serpiente...»
García Lorca, *Llanto por la muerte de Ignacio Sánchez Mejías*

Nobody is singing here, or weeping in the corner, or pricking his spurs, or frightening the snake...

«El sargento echa una ojeada a la Madre Patrocinio y el moscardón sigue allí. La lancha cabecea sobre las aguas turbias, entre dos murallas de árboles que exhalan un vaho quemante, pegajoso. Ovillados bajo el pamacari, desnudos de la cintura para arriba, los guardias duermen abrigados por el verdoso, amarillento sol del mediodía: la cabeza del Chiquito yace sobre el vientre del Pesado, el Rubio transpira a chorros, el Oscuro gruñe con la boca abierta...» «...El motor ronca parejo, se atora, ronca y el práctico Nieves lleva el timón con la izquierda, con la derecha fuma...»
Vargas Llosa, *La Casa Verde*

The sergeant takes a look at Sister Patrocinio and the botfly is still there. The launch is pitching on the muddy waters, between two walls of trees that give off a burning, sticky mist. Huddled under the canopy, stripped to the waist, the soldiers are asleep, with the greenish, yellowish noonday sun above: Shorty's head is lying on Fat's stomach, Blondy is breathing in short bursts, Blacky has his mouth open and is grunting...... ...The motor is snoring evenly, it chokes, it snores, and Nieves the pilot is holding the rudder in his left hand as he uses his right to smoke with...
(Translation by Gregory Rabasa)

3. Present tense with future perspective

The present may be used instead of the future tense in the following cases:

a. With verbs of non-durative or instantaneous action, particularly with verbs of motion: **entrar**, **salir**, **venir**, etc. But it is also used with other verbs in informal speech situations. An adverbial indicating posteriority generally co-occurs.

Salen la próxima semana.
They are leaving next week.

¿Vienes esta noche?
Are you coming tonight?

Te veo más tarde.
{ *I will see you later.*
{ *I will be seeing you later.*

Se casan el sábado.
{ *They will get married on Saturday.*
{ *They are getting married on Saturday.*

b. In **ir a** + INF constructions, equivalent to the English construction *to be going to* + INF:

Vamos a visitarla esta tarde.
We are going to call on her this afternoon.

Vamos a cenar afuera.
We are going to eat out.

c. With the verb **querer** when actual will or willingness is described, referring either to the present moment or to the immediate future. It corresponds to the English verb *will*:

¿Quieres tomar algo?	*Will you have something to eat?*
¿Quieres ir conmigo?	*Will you come with me?*
No quiere verme.	*He won't see me.*

d. In commands, when the speech situation is an informal one:

Vas (=irás) allá y le dices (=dirás) que te han engañado; y entonces, reclamas (=reclamarás) tus derechos.	*You go (=will go) there and tell (=will tell) them that you have been deceived; and then you claim (=will claim) your rights.*

In informal speech situations the present tense is not only more common in all of the above cases, but it is actually prefered over the future.

There are other instances where a future perspective is definitely implied and Spanish also uses the present tense instead of the future:

a. With verbs of volition, need, and desire, which are durative in themselves and as such refer not only to the here and now but also to a future dimension:

Pienso contárselo todo.	*I intend to tell him everything.*
Anhelo conocerla.	*I am anxious to meet her.*
Necesito verlo.	*I need to see him.*
Espero mejorarme.	*I expect to get well.*

b. In interrogative statements asking for permission and direction, which in English are rendered by *shall*:

¿Le digo que pase?	*Shall I tell him to come in?*
¿Compro el periódico o no?	*Shall I buy the newspaper or not?*
¿A dónde pongo las flores?	*Where shall I put the flowers?*
¿A dónde nos encontramos?	*Where shall we meet?*

c. In *if*-clauses stating conditions when the fulfillment of the condition is viewed as probable, as opposed to the use of the imperfect subjunctive which implies that the condition is more hypothetical, less likely to be fulfilled:

Si el médico no llega a tiempo se morirá.	*If the doctor does not get here on time, he will die.*
Si te vas, te va a extrañar mucho.	*If you leave, he is going to miss you very much.*
BUT:	
Si te fueras, te extrañaría mucho.	*If you left, he would miss you very much.*

4. Present tense for past actions

The present tense may be used in Spanish for past actions under the following circumstances:

a. For repeated or continued events begun in the past which are still ongoing within the present. This use of the present tense with indicators of continuity such as **hace ... que** and **desde ...** is equivalent in English to the present perfect progressive, or to the present perfect if the verb is one of inner life:

Hace cuatro años que vivimos aquí.	*We have been living here for four years.*
Estudia música desde la niñez.	*He has been studying music since his childhood.*
La conozco desde hace años.	*I have known her for years.*

b. For completed actions within the actual present. These are expressed through the construction **acabar de** + INF. It is equivalent in English to *to have just* + past participle:

Acaba de volver.	*He has just returned.*
Acaban de firmar un nuevo contrato.	*They have just signed a new contract.*
Acaba de llamarme.	*She has just called me.*

c. For past occurrences which were not completed. In this case the present always co-occurs with **casi** or **por poco**. English uses the past tense with *almost* or *nearly*:

Por poco se muere.	*He nearly died.*
Casi lo atropella un auto.	*A car almost hit him.*
Casi se me olvida decirte lo más importante.	*I almost forgot to tell you the most important thing.*

The Future Tense

The notion of future, grammatically speaking, responds to a concept of subsequence or posteriority in relation to a given point. The simple future describes an anticipated event as posterior to the grammatical present. The event may take place either in the mediate or immediate future, which explains why in this latter case the present may be substituted for the future as it overlaps with the extended present itself. Since the notion of subsequence refers to anticipated events, which are possible, probable, but far from certain, by extension the future has acquired several other uses.

USES OF THE FUTURE

The Spanish future corresponds to the English auxiliaries *will* and *shall*, which have basically the same functions. It is used as follows:

1. To predict or anticipate the occurrence of an event:

El tratado se firmará el mes entrante.	*The treaty will be signed next month.*
La conferencia tendrá lugar en el auditorio.	*The lecture will take place in the auditorium.*
Hablarán profesores muy distinguidos.	*Very distinguished professors will speak.*

2. To describe the intent to act:

Vendré mañana por la tarde.	*I will arrive tomorrow afternoon.*
Trataremos de conseguir entradas.	*We will try to get tickets.*
Te explicaré la importancia del asunto.	*I will explain to you the importance of the issue.*

3. To express the determination or the will to act:

Lo haré, venga lo que venga.	*I will do it, come what may.*
Nos casaremos a pesar de toda oposición.	*We will get married despite any opposition.*
Tendrás el dinero, te lo prometo.	*You shall have the money, I promise.*

4. To express a command. (By extension of the meaning of obligation or determination to act, the future functions as a command when it is used in the second person.)

No matarás.	*Thou shall not kill.*
Harás lo que te digo sin protestar.	*You shall do what I tell you without protesting.*
Irás a verlo y le comunicarás nuestra decisión.	*You shall go to him and inform him of our decision.*

5. To express conjecture:

   As a result of the fact that future events are possible, probable, but not certain, the future tense is also used to express conjecture about an ongoing or future event. Whether probability about such events is expressed cannot always be determined from the sentence alone, but must be derived from the total context. While the usage of the future expressing conjecture is a productive one in Spanish, in English it is rare. Conjecture in English is rendered by lexical paraphrases or the modal auxiliaries *must* and *should*.

¿Qué hora será?	*What time do you suppose it is?*
—Serán las ocho.	*—It must (should) be eight o'clock.*
¿Qué hará ahora?	*{ What do you suppose he is doing now? { What do you suppose he will do now?*
¿Será ésta la clave?	*Will this be the clue?*
¿Qué interés tendrá en ocultarte la verdad?	*What interest can he have in hiding the truth from you?*

6. To describe concession:

By extension of the meaning of probability, the future is also used to describe concession. In this case it is rendered in English by *might*.

Será indiscreto, pero nunca es mal intencionado.	*He might be indiscreet, but he never means any harm.*
Él será muy antipático, pero es muy eficiente.	*He might not be very personable, but he is very efficient.*

7. To express coexistent future actions:

The future may be used for two or more co-existent actions in coordinate sentences.

Yo hablaré y tú escucharás.	*I will speak and you will listen.*
Estudiarás y trabajarás como hacen todos.	*You will study and work as everybody else does.*

In subordinate sentences, on the other hand, the future cannot be used twice for simultaneous or co-existent future events. One of them is expressed by the present subjunctive.[1]

Mientras (que) yo hable, tú me escucharás.	*While I speak, you will listen.*
Me levantaré cuando den las doce.	*I will get up when the clock strikes twelve.*
Trabajarás mientras estudies como hacen todos.	*You will work while you study as everybody else does.*

ALTERNATE CONSTRUCTIONS FOR THE FUTURE

Apart from the prospective **ir a** + INF, which has displaced the future tense when intent to act is described, other auxiliaries compete with the future tense in the following instances:

1. When volition or determination to act are expressed, **querer** = *to want* and **pensar** = *to mean to, to intend*, conjugated in the present, are used instead of the future:

Quiero hacerlo, venga lo que venga.	*I want to do it, come what may.*
Pienso casarme tan pronto me gradúe.	*I intend to get married as soon as I graduate.*

2. When obligation or advisability are conveyed, **deber** = *ought to, must* and **tener que** = *to have to* may also be used in the present rather than in the future:

Debes ir a verla.	*You must go to see her.*
Tienes que informarle ya.	*You must (have to) inform her right now.*

[1] See page 152.

The same applies to **haber que** + INF, which is used only impersonally, that is, without specific reference to a definite subject:

Hay que salir temprano.

One should leave early.
We must leave early
One should . . .

The Conditional Tense

The simple future tense, as seen previously, describes an anticipated event as posterior to the grammatical present. The conditional tense, on the other hand, describes an anticipated event as subsequent to the grammatical past. But whereas the future is an absolute tense insofar as it can be used without reference to another event or temporal expression, the conditional is a relative tense. Its usage depends upon a given point of reference, expressed or implied.

The Spanish conditional corresponds to the English auxiliaries *would* and *should* which basically have the same functions.

THE CONDITIONAL AS RETROSPECTIVE FUTURE

1. The conditional is used when subsequence in relation to the grammatical past is expressed. As such, when direct discourse is rewritten into indirect discourse, the conditional occurs in place of the future and it has essentially the same functions as the future. It may be used:

DIRECT DISCOURSE	INDIRECT DISCOURSE

a. To predict or anticipate the occurrence of an event:

El tratado se firmará el mes entrante.

The treaty will be signed next month.

Anunciaron que el tratado se firmaría el mes entrante.

It was announced that the treaty would be signed next month.

b. To describe the intent to act:

Tratarán de conseguir entradas.
They will try to get tickets.

Dijeron que tratarían de conseguir entradas.
They said that they would try to get tickets.

c. To express the determination or the will to act:

Tendrás el dinero.
You shall have the money.

Afirmó que tendría el dinero.
He affirmed that I would have the money.

When the future tense expresses a command, the command cannot be rendered in indirect discourse through the conditional. Depending upon the verb used in indirect discourse to introduce the quote, either a modal auxiliary or the subjunctive should be employed.[1]

DIRECT DISCOURSE	INDIRECT DISCOURSE
Renunciará Ud. ahora mismo. *You shall resign right now.*	Me obligó a que renunciara en ese mismo momento. *He forced me to resign then and there.*
Harás lo que te dicen. *You shall do what you are told.*	Me dijo que hiciera (debería hacer) lo que me decían. *He told me I had to do what I was told.*
No irás a ningún lado. *You will not go anywhere.*	Me contestó que no podía (podría) ir a ningún lado. *He answered I could not go anywhere.*
	No me permitió que fuera a ningún lado. *He did not allow me to go anywhere.*

2. The conditional can also express conjecture in relationship to the grammatical past, just as the future expresses probability in relationship to the grammatical present. Probability in English in this case is also rendered by lexical paraphrases or the auxiliaries *must* and *could*.

¿Qué hora sería cuando regresó su marido?	*What time could it have been when her husband returned?*
¿Sería verdad lo que él decía?	*Could what he was saying be true?*
¿Qué interés tendría en ocultarle la verdad?	*What interest could he possibly have in hiding the truth from her?*
Ella tendría unos veinte años cuando se casó.	*She must have been twenty when she got married.*

THE CONDITIONAL AS HYPOTHETICAL FUTURE

When the conditional does not occur in indirect discourse, it is used in *if*-clauses where it expresses subsequence or future time in relation to a hypothetical situation or condition. The clause stating the condition is called the *if*-clause because a hypothetical, and as such, future action depends upon it. The clause stating the condition may take either the present indicative or the imperfect subjunctive, depending upon the degree of probability attached to its fulfillment. The conclusion, stated in the clause that expresses the potential consequences, may take either the future or the conditional, depending upon the meaning intended.

---

[1] See Subjunctive in Nominal Clauses, page 160.

1. When the *if*-clause takes the present indicative, the future or the conditional may occur in the conclusion. The future describes the determination to act, whereas the conditional states mere probability or contingency.

Si tú vas, yo iré.	*If you go, I will go.*
Si tú vas, yo iría.	*If you go, I would go.*
Si él renuncia, renunciaremos todos.	*If he resigns, all of us will resign.*
Si él renuncia, renunciaríamos todos.	*If he resigns, all of us would resign.*

2. When the *if*-clause takes the imperfect subjunctive, the conclusion can only take the conditional. As before, the conditional states probability.

Si él fuera, yo iría.	*If he goes, I would go.*
Si él renunciara, renunciaríamos todos.	*If he resigns, all of us would resign.*

An *if*-clause containing the imperfect subjunctive is not only used for conditions that are less likely to be fulfilled than those containing the present indicative, but also for contrary-to-fact conditions. Since these clauses may imply negation, the conclusion may also be impossible to fulfill.

Si tuviera tiempo (que no tengo), iría.	*If I had time (which I don't), I would go.*
Como no tengo tiempo no voy.	*As I have no time, I am not going.*

3. The conditional also occurs in sentences without a preceding or following clause stating conditions. This usage may be considered elliptical, the *if*-clause being implied or understood by the speakers. This construction occurs in softened assertions, requests, and suggestions.

Yo no haría eso (si fuera Ud.).	*I would not do that (if I were you).*
¿Me prestarías el dinero (si pudieras)?	*Would you lend me the money (if you could)?*
¿Te molestaría que yo fumara?	*Would it bother you if I smoke?*

THE CONDITIONAL IN RELATION TO OTHER TENSES

Since the main function of the conditional is to express subsequence, this tense does not refer to any specific temporal dimensions but to mere posteriority in relation to a point of reference. The point of reference may either be the grammatical past, or a present/future situation or condition. For these reasons, the conditional can occur with any of the following tenses and adverbials of time:

Me aseguró que vendría hoy.	*He assured me he would come today.*
Me aseguró que vendría ayer.	*He assured me he would come yesterday.*
Me aseguró que vendría mañana.	*He assured me he would come tomorrow.*
Me ha asegurado que vendría hoy.	*He has assured me he would come today.*

Me había asegurado que vendría hoy.	*He had assured me he would come today.*
Me aseguraba que vendría hoy.	*He assured (was assuring) me he would come today.*

In all of the preceding cases "his coming" is subsequent to "his assuring me of it," whether the temporal dimension is past, present, or future.

THE CONDITIONAL CONTRASTED WITH "WOULD" AND "SHOULD"

As seen before, the English auxiliaries *would* and *should* correspond to the Spanish conditional when anticipated events and intent or determination to act are described from a past perspective. There are, however, other uses of *would* and *should* which cannot be rendered in Spanish by the conditional.

1. When *would* denotes will or volition in relation to the grammatical past, **querer** in the preterit or the imperfect, depending upon the context, is its equivalent.

He would never listen to me.	Nunca quiso escucharme.
They would not do it then.	No querían hacerlo entonces.
He would not see her the following day.	No quería verla al día siguiente.

2. When *would* + INF denotes habitual events, **soler** in the imperfect + INF, or the infinitive conjugated in the imperfect are used in Spanish.

On Sundays we would spend the day with our family.	Los domingos solíamos pasar (pasábamos) el día con la familia.
She would read for hours without stopping.	Solía leer (leía) horas seguidas sin parar.
During the winter we would eat early.	En el invierno solíamos cenar (cenábamos) temprano.

3. Advisability in relation to the present/future expressed by *should* is rendered in Spanish by **deber** in the conditional.

We should leave now.	Deberíamos irnos ahora.
She should not be working so hard.	No debería trabajar tanto.

4. Wonder or suspicion in relation to the present/future expressed by *should* is rendered in Spanish by **haber de** (in the conditional) + INF.

There is no reason why the signature should have been omitted.	No hay razón por la cual habrían de omitir la firma.
Why should she stay home all the time?	¿Por qué habría de quedarse en casa todo el tiempo?
Why should he lie to you?	¿Por qué habría de mentirte?

5. The usage of *should* in *if*-clauses may be rendered in Spanish by conjugating the infinitive in the present indicative or the subjunctive, depending upon the degree of probability attached to the fulfillment of the condition.

If he should arrive earlier, tell him to wait for me.	Si llega más temprano, dile que me espere.
(If) Should you run into him, please ask him to call me.	Si llegaras a encontrarte con él, dile que me llame por favor.

6. The usage of *would* after verbs of wishing is rendered in Spanish by conjugating the infinitive in the subjunctive. The clause may be introduced by **ojalá** or a verb of wishing.

I wish he would not come.	⎰ Ojalá no viniera. ⎱ Espero que no venga.
I wish it would stop raining.	⎰ Ojalá parara de llover. ⎱ Como deseo que pare de llover.

2

PERFECT TENSES OF THE INDICATIVE

The Present Perfect[1]

The present perfect is a relative tense. It describes completed events in relation to the grammatical present of the speaker. It can be used for events which were completed in a period of time which falls within the grammatical present, and for events completed in a prior dimension which have results or consequences bearing upon the present time. Basically, both Spanish and English use the present perfect in the same way. The following discussion is, therefore, applicable to both languages. Those functions which are not shared by Spanish and English will be discussed later.

THE PRESENT PERFECT CONTRASTED WITH THE PRETERIT[2]

1. Since the present perfect connects a completed occurrence with the grammatical present, it co-occurs with adverbials indicating a space of time which falls within the speaker's present interest: **hoy, este mes, este siglo**, etc. The preterit, on the other hand, is used with adverbials which indicate a space of time which is not included in the grammatical present: **ayer, el mes pasado, el año pasado**, etc.

---

[1] Spanish grammarians refer to this tense as the past perfect. In order to be consistent with texts published in the United States, we refer to it as the present perfect, although there are compelling grammatical reasons in Spanish to consider it a past tense.

[2] For the differences between the English and Spanish preterit see Chapter 5, The Preterit.

El mes pasado no me llamó ni una sola vez.	*Last month she did not call me once.*
Esta semana de repente me ha llamado varias veces.	*This week all of a sudden she has called me several times.*
Supe ayer que estaba enferma, pero no he podido ir a verla todavía.	*I found out yesterday that she was sick, but I have not been able to go to see her yet.*
En este siglo la ciencia ha progresado muchísimo.	*In this century science has progressed tremendously.*
Sin embargo, en siglos pasados también hizo grandes avances.	*However, in previous centuries it also made great advances.*

2. When the present perfect occurs with adverbials indicating duration or repetition, the action is described as having taken place in the extended present. If the preterit occurs with the same adverbials, the event is viewed as having occurred within the past without any necessary connection with the present tense.

Nunca le ha faltado nada.	*He has never lacked anything.*
Nunca le faltó nada.	*He never lacked anything.*
No me ha hablado en toda una semana (recientemente).	*He has not spoken to me in a whole week (recently).*
No me habló en toda una semana (en aquel entonces).	*He did not speak to me for a whole week (at that time).*
Hemos ido al teatro varias veces (en las últimas semanas).	*We have gone to the theater several times (during the last few weeks).*
Fuimos al teatro varias veces (durante la temporada de invierno).	*We went to the theater several times (during the winter season).*

3. When the present perfect occurs without any modifiers, it describes a completed event either as continuing up to the present or as having consequences bearing upon the present. The preterit, on the other hand, would describe the same event as completed in the past, without necessarily implying any consequences upon the present.

Ha estado gravemente enferma (en los últimos meses).	*She has been seriously ill (during the last few months).*
Estuvo gravemente enferma (cuando dio a luz).	*She was seriously ill (when she gave birth).*
Ha sido un trabajador muy consciente (en todo momento).	*He has been a very conscientious worker (all along).*
Fue un trabajador muy consciente (mientras estuvo con esta compañía).	*He was a very conscientious worker (while he was with this company).*

4. The present perfect may also be used for events which, while not having taken place in the extended present, do have results bearing upon the present time.

Fleming ha comprobado que la penicilina es un agente contra ciertas infecciones.	*Fleming has proven that penicillin is an effective agent against certain infections.*
Se ha demostrado que el factor ambiente es tan importante como el factor hereditario en la conducta humana.	*It has been proven that the environmental factor is as important as the hereditary factor in human behaviour.*

The uses described of the present perfect are not, however, so strictly observed in all parts of the Spanish-speaking world, or in comparison to English. In certain areas of Spain and Spanish America the preterit alternates with the present perfect or simply substitutes it. Occasionally the reverse also happens.

¿Qué pasó ahora? ¿Qué ha pasado ahora?	*What has happened now?*
No vino a trabajar hoy. No ha venido a trabajar hoy.	*He hasn't come to work today.*
He venido a verte esta mañana. Vine a verte esta mañana.	*I came to see you this morning.*
Ha llovido mucho el mes pasado. Llovió mucho el mes pasado.	*It rained a lot last month.*

But since the rules previously given are grammatical in standard Spanish, regardless of regional variants, there is no reason why the English speaker should not transfer positively his own usage of the present perfect in the cases described above.

THE SPANISH AND ENGLISH PRESENT PERFECT CONTRASTED

As seen thus far, the present perfect has equivalent functions in both languages, but there are, nevertheless, two important contrasts:

1. In Spanish the present perfect may not only be used in reference to an indefinite past time, but also in relation to a definite, specific point in the past. It may, therefore, co-occur with adverbials of specific past reference. In English, the present perfect is only used in relation to an indefinite past time, while specific reference to the past is expressed by the preterit. For this reason, the Spanish present perfect signaling a definite past occurrence is rendered in English by the preterit.

Su hija se ha casado el año pasado.	*Her daughter was married last year.*
Sus padres han muerto hace cuatro años.	*His parents died four years ago.*
Ayer ha trabajado todo el día.	*Yesterday he worked all day long.*

2. The English present perfect must be used when an event which began earlier is still in progress within the actual present, provided that the event be one of non-conclusive, durative action: *to love, to wish, to aspire, to live, to remain, to work, to suffer*, etc. While in Spanish the present perfect may also be used with these verbs, the usage of the present tense is more common in this context.

How long have you lived here?	¿Cuanto tiempo hace que Ud. vive aquí?
	. . . ha vivido . . .
He has loved her ever since he saw her.	La quiere desde que la vio.
	La ha querido . . .
She has been with them ever since she became a widow.	Está con ellos desde que enviudó.
	Ha estado . . .
He has worked for them since December.	Trabaja con ellos desde diciembre.
	Ha trabajado . . .

With some verbs, however, the Spanish present perfect cannot be used when current duration is described, because these particles signal in Spanish either initiative or terminative aspect, depending upon the context: **conocido, sabido, visto, entendido, escuchado,** etc.[1] The difference between initiative and durative aspect may or may not be signaled in English by a different lexical item.

La he conocido.	*I have met her.*
Lo ha sabido ayer.	*He found out yesterday.*
Lo ha entendido.	*He has grasped it.*

With these verbs the simple present is used to describe duration from a time frame forward.

La conoce desde hace años.	*He has known her for years.*
Lo entiende desde hace tiempo.	*He has understood it for a long time.*
Lo sabe desde hace tiempo.	*He has known it for a long time.*
Nos vemos diariamente desde hace meses.	*We have seen (been seeing) each other daily for months.*

The Past Perfect[2]

The past perfect is a relative tense. Its usage is always dependent upon a given point of reference—either another completed event or a temporal expression referring to past time. The past pluperfect describes a completed event as anterior

---

[1] See Chapters 4 and 5: "Progressive Constructions," "Preterit and Imperfect."

[2] In order to be consistent with texts published in the United States, we refer to this tense as the past perfect and not the pluperfect.

to another past action, or as completed before a given time, expressed or implied. Both Spanish and English use the past perfect in the same way.

Cuando yo llegué, ellos habían salido ya.	*When I arrived, they had already left.*
Aquel día supe que me había engañado.	*That day I found out that he had deceived me.*
No la había oído hablar así hasta ahora.	*I had not heard her speak like that until now.*
Hacía mucho tiempo que no nos habíamos visto.	*It had been a long time since we had seen each other.*

In both Spanish and English, the preterit is often used instead of the past perfect. This is, of course, much more prevalent in the spoken than written language, in informal than in formal speech situations. To indicate anteriority the preterit co-occurs with one of the following relators:

en cuanto
apenas
tan pronto como   *as soon as*
en seguida que

después que
luego que   *after*

En cuanto terminó su trabajo, se fue.	*As soon as he finished his work, he left.*
Ni bien me vio, me reconoció.	*As soon as he saw me, he recognized me.*
Después que habló con ella, se convenció de su inocencia.	*After he talked to her, he became convinced of her innocence.*
Luego que terminó varios poemas, los envió a la revista.	*After he finished several poems, he sent them to the journal.*

The Preterit Perfect

The preterit perfect is no longer used today in oral speech. It is confined to literary writings of the past, being rare in contemporary literature itself. The usage of the preterit perfect is always dependent upon a given point of reference, another completed event, or an adverbial of past time. It describes the immediate anteriority of one event with respect to another completed event or adverb of past time. Thus it always co-occurs with relators of time indicating immediate anteriority.

When the pluperfect or the simple preterit co-occur with these relators, they describe the same relationships expressed by the preterit perfect. For this reason, these tenses are used today instead of the preterit perfect.

En cuanto se hubo despedido salió.	*As soon as he had bid them farewell, he*
había despedido	*left.*
despidió	

The Future Perfect

The future perfect is a relative tense. It describes an anticipated event which will be completed prior to another future event, or to a future temporal expression. The future perfect is used:

1. To describe an anticipated event as completed. It corresponds in English to *will* + perfect infinitive.

Cuando regreses, ella se habrá casado ya.	*By the time you return, she will have married already.*
Cuando llegues, habremos terminado.	*By the time you arrive, we will have finished.*
Para el lunes habremos hecho la decisión.	*By Monday we will have made the decision.*

2. To express conjecture or probability about a past event. Its equivalent in English is a phrase meaning probability or *must* + perfect infinitive.

Se habrá ido ya.	*She must have left already.*
Vi que no se hablaban. Se habrán peleado.	*I saw that they were not talking to each other. They must have had a fight.*
No me entendió. No habré sabido explicarme.	*He did not understand me. Perhaps I did not make myself clear.*

3. To express concession about a past event, which in English is rendered by *might* + perfect infinitive.

Habrá sido indiscreto, pero no fue mal intencionado.	*He might have been indiscreet, but he meant no harm.*
Ud. habrá entendido eso, pero eso no fue lo que yo dije.	*You might have understood that, but that is not what I said.*

The Conditional Perfect

The conditional perfect is a relative tense. It describes an anticipated event which will be completed prior to another future event, a future condition or situation. In all instances it describes future completion from a *past perspective*. The conditional perfect is used:

1. To describe the realization of an anticipated event from a past perspective. It corresponds in English to *would* + perfect infinitive.

Me dijo que para cuando yo regresase, ella se habría casado ya.	*She told me that by the time I returned, she would have married already.*
Me prometió que para cuando yo llegase, habría terminado.	*He promised me that by the time I returned, they would have finished.*

| Me dijo que para el lunes habrían hecho la decisión. | *He said that by Monday they would have made the decision.* |

2. To express conjecture or probability about a completed event from a past perspective. Its equivalent in English is a phrase meaning probability or *might* + perfect infinitive.

María se preguntaba si su amiga se habría ido.	*Mary was asking herself whether her friend might have left already.*
No me entendió. No habría sabido explicarme.	*He did not understand me. Perhaps I did not make myself clear.*
No podía dejar de pensar en lo que habría sido de la vida de su amiga.	*She could not stop thinking about what might have become of her friend's life.*

3. To describe the result of a condition, implied or expressed, as completed. Its equivalent in English is *would* or *should* + perfect infinitive.

Si tú hubieras estado aquí eso no habría pasado.	*If you had been here that would not have happened.*
Si tú supieras inglés, habrías entendido lo que te decía.	*If you knew English, you would have understood what he was saying.*
Yo no habría hecho eso.	*I would not have done that.*
Me habría gustado hablar contigo, pero no tuve tiempo.	*I would have liked to speak to you but I did not have time.*

3

PRONOUNS: PERSONAL, OBJECT, PREPOSITIONAL, AND NEUTER

Personal Pronouns

SUBJECT PRONOUNS

yo	*I*	nosotros, -as	*we*
tú ⎫		vosotros, -as ⎫	
usted ⎭ *you*		ustedes ⎭ *you*	
él	*he*	ellos, -as	*they*
ella	*she*		

USES OF THE SUBJECT PRONOUNS

Since the Spanish verb forms have different endings for each grammatical person (except in some tenses), the subject forms are normally omitted. They are, however, used in some cases.

1. When the verb endings are the same for the first, second, and third person singular, as in the imperfect indicative, the conditional, and all subjunctive tenses, the subject pronouns may be inserted to avoid ambiguity.

Yo quería ir, pero él no podía.　　*I wanted to go, but he couldn't.*
Es necesario que Ud. vaya.　　*It's necessary that you go.*

Es necesario que él vaya.	*It's necessary that he go.*
Si pudiera, yo iría.	*If I could, I would go.*
Si pudiera, él iría.	*If he could, he would go.*

2. When the subject pronoun is stressed in English for emphasis or for contrast, a subject form is added in Spanish.

| Tú puedes irte, ella no. | *You can go, not she.* |
| Dígale que yo lo quiero ver. | *Tell him I want to see him.* |

3. Subject pronouns are used in initial position with verbs of opinion and knowledge (**saber, suponer, dudar, pensar, creer**, etc.) when the speaker wishes to reassert his stand or opinion, and not merely convey some objective or neutral information.

Yo sé lo que te digo.	*I know what I'm telling you.*
Nosotros no podemos dudar de eso.	*We can't doubt that.*
Yo supongo que él puede hacerlo.	*I suppose that he can do it.*

4. **Usted** and **ustedes** are added for courtesy. They occur, however, no more than once per sentence. **Usted** and **ustedes** are frequently abbreviated to **Ud.**, **Uds.**, respectively.

| Si Ud. pudiera hacerme el favor le quedaría muy agradecido. | *If you could do me the favor I would be very grateful.* |
| Ud. tiene tanto trabajo que no quisiera molestarlo. | *You are so busy I wouldn't want to impose upon you.* |

5. Subject pronouns are used after the verb **ser** if the predicate is omitted, as in answering questions.

| ¿Quiénes están ahí? —Son ellos. | *Who is there? It's they.* |
| ¿Quién habla, María? —Sí, soy yo. | *Who is speaking, Maria? Yes, it's I.* |

6. Subject pronouns do not normally replace inanimate nouns or animate non-human beings in Spanish. Since there is no subject pronoun like the English *it* or its plural *they* for inanimate things, the inanimate or non-human subject nouns are either repeated, or the subject form is omitted as in the case of animate subjects.

La televisión ha facilitado la difusión internacional de noticias. La televisión nos da además una visión gráfica de los eventos.	*Television has facilitated the international diffusion of the news. It gives us also a graphic vision of events.*
La administración de los recursos del país es asunto complicado. Require talento, conocimientos y dedicación.	*The administration of the country's resources is a complicated matter. It requires talent, knowledge, and self-dedication.*
Estos muebles antiguos son del siglo XVIII. Pertenecían a sus antepasados.	*These antique pieces of furniture are from the eighteenth century. They belonged to his ancestors.*

If inanimate nouns are personified, they are more readily replaced by personal subject pronouns.

La voluntad no lo es todo. Ella es, sin embargo, la mejor aliada del hombre.

Will isn't everything. It is, however, man's best ally.

Las artes son la actividad más desinteresada del hombre. Ellas constituyen su logro más perenne.

The arts are man's most unselfish pursuit. They are his most perennial achievement.

Tú versus usted

Usted is equivalent to the conventional English *you*. It is the universal respectful form of address in all Spanish-speaking countries, and the form a foreigner should use under all circumstances unless he is invited to do otherwise, becomes intimate friends with adults of roughly his own age, or is addressing children.

Tú is the familiar or intimate form of address. Its usage is roughly equivalent to that of the first name in English. However, the latter is more widely used in English than the **tú** form in Spanish, for the first name may be used with **usted**, especially when addressing friends older than oneself.

Even though the norms for **tú** and **usted** may vary from country to country and fluctuate under special circumstances, **tú** applies generally to the following relationships: near relatives, close friends, and small children. A foreigner should not confuse its usage with the first name basis of English and employ it to address his business associates, his subordinates, or his domestic servants. The non-reciprocal **tú** in addressing inferiors is considered as either patronizing or condescending, unless personal friendship or a great age difference exists.

The normal form of address between two people may vary under certain circumstances. Formal events such as court sessions, conferences, and oral examinations require the formal **usted** between the participants, regardless of their personal relationship. The reciprocal form of address, either **tú** or **usted**, may also fluctuate temporarily to a non-reciprocal form under certain conditions. These would involve highly emotional experiences triggered by such things as love, hatred, and rage. The form used—**tú** or **usted**—would thus be expressive of temporary closeness, distance, condescendence, etc., depending upon the context.

Nosotros and vosotros

Nosotros, nosotras, is the equivalent of *we*. The masculine form refers to males; the feminine, to females. The masculine form is also used for mixed company.

Nosotros, los estudiantes, nos oponemos a esta moción.

We, the students, oppose this motion.

Nosotras, las mujeres profesionales, constituímos una minoría.

We, the professional women, constitute a minority.

Nos, equivalent to the English royal and editorial *we*, is hardly used today. When it appears, it is limited to sovereigns and high-ranking officers of the church exercising their official capacities. Writers and editors nowadays use the form **nosotros** instead.

Vosotros, vosotras, is the plural form of **tú** in Castilian. In Spanish-speaking America, it has been replaced by **ustedes**.

Object Pronouns

The object forms of the personal pronouns can only be used in connection with verbs and verbal derivatives, infinitives, and participles. All object pronouns—direct, indirect, and reflexive—are always joined in speech to a verb. They are placed immediately before a conjugated verb and a negative command. They must follow an affirmative command, a simple infinitive, and a present participle and may either precede or follow verb + INF constructions and progressive tenses. (See Position of Object Pronouns in Relation to Verbs, page 34.)

Direct object = The animate or inanimate target of an action

DIRECT OBJECT PRONOUNS

me	*me*	**nos**	*us*
te	*you*	**os**	*you*
lo[1] (masc.)	*you* / *him* / *it*	**los** (masc.)	*you* / *them*
la (fem.)	*you* / *her* / *it*	**las** (fem.)	*you* / *them*

Direct object pronouns agree in number and in gender with the direct object nouns they replace or co-occur with.

He comprado **la casa**.	**La** he comprado.
Quiero ver **a María**.	**La** quiero ver. (Quiero ver**la**.)
No mires **eso**.	No **lo** mires.
Estoy escribiendo **la carta**.	**La** estoy escribiendo. (Estoy escribiéndo**la**.)
Saluda **a los profesores**.	Salúda**los**.
Sin llamar **a Pepe**, no puedes ir.	Sin llamar**lo**, no puedes ir.
Llamando **a Pepe**, averiguarás.	Llamándo**lo**, averiguarás.

---

[1] In Peninsular Spanish the indirect object forms **le** and **les** are used when the direct object is a human masculine noun; **lo** and **los** occur with inanimate nouns.

Nouns as direct objects: the personal **a**

In English the distinction between a noun as subject or as direct object is signaled by word order. In Spanish, word order is rather flexible. Therefore, a noun as subject must be differentiated from a noun as object by the personal **a** whenever the possibility of ambiguity exists.

Los empleados supervisan. Supervisan los empleados.	*The employees supervise.*
Supervisan **a** los empleados.	*They supervise the employees.*
Mi hermano y mi tío nos acogieron muy bien. Nos acogieron muy bien mi hermano y mi tío.	*My brother and my uncle received us kindly.*
Acogieron muy bien **a** mi hermano y **a** mi tío.	*They received my brother and my uncle very kindly.*

The personal **a** is used in the following cases:

1. When the direct object is a noun that refers to a definite, particular individual:

Venció a su enemigo.	*He overcame his enemy.*
Envió a su secretaria.	*He sent his secretary.*
Cuida a los enfermos.	*She takes care of the sick.*
Vio a María.	*He saw Mary.*

2. When the subject and direct object nouns denote animals or things and the possibility of ambiguity exists as to who is the subject or object:

El perro persigue al gato.	*The dog chases the cat.*
El gato persigue al perro.	*The cat chases the dog.*
El helicóptero siguió al yate.	*The helicopter followed the yacht.*
El yate siguió al helicóptero.	*The yacht followed the helicopter.*

3. When any of the pronominal indefinites **alguien**, **alguno**, **nadie**, **ninguno**, or **cualquiera** or the demonstratives, possessives, interrogatives, or relatives refer to people:

Necesito ver a alguien.	*I need to see someone.*
Contratará a cualquiera.	*She will employ anyone.*
No encontraron a nadie mejor.	*They didn't find anyone better.*
Mándame a alguno de ellos.	*Send me one of them.*
No me envíes a ése otra vez.	*Don't send me that one again.*
Salúdame a los tuyos.	*Greet your relatives for me.*
¿A cuántos invitarás?	*How many will you invite?*
Llama a cuantos quieras.	*Call as many as you wish.*

4. When an inanimate or non-human noun is personified:

Adoro a Boston.	*I adore Boston.*
Conozco a tu patria.	*I know your homeland.*

Cuida a su perro como si fuera un niño.	*She takes care of her dog as if it were a child.*
Hay que obedecer a la ley.	*One has to obey the law.*
Hay que resistir a la tentación.	*One has to resist the temptation.*

If any of the above direct object nouns were not personified, they would occur without the **a**.

The personal **a** may be omitted if the direct object noun is indefinite, that is, when it does not refer to a particular individual. For this reason it may be left out before plural and collective nouns which denote a general class and not particular individuals (unless the possibility of ambiguity exists).

Necesito cocinero.	*I need a cook.*
Quisiéramos una secretaria bilingüe.	*We would like a bilingual secretary.*
Mañana elegirán los diputados.	*Tomorrow they will elect the representatives.*
He conocido españoles de todas partes.	*I have known (met) Spaniards from every area.*
Me marea ver tanta gente.	*It makes me dizzy to see so many people.*

BUT:

Vencieron a los enemigos.	*They overcame their enemies.*
Vencieron los enemigos.	*Their enemies overcame them.*

When **tener** can substitute for **estar**, or when it means "to hold," it takes the personal **a** before a direct object noun. When it means "to have," "to possess," it does not.

Tiene a su hijo enfermo.	*His (her) son is ill.*
Tuvo a su hijo en brazos.	*She held her son in her arms.*
Tiene un hijo.	*She has a son.*

USES OF DIRECT OBJECT PRONOUNS

1. Direct object pronouns are used to replace nouns functioning as direct objects.

Compré el libro.	Lo compré.
Compré los libros.	Los compré.
No traigas la carta.	No la traigas.
No traigas las cartas.	No las traigas.
Quiero ver a María.	La quiero ver. (Quiero verla.)
Estoy escribiendo la carta.	La estoy escribiendo. (Estoy escribiéndola.)
Saluda a los señores.	Salúdalos.

2. When a direct object noun is not deleted, and it occurs in preverbal position, an object pronoun must co-occur with it. The object pronoun follows the noun immediately.

Direct object nouns in object position—	*Direct object nouns in subject position—*
postverbal	*preverbal*
Compré los libros.	Los libros los compré yo.
I bought the books.	*The books were bought by me.*
Vestiré a los niños.	A los niños los vestiré yo.
I will dress the children.	*The children will be dressed by me.*
Es imposible localizar a Pedro.	Pedro es imposible localizar.
It is impossible to get a hold of Peter.	*Peter is impossible to get a hold of.*

3. Only an object pronoun can be used if the direct object is human and in the first person singular or plural, or in the second person **tú**.

No me vio.	*He did not see me.*
Te recogerán luego.	*They will pick you up later.*
Nos buscaron toda la mañana.	*They looked for us all morning long.*

The prepositional object forms **a mí**, **a ti**, **a nosotros**, may co-occur with the object pronouns but they cannot replace them in this instance. The sequences ***Vio a mí**, ***Recogerán a ti**, etc., are not grammatical in Spanish.

If the direct object noun is a third person noun, singular or plural, the direct object pronoun is, of course, optional unless the noun is omitted.

Vi a Juan.	*I saw John.*
Lo vi a él.⎫	
Lo vi. ⎭	*I saw him.*

4. A direct object pronoun generally co-occurs with **usted** and **ustedes** when these function as direct objects.

La vi a Ud. muy triste en ese rincón. ⎫	
A Ud. la vi muy triste en ese rincón. ⎬	*I saw you looking very sad in that corner.*
No los molestaré a Uds. más con esas cosas. ⎫	
A Uds. no los molestaré más con esas cosas. ⎬	*I won't bother you anymore with those things.*

5. A direct object always co-occurs with the personal pronoun **uno** when it functions as a direct object, in order to differentiate it from the indefinite **uno**.

¿Qué pasa que no lo saludan a uno por aquí?	*What is the matter that they don't greet one around here?*
Aquí no lo estiman a uno.	*They don't appreciate you (one) here.*

6. The verbs **haber**, **tener**, and **hacer** take a direct object pronoun when their corresponding object nouns are deleted. Their English equivalents do not.

¿Hay muchos artistas en el pueblo?	*Are there many artists in town?*
—Sí, los hay.	*—Yes, there are.*

Parece tener sesenta años, pero no
  los tiene.
Creí que nos haría el favor, pero no
  lo hizo.

*She seems sixty years old, but she
is not.*
*I believed he would do us the favor,
but he did not.*

7. Direct object pronouns cannot be used to replace the following forms when
   they function as direct objects: relative pronouns; the indefinites **algo, nada,
   alguien, nadie,** and **cualquiera.**

A quien vi es a María.   BUT NOT: ★A la vi es María.
Llama a cualquiera.   BUT NOT: ★LLámalo.

¿Buscas algo?
—No busco nada.   BUT NOT: ★No lo busco.
—Sí, busco algo.   ★Sí, lo busco.
Are you looking for something?
—No, I am not looking for anything.
—Yes, I am looking for something.

INDIRECT OBJECT PRONOUNS

me	*me*	**nos**	*us*
te	*you*	**os**	*you*
le (se)	*you* / *him* / *her* / *it*	**les** (se)	*you* / *them*

The indirect object pronouns are similar in form to direct object pronouns except
for the third person singular and plural. Indirect object pronouns agree in number
with the objects they replace, introduce, or co-occur with. The gender distinction
does not apply here.

When the indirect objects **le** and **les** are used with a third person direct object
pronoun they become **se.**

Le trajo el regalo.   **Se lo** trajo.
She brought him a gift.   *She brought it to him.*

Les explicó la situación.   **Se la** explicó.
He explained the issue to them.   *He explained it to them.*

FUNCTION OF INDIRECT OBJECT PRONOUNS

The function of indirect object pronouns covers in Spanish a wide range of
meanings. The pronoun may indicate that the person is the indirect receiver of the
action; that he stands to lose or gain by it; that he is the possessor; or that he is
emotionally involved in an event. The indirect object pronoun almost universally

refers back to an animate human being, except in literary writings where inanimate nouns are often personified. Indirect object pronouns are thus used in Spanish to signal the following relationships:

1. To denote the person *to whom* something is done, conveyed, or imparted:

Te escribiré pronto.	*I'll write you soon.*
Le hablé ayer.	*I spoke to her yesterday.*
Nos explicó la situación.	*He explained the situation to us.*
¿Qué te contestaron?	*What did they answer (say to you)?*
No me lo admitió.	*He did not admit it to me.*

2. To denote the person *for whose* benefit or *to whose* advantage something is done:

Nos diseñó la casa.	*He designed the house for us.*
Me escribió la carta.	*She wrote the letter for me.*
Le decoró la casa.	*He decorated the house for her.*
Le hizo las cortinas.	*She made the curtains for him.*
Me hizo un vestido.	*She made me a dress.*

3. To denote the person *from whom* something is taken away, bought, or removed:

Le compró la casa.	*He bought the house from him.*
Les quitaron la licencia.	*They took their license away from them.*
Le sacó las llaves.	*He took the keys from him.*
Le suspendieron el permiso.	*They took his permit away from him.*
Nos ganó la apuesta.	*He won the bet from us.*

4. To denote the person *for whom* a service or disservice is performed if the direct object is his possession: body parts, articles of clothing, and personal belongings. In these cases, English uses the possessive:

Me cortó el pelo.	*He cut my hair.*
Le curó las heridas.	*He cured his wounds.*
Le puso la mano en el hombro.	*He put his hand on her shoulder.*
Le expropiaron las tierras.	*They expropriated his lands.*
Me perdió las llaves.	*He lost my keys.*
Le suspendieron la licencia.	*They revoked his license.*

5. To denote the emotional involvement or special interest of a person in a given event. No equivalent structure exists in English, but the meaning conveyed in Spanish may be rendered lexically in English:

No me lo traten mal.	*Don't treat him badly (for my sake).*
Me lo mandaron lejos.	*They send him far away (from me).*
No me la dejen salir sola.	*Don't let her go alone (for my sake, because of me).*

6. In Spanish, indirect object pronouns are also used to signal the subject of a sentence in the following cases:

    a. In sentences with verbs of the **gustar** class, such as **parecer**, **interesar**, **importar**, **convenir**, **preocupar**, **faltar**, and **tocar**. The indirect object forms signal the logical subject of the sentence—as opposed to the grammatical subject—and tend to occur in subject position. A few of these verbs have the same structure in English, while others function differently.

Me pareció una persona atenta.	*He seemed an attentive person to me.*
Nos preocupa su estado de salud.	*His health worries us.*
No me importa tanto lo que piensa.	*What he thinks does not concern me too much.*
Me gusta mucho esta novela.	*I like this novel very much.*
Le interesa el arte moderno.	*She is interested in modern art.*
Le falta experiencia.	*She lacks experience.*
Me faltan varias páginas.	*I am missing several pages.*
Hoy te toca cocinar.	*Today is your turn to cook.*

b. In impersonal sentences, **es imposible manejar**, **es difícil volver**, etc., an indirect object pronoun may be added to specify the subject.

Le es imposible ir.	*It is impossible for her to go.*
Me es difícil asistir a la reunión.	*It is difficult for me to attend the meeting.*
Nos será muy grato volver a verlo.	*It will be a great pleasure for us to see him again.*

Spanish and English indirect object forms contrasted

In Spanish only an indirect object pronoun can signal all of the relationships previously described. English, as opposed to Spanish, does not have a fixed form for the indirect object. It may signal the indirect object through word order, immediately after the verb:

She gave the man *the book.*	Le dio al hombre el libro.
She bought him *a car.*	Le compró un auto.

It may restructure the indirect object into a prepositional phrase:

She gave the book to the man.	Le dio el libro al hombre.
She bought a car for him.	Le compró un auto.

It may express the various relationships previously shown through the prepositions *to*, *for*, *from* and *off*.

She did it to him.	Se lo hizo.
I did it for her.	Se lo hice.
I took it from her.	Se lo quité.
I took it off her.	Se lo quité.

When the indirect object is a personal possession, in English the possessive occurs.

She ironed his *shirt.*	**Le** planchó la camisa.
He pulled her *tooth out.*	**Le** sacó la muela.
He painted her *house.*	**Le** pintó la casa.

The usage of the indirect object form in Spanish may thus correspond to any one of the previously described categories in English: the indirect object signaled by word order; *to, for, from,* and *off* relationships; or the possessive. The reverse does not apply. An indirect object noun or pronoun cannot be restructured in Spanish into a prepositional phrase as in English. Furthermore, when an indirect object noun refers to a particular, specific individual, it co-occurs in Spanish with an indirect object pronoun.

No podía negarle nada a su mujer.	*He could not refuse his wife anything.*
Nos explicó el asunto a Pedro y a mí.	*He explained the issue to Peter and to me.*

This does not mean that indirect object pronouns cannot co-occur in Spanish with prepositional object forms. They do, but they cannot replace indirect object pronouns as in English. Prepositional object forms are optional and/or redundant. Sentences of the following type are therefore ungrammatical in Spanish: ***Regaló el auto a mí, *Ella cortó mi pelo, *Dio un libro a nosotros.**

Nouns and pronouns as indirect objects

1. All indirect object nouns are introduced in Spanish by the personal **a** When a noun refers to a definite, particular individual or individuals, an indirect object pronoun occurs with it. Only in a few cases is the indirect object an inanimate noun or non-human being.

Les enseñaron la ciudad a los turistas.	*They showed the city to the tourists.*
Les quitaron a los Pérez todo lo que tenían.	*They took away from the Perez' all they owned.*
No le permite fumar a su hijo.	*He does not allow his son to smoke.*

2. Relative pronouns that function as indirect objects are also introduced by **a**. They too co-occur with objective pronouns.

Es a María a quien se lo debes ocultar.	*It is Maria whom you should hide it from.*
Es a tu jefe a quien le debes pedir permiso.	*It is your boss whom you should ask for permission.*

3. When the indirect object noun phrase occurs in preverbal or subject position, an indirect object pronoun co-occurs with it.

A Luz no le dije nada.	*To Luz I did not say anything.*
A José sí se lo conté todo.	*John I did tell everything.*
A quien le debes pedir ayuda es a tu padre.	*The one you should ask for help is your father.*

4. Indirect object pronouns may be omitted if the object noun is an inanimate noun, or a collective, plural, or indefinite noun that does not refer to a specific person.

Hará Ud. un servicio al mundo civilizado.	*You will perform a service to the civilized world.*
Esos detalles no pertenecen a la historia.	*These details do not belong to history.*
Entregó los materiales a la policía.	*He handed the materials over to the police.*
Envió los documentos a los abogados.	*He sent the documents to the lawyers.*
Usted no se pertenece, pertenece a su pueblo.	*You do not belong to yourself, you belong to your people.*

5. The indefinites referring to people, **alguien**, **nadie**, **ninguno**, and **cualquiera**, when functioning as indirect objects are introduced by **a**. Object pronouns usually co-occur with them.

No se lo voy a dar a cualquiera.	*I won't give it to just anyone.*
Se lo regalaré a alguien que lo sepa apreciar.	*I will give it to someone who knows how to appreciate it.*
No le explicaré a nadie los motivos de mi decisión.	*I won't explain to anyone the reasons behind my decision.*

6. With a few verbs such as **decir**, **hablar**, **enseñar**, **preguntar**, **contestar**, and **comunicar**, which always take a direct object, the direct object noun or pronoun may be deleted when an indirect object pronoun co-occurs.

Ya le dije.	*I told her already.*
¿Le hablaste?	*Did you speak to her?*
¿Le preguntó Ud.?	*Did you ask him?*
Le enseño.	*I teach her.*

Word order

In English an indirect object noun is placed almost universally after the verb, unless it is restructured into a prepositional phrase, in which case it follows the direct object. In Spanish the preferred word order is the following: verb + direct object followed by the indirect object noun introduced by **a**. This rule is easier to remember if one keeps in mind that the direct object is more closely connected to the verb than the indirect object, in spite of its location in English.

Le enseñó los libros **al hombre**.	*He showed the man the books.* / *He showed the books to the man.*
Da**le** recuerdos **a María**.	*Give my regards to Mary.* / *Give Mary my regards.*
Les contó toda clase de mentiras **a las muchachas**.	*He told the girls all kinds of lies.*
No puede negar**le** nada **a su mujer**.	*He cannot refuse his wife anything.*

POSITION OF INDIRECT OBJECT PRONOUNS IN RELATION TO OTHER PRONOUNS

1. When two object pronouns co-occur, the indirect object form precedes the direct object.

Nos lo dieron ayer.	*They gave it to us yesterday.*
Se lo prometieron.	*They promised it to him (her).*
Véndamelo.	*Sell it to me.*
No se lo des.	*Don't give it to him.*

The English-speaking student should keep in mind that under these circumstances the indirect object pronoun is obligatory in Spanish and cannot be rendered through a prepositional form as in English. The following would be ungrammatical in Spanish:

*Lo dieron a nosotros ayer.
*Lo prometieron a él.
*Véndalo a mí.
*No lo diga a él.

2. When the indirect object is a reflexive pronoun, it must likewise precede the direct object form.

Me la quité.	*I took it off (me).*
Se lo puso.	*He put it on (himself).*
No nos lo explicamos.	*We cannot explain it to ourselves.*

3. The reflexive **se** of passive reflexives and impersonal sentences also precedes any object pronoun, direct or indirect.

Se le quemó la casa.	*His house burnt down.*
Se me perdió la llave.	*My key got lost.*
Se le informó.	*He was informed.*
Se las envió a Francia.	*They (fem.) were sent to France.*

POSITION OF OBJECT PRONOUNS IN RELATION TO VERBS

1. All object pronouns—direct, indirect, and reflexive—are always joined in speech to a verb. They are placed immediately before a conjugated verb, including the auxiliary **haber** in the compound tenses and in negative commands.

No la vi ayer.	*I didn't see her yesterday.*
Se lo ha comprado.	*He has bought it for (from) her.*
No me lo quitó.	*He didn't remove it (take it away) from me.*
No lo venda.	*Don't sell it.*

2. Object pronouns immediately follow and are attached to affirmative commands, infinitives, and present participles.

Cómprelo.	*Buy it.*
Véndaselo.	*Sell it to her (to him).*
Conocerte es quererte.	*To know you is to love you.*
Llama para saludarlo.	*Call up to greet him.*
Cuidándose mejorará.	*By taking care of himself, he will improve.*
Hablándole lo convencerá.	*By speaking to him, you'll convince him.*
No haberte conocido antes . . .	*Not to have met you before . . .*

3. In verb + INF constructions and progressive tenses, the object pronouns may either precede the verb or follow the infinitive when the conjugated verb is a true auxiliary.[1]

Voy a comprarte algo. \}	
Te voy a comprar algo.\}	*I'll buy you something.*
Acaba de llamarme.\}	
Me acaba de llamar.\}	*He (she) has just called me.*
Quiere vendértelo. \}	
Te lo quiere vender.\}	*He wants to sell it to you.*
Se está viendo en el espejo.\}	
Está viéndose en el espejo. \}	*She is looking (at herself) in the mirror.*

When the conjugated verb is not a true auxiliary, the object form should be attached to the form it logically belongs to, as the sentence might change in meaning or be awkward or ungrammatical.

Te mandé hacerlo.	*I ordered you to do it.*
Te lo mandé hacer.	*I had it done for you.*
Es inútil intentarlo.	*It is useless to try it.*
Le es inútil intentar.	*It is useless for him to try.*

There are two instances in which an object must go with the conjugated verb: when the infinitive is intransitive, and when the auxiliary is a reflexive verb.

Le hizo trabajar.	*He made her work.*
Le obligó volver.	*He made him return.*
Nos aconsejó seguir con el proyecto.	*He advised us to continue with the project.*
Se puso a llorar.	*She started to cry.*
Se puso a estudiar.	*He began to study.*
Se quedó a descansar.	*He stayed home to rest.*
Se quedará a cenar.	*He will stay for dinner.*

---

[1] See Object Pronouns in Verb + INF Constructions, page 95 .

BUT NOT:

*Hizo trabajarle.
*Obligó a volverle.
*Puso a llorarse.
*Quedó a descansarse.

If the infinitive is a reflexive form and the conjugated verb a true auxiliary, the reflexive **se** (whether a pronoun or not) may be attached to either.

Quiso irse temprano. ⎫ Se quiso ir temprano. ⎭	*He wanted to leave early.*
Tienes que vestirte. ⎫ Te tienes que vestir. ⎭	*You must get dressed.*
No debes enfadarte. ⎫ No te debes enfadar. ⎭	*You should not get angry.*

If the conjugated verb is not a true auxiliary and the infinitive is reflexive, the particle must be attached to the infinitive.

Espero no aburrirme.	*I hope not to be bored.*
Anhela casarse.	*She longs to be married.*
Aspira enriquecerse.	*He expects to become rich.*

BUT NOT:

*Me espero no aburrir.
*Me anhelo casar.
*Se aspira enriquecer.

Prepositional Pronouns

FORMS OF THE PREPOSITIONAL PRONOUNS

Prepositional pronouns are identical in Spanish to the subject pronouns, except for the first and second persons singular.

a, para:	mí	nosotros, -as
	ti	vosotros, -as
	usted	ustedes
	él	ellos
	ella	ellas

These forms occur after every preposition except **con**, which has the following special forms for the first, second informal, and third persons singular: **conmigo**, **contigo**, **consigo**. The preposition **entre** always requires subject forms.

El libro es para ella.	*The book is for her.*
Lo hizo por ti.	*He did it for (because of) you.*
Viene hacia Ud.	*He is coming towards you.*
Entre ella y yo no hay secretos.	*Between her and me there are no secrets.*
Hablan de mí.	*They are talking about me.*
Va con ellos.	*She is going with them.*

USES OF THE PREPOSITIONAL PRONOUNS

When the pronoun is governed by a preposition, the prepositional form must be used since in Spanish an object pronoun can only occur with verb forms and verbal derivatives.

Prepositional pronouns are used instead of object pronouns under the following conditions:

1. When no verb is present but implicitly given, such as in answering questions when the answer is the direct or indirect object of the verb previously expressed:

¿A quién viste?	*Whom did you see?*
—A ella.	*—Her.*
¿Se lo contaste a ellos?	*Did you tell them?*
—A ella sí, pero a él no.	*—Her, yes, but not him.*

2. When two or more pronouns governed by the same verb are brought into contrast or are emphasized:

Le compré algo a él, pero no a ella.	*I bought something for him, but not for her.*
Te lo dije a ti, y a ella también se lo diré.	*I have told you and I will tell her also.*

3. With all intransitive verbs of motion, the personal pronoun representing the direction or destination of the motion should be in the prepositional form. The prepositional pronoun doesn't represent an object but the adverbial destination. The **a** has true prepositional value and occurs with all verbs of motion in Spanish that require an adverbial complement of destination to fulfill their meaning.

Llegó a mí llorando.	*She came to me crying.*
Acudiré a él, ya que está enfermo.	*I'll go to him since he is ill.*
Recurrimos a Ud. esperanzados de que alguien nos asista.	*We resort to you in the hope that someone might assist us.*
Vino a mí en un estado deplorable.	*He came to me in a deplorable condition.*

4. With reflexive verbs (other than in true reflexive constructions where the subject and the direct or indirect object are the same person) the personal pronoun representing the destination or direction of the movement, literally or figuratively speaking, should also be in the prepositional form.

Me presenté a ella.	*I introduced myself to her.*
Te dirigiste a él en tono altivo.	*You addressed him in an arrogant tone of voice.*
Nos acercamos a él.	*We approached him.*
Me encomendé a Dios.	*I commended myself to God.*

Even though the sequences **me le acerqué**, **te le dirigiste**, **me le encomendé**, and **nos le acercamos** are often used in colloquial speech, the alternate **me acerqué a él**, etc., are preferred in the standard language.

Optional uses of prepositional object forms

The use of prepositional object forms with object pronouns is optional and redundant whenever an object pronoun occurs or is required. The redundant constructions **a mí . . . me, a ti . . . te, a él . . . le**, etc., are more frequent with indirect objects than with direct objects, and in either case they are generally limited to human objects.

Whenever the objective pronouns are stressed in English for contrast or for emphasis, a prepositional form must be used in Spanish, since the object pronouns are unstressed and as such are incapable of rendering those shades of meaning.

The prepositional forms may precede the object pronouns or follow the verb. The sequences **a mí . . . me, a él . . . le**, etc., are, however, more frequent than the reverse, **me . . . a mí, le . . . a él**, since greater emphasis is conveyed when the prepositional form precedes.

A mí me acusaron.	*It was I who was accused.*
Me acusaron a mí.	*They accused me.*
A ella no la quiero ver.	*Her I don't want to see.*
No la quiero ver a ella.	*I don't want to see her.*
A mí me regaló el auto.	*To me he gave the car.*
Me regaló el auto a mí.	*He gave the car to me.*

Since the third person pronoun is ambiguous, the prepositional forms may also be used for clarity.

Se lo voy a dar a ella.	*I will give it to her.*
A él no le diré nada.	*Him I won't tell anything.*
Le entregaré el libro a Ud. personalmente.	*I'll deliver the book to you personally.*

Neuter Pronouns *ello* and *lo*

The neuter subject and object pronouns **ello** and **lo** do not replace subject or object pronouns. These must be reproduced by their corresponding subject or object pronouns and agree with them in number and gender. **Ello** and **lo** reproduce verbs, predicates, and whole sentences previously mentioned or understood.

USES OF *ELLO*

Ello as subject is not frequently used today. In informal speech situations **eso** and **esto** are used instead. **Ello** corresponds to the English *it* and *that* when applied to concepts or ideas previously mentioned.

Te acusaron de haberlo traicionado. Y **ello** no es cierto. (ello = que tú lo hubieras traicionado)	*They accused you of having doublecrossed him. And that is not true.*
Mantienen algunos que la historia se repite. Si **ello** fuera así, no habría progreso alguno. (ello = que la historia se repite)	*Some claim that history repeats itself. If it (that) were true, there wouldn't be any progress.*

As object of a preposition **ello** occurs somewhat more frequently, but even then **eso** and **esto** tend to replace it.[1]

¿Qué fue de ello?	*What became of it?*
En ello tengo puestas todas mis esperanzas.	*All my hopes hinge upon it.*
De ello depende todo.⎱ De eso . . . ⎰	*Everything depends upon it.*
Cuenta con ello.⎱ . . . con eso. ⎰	*Count on it.*

USES OF *LO*

1. **Lo** may refer to something previously expressed, as well as anticipate what follows. As such, it may be equivalent to the English *it* or *so* when it has the same function.

Nada nos alejará. Te **lo** prometo. (lo = que nada nos alejará ya)	*Nothing will draw us apart.* *I promise (it) you.*

---

[1] See Neuter Demonstratives, page 313.

¿Crees que algún día hará algo?
—**Lo** dudo.
(lo = que nunca hará nada)

Do you believe he will ever amount to anything?
—*I doubt it.*

No tenemos teléfono. **Lo** siento.
(lo = que no tengamos teléfono)

We don't have a phone. I'm sorry (about it).

Compréndе**lo**. Nada te detiene aquí más que ella.
(lo = nada te detiene aquí más que ella)

Understand it. Nothing keeps you here but her.

Oyе**lo** bien: no quiero que te vayas sola.
(lo = no quiero que te vayas sola)

Get it straight: I don't want you to go alone.

2. With **ser**, **estar**, **parecer**, and verbs of similar meaning, **lo** reproduces the predicate. **Lo** must be used when the predicate is omitted. With *to be*, the predicate may be omitted in English, or be replaced by *so*. With *to look*, *it* is used instead of *so*.

¿Está Ud. casado?
—Sí, **lo** estoy.
(lo = casado)

Are you married?
Yes, I am.

¿Es fea?
—Sí, **lo** es, mucho.
(lo = fea)

Is she ugly?
Yes, very much so.

¿Es buen presidente?
—El cree serlo, pero no **lo** es.
(lo = buen presidente)

Is he a good president?
He thinks so, but he isn't.

Tiene sesenta años pero no **lo** parece.
(lo = que tiene sesenta años)

He is sixty, but he doesn't look it.

3. When **todo** is the direct object of a verb, **lo** co-occurs with it.

El cree saberlo todo.
Todo lo ha perdido.
¿Por qué tengo que decidirlo todo ahora?

He thinks he knows everything.
He has lost everything.
Why do I have to decide on everything now?

4. If the direct object of verbs of expression or communication is implied but not given, **lo** occurs instead. In English, *it* or *so* are used in that case. But whereas in English *it* or *so* are sometimes omitted, **lo** must be kept in Spanish.

Lo creo.
No lo creo.
Lo dije.
Lo divulgará.

I believe it.
I don't think so. or *I don't believe it.*
I said it. or *I said so.*
He'll divulge it.

Yo te lo dije.	*I told you (so).*
Lo sé.	*I know it.* or *I know so.*
Lo dudo.	*I doubt it.*

But with the verbs **decir**, **preguntar**, and **pedir**, which take a direct object in Spanish, **lo** is often omitted if an indirect object pronoun is present.

Se lo diré a ella.	*I'll tell her (it).*
Le diré.	*I'll tell her.*
Pregúntaselo.	*Ask him (about it).*
Pregúntale.	*Ask him.*
Pídeselo.	*Request it from him.*
Pídele.	*Request it.*

4

PROGRESSIVE CONSTRUCTIONS

Form of Progressives

AUXILIARY + -NDO FORM

The **-ndo** form can occur in Spanish with any of the following auxiliaries to form progressive constructions: **estar, seguir, continuar, ir, venir,** and **andar.** Excepting **seguir** and **continuar** which are entirely synonymous, the other auxiliaries are not interchangeable. Each one of them conveys a different shade of meaning and is used in a different context.

Progressive constructions are relative constructions. Their usage is dependent upon a given point of reference. They either co-occur with another event or a temporal expression of definite time, explicitly stated or implied by the speech situation or context.

DISTRIBUTION AND FUNCTION OF PROGRESSIVES

Estar + -ndo form

The distribution and function of **estar + -ndo**, the most frequently used progressive, differ substantially from that of its English equivalent. The source of these differences lies in the function of the simple, unexpanded tenses in the two languages.

In Spanish, the simple unexpanded tenses may refer to events which occurred at an indefinite time, and also to events which were occurring on a definite, specific occasion. For example, the Spanish present and imperfect tenses are not only used for habitual events—not necessarily ongoing at the time of the utterance—but also for events which were in progress at the time in question or simultaneous with another event.

¿A quién buscas?   *Whom are you looking for?*
El niño camina ya.   *The child is already walking.*
El niño caminaba ya.   *The child was already walking.*

Progressives, on the other hand, are used when attention to a specific moment is emphasized:

¿De qué te estás quejando ahora?   *What are you complaining about now?*
Ella le estaba ocultando algo.   *She was hiding something from him.*

and when ambiguity could arise as to the ongoing versus habitual or future nature of the event:

NATURE OF EVENT

Future	*Habitual*	*Ongoing*
Te espero.	Te espero.	Te estoy esperando.
I will wait for you.	*I wait for you.*	*·I am waiting for you.*
Ya cede.	Cede poco a poco.	Está cediendo.
He is about to give in.	*He gives in little by little.*	*He is giving in.*

Estar progressives are not used for actions extended or repeated over a period of time. For this reason, they do not normally co-occur with indicators of repetition, **todos los lunes, de vez en cuando, cada tanto**, etc. Either the simple unexpanded tenses or one of the other progressives constructed with **ir, venir,** or **seguir** is used instead.

She was seeing him every Monday.	Lo veía cada lunes.
He is calling her every so often.	La llama cada tanto.
He was losing all of his fortune.	Iba perdiendo toda su fortuna.
He has been causing us many difficulties.	Ha venido ocasionándonos muchas dificultades.
She has been improving slowly.	Ha ido mejorando de a poco.

In English, as opposed to Spanish, the simple unexpanded tenses are incompatible with definite time reference. Consequently, they cannot be used to indicate simultaneity with the act of speech or another event. Actions in progress on a definite occasion or simultaneous with another event are rendered by progressives. This applies whether a single event or a series of the same event is described:

What is he telling you now?	¿Qué te dice ahora?
He is spending the mornings writing.	Se pasa las mañanas escribiendo.
He has been improving.	Ha venido mejorando.

English progressives may refer to extended or repeated events provided the time period is definitely confined. This, however, could mean either a short or a prolonged stretch of time. In Spanish, extension or repetition over a prolonged period of time is not rendered by **estar** progressives but by the simple tenses or **ir**, **venir**, and **seguir** progressives.

Wherever he was going at that time, he was well received.	A donde iba en aquel entonces, era bien recibido.
Whenever he was writing, she was nagging.	Siempre que él escribía, ella lo molestaba.
He was slowly curtailing her freedom.	Poco a poco iba limitando su independencia.
She is feeling better as the days go by.	Va sintiéndose mejor a medida que pasan los días.

Further restrictions on **estar + -ndo** form

As opposed to English progressives which may have an indefinite extension provided that time is definitely specified, **estar** progressives have only limited duration and are subject to further restrictions:

1. They are standardly used when ongoing actions fall within the limits of the act of speech but not beyond it.

Estoy escribiendo, no me interrumpas.	*I am writing, do not interrupt me.*
Cuando lo fui a ver, estaban cenando.	*When I went to see him, they were having dinner.*

BUT:

I am enclosing the materials you have requested.	Adjunto los materiales que Ud. ha solicitado.
We are sending you the application form and all pertinent information.	Le enviamos la solicitud y toda la información pertinente.

2. **Estar** progressives cannot be used to express future time or intent to act, as is the case with English progressives. In Spanish, a simple tense equivalent to the time of the English progressive occurs instead.

He is arriving this afternoon.	Llega (llegará) esta tarde.
She is speaking tomorrow.	Habla (hablará) mañana.
We are sending her flowers for her birthday.	Le enviaremos flores para su cumpleaños.
I was told he would be returning soon.	Me dijeron que volvería pronto.

The use of *is going to* + INF as a prospective present and *was going to* + INF as a prospective past is rendered in Spanish by the present and imperfect of **ir a** + INF.

I am going to call her later on.	Voy a llamarla después.
He was going to leave the following day.	Iba a irse al día siguiente.
They are going to study tonight.	Van a estudiar esta noche.

3. **Estar** progressives are seldom used in standard Spanish with verbs of motion of instantaneous action: **ir**, **venir**, **regresar**, **volver**, **entrar**, etc. Whether the English progressive describes an ongoing or a subsequent event in relation to the past or present, Spanish uses a simple tense instead.

I am going to Chicago.	Voy a Chicago.
As I was leaving, the phone rang.	Cuando me iba, sonó el teléfono.
He was told that she would be arriving the following week.	Le dijeron que ella llegaría la semana entrante.

Although **estar** progressives do sometimes occur with these verbs in informal speech, they are not considered grammatical by Spanish grammarians.

Ya me voy.	*I am already leaving.*
Ya vuelvo.	*I am already returning.*

BUT NOT:

★Ya me estoy yendo.
★Ya estoy volviendo.

Verbs of motion which refer to durative actions can take **estar** progressives.

Estábamos caminando en el centro cuando vimos a María.	*We were walking downtown when we saw Maria.*
Estaba paseando con su novio por la tarde.	*She was walking with her boyfriend in the afternoon.*

4. Progressive constructions do not occur with stative verbs in either Spanish or English, that is, with those verbs that do not refer to actions or processes: **tener**, **poseer**, **saber**, **caber**, etc. But some stative verbs may function as process verbs as well. There is no one-to-one correspondence between Spanish and English as to which verbs function as either stative or process verbs, or both. *Have* and *be*, which in English may either be stative or process verbs, only function as statives in standard Spanish.[1] They are rendered in Spanish by some other lexical item when functioning as process verbs in English.

He is having a hard time.	El la está pasando muy mal.
You are being very unfair.	Estás actuando muy injustamente.
They are being very cautious.	Están procediendo con mucha cautela.
He is having a dinner party.	Tiene una cena.

The same applies in reverse. Spanish may use some stative verbs as action verbs in certain contexts where English does not.

Te estoy oyendo, sigue.	*I am listening, continue.*
Los estoy viendo desde la ventana.	*I am watching them from the window.*
Está aburriéndose como nunca.	*She is as bored as she can be.*

---

[1] Sentences such as **El gobierno está siendo atacado por la oposición** and **La reina está siendo agasajada** do occur occasionally in Spanish, particularly in the news media. But these are transfers or calques from English.

5. Since **estar** progressives are only used with action verbs, the **-ndo** form cannot be used for stative adjectives of posture. The past participle **-do** form must be used for the English *-ing* form.[1]

He was standing on the corner.	Estaba parado en la esquina.
She was lying down, resting.	Estaba acostada, descansando.
He was sitting next to her.	Estaba sentado junto a ella.

Continuar, seguir + -ndo forms

This construction describes the *duration* or *repetition* of an action which has begun in the past and is still ongoing at a given time. As such, it can be used for repeated or habitual events. If the meaning of the verb refers to a conclusive event, repetition and extension in time are suggested. If the event is non-conclusive, durative, only continuance is described.

The **seguir/continuar + -ndo** form may co-occur with adverbials indicating repeated or habitual events: **todos los días, de vez en cuando, cada tanto**, etc.

Seguía escribiéndole todos los lunes.	*She kept on writing him every Monday. (She continued to write him. . .)*
A pesar de los consejos del médico continuaba trabajando tanto como antes.	*Despite his doctor's advice he kept on working as hard as before.*
Seguirá odiándolo hasta que se muera.	*He will continue hating him (to hate him) until he dies.*
Seguía llamándome de vez en cuando.	*She kept on calling me every so often.*

The only significant difference between this construction and its English equivalent *to continue* is that in English the verb may occur with an *-ing* form or an infinitive, whereas in Spanish it can only take an **-ndo** form.

Ir, venir, andar + -ndo forms

These constructions describe the continuance or repetition of an action, implying at the same time an idea of progressive movement in space or in time. They have no direct equivalent in English. **Ir** is used when duration from a time frame forward and realization by degree are stressed. **Ir** progressives may, therefore, co-occur with adverbials of comparison, intensity, and manner.

Va entendiendo la materia mejor que antes.	*He is grasping the subject matter better than before.*
Iba queriéndolo cada día más.	*Her affection for him was growing daily.*
Se va haciendo de noche.	*It is beginning to get dark.*
Se va haciendo tarde.	*It is getting late.*

---

[1] See Chapter 7, The Gerund.

Poco a poco iba añadiendo libros a su colección.	*Little by little he continued adding books to his collection.*
Ve siguiendo paso a paso las instrucciones que te he dado.	*Follow step by step the instructions I have given you.*
Al principio bebía poco, pero despúes fue abusando.	*In the beginning he drank moderately, but later on he started overdoing it.*

Venir occurs when continuance from the past towards the present and realization by degree are described. **Venir** progressives may, therefore, co-occur with indicators of temporal continuity: **desde hace . . ., hace . . . que.**

Hace años que viene luchando por forjarse un porvenir.	*He has been struggling for years to forge for himself a better future.*
Vengo esperándote desde las dos.	*I have been waiting for you since two o'clock.*
Venía pidiendo justicia desde hacía años.	*He had been asking for justice for years.*
Viene queriéndola desde la adolescencia.	*He has been in love with her since his teens.*
Vengo advirtiéndotelo desde hace meses.	*I have been warning you about it for months.*
Viene empeorándose desde anoche.	*He has been getting progressively worse since last night.*

Andar is used when continuance and motion with indefinite direction are implied. **Andar** progressives may, therefore, co-occur with adverbials of temporal extension.

Anda buscándote desde ayer.	*He has been looking for you since yesterday.*
Anda haciendo disparates.	*He goes about making blunders.*
Andaba viajando por Europa.	*He was traveling in Europe.*
Anda enamorando a todas las muchachas del pueblo.	*He goes about courting all the girls in town.*

The Present and Imperfect Progressives

In Spanish the present and the imperfect tenses may be used for actual ongoing events and for habitual and future actions. The present progressive and its back-shifted equivalent, the imperfect progressive, also have parallel functions and are used essentially under the same conditions:

1. When a contrast between a habitual and an ongoing happening is made:

No está mintiendo. El no miente nunca ni tiene por qué hacerlo ahora. *He is not lying. He never lies and has no reason to do it now.*	No estaba mintiendo. El no mentía nunca y no tenía por qué hacerlo entonces. *He was not lying. He never lied and had no reason to do it then.*

Está dándole de comer al niño.
Siempre le da de comer temprano.
She is feeding the child. She always feeds him early.

Estaba dándole de comer al niño.
Siempre le daba de comer temprano.
She was feeding the child. She always fed him early.

2. When, depending upon the nature of the event itself, there could be ambiguity as to ongoing, habitual, or future meaning:

a. Verbs which refer to conclusive, non-durative actions (**traicionar, recobrar, dar, saludar, despedir, ahuyentar**, etc.) can only refer to habitual or future events in the present and the imperfect. The unfolding of the action or its co-occurence with another event is rendered by the present and imperfect progressives, depending upon temporal perspectives.

Future	*Habitual*	*Ongoing*
Ya se lo explica. *He will explain it to her in a second.*	Se lo explica. *He explains it to her.*	Se lo está explicando. *He is explaining it to her.*
Ya se lo explicaba. *He was going to explain it to her in a second.*	Se lo explicaba. *He used to explain it to her.*	Se lo estaba explicando. *He was explaining it to her.*
Ya cede. *He is about to give in.*	Cede fácilmente. *He gives in easily.*	Está cediendo. *He is giving in.*
Ya cedía. *He was about to give in.*	Cedía fácilmente. *He gave in easily.*	Estaba cediendo. *He was giving in.*
Me lo da luego. *He will give it to me later.*	Me da cuanto le pido. *He gives me what I ask for.*	Me está dando lo que le pedí. *He is giving me what I asked for.*
Me lo daba luego. *He would give it to me later.*	Me daba cuanto le pedía. *He would give me what I asked for.*	Me estaba dando lo que le había pedido. *He was giving me what I had asked for.*

b. Verbs which signal the entry into a state of being (**enfermarse, enamorarse, impacientarse, fastidiarse, acomplejarse, acobardarse**, etc.) can only refer to habitual events when in the simple present or imperfect. To signal the ongoingness of the event or the approximation to its completion, the progressives are used.

Ella se acostumbra a todo.
She gets used to everything.

Veo que se está acostumbrando a su presencia.
I see that she is getting accustomed to his presence.

Ella se acostumbraba a todo.
She would get used to everything.

Veía que se estaba acostumbrando
a su presencia.
*I saw that she was getting accustomed
to his presence.*

Te cansas rápido.
You tire quickly.

Déjalo ya porque te estás cansando
demasiado.
*Leave it alone now because you are
getting tired.*

Te cansabas rápido.
You would tire quickly.

Insistí que lo dejaras porque te
estabas cansando demasiado.
*I insisted that you leave it alone
because you were getting too tired.*

c. Occasionally there might also be ambiguity with verbs which refer to non-conclusive, durative events, depending upon the context. In such cases the progressives would also be used to convey ongoingness.

Dice que los niños están jugando
en el jardín.
(**juegan** would imply habitual
action)

*She says the children are playing in
the garden.*

Dijo que los niños estaban jugando
en el jardín.
(**jugaban** would imply habitual
action)

*She said the children were playing in
the garden.*

Te estoy esperando.
(**espero** could mean either future,
ongoing, or habitual action)

I am waiting for you.

Te estaba esperando.
(**esperaba** could mean either
future, ongoing, or habitual
action)

I was waiting for you.

If no ambiguity is possible, and no special emphasis upon ongoingness is intended, then the simple tenses are more commonly used.

Voy a salir aunque llueve.
*I will go out even though it is
raining.*

Iba a salir aunque llovía.
*I was going to go out even though
it was raining.*

Veo que habla con alguien.
I see her talking to someone.

Vi que hablaba con alguien.
I saw her talking to someone.

Ya que insistes, acepto.
Since you are insisting, I accept.

Ya que insistías, acepté.
Since you were insisting, I accepted.

3. English progressives describing current ongoingness of repeated or extended events are rendered in Spanish by the simple tenses. Future time or intent is rendered by **ir a** + INF or the simple tenses, if the meaning of the verb allows it.

He is accepting his fate with great courage.	Acepta su destino con gran valentía.
He was always needing money.	Siempre necesitaba dinero.
Whenever he was writing, his wife was nagging.	Siempre que él escribía, su mujer lo molestaba.
I am seeing her tomorrow.	Mañana la veo (veré, voy a ver).
He was returning the following week.	Regresaba (iba a regresar, regresaría) la semana siguiente.

When realization by degree is suggested or implied, then **ir** or **venir** progressives occur instead.

His strength is failing him little by little.	Sus fuerzas le van fallando de a poco.
The people were coming out of church.	La gente venía saliendo de la iglesia.
The wedding party was entering the church.	El cortejo nupcial iba entrando a la iglesia.
He is regaining his strength.	Va recobrando las fuerzas.

The Preterit Progressive

The simple preterit describes a past event as completed and as a point in time, regardless of the durative or non-durative nature of the event itself. When a past and *terminated* event is described as having been ongoing, the preterit progressive occurs instead. The Spanish preterit progressive cannot be used to describe the co-existence of events because it always describes an event as terminated at the time in question. In English the simple preterit describes a past event as completed but not as a point in time. Consequently, it may be used for terminated and for continued actions within the past. The preterit progressive, on the other hand, occurs when ongoingness at a specific time is described. The English preterit progressive, as opposed to the Spanish progressive, does not imply at all the event's completion or termination; it only describes the action in its progression. For this reason, the two progressives are not equivalent insofar as functions are concerned. The Spanish preterit progressive will correspond to the English simple preterit or to the past perfect progressive, but not to the preterit progressive itself.

Estuve llamándote toda la mañana.	*I spent the whole morning calling you.*
Estuvo esperándola por dos horas.	{*He spent two hours waiting for her.* {*He waited for her for two hours.*
Estuvo trabajando hasta que ella llegó.	*He had been working until she arrived.*
Estuvo buscando trabajo por meses antes de encontrar algo.	*He had been looking for a job for months before he found something.*

Since the Spanish preterit progressive cannot be used to describe the co-occurrence of two events,[1] it cannot co-occur with adverbials of unconfined time either. It may only co-occur with adverbials that are definitely confined—those which cover a time period from one point to another, or as up to a given point in time. Coexistence between two ongoing events or ongoingness of one event at a given time, within a past dimension, can only be rendered in Spanish by the imperfect progressive or the simple imperfect tense.

Preterit Progressive	*Imperfect Progressive and Imperfect*
Definitely confined time-adverbials.	Non-confined time-adverbials.
Ongoing event is terminated.	Ongoing event is in progress.
	Cuando yo llamé, él estaba estudiando (estudiaba). *When I called, he was studying.*
Estuvo trabajando de tres a cinco. *He had been working from three to five.*	A las cinco todavía estaba trabajando (trabajaba). *At five he was still working.*
Estuvo estudiando hasta medianoche. *He had been studying until midnight.*	A medianoche todavía estaba estudiando (estudiaba). *At midnight he was still studying.*

The Present and Past Perfect Progressives

The present perfect describes an event which was completed within the grammatical present of the speaker, and which may, depending upon the nature of the event, continue within the actual present or have consequences bearing upon it. The past perfect describes the completed occurrence of an event which took place before another event or an adverbial of past time. The present and past perfect progressives, on the other hand, are used when continuance or ongoingness of an event at a definite time—within the actual present and the past, respectively—are being described.

He estado pensando en ti toda la tarde.	*I have been thinking about you all afternoon.*
Había estado pensando en ti toda la tarde.	*I had been thinking about you all afternoon.*
Hemos estado trabajando todo el día.	*We have been working all day long.*
Habíamos estado trabajando todo el día.	*We had been working all day long.*

In English the present and past perfect progressives must be used when describing events begun at an earlier point but still ongoing at a later and specific time.[2] In

---

[1] ***Cuando yo llegué, él estuvo estudiando** and all other sentences of this type are ungrammatical in Spanish.

[2] Stative verbs, of course, do not take progressives in English: *She has known it for weeks, He has loved her for years.*

Spanish the simple present and imperfect tenses, respectively, with the temporal expressions of continuity **hace . . . que** and **desde hace . . .** are more idiomatic than progressives if the meaning of the verb refers to a durative, non-conclusive action, or to a conclusive but repeated event.

We have been living here for years.	Hace años que vivimos aquí.
We had been living there for years.	Hacía años que vivíamos allí.
She has been dating him for months.	Sale con él desde hace meses.
She had been dating him for months.	Salía con él desde hacía meses.
She has not been eating for a week.	Hace una semana que no come.

When the meaning of the verb refers to a conclusive event and ongoingness is confined to a short period of time, then the progressive is also obligatory in Spanish. But in Spanish the present and imperfect progressives are used rather than the present and past perfect progressives as in English.

Hace horas que se lo estoy explicando.	*I have been explaining it to him for hours.*
Hace rato que te lo estoy suplicando.	*I have been begging you for quite a while.*
Hacía horas que se lo estaba explicando.	*I had been explaining it to him for hours.*
Hacía rato que se lo estaba suplicando.	*I had been begging him for quite a while.*

When repetition and realization by degree from a time frame forward are stressed, then **ir** or **venir** progressives or the simple tenses occur instead of **estar** progressives.

Desde que murió su padre ha ido malgastando la fortuna de la familia.	*Since his father died he has been squandering the family's fortune.*
Poco a poco ha ido limitando (. . . limitaba) su independencia.	*He has been curtailing her freedom little by little.*
Desde que había muerto el padre había ido malgastando la fortuna de la familia.	*Since his father had died he had been squandering the family's fortune.*
A medida que se mejoraba había ido recobrando el uso de sus facultades.	*At the same rate he was recovering he was regaining the use of his faculties.*

The Future and Conditional Progressives

The simple future and conditional tenses describe the occurrence of an event as subsequent to the grammatical present and past, respectively. Since the notion of subsequence is incompatible with the notion of co-existence, the future and conditional progressives are used under the following conditions:

1. When a future event is viewed as co-occurring with another subsequent event:

Cuando llegues estaremos esperándote en el aeropuerto.	*When you arrive we will be waiting for you at the airport.*

Convenimos que cuando llegara estaríamos esperándolo en el aeropuerto.	*We agreed that when he arrived we would be waiting for him at the airport.*

2. When an anticipated event is viewed as ongoing at a specific future time:

Mañana a estas horas estaré escribiéndote.	*Tomorrow at this time I will be writing to you.*
La semana que viene estaremos cruzando el ecuador.	*Next week we will be crossing the equator.*

3. When probability or conjecture about present and past ongoing events is described, the future and conditional progressives are used respectively. This is their most productive occurrence in Spanish because the simple future and conditional could either express subsequence or conjecture, and thus be ambiguous. In English the present and preterit progressives with expressions of probability occur in these contexts.

¿En qué estará pensando ella?	*I wonder what she is thinking about?*
¿Qué estará haciendo el niño?	*I wonder what the child is doing?*
¿Qué estarán diciendo?	*I wonder what they are saying?*
Ella se preguntaba si entre esa mujer y su marido no estaría pasando algo.	*She was wondering whether something wasn't going on between her husband and that woman.*

BUT:

¿Qué le dirá a ella?	$\begin{cases} \textit{What will he tell her?} \\ \textit{What could he be telling her?} \end{cases}$
¿Qué pasaría allí?	$\begin{cases} \textit{What would happen there?} \\ \textit{What was going on there?} \end{cases}$

Spanish future and conditional progressives are not used to express the intent to act, which is the most productive usage of these tenses in English. In Spanish, the simple future, **ir a**+INF in the present or the imperfect (depending upon temporal perspective), or the conditional is used instead.

We will be sending her flowers for her birthday.	Vamos a enviarle flores para su cumpleaños.
She said she would be leaving soon.	Dijo que se iría (iba a ir) pronto.
I was told they would be marrying soon.	Me dijeron que se casarían (iban a casarse) pronto.

5

SIMPLE PAST TENSES OF THE INDICATIVE: PRETERIT AND IMPERFECT

The Simple Past Tenses

Spanish has two simple past tenses, the preterit and the imperfect. The selection of one tense over the other is not determined by different temporal dimensions (both may refer to definite and indefinite past events) but by differences in the aspect of the action.

Aspectual differences arise from different conceptualizations of events. Any event can be viewed, potentially speaking, at different stages of its occurrence: at its beginning, its end, globally (beginning and end included), and in the course of its unfolding—without reference to either beginning or termination. Conceptualizing an event at its beginning corresponds to initiative aspect; at its end or globally (beginning and end included) represents terminative aspect. Viewing an event without reference to beginning or end is equivalent to durative or imperfective aspect. The Spanish preterit is characterized by initiative and terminative aspects, both of which depict an event as a point in time. The Spanish imperfect is characterized by durative or imperfective aspects, which describe an event as a continuum in time.

The aspectual differences described above are lacking in English. Thus, there is no one-to-one correspondence between the preterit and imperfect tenses and any single English verbal form. The equivalences that can be established between any two forms, for example, the Spanish and English preterits—both past and perfective—and the Spanish imperfect and English past progressive—both durative and imperfective—are incomplete and, if not qualified, misleading. The lack of true correspondences, and the complexities that arise in attempting to establish them, result not merely from the aspectual differences that exist in Spanish but also from the range of options within a given context and the restrictions in usage that characterize potential English equivalents. For these reasons, and others to be mentioned later, the Spanish preterit and imperfect, depending upon the context in which they occur and the meaning being signaled, may correspond to one or to more than one of the following English forms:

PRETERIT

Vivió en Madrid un año.	*He* lived *in Madrid for one year.*
Fue embajador en Francia.	*He* used to be (*was*) *ambassador to France.*
Ya se fue.	*He* has *already* left.
La boda fue el sábado.	*The wedding* had been *on Saturday.*

IMPERFECT

Mientras escribía, fumaba.	*When he* was writing, *he* was smoking. *While he* wrote, *he* smoked. *When he* was writing, *he* would smoke.
Cuando llegué, él estudiaba.	*When I arrived, he* was studying.
Cuando yo llegaba, él salía.	*As I* was arriving, *he* was leaving. *Whenever I* would arrive, *he* would leave.
Se veían a menudo como suele ser con los buenos amigos.	*They* used to see *each other often, as is the case with good friends.*
Hacía años que estudiaba música.	*She* had been studying *music for years.*
La conocía desde hacía años.	*She* had known *her for years.*
Me informó que regresaba la semana siguiente.	*He informed me he would return the following week.* *He informed me he* would be returning . . . *He informed me he* was returning . . .
Si tuviera tiempo, iba.	*If I had time, I* would go.
Era encantador.	*He* was *charming.*

The Preterit

TIME

The Spanish preterit is an absolute tense. It is absolute in the sense that it can refer to a definite or indefinite past time and describe a single event or series of events, without reference to another action or temporal expression. But since all absolute tenses can be used in a relative way as well, the preterit may also be used in relation to other events and temporal expressions.

Nunca fue amigo mío.	*He was never a friend of mine.*
Nació, vivió y murió en Salamanca	*He was born, lived, and died in Salamanca.*
Entró, saludó a todos y al rato se retiró a su cuarto.	*He came in, greeted everyone, and shortly thereafter retired to his room.*
Ni bien me vio, vino a saludarme.	*As soon as he saw me, he came to greet me.*

Whereas in Spanish the preterit can refer to a definite or indefinite past time, the English preterit generally occurs only in reference to a definite past dimension, expressed or implied.[1] When the Spanish preterit refers to an indefinite past time, it is equivalent to the English *used to* + INF construction, which occurs in these contexts.

Vivió en Madrid diez años.	*He lived in Madrid for ten years.*
Fue embajador en Francia de 1956 a 1960.	*He was ambassador to France from 1956 to 1960.*
El verano pasado trabajó en Europa.	*Last summer he worked in Europe.*

BUT:

Fue embajador en Francia.	*He used to be ambassador to France.*
Trabajó en el Departamento de Estado.	*He used to work for the State Department.*
Vivió en el extranjero.	*He used to live abroad.*

The temporal distinctions between the Spanish preterit and present perfect are often neutralized. While this is far more frequent in American than Castillian Spanish, in both the preterit is generally used for completed actions within the extended present. Since English observes more strictly than Spanish the connection of a perfective event in relation to the present, the Spanish preterit will be equivalent to the English past perfect in this context.

¿Se fue ya para su casa?	*Has he already left for home?*
Terminé todas las cartas.	*I have finished all the letters.*
¿Acabaste la tarea ya?	*Have you finished your homework?*
Por fin entendiste lo que quiero decir.	*At last you have understood what I mean.*

The Spanish preterit is used instead of the past perfect to indicate the immediate anteriority of an event in relation to another. The English preterit, having no punctual aspect, is not always interchangeable with the past perfect. Consequently, the Spanish preterit may also correspond to the English past perfect.

Dijo que estuvo gravemente enfermo.	*He said he had been gravely ill.*

---

[1] An exception is comparative sentences in which the preterit does occur for indefinite past time: *Spain is no longer what she was, He is no longer as powerful as he was once upon a time.*

Supimos que la boda fue el sábado.

We learned that the wedding had been on Saturday.

Me contó que tuvo dificultades con su jefe.

He told me he had had difficulties with his boss.

Had the English preterit been used in the above sentences it would have indicated co-existence or subsequence in relation to the subordinating verb—but not anteriority.

He said he was gravely ill.
We learned that the wedding was (would be) on Saturday.
He told me he had (was having) difficulties with his boss.

Dijo que estaba gravemente enfermo.
Supimos que la boda era el sábado.

Me contó que tenía dificultades con su jefe.

ASPECT

The aspect of the Spanish preterit is perfective and punctual. *Perfective* means completed action, whether a single event or a series of the same event is described. *Punctual* means that the action or state of being is depicted as a point in time rather than a continuum, even when the event was durative or extended through repetition.

The differences in usage between the Spanish and English preterits arise from the punctual aspect of the Spanish form. The English preterit also implies perfective, completed action, but it does not imply punctual action. Thus, it can be used for non-conclusive events which were indefinitely extended, and which in Spanish can only be rendered by the imperfect. Since the Spanish preterit has perfective and punctual aspect it may co-occur with indicators of specific, definite time: **a las cuatro, a mediodía**, etc. When repeated actions are described, the preterit occurs only with adverbials that are definitely confined: **diez años, varias veces, el año pasado**, etc.

El tratado se firmó a las tres.
Llegó a las siete.
Ayer estudió todo el día.
Vivió toda la vida en Salamanca.

The treaty was signed at three.
He arrived at seven.
Yesterday he studied all day long.
He lived in Salamanca all his life.

Conversely, the preterit does not co-occur with adverbials that are indefinitely extended, such as **de vez en cuando, generalmente, habitualmente**, and **cada tanto**. When an adverbial of indefinite repetition occurs with the preterit, another adverbial of definite extension co-occurs with it, explicitly or implicitly.

El mes pasado trabajó todos los fines de semana.

Last month he worked every weekend.

La fue a ver todos los días mientras estuvo enferma.

He went to see her daily while she was sick.

No faltó al trabajo nunca.

He never missed a day's work (while he worked).

ASPECT AND MANNER OF THE ACTION

The Spanish preterit, as stated initially, may refer to either initiative or terminative aspect. Whether initiative or terminative aspect is signaled depends upon the manner of the action, that is, the intrinsic nature of the event itself and the context in which it occurs.

1. When a verb refers to a conclusive, non-durative event—one that must be terminated in order to be completed—the preterit describes it as perfected and terminated. This is the case with all verbs of brief or instantaneous action. In this case, both Spanish and English convey the same information.

Se fue ayer.	*He left yesterday.*
Envió la carta.	*He sent the letter.*
Cerró ventanas y puertas.	*He shut all doors and windows.*
Señaló al culpable.	*She pointed out the offender.*
Lo expulsaron del club.	*They expelled him from the club.*
La primera guerra mundial estalló en 1914.	*World War I broke out in 1914.*

2. When a verb refers to a non-conclusive event (action or state of being) which is durative in itself two possibilities arise. The preterit may either refer to the moment of the completion of the event, which coincides with the moment of its beginning, or to the end of the event, which coincides with its termination.

   a. With a limited number of verbs of knowledge, perception, emotion, and being, the preterit refers to the beginning of the event, but the event is perfected and completed when it takes place. Consequently, initiative aspect contains no necessary reference to duration. It only stresses the perfection of the event itself. The English preterit does not differentiate between initiative and terminative aspect. The Spanish preterit signaling initiative aspect may be rendered in English lexically, by other alternate constructions, or by the preterit itself.

   With verbs of knowledge, the difference between initiative and durative aspect may be rendered in English by different lexical items.

INITIATIVE	DURATIVE
Supe que te ibas.	Sabía que te ibas.
I learned (found out) that you were leaving.	*I knew that you were leaving.*
La conocí anoche.	La conocía bien.
I met her last night.	*I knew her well.*
Comprendí por qué no quería casarse.	Comprendía por qué no quería casarse.
I grasped why she did not want to get married.	*I understood why she did not want to get married (could see her point, shared her view).*

Verbs of perception, regardless of initiative or terminative aspect, are rendered in English by the preterit.

De repente oímos un ruido espantoso.	All of a sudden we heard a terrible crash.
Vi que se iba.	I saw her leaving.
En ese momento sentí tremenda compasión por la mujer.	At that moment I felt great compassion for the woman.
Al verla tan frágil tuve la sensación de que era sólo una niña.	Upon seeing her so fragile I had the feeling she was just a little girl.
Un sentimiento de bienestar inundó su ser.	A feeling of well-being overcame him.

With reflexive verbs which in the preterit signal the entry into a state of being (whether these be of emotion or of a different nature), several English constructions may be used to signal initiative aspect: *get* or *become* + past participle or adjective; *to fall* + noun or past participle, and the preterit when the verb is intransitive.

Al oírme hablar, se espantó.	Upon hearing me talk, she became frightened.
Cuando se lo dije, se enfureció.	When I told her, she became furious.
Al rato se tranquilizó.	A while later he calmed down.
Ni bien la vio, se enamoró.	The minute he saw her, he fell in love.
Ni bien se acostó, se durmió.	As soon as he went to bed, he fell asleep.
Se hizo famoso.	He became famous.

With the verb of being **ser**, contextual clues indicate whether initiative or terminative aspect is conveyed. When existence from a given point on is conveyed, then initiative aspect applies. Excepting terminative aspect which may be rendered in English by the past perfect, Spanish initiative and durative aspect with **ser** are rendered in English by the preterit.

INITIATIVE	TERMINATIVE
Dios dijo: Sea la luz y la luz fue. *God said: Let there be light and there was light.*	Hacerle cambiar de opinión fue muy difícil. *Making him change his mind had been very difficult.*
Desde ese día ya no fue la misma mujer. *From that day on she no longer was the same woman.*	Cárdenas fue maestro de escuela antes de ser presidente. *Cardenas had been a school teacher before he was president.*
Aunque se habían reconciliado, desde entonces la relación entre ambos fue diferente. *Even though they had made amends, from that point on the relationship between them was (became) different.*	Fue un gran presidente. *He was (had been) a great president.*

DURATIVE

Hacerle cambiar de opinión era muy difícil.	*Making him change his mind was very difficult.*
Era maestro de escuela.	*He was a school teacher.*
Era muy guapa de joven.	*She was very beautiful as a young woman.*

b. When the preterit occurs with other verbs which refer to non-conclusive events, it describes them globally, beginning and end included. The event is not only perfected but terminated. Even though the event might have had considerable extension in time, it is not described as durative or as ongoing within the past. The preterit depicts it as a point in time. Extension beyond that point is impossible.

Vivió toda la vida en Salamanca.	*He lived in Salamanca all his life.*
Luchó por la emancipación de los oprimidos por muchos años.	*He fought for the emancipation of the oppressed for several years.*
Estuvo enfermo varios meses.	*He was (had been) ill for several months.*

Temporal dimensions: anteriority versus co-existence

Since the Spanish preterit depicts an event as a point in time, it cannot occur in indirect discourse as a backshifted present, as does the English preterit. The English preterit in this context, which may describe co-existence or subsequence in relation to the subordinating verb, is rendered in Spanish by the imperfect.

He said he had to study. (The event is either co-existent with the moment of utterance or subsequent to it.)	Dijo que tenía que estudiar.
He said he was sick. (Co-existence only.)	Dijo que estaba enferma.

The Spanish preterit in this context would always signal anteriority in relation to the subordinating verb.

Dijo que no pudo (había podido) ir.	*He said he had not been able to go.*
Quiso (había querido) ir pero no pudo.	*He had wanted to go but could not.*
Dijo que tuvo (había tenido) que estudiar.	*He said he had had to study.*

Due to its punctual aspect, the Spanish preterit cannot occur in subordinate sentences to express co-existence, as the English preterit does with stative and durative verbs. Nor can it be used in comparative sentences where a contrast between a former and subsequent event is stated. The imperfect applies in both cases.

While she was a student she earned her living as a waitress.	Cuando era estudiante se ganaba la vida como camarera.
When he wrote, he smoked a pipe.	Cuando escribía, fumaba pipa.

| While she studied, she drank coffee to stay awake. | Mientras estudiaba, tomaba café para mantenerse despierta. |
| Even though he had been promoted, he still worked as hard as before. | Aunque lo habían ascendido, trabajaba tanto como antes. |

Co-existence is not signaled by the Spanish preterit in subordinate clauses, regardless of the manner of the action and the initiative or terminative aspect of the verb. Even in those subordinate sentences in which the preterit has initiative aspect, sequential events are described. This is evident from the fact that the clause containing the preterit with initiative aspect can be rewritten—without altering the meaning of the sentence—as an adverbial clause implying anteriority.

| Cuando me acostumbré a su voz, pude seguir la conferencia. Después que me acostumbré a su voz pude seguir la conferencia. | Once I got used to his voice, I could follow the lecture. |
| Cuando le habló calmadamente, lo escuchó. Después que (una vez que) le habló calmadamente, lo escuchó. | Once he spoke to her calmly, she listened. |

The Imperfect Indicative

ASPECT AND TIME

The imperfect indicative describes a past action, state, or condition as a continuum in time without any reference to its beginning or end. Since it never implies the termination of an event, its durative aspect may be one of definite or indefinite extension in time. For this reason, the imperfect functions as a backshifted present. As a backshifted present it describes, in relation to the grammatical past, what the present tense describes in relation to the grammatical present: (1) ongoing events; (2) repeated or continued actions; (3) the existence of states and conditions, either short or long lasting; (4) future time or intent; and (5) actions begun in prior dimensions which were still in progress at a later stage within the grammatical past. Whether the imperfect tense describes an ongoing event simultaneous with another event, habitual actions, future events, or perfective but still ongoing actions, depends largely upon the manner of the action, that is, the intrinsic nature of the event itself and the linguistic or extra-linguistic context in which it occurs.

Present Tense	*Imperfect Tense*
ONGOING EVENTS AT THE TIME IN QUESTION	
¿Qué hace en la cocina a estas horas? *What is she doing in the kitchen at this hour?*	¿Qué hacía en la cocina a esas horas? *What was she doing in the kitchen at that hour?*

Veo que viene solo.
I see that he is coming alone.

Vi que venía solo.
I saw that he was coming alone.

Creo que habla con alguien.
I think that she is talking to someone.

Creía que hablaba con alguien.
I thought that she was talking to someone.

REPEATED OR CONTINUED ACTIONS

La llamo todos los lunes.
I call her every Monday.

La llamaba todos los lunes.
I would call her every Monday.

Cenan a las siete generalmente.
They dine at seven generally.

Cenaban a las siete generalmente.
They would dine at seven generally.

No se llevan bien.
They do not get along.

No se llevaban bien.
They did not get along.

STATES OF BEING AND CONDITIONS, SHORT OR LONG LASTING

Se ve que está triste.
One can see that he is sad.

Se veía que estaba triste.
One could see that he was sad.

La situación política es inquietante.
The political situation is disturbing.

La situación política era inquietante.
The political situation was disturbing.

El Perú abarca una gran extensión territorial.
Peru embraces a large territorial expanse.

El Antiguo Perú abarcaba una gran extensión territorial.
Old Peru embraced a large territorial expanse.

FUTURE TIME OR INTENT

Dicen que parten mañana.
They say they will leave (are leaving) tomorrow.

Dijeron que partían mañana.
They said they would leave (were, would be leaving) tomorrow.

María se recibe la semana entrante.
Maria will graduate next week.

María se recibía la semana siguiente.
Maria would graduate the following week.

Se comprometen mañana.
They will get engaged tomorrow.

Se comprometían al día siguiente.
They would get engaged the following day.

EVENTS BEGUN IN A PRIOR DIMENSION, STILL IN PROGRESS AT THE TIME IN QUESTION

La conoce desde hace años.
He has known her for years.

La conocía desde hacía años.
He had known her for years.

Trabaja allí desde enero.
He has been working there since
  January.

Trabajaba allí desde enero.
He had been working there since
  January.

Salen juntos desde hace tiempo.
They have been going together for a
  long time.

Salían juntos desde hacía tiempo.
They had been going together for a long
  time.

Temporal dimension : co-existence

Although the imperfect tense can assume any of the functions of the present tense, the imperfect is not an absolute but a relative tense. The present tense is absolute in the sense that it can be used with or without reference to the actual present, and may occur independently of other anterior or co-existent events. The usage of the imperfect, on the other hand, is generally dependent upon some specific time reference. Time reference may either be conveyed by the co-occurrence of another event (in a different tense) or by an adverbial of past time. But just as the present tense describes co-existence with the moment of utterance, the imperfect describes co-existence in relation to another past event or a given past perspective. The imperfect describing co-existence tends to occur most often in relation to the preterit, but it may also be used in connection with other verbs.

La llamé pero no estaba en casa.
I called her but she was not at home.

Cuando la conocí tenía veinte años.
When I met her she was twenty years
  old.

Cuando tú llegabas, él salía.
As you were arriving, he was leaving.

No me ha dicho lo que yo esperaba
oír.
He has not told me what I expected
  (was expecting) to hear.

¿No te das cuenta de que podías ser
su padre?
Don't you realize that you could be her
  father?

Sabía que tú lo harías.
He knew you would do it.

Vimos su casa que estaba situada en
una colina y tenía una vista
magnífica. Hermosos jardines la
rodeaban.
We saw his house which was located on
  a hill and had a magnificent view. Beau-
  tiful gardens surrounded it.

When the imperfect does not occur in relation to another verb, it generally co-occurs with adverbials of past time. Occasionally, however, it may be used without any reference to a specific point in the past.

El año pasado cenábamos a las siete.
Last year we would dine at seven.

Cuando él hablaba anoche todos lo
escuchaban con gran interés.
While he was speaking last night
  everyone listened with great interest.

En aquellos tiempos no estaba de
moda asolearse.
In those days it was not fashionable to
  sunbathe.

Antes el matrimonio significaba un
lazo indisoluble.
In former times, marriage meant an
  indissoluble bond.

Cuando él hablaba, todos temblaban.	*Whenever he would speak, everyone would tremble.*
Inglaterra ya no es lo que era.	*England no longer is what she used to be.*

Aspect and manner of the action

The aspect of the imperfect, as already stated, is one of durative, non-terminated action. For this reason the imperfect can describe an event as ongoing at a given time; as repeated or continued (definitely or indefinitely); or as subsequent to the time in question. The interpretation of a given event is determined by the intrinsic nature of the event itself and the linguistic or extra-linguistic context in which it occurs.

1. When the meaning of the verb refers to a conclusive action, one that must be terminated in order to be completed, ongoingness at the time in question is described.

   a. The imperfect describes a single or repeated ongoing action of either short or long duration. Ongoingness is conveyed by the co-occurence of another event or an adverbial that signals specific past time.

SINGLE ONGOING EVENT

Se moría lentemente. Su cuerpo se consumía y su espíritu se enflaquecía.	*He was slowly dying. His body was wasting away and his spirit was failing.*
La vida se le escapaba.	*His life was slipping away.*
Cuando yo llegué, ella acostaba al niño.	*When I arrived, she was putting the child to bed.*
Cuando yo llegaba ayer, él partía.	*As I was arriving yesterday, he was leaving.*

REPEATED ONGOING EVENTS

Era mediodía. Iba y venía de un lado para otro sin poder refrenarse. No era para menos, su hijo estaba a punto de nacer.	*It was noon. He was pacing up and down without being able to restrain himself. It was understandable, for his son was about to be born.*
El niño tocaba cuanto objeto había en la sala. Su madre se desesperaba y no veía la hora de que se fueran las visitas.	*The child was touching every object in the living room. His mother was in a state of frenzy and could hardly wait for the guests to leave.*
Marido y mujer discutían anoche. Yo los oía desde mi cuarto. A ratos parecían calmarse pero a los pocos minutos volvían a comenzar.	*The husband and wife were arguing last night. I could hear them from my room. At moments they seemed to calm down, but they would begin again a few minutes later.*

Los invitados llegaban unos tras otros. El anfitrión los hacía pasar.	*The guests were arriving one after the other. The host was showing them in.*
Estaba agitadísimo esa mañana. Fumaba un cigarillo detrás de otro y se retorcía las manos frenéticamente.	*He was very agitated that morning. He was smoking one cigarette after another and wringing his hands frantically.*

b. The imperfect describes habitually repeated events. Repetition is conveyed by the context, adverbials of repetition (**todos los días, cada año, generalmente, constantemente**, etc.), or adverbials of manner (**muy bien, mal, magníficamente**, etc.).

Cada tanto llegaba tarde al trabajo.	*Every so often he was (would be) late for work.*
Los negocios cerraban a las siete en verano.	*The stores closed at seven in the summer.*
Salían juntos casi siempre.	*They went out together most of the time.*
El cartero llegaba a mediodía.	*The mailman used to arrive at noon.*
Generalmente nos recibía con mucha cordialidad.	*Generally he would receive us very cordially.*
Cuando hacía mucho calor abrían puertas y ventanas, pero nunca prendían el aire acondicionado.	*When it was very hot they would open doors and windows, but never turn on the air-conditioning.*

2. When the imperfect refers to non-conclusive events, durative actions, and states of being, the duration may be definitely or indefinitely confined.

a. Durative actions and inner processes may be definitely or indefinitely extended in time, depending upon the intent of the speaker.

Sabía su materia como nadie.	*He knew his subject matter better than anyone else.*
Ayer no sabía nada en clase.	*Yesterday he did not know a thing in class.*
Dudaba de todo y de todos.	*He doubted everything and everyone.*
Hasta hace poco dudaba de ella, pero ahora ya no.	*Until recently he was unsure of her, but now that is no longer the case.*
Vivían en Madrid.	*They were living (used to live) in Madrid.*
Hasta al año pasado vivían en Madrid.	*Until last year they lived in Madrid.*
Al entrar me di cuenta que discutían.	*When I walked in I realized that they were arguing.*
Discutían muy frecuentemente.	*They used to argue very often.*

b. States of being and conditions may be short or long lasting, depending upon the nature of the state of being and the context in which it occurs.

El verano estaba calurosísimo.	*The summer was very hot.*
El día estaba muy caluroso.	*The day was very hot.*
Esa semana se encontraba agotado.	*That week he was exhausted.*
Nunca le faltaban energías.	*He never lacked energy.*
Al llegar los españoles a América, se encontraron con diversas razas indígenas que tenían diversos niveles de civilización.	*Upon arriving to America, the Spaniards encountered diverse indigenous races which exhibited different levels of civilization.*
Al ver el mar Caribe me di cuenta que sus aguas eran magníficas.	*When I saw the Caribbean I realized that its waters were magnificent.*

3. Since the imperfect may have indefinite extension in time, a state of being or event perfected in a prior dimension

a. may continue to exist or still be in progress at a later stage in the past:

Se conocían desde la infancia.	*They had known each other since early childhood.*
Estudiaba música desde hacía años.	*She had been studying music for years.*
Veraneaban en el mismo lugar desde hacía años.	*They had been spending the summers at the same resort for years.*
Estaban muy descontentos desde que se habían mudado.	*They had been very unhappy ever since they had moved.*
Estaba muy enferma desde el año pasado.	*She had been very ill since last year.*

b. may continue to exist within the present time itself. For this reason the imperfect is also used to describe current truths which were equally applicable to former times. In this context the imperfect tends to be subordinated to a verb in the preterit or the imperfect:

Copérnico demostró que la tierra giraba (gira) alreador del sol.	*Copernicus has demonstrated that the earth revolves around the sun.*
Fleming descubrió que la penicilina era (es) un agente efectivo contra ciertas infecciones.	*Fleming has discovered that penicillin is an effective agent against certain infections.*
Yo creía que era (es) tu amigo.	*I thought he was (is) your friend.*
No sabía que él estaba (está) aquí.	*I didn't know he was (is) here.*
Traté de olvidarme de quien era (soy).	*I tried to forget who I was (am).*

The imperfect as a backshifted future

Because the imperfect describes an event as a continuum in time which may have indefinite extension, it is also used as a backshifted future to express intent or future time in relation to the grammatical past.

1. The most frequent occurrence of the imperfect expressing future time is its usage in indirect discourse. In indirect discourse one reports what someone else said or thought. The quote is introduced by a verb of saying in the preterit, such as **decir**, **contestar**, and **explicar**. The persons are shifted and the tenses are changed. The quote may, however, also occur without an introducing verb. Verbs most likely to be used in this context are the same ones used in the present tense: verbs of motion of short duration or instantaneous action; and verbs of volition, need, and desire which are durative in themselves.

DIRECT DISCOURSE	INDIRECT DISCOURSE
Present	*Imperfect*
Salgo mañana a las tres. *I will leave (be leaving) tomorrow at three.*	Dijo que salía mañana a las tres. *He said he would leave (be leaving, was leaving) tomorrow at three.*
Regresa la semana próxima. *He will return (is returning) next week.*	Anunciaron que regresaba la semana próxima. *They announced that he would return (**be** returning, was returning) next week.*
Quiere verla mañana por la tarde. *He wants to see her tomorrow afternoon.*	Dijo que quería verla mañana por la tarde. *He said that he wanted to see her tomorrow afternoon.*
Quiero ir pero no puedo. *I want to go but I cannot.*	(Explicó que . . .) Quería ir pero no podía. *(He explained that . . .) He wanted to go but couldn't.*
Espero poder asistir a la conferencia. *I hope to be able to attend the lecture.*	(Me contestó que . . .) Esperaba poder asistir a la conferencia. *(He replied that . . .) He hoped to be able to attend the lecture.*

2. Very frequently, however, the shifting of tenses is not due to indirect discourse, but to the fact that the subordinating verb is in the past and that the depending verb—logically in the present or the future—is therefore shifted.

No sabía que llegaban hoy. . . . llegan . . . van a llegar . . .	*I did not know that they were arriving today.* *. . . are arriving . . .* *. . . will arrive . . .*
No me dijeron que hablaba esta tarde. . . . que habla . . . . . . que va a hablar . . .	*They did not tell me that he was speaking this afternoon.* *. . . is speaking . . .* *. . . will speak . . .*

3. The prospective present **ir a** + INF is rendered in the past by the imperfect.

Iba a ir, si podía.	*She was going to go if she could.*
¡Cómo iba a dejarlo solo si estaba enfermo!	*How was I going to leave him alone when he was sick!*
¡Cómo iba a pagarle si no tenía dinero!	*How was I going to pay him when I had no money!*
Iban a entrevistarlo esta tarde.	*They were going to interview him this afternoon.*

In other than the above cases the imperfect expressing intent is used in requests in direct or indirect discourse. In direct discourse the action can be viewed as having begun in a prior dimension and continuing at the time of the utterance.

Dijo que necesitaba hablarle.	*He said he needed to talk to you.*
Quería verte para pedirte un favor.	*I wanted to see you to ask for a favor.*
Venía a pedirle permiso para irme.	*I came to request permission to leave.*
¿Qué deseaba Ud?	*What did you wish?*

In informal speech the imperfect occurs instead of the conditional in *if*-clauses.

Si pudiera, iría. ⎫ Si pudiera ir, iba.⎭	*If I could go, I would.*
Si tuviera dinero, compraba (= compraría) esa casa.	*If I had money, I would buy that house.*
Dijo que si tenía tiempo, pasaba (= pasaría) a vernos.	*He said that if he had time he would stop by to see us.*

ENGLISH EQUIVALENTS FOR THE SPANISH IMPERFECT

The English equivalents for the Spanish imperfect are numerous: the preterit; the preterit progressive; *would* or *used to* + INF; the past perfect; the past perfect progressive; the conditional; and the conditional progressive. These equivalents respond to the varied functions that the imperfect may assume and to the functions that each of the English simple, perfect, and progressive tenses can have. Therefore, English equivalents for the imperfect depend upon the function of a Spanish imperfect in a given context, as well as the usage restrictions or limitations that characterize the English forms. For these reasons, the English equivalents of the imperfect are not interchangeable in most contexts.

English preterit for Spanish imperfect

The Spanish imperfect describing the co-existence of a state or condition with another event or in relation to a definite past time functions as a retrospective present. In these cases it corresponds to the English preterit. The English preterit is perfective but not punctual. It may, therefore, have indefinite extension in time and function as a retrospective present with stative and durative verbs. The Spanish preterit, on the other hand, could never occur in this context because it is not only perfective but punctual as well. It depicts an event as a point in time and cannot, therefore, describe extension beyond that point.

Extended Present	*Extended Retrospective Present*
Me siento decepcionada y no sé por qué. *I feel disappointed but I do not know why.*	Me sentía decepcionada y no sabía por qué. *I felt disappointed but I did not know why.*
Son las siete. Todos estamos sentados alrededor de la mesa. *It is seven o'clock. All of us are seated at the table.*	Eran las siete. Todos estábamos sentados alrededor de la mesa. *It was seven o'clock. All of us were seated at the table.*
Es especialista en medicina interna. *He is a specialist in internal medicine.*	Era especialista en medicina interna. *He was a specialist in internal medicine.*
Estudia y trabaja de camarera para pagarse los gastos. *She studies and also works as a waitress to pay for her expenses.*	Estudiaba y trabajaba de camarera para pagarse los gastos. *She studied and also worked as a waitress to pay for her expenses.*

If an inner process is described—either as co-existent with another event or in relation to a definite past time—it also corresponds to the English preterit.

No le gustan las fiestas. *He does not like parties.*	No le gustaban las fiestas. *He did not like parties.*
No le interesa la política. *He is not interested in politics.*	No le interesaba la política. *He was not interested in politics.*
Ya no confía en nadie. *He no longer trusts anyone.*	Ya no confiaba en nadie. *He no longer trusted anyone.*

English preterit progressive for Spanish imperfect

When the imperfect describes an ongoing action, or two simultaneous ongoing actions which occurred at a *specific* time (*at nine o'clock, at that very moment,* etc.), in English the preterit progressive will be equivalent to the Spanish imperfect. The English preterit does not generally occur in these contexts because it does not describe the simultaneous occurrence of two events on a specific occasion, nor does it emphasize the ongoingness of an event at a specific time.[1]

Cuando se despidieron, la mujer lloraba amargamente.	*When they said good-bye to each other, the woman was crying bitterly.*

---

[1] See Chapter 4, Progressive Constructions.

Cuando la conocí, ella trabajaba en la Embajada de Francia.	When I met her, she was working at the French Embassy.
Eran las nueve. El niño dormía tranquilamente.	It was nine o'clock. The child was sleeping peacefully.
¿En qué pensaba esa mujer en ese momento?	What was the woman thinking about at that moment?
Al oirla hablar, dudaba de su propia cordura.	As he was listening to her speak, he was doubting his own sanity.
¿Qué hacía Pablo el martes pasado?	What was Paul doing last Tuesday?
—Jugaba golf con sus amigos.	—He was playing golf with his friends.

But when the imperfect describes repeated or habitual events, the co-occurrence of two events which did not take place at the very same time, then the simple preterit modified by indicators of repetition can also correspond to the Spanish imperfect.

Cada vez que íbamos de merienda, llovía.	Every time we went on a picnic, it rained.
Mientras vivíamos en Francia, íbamos al teatro con frecuencia.	While we lived in France, we went to the theater often.
Los martes jugaba golf.	On Tuesdays he played golf.
Por las tardes estudiaba.	In the afternoons she studied.
Dormía de día porque trabajaba de noche.	He slept in the daytime because he worked nights.
Cuando leía, fumaba.	When he read, he smoked.

"Used to" and "would"+ INF for Spanish imperfect

Neither the English preterit nor the preterit progressive is used for events which occurred at an indefinite past time. When the imperfect describes habitual events which occurred in the indefinite past, in English *would* or *used to*+INF corresponds to the imperfect.

Llegaba tarde al trabajo con frecuencia.	He often used to be late for work.

"He was frequently late for work" would imply repetition at some definite point, such as "during the last few weeks," "while he was sick," or some other time.

Su abuelo era un tirano. Cuando hablaba todos temblaban.	His grandfather used to be a tyrant. When he spoke, everyone would tremble.
Se veían muy a menudo, como suele ser con los amigos de verdad.	They used to see each other often, as is the case with true friends.

Both *would* and *used to* + INF may also occur in relation to a specific past time when repetition is implied. They may, therefore, also be used in that context.

El verano pasado, salíamos más seguido.	{ *Last year we used to go out more often.* { *Last year we would go out more often.*
Cuando trabajaba en el centro, él me esperaba para que regresáramos juntos.	{ *When I worked downtown, he would wait for me so that we could return together.* *When I worked downtown, he used to wait for me so that we could return together.*

English past perfect and past perfect progressive for Spanish imperfect

When the imperfect describes an event which had begun at some earlier point but was going on at a later stage in the past, in English the past perfect progressive will correspond to the imperfect, unless the verb is one of inner life. Inner life processes are rendered in this case by the simple past perfect.

Trabajaba allí desde enero.	*He had been working there since January.*
Estudiaba música desde hacía años.	*She had been studying music for years.*
Se querían desde la adolescencia.	*They had been in love with each other since their teens.*
Estaban muy descontentos desde que se habían mudado.	*They had been very unhappy ever since they had moved.*

English conditional and conditional progressive for Spanish imperfect

The imperfect expressing future time or intent is rendered in English by either the simple or the progressive conditional, except in *if*-clauses where only the simple conditional may occur. But since intent and future time can also be rendered by the preterit progressive, this tense may also occur in this context.

Me informó que regresaba esa noche.	*He informed me that he would return (would be, was returning) that evening.*
Supe que se casaban mañana.	*I learned that they would get married (would be, were getting married) tomorrow.*
Si tuviera tiempo, iba.	*If I had time, I would go.*
Dijo que si tenía dinero, lo compraba.	*He said that if he had money, he would buy it.*

The Preterit Contrasted with the Imperfect

THE PRETERIT CONTRASTED WITH THE IMPERFECT

Preterit	*Imperfect*

OVERVIEW

Absolute past tense. It reports past actions *independently* of a previous action or a temporal expression. It may refer to a definite or an indefinite past time.	Relative past tense. It generally occurs *subordinated* to another event or a definite point in the past. Occasionally it may occur without reference to a specific past moment. When used in this way it co-occurs with indicators of habitual or repeated action, expressed or implied.
Entró, saludó a todos y al rato se retiró a su cuarto. *He came in, greeted everyone, and a few minutes later retired to his room.*	Cuando la fuí a ver, estaba enferma. *When I went to see her, she was ill.*
	El año pasado vivía en Nueva York. *Last year he was living in New York.*
Nació, vivió y murió en Salamanca. *He was born, lived, and died in Salamanca.*	Releía a los clásicos frecuentemente. *He used to reread the classics frequently.*
Fuimos a su casa varias veces. *We went to his house several times.*	Ibamos a su casa todos los domingos. *We used to go to his house every Sunday.*

ASPECT

Perfective and punctual. The action is described as *completed*. It is also viewed as a *point* in time (punctual). If a series of events of the same kind is reported, it is always definitely confined, once, twice, twenty times.	Imperfective. The event is described as *non-completed* and *durative*. It is viewed as a *continuum* in time, as existing or ongoing. The event may have definite or indefinite extension in time, depending upon the nature of the event itself and its context.

TIME

Retrospective past:	Retrospective present, future, and past:
The action is always a past event in relation to the moment of utterance.	When subordinated to another tense the action may be a retrospective present or a future event in relation to the moment of utterance. When the imperfect occurs alone, it generally refers to a past event, habitual or ongoing at that time.

The preterit reports, narrates, what *took place*, and *what was = had been*.

The imperfect describes what was (a) *co-existent* with another event; (b) *what was going* on at a given time; (c) *what used to be:* mental and emotional processes or states, physical and material conditions; (d) *what used to happen:* continuous or habitually repeated actions; (e) *what still is:* events, states, and conditions in indirect discourse; (f) *what will be:* mostly in indirect discourse with a limited class of verbs.

ANTERIORITY VERSUS CO-EXISTENCE

Tuvieron un hijo ayer.
A child was born to them yesterday.

Tenían un hijo.
They had a child.

Le costó mucho esfuerzo aprender el inglés.
It was (had been) very hard for him to learn English.

Le costaba esfuerzo hablar inglés aunque lo comprendía perfectamente.
It was hard for him to speak English, even though he could understand it perfectly.

SEQUENTIAL EVENTS VERSUS CO-EXISTENT EVENTS

Cuando yo entré, él salió.
When I came in, he left the room.

Cuando yo llegaba, él salía.
As I was arriving, he was leaving.

Me contó que tuvo (había tenido) dificultades con su jefe.
He told me he had had difficulties with his boss.

Me contó que tenía dificultades con su jefe.
He told me he was having difficulties with his boss.

ANTERIORITY VERSUS SUBSEQUENCE

La boda fue el sábado.
The wedding took place on Saturday.

La boda era el sábado.
The wedding was going to take place on Saturday.

No quiso ir.
He did not want (had not wanted) to go.

Quería ir a México el verano siguiente.
He wanted to go to Mexico the following summer.

6

PRONOUNS: REFLEXIVES AND REFLEXIVE CONSTRUCTIONS

Reflexive Pronouns

FORMS

me	*myself*	**nos**	*ourselves*
te	*yourself*	**os**	*yourselves* (**vosotros**)
se	*himself* *herself* *itself*	**se**	*themselves* *yourselves* (**Uds.**)

Reflexive pronouns are similar in form to object pronouns except for the third person. The same set of pronouns is used for direct and indirect reflexive objects. Reflexive object pronouns must agree in number with their respective subjects. Gender distinction does not apply here.

1. PRONOMINAL REFLEXIVE CONSTRUCTIONS WITH ANIMATE SUBJECTS

A true reflexive construction is one in which the subject is the same as the direct or indirect object, that is, the subject is both the actor and the receiver of the action. Any transitive verb may take a reflexive object if its meaning permits.

El me curó.
Yo me curé.

He cured me.
I cured myself.

María vistió al niño.	*Mary dressed the child.*
María se vistió.	*Mary dressed herself.*

No se lo puedo explicar.	*I can't explain it to him.*
No me lo puedo explicar.	*I can't explain it to myself.*

Reflexive pronouns as direct objects

When the target of the action is the same person as the subject, the reflexive pronoun marks the identity between the subject and the direct object. These sentences have equivalent structures in English. However, while in English the reflexive pronouns may be omitted when no ambiguity exists, in Spanish the reflexive pronouns are obligatory.

Ella se bañó antes de vestirse.	*She bathed (herself) before dressing.*
El se afeitó.	*He shaved (himself).*
Se cortó al afeitarse.	*He cut himself while shaving.*
María se defendió.	*Maria defended herself.*
Te juzgas mal.	*You judge yourself inaccurately.*

Reflexive pronouns as indirect objects

When the person involved in the action is the same as the subject, the reflexive pronoun marks the identity between the subject and the indirect object. The functions of the reflexive indirect objects are equivalent to those of non-reflexive indirect objects. The reflexive indirect object may indicate that the subject is the receiver of the action, that he stands to gain or lose by it, that he is the possessor, or that he is merely interested in a given event.

INDIRECT OBJECTS

Reflexive	*Non-reflexive*
RECEIVER OF THE VERBAL ACTION	
No **me** lo puedo explicar.	No **me** lo pudo explicar.
I can't explain it to myself.	*He could not explain it to me.*
BENEFIT	
Me compré los libros.	**Me** compró los libros.
I bought the books for myself.	*He bought the books for me.*
POSSESSION	
Me rompí la pierna.	**Me** rompió la pierna al chocarme.
I broke my leg.	*He broke my leg when he collided with me.*

INTEREST

Se guardó la carta.	**Le** guardó la carta.
She kept the letter for herself.	*He kept the letter* for her.

Reflexive pronouns, just as indirect object non-reflexive forms, may correspond in English to the reflexive indirect object signaled by word order, or to *to, for, from, off,* and *on* relationships.

Reflexive object pronouns, direct and indirect, have the same patterns as non-reflexive object pronouns. Therefore, they cannot be rendered through prepositional reflexives alone. If the latter occur, the object pronouns co-occur with them. When in English a reflexive pronoun is or may be omitted, it still must be retained in Spanish.

Reflexive indirect object forms are used as follows:

1. When the verb takes a direct object and the person involved in the action is the same as the subject of the sentence, the reflexive pronouns must be used.

No se puede permitir ese lujo.	*He cannot allow* himself *that luxury.*
Yo me dije a mi misma: esto tiene que acabar.	*I told* myself: *this has to come to an end.*
No me lo explico.	*I cannot explain it* to myself.
Me compré varias cosas.	{*I bought* myself *several things.* {*I bought several things* for myself.
Se hizo un vestido.	{*She made* herself *a dress.* {*She made a dress* for herself.
Se consiguió un trabajo.	{*He found* himself *a job.* {*He found a job* (for himself).
Se quitó la venda.	*He removed the bandage* (from himself).
Sácate esa ropa.	*Take those clothes* off (yourself).

2. When the direct object is a personal possession, such as body parts or items of clothing, the indirect reflexive is used in Spanish. In English, the possessive occurs instead.

Juan se lavó las manos.	*John washed his hands.*
El se rompió el brazo.	*He broke his arm.*
Quítate el saco.	*Take your coat off.*
Ponte los guantes.	*Put your gloves on.*
Se estropeó las uñas.	*She ruined her nails.*
No se pinta los ojos.	*She does not make up her eyes.*

3. The indirect reflexive may also be used to signal the involvement of a person in an action or his special interest in it, just as the non-reflexive indirect pronoun. This usage has no parallel in English, but its meaning may sometimes be rendered by prepositional phrases or lexically.

Se guardó la carta.	*She kept the letter* (*for herself*).
Me tomaré la medicina, ya que insistes.	*I'll take the medicine* (*for my benefit*) *since you insist.*

Se tomó la libertad de entrar sin anunciarse.	*He took the liberty of entering without announcing himself.* *(He did it "on his own.")*
Se lo comió todo.	*He ate it all up.*
Me hice un vestido.	*I had a dress made (for myself).*
Se cortó el pelo.	*He had his hair cut.*

Reflexive versus reciprocal action

When the verb is in the first, second, or third person plural, the sentence can be ambiguous in Spanish. It can either mean true reflexive or reciprocal action. In English, on the other hand, such ambiguity would not arise since either the reflexive pronouns *ourselves, themselves*, or the reciprocal pronouns *each other, one another*, would be used.

Ellos se alaban.
Nosotros nos conocemos bien.

These sentences can either mean:

Ellos se alaban a sí mismos.	*They praise themselves.*
Nosotros nos conocemos bien a nosotros mismos.	*We know ourselves well.*

or they can imply reciprocal action:

Ellos se alaban el uno al otro.	*They praise one another.*
Nosotros nos conocemos bien la una a la otra.	*We know each other well.*

To prevent ambiguity, the prepositional reflexive **a sí (mismo)** is added to the objective reflexive **se** to show that the action of each of the several actors falls upon himself. If a reciprocal meaning is intended, the reciprocal pronouns **mutuamente, recíprocamente, entre sí, uno-s a otro-s** may be added.

Whereas in English the reciprocal pronouns may be omitted with some verbs, in Spanish **se** is obligatory with verbs that can take a reflexive object. The reciprocal pronouns, like prepositional reflexive pronouns, are optional.

Nos encontrábamos todos los sábados.	*We met every Saturday.*
Se besaron unos a los otros y partieron.	*They kissed each other and parted.*

When the verb is intransitive—cannot take object nouns or pronouns—the reciprocal meaning is rendered by **uno**, the appropriate preposition, and **otro**.

No pueden vivir el uno sin el otro.	*They cannot live without each other.*
Nacieron el uno para el otro.	*They were born for each other.*
Existen el uno para el otro.	*They exist only for each other.*

2. NON-PRONOMINAL REFLEXIVES WITH ANIMATE SUBJECTS

Inherent reflexives

Some Spanish verbs require the obligatory presence of the reflexive forms without any sintactic or semantic meaning attached to them. Except for at least three verbs in English which also demand reflexive pronouns (*to absent oneself, to perjure oneself,* and *to pride oneself*), Spanish inherent reflexives have no equivalents in English, and must be learned as such.

atreverse a	*to dare*	quejarse	*to complain*
arrepentirse de	*to repent,*	fugarse	*to escape*
	to be sorry	comportarse	*to behave*
abstenerse de	*to abstain*	portarse	*to behave*
acordarse de	*to remember*	burlarse de	*to make fun of*
empeñarse en	*to insist upon*	obstinarse	
cerciorarse de	*to make certain,*	(empecinarse)	*to insist upon*
	to ascertain	dignarse	*to deign*
darse cuenta de	*to realize*	preciarse de	*to boast of*
jactarse de	*to boast of*	vanagloriarse	*to boast of*

Reflexives with verbs of inner life

The reflexive **se** with verbs of inner life does not represent an object pronoun since the subject cannot be said to be acting upon himself directly. Feelings and memories arise within him with a certain degree of autonomy. The **se** marks in these constructions the subject as source of the action or as participant in it, because inner events are not caused solely by experiences received from without but from the subject's inner self as well.

Spanish reflexives of inner life are generally equivalent to English passives with *get, become,* and *be.* Occasionally they can be rendered in English by reflexive or intransitive verbs. English *be* passives with verbs of inner life cannot, however, be rendered in Spanish by **ser** passives, because the **ser** passive is not grammatical in this instance.[1]

With transitive verbs of inner life the reflexive has an intransitivising function.

Transitive Value		*Intransitive Value*	
The verb has a subject and needs an object in order to complete its meaning. The subject acts directly upon some person or thing.		The action is complete in itself. It does not pass to a second person or thing.	
alegrar	*to gladden*	alegrarse	*to be or become glad*
asombrar	*to astonish*	asombrarse	*to be or become surprised*

---

[1] See **Ser** Passives, page 258.

Transitive Value		Intransitive Value	
ajustar	*to adjust*	ajustarse	*to adapt or adjust oneself*
afligir	*to worry*	afligirse	*to be or become worried*
arriesgar	*to risk*	arriesgarse	*to risk or expose oneself*
asustar	*to scare*	asustarse	*to be or to get scared*
emocionar	*to move someone*	emocionarse	*to be or become moved*
entristecer	*to sadden*	entristecerse	*to be or become sad*
enojar	*to anger*	enojarse	*to get or become angry*
escandalizar	*to scandalize*	escandalizarse	*to be shocked, scandalized*
enamorar	*to court*	enamorarse	*to fall in love*
equivocar	*to mistake*	equivocarse	*to make a mistake*
entregar	*to hand over*	entregarse	*to surrender, to give oneself up*
esconder	*to hide*	esconderse	*to hide oneself*
complacer	*to please*	complacerse	*to be pleased*
mejorar	*to improve*	mejorarse	*to improve*
ofender	*to offend*	ofenderse	*to be or to get offended*
tranquilizar	*to calm or to reassure*	tranquilizarse	*to calm down*
preocupar	*to worry*	preocuparse	*to be worried, to worry*
comprometer	*to compromise*	comprometerse	*to commit oneself or to be committed*
decidir	*to decide*	decidirse	*to make up one's mind*
resolver	*to resolve*	resolverse	*to decide to*
acordar	*to agree upon*	acordarse	*to remember*
olvidar	*to forget*	olvidarse	*to forget to (about)*
sentir	*to feel*	sentirse	*to feel*

Tus palabras me asombran.	*Your words astonish me.*
Ella se asombró al oír sus palabras.	*She was astonished by his words.*
Ajusta el aire-acondicionado.	*Adjust the air-conditioner.*
Tienes que ajustarte a ese cambio.	*You have to adjust to this change.*
El gerente ha mejorado las condiciones de trabajo.	*The manager has improved working conditions.*
Ella se ha mejorado.	*She has improved.*
La ofendiste.	*You offended her.*
Ella se ofendió.	*She got offended.*
Ella se ofendió por su falta de cortesía.	*She was offended by his lack of courtesy.*
La hiciste enojar.	*You made her angry.*
Se enojó.	*She got (became) angry.*
Ella se enojó por tus flirteos con otras mujeres.	*She was angered by your flirting with other women.*

Me preocupa su salud.　　　　　　　　His health worries me.
Yo me preocupo por su salud.　　　　　I worry on account of his health.
　　　　　　　　　　　　　　　　　　I am worried because of his health.

Sintió el marmól frío bajo sus pies.　　She felt the cold marble under her feet.
Se sintió mal (enferma).　　　　　　　She felt ill.

Reflexives with verbs of motion

The reflexive particle with verbs of motion does not represent an object pronoun. With transitive verbs of motion as with verbs of inner life **se** has an intransitivizing function.

Transitive Value		*Intransitive Value*	
acostar	to put to bed	acostarse	to lie down or go to bed
acercar	to bring near to, to pass	acercarse	to come close to
alejar	to move something away	alejarse	to move away
bajar	to bring something down	bajarse	to get off or come down
enderezar	to straighten	enderezarse	to rise upward
levantar	to lift	levantarse	to get up or stand up
mover	to move	moverse	to move about
subir	to raise	subirse	to climb up
retirar	to withdraw	retirarse	to retire
meter	to put into	meterse	to get into or to meddle
sentar	to seat	sentarse	to sit down

Even though verbs like **sentarse**, **acostarse**, and **levantarse** are commonly translated into English as *to seat oneself, to put oneself to bed, to raise oneself*, the intransitive equivalents *to sit down, to lie down,* and *to get up* correspond more accurately to the Spanish reflexives.

La madre acostó a los niños.　　　　　The mother put the children to bed.
Luego se acostó ella a descansar.　　　Later she lied down to rest.

No levantes la maleta, es demasiado　　Don't lift the suitcase, it is too heavy
　pesada para ti.　　　　　　　　　　for you.
Cuando entren las señoras, tienes que　When the ladies come in you have to
　levantarte.　　　　　　　　　　　stand up.

No muevas eso.　　　　　　　　　　Don't move that.
Ese niño no deja de moverse.　　　　　That child does not stop moving about.

Sentó a la invitada de honor a la　　　She seated the guest of honor at the right
　derecha de su marido.　　　　　　　of her husband.
Ella se sentó junto a Fernando.　　　　She sat down next to Fernando.

Mete el sobre en mi escritorio.　　　　Put the envelope in my desk.
Métete en la cama.　　　　　　　　　Get into bed.
No te metas en asuntos ajenos.　　　　Don't meddle in someone else's affairs.

The reflexive particle with intransitive verbs of motion may or may not change the meaning of the verb. If it makes a semantic difference the **se** is naturally obligatory, and the two forms must be learned as two different verbs.

ir	*to go*	irse	*to leave, to depart*
salir	*to go out, to leave*	salirse	*to get out of something or some place*
marchar	*to march*	marcharse	*to leave or depart*
volver	*to return*	volverse	*to turn around or turn back*
entrar	*to go in*	entrarse	*to slip into or to go into*
parar	*to stop*	pararse	*to stand up, to get up, or to stop*

With the following verbs the reflexive is optional. It doesn't make a significant change in meaning:

venir	venirse	*to come*
escapar	escaparse	*to escape or to run away*
pasear	pasearse	*to stroll*

A few verbs of motion occur with the reflexive only:

fugarse	*to run away or to elope*
agacharse	*to stoop or to squat*

3. NON-PRONOMINAL REFLEXIVES WITH INANIMATE SUBJECTS

Reflexive constructions with inanimate subjects are generally referred to as passive reflexives. They are considered passives because the grammatical subjects (logically objects since inanimates cannot act upon themselves) are not the actors but are acted upon by an agent. The reflexive with inanimate subject does not occur with an agent, but it may occur with a causative phrase. While most reflexives with inanimate subjects may be considered passives, not all of them are, as will be seen below.

A reflexive construction with inanimate subjects is used whenever an event is described for which no agent is specified or specifiable; when an event refers to processes for which no human agent could be postulated such as in natural phenomena; or when inanimate nouns are personified. The verb occurs in the third person, singular or plural, depending upon the subject. The subject does not normally assume subject position (preceding the verb) but object position (immediately after the verb), unless the inanimate nouns are personified.

Se quemaron las casas.	*The houses burnt down.*
Se ensució la pared.	*The wall got dirty.*
Se contaminó el aire.	*The air became polluted.*
Se inundaron las calles con las lluvias.	*The streets were flooded due to rains.*
Se derrumbó el edificio.	*The building caved in.*
Se hundió el techo de la casa.	*The roof of the house fell in.*

Se fundió el motor del coche.	*The motor of the car broke down.*
Se paró el reloj.	*The clock stopped.*

When inanimates are personified the nouns are attributed self-agency and as such they precede the verb, just as animate subjects do.

La luz se iba haciendo más tenua.	*The light grew dimmer and dimmer.*
En verano el sol se pone más tarde.	*During the summer the sun goes down later.*
Los días se van haciendo más largos.	*The days are becoming longer.*
Las flores se han marchitado.	*The flowers have wilted.*
La historia se repite.	*History repeats itself.*
La vida se pasa rápido.	*Life goes by quickly.*
La naturaleza se renueva constantemente.	*Nature regenerates itself constantly.*
Los Estados Unidos no se verán cohibidos por las amenazas del comunismo.	*The United States will not be intimidated by communist threats.*
Canadá se unirá a la O.E.A.	*Canada will join the O.A.S.*

Reflexive sentences with inanimate subjects may correspond in English to intransitive verbs, to passives with *get*, *become*, and *be*, and to reflexive verbs occasionally when an inanimate noun is personified.

4. THE *SE ME* CONSTRUCTIONS

The **se me** construction is used in Spanish to express unplanned or involuntary happenings. Like the passive reflexive it contains an inanimate noun as grammatical subject (logically object since inanimates cannot act upon themselves), and an obligatory indirect object pronoun to signal the person involved in the action or affected by it. There are various uses of the **se me** sentences, none of which has parallels in English.

1. The inanimate nouns are the grammatical subjects but not the agents. The indirect object pronoun, obligatory here, represents the agent that unintentionally brings about the action.

Se me rompió el jarrón.	*I broke the vase.*
Se me rompieron los vasos.	*I broke the glasses.*
Se me agotaron los recursos.	*I have exhausted all means.*
Se me olvidó el libro.	*I forgot the book.*
Se le escapó un grito.	*He let out a scream.*

If these actions are thought of as being deliberate and not accidental, active construction with the indirect object as subject would be used instead.

Rompí el jarrón.
Agoté todos los recursos.
No traje el libro o lo dejé en casa.
Lanzó un grito.

Since certain actions such as **olvidar** and **escapar** cannot be consciously deliberate acts, different verbs are used instead: **dejar**, **lanzar**, etc.

2. The **se me** construction must also be used for physiological or affective processes that arise within a person. The subject noun phrases are not the agents. The indirect object pronoun is the source of the action, as well as the person affected by the process that arises within him. The equivalent in English is the possessive.

Se le subió la fiebre.	*His fever rose.*
Se le bajó la presión.	*His blood pressure dropped.*
Se le llenaron los ojos de lágrimas.	*His eyes filled with tears.*
Se le doblaban las rodillas.	*His knees were shaky (shaking).*

3. An indirect object pronoun can also be used in reflexive sentences—with animate and inanimate subjects—to signal the emotional involvement or interest of a second person. When in Spanish a relationship of belongingness or possession is expressed, in English the possessive occurs. In most other cases there is no structural equivalent.

Se le enfermó el hijo.	*His son became ill.*
Se le fue la mujer.	*His wife left him.*
Se le casó la hija.	*Her daughter got married.*
Se me rompió el jarrón.	*My vase got broken.*
Se nos descompuso el coche.	*Our car broke down.*
Se le echó a perder la comida.	*His food got spoiled.*
No te me vayas.	*Don't leave for my sake.*
No te me enfermes ahora.	*Don't get sick on me now.*
No te me asustes, por favor.	*Don't get scared, please.*

5. *SE* AS AN INDEFINITE SUBJECT REFERENCE

Se also functions as an indefinite subject reference in Spanish. As an indefinite subject it is equivalent in English to the indefinite subjects *one*, *they*, *it*; to the colloquial *you*; and to the *be* passive without an agent.

Se occurs with both transitive and intransitive verbs. The verb may be in the third person, singular or plural, depending upon the transitive or intransitive nature of the verb and the kind of objects a transitive verb takes. There is never any mention of an agent.

1. The verb occurs in the third person singular in all of the following cases:

   a. With intransitive verbs, i.e., those which do not take an object:

Aquí se trabaja mucho.	*One works a lot here.*
En los Estados Unidos se vive bien.	*In the United States one lives well.*

b. With transitive verbs when the direct object is an infinitive or a clause:

Se prohíbe fumar.	*Smoking (is) forbidden.*[1]
Se espera que renuncie pronto.	*It is expected that he will resign soon.*

c. With the copulative verb **ser**:

O se es honesto o deshonesto, pero no las dos cosas.	*Either one is honest or dishonest but not both.*
Se es lo que se debe ser.	*One is what one is meant to be.*

d. With transitive verbs which have a human noun as direct object. The direct object must be introduced by **a** in order to differentiate an impersonal **se** sentence from a reciprocal or reflexive sentence.[2] The equivalent in English in these cases is the *be* passive without an agent.

Se ayuda a los pobres.	*The poor are helped.*
Se persigue a los delincuentes.	*Delinquents are persecuted.*
Se condenó al acusado a cinco años de prisión.	*The defendant was sentenced to five years in prison.*

Se ayudan los pobres could either mean **Se ayudan los pobres a sí mismos** or **Se ayudan los pobres los unos a los otros**.

2. When the verb is transitive and the object is an inanimate noun, the verb agrees in number with the object.

Se rechazó su propuesta.	*His proposal was rejected.*
Se rechazaron sus propuestas.	*His proposals were rejected.*
No se dice nada malo de él.	*Nothing bad is said about him.*
No se dicen muchas cosas malas de él.	*Not many bad things are said about him.*

3. When an impersonal sentence is formed with a reflexive verb, the impersonal **uno** replaces the indefinite **se** to avoid ambiguity.

Uno se acostumbra a todo.	*One adjusts to everything.*
Uno se aburre en este pueblo.	*One is bored in this town.*

---

[1] **Se** sentences dealing with regulations, prohibitions, and advertisements are rendered in English by the abbreviated passive without *be*.

Se prohíbe entrar.	*Entrance forbidden.*
Se afinan pianos.	*Pianos tuned.*
Se arreglan relojes aquí.	*Watches repaired here.*

[2] With a limited class of verbs used in advertisements which take indefinite human objects (such as **buscar, necesitar, solicitar**, etc.), the personal **a** does not occur. The verb may either be in the third person singular or plural, depending upon the object.

Se busca secretaria.	*Secretary needed.*
Se buscan secretarias.	*Secretaries needed.*
Se solicita cocinera.	*Cook wanted.*
Se necesitan médicos.	*Physicians needed.*

BUT:

Se acostumbra a todo.	*She adjusts to everything.*
Se aburre en este pueblo.	*He is bored in this town.*

Se sentences with transitive verbs may take direct and indirect objects, but the direct object noun cannot be pronominalized when an indirect object form co-occurs.

Se hicieron muchas preguntas difíciles en el examen.	Se le hicieron muchas preguntas difíciles en el examen.
Many difficult questions were asked on the exam.	*He was asked many difficult questions on the exam.*
Se dieron instrucciones explícitas.	Se le dieron instrucciones explícitas.
Explicit instructions were given.	*He was given explicit instructions.*
Se entregó el dinero.	Se le entregó el dinero.
The money was delivered.	*He was given the money.*

In informal speech situations, the indefinite **se** is not frequently used, particularly when the direct or indirect object is a person. An impersonal sentence with the verb in the third person plural occurs instead.

Se recibió al embajador.	Recibieron al embajador.
The ambassador was received.	*They received the ambassador.*
Se ayudó a los pobres.	Ayudaron a los pobres.
The poor were helped.	*They helped the poor.*
Se le dieron muchas instrucciones.	Le dieron muchas instrucciones.
He was given many instructions.	*They gave him many instructions.*

Prepositional Reflexive Pronouns

FORMS

(a) mí	*(to) myself*		yourself
(a) ti	*yourself*	**(a) sí**	himself / herself
(a) nosotros	*ourselves*		itself / themselves

The prepositional reflexive pronouns can occur after any preposition with the exception of **con** and **entre**. After **con** the forms **conmigo**, **contigo**, and **consigo** are required. **Consigo**, however, alternates with the subject forms **con él**, **con Ud.**, **con ellos**. The preposition **entre** requires the subject forms **entre tú y yo**, **entre nosotros**, etc.

USE OF PREPOSITIONAL REFLEXIVE PRONOUNS

1. Prepositional reflexive pronouns, to which the adjective **mismo** is normally added, can only be used with true reflexive constructions—those in which the grammatical subject is both the actor and the direct or indirect object. The prepositional reflexives are optional, while the object forms are obligatory. The redundant construction is used for contrast or emphasis with indirect reflexive objects. With direct reflexive objects its usage is rare. In general, it is much less frequent than the redundant use with non-reflexive object pronouns.

No me lo puedo explicar ni a mí misma.	*I can't even explain it to myself.*
A mí me compré un reloj, y a ella una pulsera.	*I bought myself a watch, and her a bracelet.*

Prepositional reflexive pronouns *cannot* occur with inherent reflexives, reflexive verbs of inner life and motion, passive reflexives, or **se me** sentences, since in none of these does the particle **se** represent a pronoun.

2. A prepositional reflexive may be used to differentiate a reflexive sentence from a reciprocal sentence, when the verb is in the first, second, or third person plural.

Ellos se alaban.	{ *They praise themselves* { *They praise each other.*
Los artistas se alaban a sí mismos.	*Artists praise themselves.*
Los artistas se alaban entre sí.	*Artists praise each other.*
Ustedes se engañan a sí mismos.	*You are deceiving yourselves.*
Ustedes se engañan entre sí.	*You are deceiving each other.*

3. Prepositional reflexives occur after prepositions. The reflexive **sí** generally occurs after **a**, **de**, or **en**. After compound prepositions, except for the first and informal second personal singular, subject forms may occur instead of **sí**: **alrededor de, cerca de, delante de, dentro de, encima de, frente a**, etc.

Viéndome a mí misma en ese estado comprendía mejor a mi amiga.	*Seeing myself in that predicament, I could better understand my friend.*
El egoísmo te impedía pensar en otra cosa que en ti mismo.	*Your egotism prevented you from thinking about anything but yourself.*
Dentro de él sólo había odio.	*Inside himself there was only hatred.*
Tenía a toda su familia alrededor de ella.	*She had her whole family surrounding her.*

Uses of **mismo**

As seen before, the adjective **mismo** is added to prepositional reflexives for emphasis or clarity.

El niño se vistió a sí mismo.	*The child dressed herself.*
Se compró un traje a sí misma.	*She bought herself a dress.*

Mismo can also be used to stress the identity of the grammatical subject as *agent* of the action. In this case it immediately follows the subject.

El niño mismo se vistió.	*The child himself put his clothes on.*
Se educó él mismo.	*He is self-educated.*
El mismo no sabe lo que quiere.	*He himself does not know what he wants.*

7

THE INFINITIVE, THE GERUND, AND THE PAST PARTICIPLE

The Infinitive

FUNCTION OF THE INFINITIVE

The Spanish infinitive when not used with a true auxiliary verb functions as a noun. As a noun it represents the abstract action of the verb without reference to time, number, or person. But since the infinitive is a verbal noun it has features of both nouns and verbs; it may co-occur with nominal determiners and verbal modifiers as well.

The Spanish infinitive is morphologically marked by the endings **-ar**, **-er**, and **-ir**. Therefore, it needs no preposition or any other device to be differentiated from other verbal forms. The English infinitive, on the other hand, is always signaled by the meaningless device *to*, except after auxiliaries (*can*, *may*, *must*, *will*, *shall*) and a few other verbs which can take a bare infinitive.

The functions assumed by the Spanish infinitive are not only fulfilled by the English infinitive but by its gerund, *-ing* form, as well. Since in English these two forms have overlapping functions the Spanish infinitive may either correspond to the English infinitive, the English gerund, or to both, depending upon the context.

As a noun the Spanish infinitive may assume any of the following functions which characterize true nouns:

1. Subject:

(El) Errar es humano, perdonar es divino.	*To err is human, to forgive, divine.*
Su constante llorar me irrita.	*Her constant crying irritates me.*
Este perenne batallar ...	*This perennial fighting...*

2. Predicate noun:

Partir es morir un poco.	*To leave is to die a little.*
Conocerla es estimarla.	*To know her is to esteem her.*

3. Modifier, introduced by prepositions:

Es buen sitio para descansar.	*It is a good place to rest.*
Está interesado en vender la casa.	*He is interested in selling the house.*
Salió sin saludarnos.	*He left without greeting us.*

4. Object of a verb:

Necesita estudiar más.	*He has to study more.*
Espera curarse.	*He hopes to get well.*
No niega haberla visto.	*He does not deny having seen her.*

The infinitive as subject

The Spanish infinitive as subject may occur alone or be modified by an article (in the masculine singular form), a demonstrative, or a possessive. It may also take adjectives and adverbs; object pronouns; a subject pronoun; or a noun phrase introduced by **de** to signal the subject.

The infinitive as subject may correspond either to the English infinitive or to its *-ing* form, since both are verbal nouns and as such may function as nouns. The reverse is not true, however. The English gerund as subject cannot be rendered into Spanish by the **-ndo** form since the latter only functions as an adverbial.[1] Whether the Spanish infinitive will correspond to the English infinitive or the gerund depends upon the modifiers it co-occurs with. In English, except for adverbs, the infinitive does not take any determiners and/or modifiers; only the *-ing* form co-occurs with them.

The Spanish infinitive as subject may be modified or determined as follows:

1. By the definite article in the masculine singular form. Its occurrence is optional and the rules of usage with the infinitive follow the general pattern of usage with nouns.[2] In English both the infinitive and the gerund may occur in this case.

(El) Errar es humano, perdonar, divino.	*To err is human, to forgive, divine.* / *Erring is human, forgiving, divine.*
Pensar es atributo exclusivo del hombre.	*Thinking is man's exclusive attribute.* / *To think is an attribute exclusive of man.*
Conocerla es estimarla.	*To know her is to esteem her.*

2. Modified or determined by a demonstrative or a possessive (in masculine singular form), the Spanish infinitive is equivalent to the English *-ing* form.

---

[1] See The Gerund, page 100.
[2] See Uses of the Definite Article, page 274.

The possessive in this case signals the subject of the Spanish infinitive and the English gerund.

Ese gritar me exaspera.	*That screaming exasperates me.*
Su constante lamentar la ha dejado con pocos amigos.	*Her constant complaining has left her with few friends.*

3. When modified by an adjective,[1] the infinitive requires either an article, a demonstrative, or a possessive (in masculine singular form). In these cases, English uses the *-ing* form.

El gastar desenfrenado la arruinó.	*The unrestrained spending ruined her.*
Un buen empezar ayuda siempre.	*A good beginning always helps.*
Este fumar exagerado es peligroso.	*This exaggerated smoking is hazardous.*
Su constante murmurar de la gente es detestable.	*Her endless gossiping about people is despicable.*

4. When modified by an adverb, the occurrence of an article is optional. It corresponds to either the English infinitive or the *-ing* form.

(El) Fumar contínuamente es malo para la salud.	*To chain-smoke is hazardous to one's health.* *Chain-smoking is hazardous to one's health.*

The Spanish infinitive in subject position can also be followed by a subject pronoun or by a noun phrase introduced by **de**, for clarity and/or emphasis. In these cases, it requires the masculine singular form of the definite article. English uses the *-ing* form with a possessive or with the genitive respectively, since the English infinitive cannot take subject pronouns.

El decirlo Ud. la convencerá.	*Your saying it (so) will convince her.*
El aceptarlo ellos es buena señal.	*Their accepting it is a good omen.*
El despertar de María a la realidad fue doloroso.	*Maria's awakening to reality was painful.*
El murmurar de las fuentes era el único ruido que se oía.	*The bubbling of the springs was the only noise to be heard.*

The infinitive as predicate noun

The infinitive as a predicate noun generally occurs in sentences where the subject is also an infinitive. It is linked by the copulative verb **ser**. The same features that characterize the infinitive as subject also characterize the infinitive as predicate

---

[1] The rules governing the position of adjectives with the infinitive follow the general pattern of adjective position with respect to nouns. Roughly speaking, if the adjective precedes, emphasis is given to the "action" described by the infinitive: Su constante **gastar** = Her constant *spending* . . . If it follows, more emphasis is given to the "type" or "kind" of this action: Su gastar **constante** = Her *constant* spending. However, style must be kept in mind along with these considerations. To be safe, it could be said that with infinitives, adjectives tend to follow, except those with a shortened form which tend to precede: **un buen empezar, un mal acabar** as opposed to **un empezar malo, un acabar malo** (See The Position of Descriptive Adjectives, page 230).

noun. Thus, in English the Spanish infinitive as predicate noun may correspond to the infinitive or the gerund, depending upon the modifiers or determiners the Spanish infinitive co-occurs with. The predicate noun function of the infinitive is rare in the spoken language. It is a construction more commonly used in proverbs and poetic language.

Ver es creer.	*To see is to believe.* / *Seeing is believing.*
Partir es morir un poco.	*To depart is to die a little.* / *Departing is (like) dying a little.*
El rendirse ante el enemigo sería humillarse ante el mundo.	*To surrender to the enemy would be to humiliate oneself in the eyes of the world.* / *Surrendering to the enemy would be (like) humiliating oneself in the eyes of the world.*
El buen comer es buen vivir.	*Good eating is good living.*
El comer bien es vivir bien.	*To eat well is to live well.* / *Eating well is living well.*

The infinitive as modifier

Since the Spanish infinitive functions as a noun, it cannot, like true nouns, modify other nouns, adjectives, or verbs directly, but must be introduced by a preposition. In English, except in the case of *to* which in some instances still retains its original meaning of purpose or direction, after all other prepositions only the gerund occurs. Thus, whether the Spanish infinitive functions as an adjectival or adverbial modifier, it will be equivalent to the gerund, or a clause in some cases, except after *in order to* (the first particles are generally omitted) which takes an infinitive.

The most commonly used patterns are the following:

para + INF   (*in order*) *to* + INF

To denote purpose or intent:

Es buen sitio para descansar.	*It is a good place to rest.*
Es mala hora para verlo.	*It is a bad time to see him.*
Estoy listo para ayudarte.	*I am ready to help you.*
Vino para llevársela.	*He came to take her with him.*

To denote condition:

Para ser respetado hay que respetar a los demás.	*In order to be respected one has to respect others.*

Para estudiar hay que tener tiempo y dinero.	*In order to study one has to have time and money.*
Hay que hacer algo para sobrevivir.	*One has to do something to survive.*

To denote result:

¿Qué hice para ofenderla?	*What have I done to offend her?*
¿Qué habrá hecho para merecer esa suerte?	*What has he done to deserve such luck?*
Se lo dije para tranquilizarla.	*I told her to appease her.*

de + INF

To qualify nouns or words functioning as nouns:

Es la hora de comer.	*It is time to eat.*
El derecho de opinar libremente . . .	*The right to free expression . . .*
El temor de perderlo . . .	*The fear of losing him . . .*
La necesidad de verlo . . .	*The need of seeing him . . .*

en + INF

Occurs with **único** and adjectives of order: **primera, segunda,** etc.

Fue el único en escucharme.	*He was the only one to listen to me.*
Ella sería la última en pensar eso.	*She would be the last one to think that.*
Fuimos los primeros en llegar.	*We were the first ones to arrive.*

al + INF	*on, upon + -ing or clause introduced by when*

To denote the co-existence of two events:

Al llegar te llamaré.	*Upon arriving, I will call you.* / *When I arrive I will call you.*
Al verla me di cuenta de cuanto había envejecido.	*Upon seeing her I realized how much she had aged.*
To denote cause:	Clause introduced by *since* or *because.*
Al no hablarme ella, me fui.	*Since she did not speak to me, I left.*
Al no obtener respuesta se dio por vencido.	*Because he received no answer, he gave up.*

Other prepositions + INF	Preposition + -ing
No tiene ganas de salir.	*He does not feel like going out.*
No está interesado en vender la casa.	*He is not interested in selling the house.*
No piensa más que en divertirse.	*He only thinks about amusing himself.*
Llámalo en vez de escribirle.	*Call him instead of writing.*
Se fue sin despedirse.	*He left without saying good-bye.*
Se lo entregó sin haberlo terminado.	*He delivered it without having finished it.*
No le concedieron la entrevista por haber llegado demasiado tarde.	*He was not granted an interview for having arrived too late (because he had arrived too late).*

The infinitive as verbal object: Verb + INF

The infinitive constructed with a verb is always the object of that verb, except in constructions with auxiliaries in which case it must be considered the main verb (i.e., **Quiero ir** versus **Me alegro de ir** = *I want to go* versus *I am happy to go*).

Whereas in English some verbs take only infinitive objects:

I want to go.	Quiero ir.
I hope to go.	Espero ir.
I need to go.	Necesito ir.

others take only *-ing* form objects:

He avoided going.	Evitaba ir.
He denied knowing it.	Negaba saberlo.
He gave up smoking.	Dejó de fumar.

while some can take either form:

I began speaking.	. . . *to speak.*	Empecé a hablar.
He continued writing.	. . . *to write.*	Continuó escribiendo.
I preferred painting.	. . . *to paint.*	Prefería pintar.

in Spanish all of these verbs take only the infinitive, with the exception of **continuar** and **seguir**, which occur only with the **-ndo** form. If an English verb + INF or verb + *-ing* construction has a single subject, then it is equivalent to Spanish verb + INF constructions.[1]

Some verb + INF constructions occur in Spanish without a preposition, while others take a preposition obligatorily. The verb + INF construction in English occurs without a preposition. The *to* signaling the infinitive is in most cases a grammatical device with no meaning. Even in those cases where it retains its original meaning of purpose or direction, it should not be rendered into Spanish by **a** on the basis of analogy with verbs that require the preposition, such as many verbs of motion: **venir, ir, llegar**, etc.

I am coming (in order) to work.	Vengo a (= para) trabajar.
I went (in order) to help her.	Fui a (= para) ayudarla.

BUT:

I want to work.	Quiero trabajar.
I need to help her.	Necesito ayudarla.

When an English verb occurs with a preposition, an *-ing* object follows. Its Spanish equivalent may or may not take a preposition.

She dreamt about graduating.	Soñaba con graduarse.
He thought about changing jobs.	Pensaba en cambiar de trabajo.

BUT:

He prevented her from going.	Le impidió ir.
He succeeded in convincing her.	Logró convencerla.

---

[1] See Subjects in Verb + INF, page 96.

Verbs that take a preposition before an object can only be learned through observation since the relational meanings of prepositions are rather abstract. The preposition is usually the same whether the object of a verb is a noun, an infinitive, or a clause.

Se cansó de María.	*He got tired of Maria.*
Se cansó de estudiar.	*He got tired of studying.*
Se cansó de que lo molestaran.	*He got tired of their bothering him.*

The following are some verbs that require a preposition before an object:

acostumbrarse a	*to get used to*	insistir en	*to insist on*
atreverse a	*to dare*	empeñarse en	*to insist on*
dedicarse a	*to devote oneself*	convenir en	*to agree on*
resignarse a	*to resign oneself*	consistir en	*to consist of*
comenzar a	*to begin*	vacilar en	*to hesitate to*
aprender a	*to learn*	cansarse de	*to get tired of*
enseñar a	*to teach*	alegrarse de	*to be glad about*
soñar con	*to dream about*	olvidarse de	*to forget*
amenazar con	*to threaten*	acordarse de	*to remember*
tardar en	*to delay, to be late in*	darse cuenta de	*to realize, to become aware of*
complacerse en	*to take pleasure in*		

AUXILIARIES WITH INFINITIVES

When the infinitive occurs with one of the following auxiliaries it must be considered the main verb. The auxiliary expresses special characteristics of the action indicated by the infinitive. Some of these auxiliaries require a preposition or relator.

poder	*to be able to*
soler	*to use to*
deber	*to have to, to ought to, must*
tener que	*to have to*
haber que	*to have to* (used in third person singular with an indefinite subject)
dejar de	*to stop, to quit*
tratar de	*to try to*
acabar de	*to have just* + past participle
empezar a	*to begin*
volver a	verb + *again*
ir a	*to be going to*
venir a	*to come to*
ponerse a	*to begin to*

Debe trabajar.	*He must (ought to) work.*
Tiene que trabajar.	*He has to work.*
Hay que trabajar.	*One has to work.*
Dejó de llover.	*It stopped raining.*
Trató de ayudarla.	*He tried to help her.*
Acaba de hablar.	*She has just finished talking.*
Empezó a nevar.	*{It began to snow.*
	{It began snowing.
Iba a estudiar medicina.	*He was going to study medicine.*
No volví a verla más.	*I never saw her again.*
¿Volvió a mencionártelo?	*Did he mention it to you again?*

OBJECT PRONOUNS IN VERB +INF CONSTRUCTIONS

Object pronouns—direct, indirect, and reflexive—may either be attached to the infinitive or may go before the conjugated verb when the latter is an auxiliary:

Puedo verlo. }	
Lo puedo ver. }	*I can see him.*
Dejó de hablarle. }	
Le dejó de hablar. }	*He stopped talking to her.*
Debe lavarse las manos. }	
Se debe lavar las manos. }	*He must wash his hands.*

except in the following two cases:

1. When the infinitive is intransitive the pronouns must go with the conjugated verb:

Le permitió volver.	*He allowed her to return.*
Le enseña a bailar.	*He teaches her how to dance.*

BUT NOT:

⋆Permitió volverle.
⋆Enseña a bailarle.

2. When the auxiliary is a reflexive verb the pronouns go with it and not with the infinitive:

Se puso a cantar.	*He began to sing.*
Se puso a trabajar.	*He began to work.*

BUT NOT:

⋆Puso a cantarse.
⋆Puso a trabajarse.

When the conjugated verb is not a true auxiliary the object pronouns must go with the form they logically belong to, either before the verb or attached to the infinitive, since the meaning of the sentence might change.

Nos prometió estudiar.	*He promised us to study.*
Prometió estudiarnos.	*He promised to study us.*
Me lo mandó hacer.	*He had it done for me.*
Me mandó hacerlo.	*He had me do it.*

SUBJECTS IN VERB + INF CONSTRUCTIONS

In Spanish only a small class of verbs can take an infinitive with a different subject from that of the verb in verb + INF constructions. In English, on the other hand, it is quite common to introduce different subjects in both verb + INF and verb + -*ing* constructions. The infinitive with a different subject from the verb may only be used in Spanish with the following categories of verbs. The subject of the infinitive is signaled by direct and indirect objects respectively.

VERBS OF PERCEPTION

oír
escuchar
ver
sentir
} + Direct object, pronominal form or noun phrase

Vi llegar el tren.	*I saw the train arrive (arriving).*
Lo vi llegar.	*I saw it arrive (arriving).*
Oía llorar a los niños.	*I heard the children cry (crying).*
Los oía llorar.	*I heard them cry (crying).*
Sentía venir la tormenta.	*I felt the storm coming.*
La sentía venir.	*I felt it coming.*

SOME VERBS OF PERSUASION

dejar
hacer
} + Direct object, pronominal form or noun phrase

Dejó salir a la criada.	*She let the maid go out.*
La dejó salir.	*She let her go out.*
Hacía reír a la gente.	*He made the people laugh.*
Los hacía reír.	*He made them laugh.*

aconsejar
impedir
mandar
permitir
prohibir
prometer
} + Indirect object, pronominal form. If a noun phrase occurs, an indirect object pronominal form co-occurs with it.

Le permitió ir.	*He permitted her to go.*
Le prohibió fumar.	*He forbade him to smoke.*
Le mandó hacer dieta.	*He ordered her to diet.*
Le permitió a María salir.	*He permitted Maria to go out.*
Le prohibió a Jorge fumar.	*He forbade George to smoke.*
Le aconsejó a María descansar más.	*He suggested to Maria to rest more.*

In all other instances where the English infinitive or *-ing* form has a different subject from the conjugated verb (the subject may be expressed through object nouns or pronouns, or possessives), a clause with a conjugated verb must be used in Spanish. The verb in the clause will either be in the indicative or the subjunctive, depending upon the governing notion.[1]

ENGLISH   SPANISH

SUBJECTS THE SAME

Verb + INF
or   Verb + INF
Verb + *-ing*

I expect to go.   Espero ir.
I don't like going there.   No me gusta ir allá.

SUBJECTS DIFFERENT

Verb + INF
or   **Clause with a conjugated verb in the**
Verb + *-ing*   **indicative or subjunctive**

I expect them to go.   Espero que vayan.
He has asked us to come.   Nos ha pedido que viniéramos.
I know him to be serious.   Sé que es serio.

They said for you to come.   Dijeron que vinieras.
He waited for her to arrive.   Esperaba que ella llegara.
This is too big for you to carry.   Esto es demasiado grande para que
                                              tú lo cargues.

I don't like Maria's going there.   No me gusta que María vaya allá.
He does not approve of her studying   No está de acuerdo con que ella
medicine.   estudie medicina.
She was surprised at his coming alone.   Se sorprendió de que él viniera solo.

---

[1] See Chapter 11, Subjunctive and Indicative in Nominal Clauses; Chapter 12, Subjunctive and Indicative in Conditional, Relative, and Independent Clauses.

In impersonal constructions the verb+INF is used in both languages when the subject is not specified or determined. But if a definite subject is introduced for the infinitive in English, then in Spanish a clause occurs instead of an infinitive.

Subject Indefinite	*Subject Definite*
Es difícil ganar. *It is difficult to win.*	Es difícil que tú ganes. *It is difficult for you to win.*
Es imposible perder. *It impossible to lose.*	Es imposible que yo pierda. *It is impossible for me to lose.*
Es bueno trabajar. *It is good to work.*	Es bueno que ellos trabajen. *It is good for them to work.*
Es posible triunfar. *It is possible to succeed.*	Es posible que Uds. triunfen. *It is possible for you to succeed.*
Es importante asistir. *It is important to attend.*	Es importante que nosotros asistamos. *It is important for us to attend.*
Es necesario descansar. *It is necessary to rest.*	Es necesario que tú descanses. *It is necessary for you to rest.*

Only in a few cases may constructions such as **es posible, es imposible, es difícil**, and **es importante** take an indirect object pronoun in order to define or specify the subject:

Subject Indefinite	*Subject Definite*
Es difícil ganar.	Te es difícil ganar. (= que tú ganes) *It is difficult for you to win.*
Es imposible perder.	Me es imposible perder. (= que yo pierda) *It is impossible for me to lose.*
Es posible triunfar.	Les es posible triunfar. (= que ellos triunfen) *It is possible for them to succeed.*
Es importante asistir.	Nos es importante asistir. (= que asistamos) *It is important for us to attend.*

VERB + CLAUSE INSTEAD OF INFINITIVE

Not all verbs take infinitives as objects. Some verbs take clauses even though there is no change of subject. Verbs of believing, knowing, thinking, and saying generally take clauses rather than infinitives as objects. This applies to Spanish and English as well. The only significant difference between the two languages is that the relator, *that*, is omitted in English, whereas **que** must be retained in Spanish.

Cree que está enfermo.[1]	*He believes (that) he is ill.*
Sé que no voy a ir.	*I know (that) I won't go.*
Pienso que no podré venir.	*I think (that) I won't be able to come.*
Teme que no va a pasar los exámenes.	*He fears (that) he won't pass the exams.*
Sospecho que tengo que ir a la reunión.	*I suspect (that) I have to go to the meeting.*
Dije que no necesito nada.	*I said (that) I need nothing.*

THE PERFECT INFINITIVE

In verb + INF constructions the simple infinitive expresses coexistent actions regardless of time perspectives. To describe events which were anterior to the action indicated by the main verb, the perfect infinitive is used instead. The perfect infinitive is formed by **haber** + past participle.

Coexistent Events	*Consecutive Events*
Me alegro de conocerte. *I am happy to meet you.*	Me alegro de haberte conocido. *I am happy to have met you.*
Espero hacerlo bien. *I hope to do it well.*	Espero haberlo hecho bien. *I hope to have done it well.*
Siento tener que llegar tarde. *I am sorry to have to be late.*	Siento haber tenido que llegar tarde. *I am sorry to have had to be late.*
No pudo ir ayer. *He could not go yesterday.*	No pudo haber ido ayer. *He could not have gone yesterday.*
Niega saber los detalles del asunto. *He denies knowing any of the details of the issue.*[2]	Niega haber sabido los detalles del asunto. *He denies having found out any of the details of the issue.*

PERMANENTLY NOMINALIZED INFINITIVES

Some Spanish infinitives and some English infinitives and gerunds have become permanently nominalized. As such they are subject to the same rules as true nouns.

---

[1] **Creer, sospechar,** and **temer** may take an infinitive as well as a clause in Spanish: **Cree estar enfermo, Teme no pasar los exámenes, Sospecho tener que ir.**

[2] It must be kept in mind that some English verbs require the *-ing* form as an object, and that therefore the perfect infinitive will not only correspond to the perfect infinitive but to the perfect *-ing* form as well. In this particular sentence the perfect infinitive signals initiative aspect, hence the lexical change in the English version.

However, there is no direct correspondence of these nominalized forms between the two languages; normally, their equivalent is a regular noun.

SPANISH		ENGLISH	
Permanently nominalized infinitives:		*Permanently nominalized infinitives and gerunds:*	
amanecer	*dawn*	*wish*	deseo
atardecer	*dusk*	*smile*	sonrisa, sonreir
anochecer	*dusk*	*walk*	andar, caminar
deber	*obligation*	*building*	edificio, construcción
haber	*assets*	*drawing*	dibujo
parecer	*opinion*	*blessing*	bendición
pesar	*sorrow*	*painting*	pintura
poder	*power*	*shipping*	embarque, navegación
saber	*knowledge*	*meeting*	reunión

The Gerund (-*ndo* form)

FUNCTION OF THE GERUND

The function of the Spanish **-ndo** form when not occurring with an auxiliary to form progressive constructions is essentially adverbial. Even though the verb + **-ndo** construction expresses a secondary action, that action describes at the same time the general circumstances in which the main event is carried out.

Salió llorando.	*She left crying.*
Volvió corriendo.	*He came back running.*
El niño se duerme abrazando el oso.	*The child falls asleep hugging his bear.*
Perdimos una semana buscando casa.	*We spent a week looking for a house.*
Escuchando las noticias me enteré del accidente.	*While listening to the news I found out about the accident.*
Es Ud. muy amable dejándome salir antes.	*You are very kind in letting me leave earlier.*

Whereas in English the -*ing* form can be used as (1) subject, (2) object of a verb, (3) object of a preposition, or (4) adjective, the Spanish **-ndo** form cannot. The English -*ing* form functioning as a noun can only be rendered in Spanish through a nominal, an infinitive, or a noun. The English -*ing* form used as an adjective is rendered in Spanish by an adjectival, adjective, past participle, noun phrase, or relative clause.

Uses of English "-ing"

1. As subject:

Complementing is lying.	Echar cumplidos es mentir.
Walking is a good exercise.	Caminar es buen ejercicio.

2. As object of a verb:

She deserved punishing.	Merecía castigo.
He hates skiing.	Detesta esquiar.

3. As object of a preposition:

He left without notifying us.	Salió sin avisarnos.
There is little harm in daydreaming.	Hay poco daño en soñar despierto.

4. As an adjective:

This is an interesting book.	Este es un libro interesante.
Where is your wedding ring?	¿Dónde está tu anillo de bodas?
He is boring.	El es aburrido.
The box containing books is for him.	La caja que contiene libros es para él.

Spanish adjectivals for English "-ing"

Since the Spanish **–ndo** form cannot be used as an adjective,[1] whenever the English *-ing* form is used as a noun modifier, in Spanish one of the following adjectivals will be equivalent to it:

1. Adjective:

an interesting book	un libro interesante
a dying man	un hombre moribundo
running water	agua corriente
flying saucer	platillo volador

2. **de** + noun or INF:

wedding ring	anillo de bodas
writing paper	papel de escribir
housing expenses	gastos de vivienda
singing lessons	lecciones de canto

3. Clause:

When a clause could be used in English instead of the *-ing* form, then a clause should be used in Spanish.

The house standing on the corner . . .	La casa que está en la esquina . . .
that stands . . .	

---

[1] The **–ndo** does occur occasionally as an adjective instead of a clause. This usage, however, should not be encouraged as it is not considered fully acceptable and is restricted to certain expressions.

Hay alguien llamando a la puerta.	*There is someone knocking at the door.*
Recibí su carta diciendo que venía.	*I received his letter saying he would come.*

The box containing books . . . *that contains . . .*	La caja que contiene libros . . .
People living in cities . . . *that live . . .*	La gente que vive en ciudades . . .
Anyone conspiring . . . *that conspires . . .*	El que conspire . . .

4. Past participle:

The past participle must be used when postures are described.

standing	parado
sitting	sentado
lying down	acostado
reclining	reclinado

Except for **ardiendo** and **hirviendo**, a past participle must also be used to express a quality or condition when no adjective in **–or** or **–nte** exists.

boring	aburrido
daring	atrevido
amusing	divertido
entertaining	entretenido
good-looking	bien parecido
etc.	

ADVERBIAL USES OF THE GERUND

The **–ndo** form as an adverbial occurs subordinated to some other verb, except in stereotyped expressions where it is unattached to any verb. It may be used immediately after a verb to modify the main action, and in a clause *without* a relator to modify the main sentence. Even though the gerund describes manner, cause, and condition, it expresses at the same time a secondary action which may co-exist or be anterior to the action of the main verb, but not be subsequent to it.

Since the English gerund has many functions its occurrence as an adverbial is less productive than in Spanish. For this reason the **–ndo** form does not always correspond to the *-ing* form, but may have to be rendered by adverbial phrases or clauses introduced by *while, when, by+-ing, since, because, if, as,* or *when,* depending upon the meaning involved. Occasionally, the most idiomatic equivalent in English will be a coordinate sentence and not an adverbial phrase or clause.

Lavó las ventanas cantando.	*He washed the windows and sang while he worked.*
Lavó el piso fregándolo.	*She washed the floor by scrubbing it.*
Estando él de jefe, tal cosa no ocurrirá.	*Since (while) he is in charge, such a thing will not happen.*

Llegando temprano, tendremos tiempo de sobra para todo.	*If we arrive early, we will have more than enough time for everything.*
Llegando ella, se acaba este lío.	*When she arrives, this confusion will come to an end.*
Escuchando las noticias, me enteré del accidente.	*As (while) I was listening to the news, I found out about the accident.*

Manner

When the gerund describes how the action is carried out, it may either precede or follow the verb. Generally, it occurs after the verb. The modification of manner is the most productive construction of the gerund in Spanish. It is also the only one for which no alternative structure, wholly synonymous, can be given.

Se fue llorando.	*She left crying.*
Entró gritando.	*He came in screaming.*
Nos pasamos la mañana limpiando la casa.	*We spent the morning cleaning the house.*
Lavó las ventanas cantando.	*He washed the windows and sang while he worked.*
Me aburrí esperándote.	*I got bored waiting for you.*
Lavó el piso fregándolo.	*She washed the floor by scrubbing it.*
Pasó el exámen estudiando.	*She passed the exam by studying for it.*
Diciéndole la verdad lograrás convencerla.	*By telling her the truth, you will succeed in convincing her.*

Cause

The gerund used to express the cause of an action may be rendered in Spanish by various alternate constructions.

para + INF:

Se quedó escondida escuchando. ⎫ Se quedó escondida para escuchar. ⎭	*She stayed hidden and listened.*
Prefiero partir sin despedirme, evitándole ese dolor.	*I prefer to leave without saying good-bye, thus sparing her the pain.*
Prefiero partir sin despedirme para evitarle ese dolor.	*I prefer to leave without saying good-bye to spare her the pain.*

porque + CLAUSE:

Se casó con él creyéndolo rico.	*She married him thinking he was rich.*
Se casó con él porque lo creía rico.	*She married him because she thought he was rich.*
Lo hice pensando en tu porvenir.	*I did it thinking about your future.*
Lo hice porque pensaba en tu porvenir.	*I did it because I thought about your future.*

al + INF:

Teniéndote a mi lado, nada temo.	*Having you on my side, I fear nothing.*
Al tenerte a mi lado nada temo.	*While I have you on my side, I fear nothing.*

Es Ud. muy amable disculpándome.	*You are very kind in excusing me.*
Es Ud. muy amable al disculparme.	

puesto que + CLAUSE:

Siendo Ud. tan joven, debería esperar para casarse.	*Being so young you should wait to get married.*
Puesto que es Ud. tan joven, debería esperar para casarse.	*Since you are so young you should wait to get married.*
Siendo él tan enfermizo, deberían cuidarlo mejor.	*He being so sickly they should take better care of him.*
Puesto que él es tan enfermizo, deberían cuidarlo mejor.	*Since he is so sickly they should take better care of him.*

como + CLAUSE:

Viendo que se iban a casar de todos modos, consintió en ello.	*Seeing that they would marry anyway, he consented to it.*
Como vio que se iban a casar de todos modos, consintió en ello.	*Since he saw that they would get married anyway, he consented to it.*
Sabiendo que ella estaba muy enferma, le ocultarían la noticia.	*Knowing that she was very ill, they would conceal the news from her.*
Como sabían que ella estaba muy enferma, le ocultarían la noticia.	*Since they knew that she was very ill, they would conceal the news from her.*
No teniendo dinero empeñó sus joyas.	*As she had no money she pawned her jewels.*
Como no tenía dinero, empeñó sus joyas.	
Estando él de jefe tal cosa no ocurrirá.	*Since he is in charge such a thing will not happen.*
Como él está de jefe, tal cosa no ocurrirá.	

Condition

The gerund used to express condition is most common in stereotyped expressions where it occurs unattached to any verb. It must be in absolute initial position (unless an adverb in **-mente** precedes it). This applies to Spanish and English as well.

Less often it may be subordinated to a verb in which case it must be rendered in English by an *if*-clause.

Pensándolo bien, debería ir.	*Thinking it over, I think I should go.*
Hablando claro, ese hombre es un sinvergüenza.	*Speaking clearly, that man is a rascal.*
Legalmente hablando, eso no se puede hacer.	*Legally speaking, that cannot be done.*
Viéndolo bien, él tiene razón.	*Looking at it objectively, he is right.*
Objetivamente hablando, ella no es gran cosa.	*Objectively speaking, she does not amount to much.*
Considerando su edad, trabaja muy bien.	*Considering his age, he works very well.*
Llegando temprano, tendremos tiempo para hablarle antes de la reunión.	*If we arrive early, we will have time to speak to him before the meeting.*
Quejándote constantemente, perderás todos tus amigos.	*If you complain all the time you will lose all your friends.*

SUBJECT AND OBJECT FORMS WITH THE GERUND

The gerund used as an adverbial generally has the same subject as the main verb.

Me aburrí estudiando.	*I was bored (got bored) while studying.*
Diciéndole la verdad, lograrás convencerlos.	*By telling them the truth you will convince them.*

If the gerund has a different subject from the main verb, a subject noun or pronoun follows it.

Llegando ella, se acaba este lío.	*When she arrives (as soon as she arrives), this confusion will come to an end.*
Permitiéndolo tú, me iría mañana.	*If you allow it, I would leave tomorrow.*
Estando ella aquí, nada temo.	*While she is here (as long as she is here) I fear nothing.*
Habiendo llegado el maestro, se callaron los niños.	*The teacher having arrived, the children calmed down.*

The gerund may also be used to refer to the *direct object* of a sentence if the verb is one of "perception" (**oír**, **sentir**, **ver**, **encontrar**, etc.) or of "representation" (**dibujar**, **pintar**, **describir**, **representar**, etc.).

Oí a la muchacha llorando.	*I heard the girl crying.*
Vi a los niños jugando.	*I saw the children playing.*
Encontré a mi amigo estudiando.	*I found my friend studying.*
Picasso la pintó planchando ropa.	*Picasso painted her ironing clothes.*
Lo representó acometiendo contra todo.	*He depicted him fighting against everything.*
Lo describe peleando contra toda injusticia.	*He describes him fighting against every injustice.*

The gerund may take object pronouns—direct, indirect, and reflexive. The pronouns follow the gerund and are attached to it.

Nos pasamos la tarde explicándoselo.	*We spent the afternoon explaining it to him.*
Prometiéndoselo la calmarás.	*By promising it to her you will appease her.*
Vivía preocupándose.	*She spent her life worrying.*
Se pasó toda la mañana vistiéndose.	*She spent the whole morning getting dressed.*
Duérmelo cantándole.	*Put him to sleep by singing to him.*

TIME AND ASPECT OF THE GERUND

The gerund as an adverbial can be used to express the temporal co-existence of two actions, or the immediate anteriority of one event with respect to another.

CO-EXISTENCE

Yendo a su casa, se encontró con su amigo en el parque.	*While walking home he found his friend in the park.*
Trabajando de día y de noche, vive cansado.	*Working day and night, he is constantly exhausted.*
Paseando por el centro, vi a tus amigos.	*While taking a stroll downtown, I saw your friends.*

IMMEDIATE ANTERIORITY

Habiendo ayudado, es justo que Ud. participe.	*Having helped, it is fair that you should participate.*
Habiéndote advertido ayer, ¿cómo has podido hacer eso?	*Having warned you yesterday, how could you have done that?*

The usage of the gerund for an action *subsequent* to the main verb is considered ungrammatical in Spanish, in spite of its occurrence in the news media and legal contexts. A clause should be used in such cases. In this respect the gerund as an adverbial has the same restriction as when it occurs with an auxiliary in progressives. In neither case can it be used for subsequence.

Su asunto será pasado a la oficina correspondiente, quedando Ud. borrado de la lista (y quedará Ud. borrado de la lista).	*The matter will be handed over to the office in question, your name being thereafter erased from the list.*
Aumentó el ingreso nacional, excediendo más de 20.000.000 de dólares (y excedío más de . . .).	*The national income has increased, surpassing 20,000,000 dollars.*

The Spanish **-ndo** form always expresses ongoingness, whether in progressive or adverbial constructions. The secondary action described by an adverbial is thus also described in its progression.

Salió gritando.	*She walked out screaming.*
Vino corriendo.	*He came running.*

This applies also to the use of the gerund with a different subject, which in Spanish is limited to verbs of perception and representation.

La oí gritando.	*I heard her screaming.*
Encontró a su amigo estudiando.	*He found his friend studying.*
Picasso la pintó planchando ropa.	*Picasso painted her ironing clothes.*

When these same verbs occur with an infinitive, a more common construction in Spanish than the above, the action is depicted as completed, terminated.

La oí gritar (cuando gritó).	*I heard her scream.*
La vi llorar (cuando lloró).	*I saw her cry.*

Just as the **-ndo** form is not used in **estar** progressives with verbs of motion of instantaneous actions, it does not occur as an adverbial either. A verb + INF construction is used in these cases.

I saw her arriving.	La vi llegar.
I heard her coming in.	La oí entrar.
We saw them leaving.	Los vimos partir.

IDIOMATIC EXPRESSIONS

The **-ndo** form of a few verbs of motion is used in Spanish to denote location.

Vivo pasando la catedral. (más allá de la catedral)	*I live beyond the cathedral.*
Su oficina está entrando a la derecha. (a mano derecha de la entrada)	*His office is at the right of the entrance.*
El negocio está bajando la plaza. (más allá de la plaza)	*The shop is beyond the park.*

The Past Participle (-*do* form)

VERBAL USAGE

The past participle is used with **haber** to form compound tenses. When constructed with **haber** it is invariable in form, as opposed to its usage with **ser**, **estar**, **tener**, etc., where the past participle agrees in number and gender with the subject.

Hemos seguido con gran interés los juegos olímpicos.	*We have followed the Olympic Games with great interest.*
Han expulsado a varios atletas.	*They have expelled several athletes.*

BUT:

Uno de los jugadores fue expulsado.	*One of the players was expelled.*
Varios jugadores fueron expulsados.	*Several players were expelled.*
La nadadora está expulsada para siempre.	*The female swimmer is expelled for good.*

ADJECTIVAL USAGE

When the past participle is not constructed with **haber**, it functions as an adjective. As an adjective it agrees in number and gender with the noun it modifies. Since the past participle represents completed, perfected action, the state of being described may be thought of as the result of a previous or simultaneous action.[1]

El hombre sentado junto a la ventana es su marido.	*The man sitting next to her is her husband.*
Tiene las casas alquiladas.	*His houses are rented.*
Está tan aburrido que se duerme.	*He is so bored that he is on the verge of falling asleep.*

Depending upon the meaning of the sentence, the past particle may also modify a noun without reference to a previous action. In this instance it describes states of a habitual or durative nature which cannot be thought of as resulting from a previous or simultaneous action.

La tierra está rodeada de mares.	*The earth is surrounded by seas.*
El pueblo está alejado del mar.	*The town is situated far away from the sea.*

ADVERBIAL USAGE

In a limited number of cases the past participle may be used to modify both the subject and the verb. This usage is parallel to that of adjectives functioning as adverbials.[2]

Llegó exhausta.	*She arrived exhausted.*
Se marchó indignado.	*He left indignant.*
Partió entristecido por la pelea.	*He left saddened by the fight.*

The past particle may also be used in a detached clause, without being connected to a verb. It may refer to the subject of a sentence:

Traducido el manuscrito, lo enviaron enseguida.	*The manuscript having been translated, it was sent out immediately.*
Arrepentido de sus errores, intentaba excusarse.	*Being sorry for his mistakes, he was trying to excuse himself.*

or be completely unrelated to it:

Vendida la casa, se mudaron.	*Having sold the house, they moved.*
Arreglado el auto, prosiguieron.	*Having repaired the car, they moved on.*

A past participle in a detached clause modifies the whole sentence. It can describe states or events anterior to or co-existent with the ones expressed by the main

---

[1] See Chapter 15, **Ser** and **Estar**.
[2] See Adjectives as Adverbials, page 240.

verb. This usage, however, is limited to formal speech and writing. In informal speech situations an adverbial clause introduced by **después de** or **cuando** for anteriority and **mientras** or **como** for coexistence would be used instead.

ANTERIORITY

Informados los padres, decidieron casarse.	*Having informed their parents, they decided to marry.*
Después de informar a los padres decidieron casarse.	*After they had informed their parents, they decided to marry.*
Resuelto el problema, todos quedaron contentos.	*The problem having been solved, everybody was happy.*
Después de resolver el problema, todos quedaron contentos.	*Once the problem had been solved, everybody was happy.*

CO-EXISTENCE

Encerrado el hijo, no podía ser feliz la madre.	*Her son being imprisoned, the mother could not be happy.*
Como estaba encerrado el hijo, no podía ser feliz la madre.	*Since her son was imprisoned, the mother could not be happy.*
Descontento el marido, la familia tampoco podía estar contenta.	*The husband being discontented, the family could not be happy either.*
Mientras el marido estuviera descontento, tampoco podía estar contenta la familia.	*For as long as the husband remained discontented, the family could not be happy either.*

As seen in these examples, in Spanish the noun follows the past participle, whereas in English it precedes *having been* + past participle (for anteriority) and *being* + past participle (for co-existence).

The past participle is also used occasionally to describe anteriority within the future. In these cases it would be rendered in informal speech situations by clauses with **ni bien** or **cuando**.

Vendida la casa, tendremos suficiente para pagar las deudas. Ni bien se venda la casa, tendremos suficiente para pagar las deudas.	*As soon as the house is sold, we will have enough to pay the debts.*
Curada la niña, saldrán de viaje. Cuando se cure la niña, saldrán de viaje.	*As soon as the girl is well, they will go on a trip.*

NOMINAL USAGE

Some past participles have been nominalized so often that they have become permanently nominalized. Most of them do not correspond to English past participles but to other parts of speech.

invitado	guest	graduado	graduate
herido	wounded	juzgado	court of justice
puesto	job, position, stand	fracasado	failure
empleado	employee	acabado	finish
delegado	delegate	pecado	sin
hecho	deed, fact	pedido	order, request
bordado	embroidery	impuesto	tax
dicho	saying	vuelto	change
desconocido	stranger		

Other past participles may be nominalized through noun deletion or by the neuter **lo.**

Dame el vestido recién planchado.
Give me the dress that has just been ironed.

Dame el recién planchado.
Give me the one that has just been ironed.

Lo dicho, dicho está.

What is said, is said.

When nominalized, past participles may function as subjects or objects. But unlike regular nouns, nominalized participles with **lo** do not take the plural and are only rarely modified by adjectives; instead they are modified by adverbs. When a past participle is nominalized, it always retains its meaning of completed action. **Lo** + past participle is equivalent to a relative clause introduced by *what* in English.[1]

Lo aprendido en la niñez difícilmente se olvida.

What is learned in childhood is unlearned with difficulty.

Lo escrito queda de testimonio.

What is written remains as testimony.

Lo confesado no puede retraerse.

What is confessed (admitted) cannot be retracted.

Pasa a máquina lo corregido.

Type what is (has been) corrected.

The Spanish and English Infinitive Contrasted

THE INFINITIVE	
Spanish	*English*

FORM

Marked by **-ar, -er, -ir** endings (never by a preposition).	Marked by *to* (a meaningless grammatical device in most cases) except after auxiliaries *can, may, shall,* etc., and a few other verbs which take a bare infinitive.

---

[1] See The Neuter **lo**, page 294, and Nominalization of Descriptive Adjectives, page 218.

VERBAL NOUN

Characteristic of infinitive when not used with a true auxiliary.	Characteristic of the infinitive and the gerund, *-ing* form. Since these two forms have overlapping functions in English, the Spanish infinitive may correspond to one form or the other, or to both.

AS SUBJECT

Assumed by infinitive It can occur alone or be determined by a definite article (in the masculine singular), by a demonstrative, or by a possessive. It can be modified further by adjectives, adverbs; take subject and object pronouns, and **de** noun phrases to signal the subject.	Assumed by both the infinitive and the gerund. If determiners co-occur (excepting adverbs), only the gerund is used. Both the infinitive and the gerund may take adverbs; but only the gerund can take adjectives, demonstratives, and a possessive to signal the subject.
El despertar temprano es saludable.	*To wake up early is healthy.* *Waking up early is healthy.*
Ese llorar . . . Su llorar . . . Un buen empezar . . .	*That wining . . .* *Her wining . . .* *A good beginning . . .*
Un mal terminar . . . Su gastar desenfrenado . . . El habérselo dicho fue un error. El hacerlo tú . . . El despertar de María . . .	*A bad ending . . .* *Her unrestrained spending . . .* *Telling her (to have told her) was a mistake.* *Your doing it . . .* *Maria's awakening . . .*

AS PREDICATE NOUN

Occurs in sentences where the subject is another infinitive. Linked by **ser**. Not very productive in the in the spoken language. More commonly used in proverbs and poetic language.	Infinitive or gerund, depending on whether determiners and/or modifiers co-occur with it.
Verte es quererte. Ver es creer.	*To see you is to love you.* *To see is to believe.* *Seeing is believing.*

AS MODIFIER

Adjectival or adverbial modifier. Must be introduced by prepositions.	Except after *to*—when it retains its original meaning of purpose—only the gerund occurs after prepositions.

Te escribo para pedirte un favor.	*I am writing (in order) to ask for a favor.*
No estoy dispuesto a ayudarla.	*I am not inclined to help her.*
Se fue sin saludarnos.	*He left without greeting us.*
Está interesado en vender su casa.	*He is interested in selling his house.*
No puedes pasar sin estudiar.	*You cannot pass without studying.*
Te agradezco por leer el manuscrito.	*I thank you for reading the manuscript.*

AS OBJECT OF A VERB

The infinitive only (except after **continuar** and **seguir** which take the **-ndo** form) if the verb has the *same subject* as the infinitive.	The infinitive and/or the gerund, depending upon the verb, with the same and a different subject.
Quiero ir.	*I want to go.*
Evitaba ir a su casa.	*He avoided going to her house.*
Continúa estudiando.	*He continued to study (studying).*
With a different subject not the infinitive but a clause with a conjugated verb.	Verb + INF or Verb + *ing* with a different subject.
Espero que vayan.	*I expect them to go.*
No estoy de acuerdo con que ella vaya.	*I don't approve of her going.*
Nos ha pedido que viniéramos.	*He has asked us to come.*
Se sorprendió de que él viniera solo.	*She was surprised at his coming alone.*

The Spanish and English Gerund Contrasted

THE GERUND

Spanish **-ndo** form	English -ing form

FUNCTION

The **-ndo** form is not a verbal noun. Only the infinitive is a verbal noun.	Both the gerund and the infinitive are verbal nouns.
The **-ndo** form cannot, therefore, have any nominal function.	The *-ing* form may assume nominal functions.
Nominal functions of the *-ing* form are rendered by infinitives or nouns.	It can be subject of a sentence:
Cantar de divertido.	Singing *is fun.*
Fumar es peligroso.	*Smoking is hazardous.*
	Object of a verb:
Soñaba con **ir** a Europa.	*She dreamt about going to Europe.*
Insisto en ir.	*I insist in going.*

Entró sin anunciarse.
No puedes dejarlo sin tratar antes.

Object of a preposition:

He walked in without announcing himself.
You can't give up without trying.

The **-ndo** form cannot be an adjectival. Adjectives, past participles, noun phrases and clauses correspond to the *-ing* form.

Adjectival modifier:

un libro interestante
un hombre atrevido
anillo de boda
el hombre que está sentado junto a ella . . .

an interesting book
a daring man
wedding ring
the man sitting next to her . . .

ADVERBIAL USAGE

The primary function of the **-ndo** form, when not used with auxiliaries to form progressive constructions, is adverbial. While functioning as an adverbial it describes at the same time a secondary action which may coexist with or be anterior to the main action, but not be subsequent to it. The **-ndo** form may occur immediately after a verb, modifying the main action, or in a clause without a relator to modify the whole sentence.

It occurs unattached only in stereotyped expressions. As an adverbial, the **-ndo** form may describe manner, cause, and condition.

Its occurrence as an adverbial is much less frequent than in Spanish. The **-ndo** form must often be rendered by an adverbial phrase introduced by *while, when, by+-ing* or an adverbial clause introduced by *because, if, as, when,* etc., depending upon the meaning. Occasionally the most idiomatic equivalent is a coordinate sentence.

Se fue llorando.
Lavó las ventanas cantando.

She left crying.
He washed the windows and sang while he worked.

Diciéndole la verdad, la convencerás.

By telling her the truth you will convince her.

Se quedó escondida escuchando.
No teniendo dinero, vendió sus joyas.
Estando ella aquí, nada temo.

She remained hidden and listened.
As she had no money, she sold her jewels.
While she is here I fear nothing.

Legalmente hablando, no hay problema.
Pensándolo bien, no debería ir.

Legally speaking, there is no problem.
Thinking it over, I should not go.

8

RELATIVE PRONOUNS

Function of Relative Pronouns

Relative pronouns connect two clauses which have a given form in common. The relative pronoun not only connects the two clauses but also reproduces a noun or pronoun contained in one of them, and in some cases reduplicates the whole clause itself. The form the pronoun refers back to is called its *antecedent*.

Pedro tiene ambiciones. Conozco las ambiciones de Pedro.	*Pedro has ambitions. I know Pedro's ambitions.*
Conozco las ambiciones que tiene Pedro.	*I know the ambitions (that) Pedro has.*

Sentences containing relative clauses can be considered recasts of two independent sentences in which one of them becomes subordinated to the other. Thus the function of the antecedent noun in the main clause need not coincide with the function of the relative pronoun in the subordinate clause.

1. Relative as subject:

La casa es muy cara. La casa se vende.	*The house is very expensive. The house is for sale.*
La casa **que** se vende es muy cara.	*The house that is for sale is very expensive.*

2. Relative as direct object:

La casa me gusta. Tú compraste la casa.	*I like the house. You bought the house.*
La casa **que** tú compraste me gusta.	*The house that you bought I like.*

3. Relative as adverbial:

El apartamento es muy cómodo. El vive en el apartamento.	*The apartment is very comfortable. He lives in the apartment.*
El apartamento **en que** vive es muy cómodo.	*The apartment that he lives in is very comfortable.*

4. Relative as complement:

El asunto me aburre. Tú me hablas del asunto.	*The issue bores me. You are telling me about the issue.*
El asunto **del que** me hablas me aburre.	*The issue that you are telling me about bores me.*

Clause Formation

Relative clauses are formed in Spanish essentially in the same way as in English, with the following exceptions:

1. Relative pronouns cannot be omitted in Spanish as they are in English.

La novela que escribió es muy original.	*The novel (that) he wrote is very original.*
La mujer con quien se casó es mucho más joven que él.	*The woman (that) he married is much younger than he.*
Las conferencias que dio eran aburridísimas.	*The lectures (that) he gave were very boring.*

2. When a relative pronoun occurs with a preposition in Spanish, the preposition must occur before the clause. In English it is placed at the end of the clause when the relative is omitted and in set phrases such as *to long for, to aim at, to insist on, to speak about,* and *to complain about.*

La mujer por quien se desvive es mi hermana.	*The woman he longs for is my sister.*
La persona de quien hablé no es de fiar.	*The person I spoke of is not to be trusted.*
La mujer de quien está enamorado es mucho mayor que él.	*The woman he is in love with is much older than he.*

RESTRICTIVE AND NON-RESTRICTIVE CLAUSES

Relative clauses may be restrictive and non-restrictive. Restrictive clauses identify which one of the possible items of a given class is being referred to.

El libro que me regalaste es muy interestante.	*The book (that) you gave me is very interesting.*
El hombre que vive al lado es médico.	*The man who lives next door is a physician.*

Non-restrictive clauses, on the other hand, provide additional information about things already identified.

El libro, que trata de los Hapsburgos, es muy interestante.	*The book, which is about the Hapsburgs, is very interesting.*
Mi amigo, quien vive al lado, es médico.	*My friend, who lives next door, is a physician.*

The difference in meaning between the two types of clauses is signaled in speech by the use of pauses which separate non-restrictive clauses from the antecedent. In writing, non-restrictive clauses are identified by commas. Not all antecedents can take restrictive clauses. Unique referents, such as proper names and pronouns, can only take non-restrictive clauses since the antecedents are already identified and cannot be further restricted.

El, que es muy comprensivo, me dio permiso.	*He, who is very understanding, gave me permission.*
Juan, que no es tonto, se dejó convencer por ese hombre.	*John, who is not stupid, let himself be convinced by that man.*
Madrid, que es la capital de España, es una ciudad muy interesante.	*Madrid, which is the capital of Spain, is a very interesting city.*

Usage of Forms

---

que = *that, which, who*

The relative **que** is invariable in form. It is used for persons and for things. It occurs as subject and direct object. It may also occur as object of a preposition when the antecedent is a thing, but not when it is a person. Even when **que** is a direct object referring back to a person it does not take the personal **a**. **Que** is the most commonly employed relative in Spanish, and it is the only form that occurs in restrictive clauses, which are the most frequent in Spanish.

De todas las personas **que** hemos entrevistado hasta la fecha no nos interesa ninguna. (**que** = direct object of **hemos entrevistado**)	*Of all the persons we have interviewed thus far we are not interested in anyone.*
La mujer **que** entró a su casa no era su esposa. (**que** = subject of **entró**)	*The woman that went into his house was not his wife.*
Admitió el error en **que** estaba. (**que** = object of **en**)	*He admitted the error that he had committed.*

Las leyes a **que** estamos sujetos no son perfectas.	*The laws which we are subject to are not perfect.*
Me asombra la facilidad con **que** escribe.	*I am amazed by the facility with which he writes.*
La velocidad a **que** vas es excesiva.	*The speed at which you are going is excessive.*
La novela **que** escribió es muy original.	*The novel (that) he wrote is very original.*
María, **que** llegó muy cansada, se retiró enseguida.	*Maria, who arrived exhausted, retired immediately.*

---

quien = *whom, that, who*

The relative **quien** (plural **quienes**) is limited to human nouns or inanimate nouns when these are personified, It is invariable for gender but inflected for number, singular/plural. It must be used instead of **que** for persons when the relative is object of a preposition. It occurs as indirect object and object of prepositions in restrictive clauses. As subject it can only be used in non-restrictive clauses.

La persona a **quien** me enviaste prometió ayudarme.	*The person whom you sent me to promised to help me.*
Es la conciencia **quien** nos impone límites.	*It is our conscience who imposes limits upon us.*
No tengo en **quien** confiar.	*I have no one that I can trust.*
Mucho depende en la vida de las personas con **quienes** uno se asocia.	*Much depends in life upon the persons with whom one associates.*
El gerente, con **quien** acabo de hablar, prometió devolverme el dinero.	*The manager, with whom I have just spoken, promised to give me a refund.*
El hombre con **quien** hablaba es mi jefe.	*The man that she was talking with (with whom she was talking) is my boss.*
María, **quien** llegó muy cansada, se retiró enseguida.	*Maria, who arrived exhausted, retired immediately.*
Vi a tu hermano, **quien** me dijo que habías estado en el extranjero.	*I saw your brother, who told me (that) you had been abroad.*

---

el, la cual
el, la que } *which, who*

The relative **cual**, which is inflected for number, is a more precise relative than **que**, which is invariable in form. Both can occur with the definite article (in the feminine or masculine, depending upon the antecedent) when a precise identification of the thing or person referred to is necessary. Of the two forms **el cual** is preferred over **el que** in the written language.

El cual and **el que** are used under the following conditions:

1. **El cual** occurs in non-restrictive clauses when the antecedent (person or thing) is at some distance from the relative pronoun and/or when ambiguity could arise as to which noun the relative refers back to. When **el cual** and **la cual** refer to human nouns, they may be interchanged with **quien** when no ambiguity exists.

Me prestó sus apuntes de la clase de historia, **los cuales** eran muy confusos.	He lent me his history class notes, which were very confusing.
Me prestó los apuntes de la clase de historia, **la cual** es muy difícil.	He lent me his notes from his history class, which is very difficult.
Siempre nos contaba anécdotas de su juventud, **la cual (la que)** había sido muy interesante.	He would always tell us anecdotes about his youth, which had been very interesting.

BUT:

El marido de mi hermana, **el cual (quien)** tiene un puesto muy malo, apenas gana lo suficiente para mantener a su familia.	My sister's husband, who has a very poor job, barely makes enough money to support his family.

2. **El cual** occurs instead of **que** after prepositions of two or more syllables (**hacia, para, contra, dentro, desde, sobre**, etc.) and after prepositional phrases (**antes de, después de, cerca de, lejos de, enfrente de, al frente de, a partir de**, etc.)

El cajón **dentro del cual** había guardado sus joyas estaba vacío.	The drawer in which she had put her jewels was empty.
La empresa **al frente de la cual** estaba mi amigo ha quebrado.	The enterprise which was headed by my friend has gone bankrupt.
Había llegado la fecha **a partir de la cual** comenzaba a correr el plazo.	The day had come on which payments would have to be made.
No encontró argumento **sobre el cual** entablar demanda.	He found no arguments on the basis of which to initiate a legal suit.

3. **El cual** also occurs after the monosyllabic prepositions **por, sin**, and **tras**, in order to avoid confusion with the relator **que** which introduces nominal clauses after these prepositions.

No había razón **por la cual** había de renunciar.	There was no reason for which he should resign.
Es un documento **sin el cual** no puedo continuar la investigación.	It is a document without which I cannot continue the investigation.

But after other monosyllabic prepositions, **de, en, con**, etc., **el cual** is used interchangeably with **el que**.

Es un tópico **del que** (**del cual**) no sabe nada.	*It is a topic about which he knows nothing.*
El problema **del cual** (**del que**) te hablé, ya se resolvió.	*The problem I spoke to you about has already been solved.*
Es una amiga **en la cual** (**en la que**) tengo entera confianza.	*She is a friend in whom I have absolute faith.*

---

cuyo = *whose*

The relative **cuyo**, used for persons and for things, is inflected for number and gender. **Cuyo** agrees with the thing possessed and not the possessor. The antecedent precedes it immediately. It is generally restricted to the literary language; in oral and colloquial speech alternate constructions replace **cuyo**.

Acaba de morir Picasso, **cuyos** méritos artísticos son indiscutibles.	*Picasso, whose artistic merits are indisputable, has just died.*
Quería visitar Italia, **cuyos** tesoros conocía a través de sus lecturas.	*She wanted to visit Italy, whose treasures she knew from her readings.*
Cervantes, **de cuya** vida íntima poco se sabe, es el precursor de la novela moderna.	*Cervantes, about whose intimate life little is known, is the forerunner of the modern novel.*

If the thing possessed is a body part, an item of clothing, or a personal possession, **cuyo** does not occur. The relative **quien** with a reflexive or indirect object pronoun —signaling possession— is used instead.

María, a **quien** le duele la cabeza con frecuencia, debería ver un especialista.	*Maria, who frequently has headaches, should see a specialist.*
El soldado a **quien** le amputaron la pierna se siente muy deprimido.	*The soldier whose leg was amputated is very depressed.*
La niña, a **quien** se le había ensuciado el vestido, lloraba.	*The girl, whose dress had gotten dirty, was crying.*

NEUTER RELATIVES

---

lo cual, lo que = *which*

The neuter relatives **lo cual** and **lo que**, which are invariable, are used when the antecedent is a whole clause rather than a noun, or when it is an indefinite neuter noun and the relative occurs as object of a preposition. **Lo cual** occurs more frequently than **lo que**.

1. When the antecedent is a clause **lo cual** and **lo que** are the only relatives that occur in Spanish. Either serves to introduce a comment, cause, or reason for what precedes.

Picasso ha sido uno de los pintores más productivos y originales del siglo, **lo cual** explica su popularidad.	*Picasso was one of the most productive and original painters of the century, which explains his popularity.*
Cuando se enojaba, **lo cual** no ocurría muchas veces, era tremendo.	*When he got angry, which was not very often, he was terrible.*
Hizo las paces con su familia, **lo cual** nos confortó.	*He made peace with his family, which was comforting to us.*

2. When the antecedent is an indefinite neuter noun — **algo**, **nada** — and the relative is object of a preposition, **lo cual** is used instead of **que**. If it is not preceded by a preposition, **que** occurs instead.

Es algo **a lo cual** no acabo de acostumbrarme.	*It is something I cannot get accustomed to.*
Es necesario que no des motivo alguno **del cual** puedan quejarse.	*It is necessary that you give no motive whatsoever for them to complain.*

BUT:

Dale algo **que** sea diferente.	*Give her something that is different.*

3. The neuter **lo cual** must be differentiated from the relative **cual** which is inflected for number and occurs with the definite article. The latter refers to a specific noun, the former to the whole preceding phrase. In English this distinction is not made, and in both cases *which* translates the Spanish relatives.

Nos envió todos los datos pertinentes, **lo cual** nos será muy útil.	*He sent us all the pertinent information, which will be very useful to us. (something which will be . . .)*
Nos envió todos los datos pertinentes, **los cuales** nos serán muy útiles.	*He sent us all the pertinent information, which will be very useful to us. (information which will be . . .)*
Habla muy bien de tus obras, **lo cual** me impresiona.	*He speaks very highly of your works, which impresses me. (the fact that he speaks well)*
Habla muy bien de tus obras, **las cuales** le impresionan.	*He speaks very highly of your works, which impress him. (the works impress him)*

A more colloquial rendering of **lo cual** is achieved by **cosa que**=*something which*, or the simple demonstrative.

Picasso ha sido uno de los pintores más productivos y originales del siglo, **cosa que** (**esto**) explica su popularidad.	*Picasso was one of the most productive and original painters of the century, which explains his popularity.*
Hizo las paces con su familia; **esto** nos confortó muchísimo.	*He made peace with his family; this was most comforting to us.*

RELATIVE ADVERBS FOR RELATIVE PRONOUNS

When the antecedent nouns refer to place, time, and manner, and the relatives function as adverbials, the relative adverbs **donde**, **cuando**, and **como** may be used instead of relative pronouns. When functioning as adverbials, relative pronouns are introduced by prepositions just like nouns. The prepositions are retained before the relative adverb **donde**, because place can refer to location, origin, destination, source, etc. To differentiate one adverbial from the other, a different preposition occurs. The exception is **en donde** which alternates freely with **donde**. **Donde** is the most frequently used relative adverb.

LOCATION

La casa **en que vivo** es muy húmeda.⎫	*The house I live in is very humid.*
La casa **donde vivo** es muy húmeda.⎭	*The house where I live is very humid.*

ORIGIN

La familia **de la que** procede es muy⎫ distinguida.	*The family which he descends from is*
La familia **de donde** procede es muy⎬ distinguida.	*very distinguished.*

DESTINATION

El sitio **al que** lo trasladaron está ⎫ muy lejos.	*The place to which he was transferred*
El sitio **a donde** lo trasladaron está⎬ muy lejos.	*is very far away.*

SOURCE

No recuerdo el lugar **en que** lo leí.⎫	*I don't remember the source where I*
No recuerdo el lugar **donde** lo leí. ⎭	*read it.*

The prepositions are omitted when **como** and **cuando** occur instead of relative pronouns. **Como** and **cuando** are far more restricted in usage than **donde** and rarely occur with expressed antecedents.

La manera **en que** te habla ⎫ es chocante.	*The way in which he speaks to you is*
La manera **como** te habla es⎬ chocante.	*offensive.*

El momento **en que** llegó era muy⎫ inoportuno.	*He arrived at a very inopportune*
El momento **cuando** llegó era muy⎬ inoportuno.	*moment.*

Donde can occur instead of the neuter relative **lo cual** when the antecedent clause refers to source in a metaphorical sense.

No se hablan, **de lo cual** deduzco
que se han peleado.
No se hablan, **de donde** deduzco
que se han peleado.

They are not speaking to each other, from which I conclude that they must have had a falling out.

RELATIVES WITHOUT OVERT, EXPRESSED ANTECEDENTS

Relative pronouns and adverbs may occur with or without expressed antecedents. Relative forms occur without antecedents when the referent is indefinite or is implicitly understood by the speaker. In either case the relative form can only refer to a member of a particular class.

Quien, quienes:

Quien can only have an indefinite person as an antecedent. It covers various English equivalents: *anyone who, whoever, someone who, the one who, who, whom.*

Quien te lo dijo te miente. (= La persona que te lo dijo te miente.)	*Whoever has told you that is lying.*
Quien no coopere será despedido.	*Anyone who does not cooperate will be fired.*
Se lo daré a quien más lo necesite.	*I will give it to whoever needs it the most.*
Buscaré quien la cuide.	*I will look for someone to take care of her.*
Por quien doblan las campanas.	*For whom the bells toll.*

When in English "someone" refers to a specific antecedent, in Spanish **quien** cannot be used; **alguien** must occur instead.

Someone who called this morning left this message for you.

Alguien que llamó esta mañana dejó este mensaje para ti.

El/la que; los/las que:

These forms when occurring without an expressed antecedent can only refer to a non-specific person. Their equivalents in English are *the one (ones) who, whoever.*[1]

El que te lo haya dicho te miente.	*Whoever has told you that is lying.*
La que sea más competente será tu secretaria.	*The one who proves most competent shall be your secretary.*
Los que no trabajan, no comen.	*The ones who do not work, do not eat.*

Lo que:

This form may refer to an indefinite or to a specific thing. If the main verb is in the future and the relative clause has a verb in the subjunctive, **lo que** refers to

---

[1] See Relative Clauses, page 187.

an indefinite thing. If the relative clause has a verb in the indicative, the antecedent is specific since it would be known as a fact by the speaker. Its equivalents in English are *whatever* and *what*.

Te daré lo que me pidas.	*I will give you whatever you might ask for.*
Te daré lo que me pediste.	*I will give you what you asked for.*
Dile lo que te de la gana.	*Tell him whatever you wish.*
Dile lo que significa.	*Tell him what it means.*

Cuanto/cuanta; cuantos/cuantas:

The antecedent may be a person or a thing plus quantifier, equivalent to **todo(-s) lo(-s) que, toda(-s) la(-s) que** in an indefinite sense. Their equivalents in English are *whatever (all that), whoever (all those that), as much as.*

Cuanto ocurre es culpa suya.	*Whatever is happening is his fault.*
Todo lo que . . .	*All that . . .*
Cuantos vengan serán bienvenidos.	*Whoever might come will be welcome.*
Todos los que . . . ⎫ Cuantas . . . ⎬ Todas las que . . . ⎭	*All those that . . .*
Cuantos los vieron se sorprendieron.	*All those who saw him were surprised.*
Dejé que dijera cuanto quisiera.	*I let him say whatever (as much as) he wanted.*
Te daré cuanto necesites.	*I will give you as much as (whatever) you need.*

Cuanto when referring to an antecedent implicitly understood by the speaker functions as a quantifier, and as such may be inflected for gender and for number, meaning in English *as many as.*

Le di cuantos (libros) quiso.	*I gave him as many (books) as he wanted.*
Le daré cuantas (solicitudes) quiera.	*I will give him as many (applications) as he may want.*

When the English "whatever" does not refer to quantity of an indefinite thing but to any one thing, then **cuanto** cannot be used. **Cualquier cosa . . . que** or **lo que** must occur instead.

Dile lo que consideres apropiado. cualquier cosa que . . .	*Tell him whatever you consider appropriate.*
Dale lo que te sobre. cualquier cosa que . . .	*Give him whatever you might have left over.*

Donde, cuando, como:

These relative forms can only have antecedents meaning place, time, or manner.

The antecedents must function as adverbials. The equivalents in English are *where*, *when*, and *how*; *wherever* and *however*.

A donde iba él, iba ella.	*Wherever he went, she went.*
No quiero vivir donde vive ella.	*I don't want to live where she lives.*
Te avisaré ni bien llegue.	*I'll let you know as soon as he arrives.*
Cuando sea que llegue será bienvenido.	*Whenever he comes he will be welcome.*
Hazlo como quieras.	*Do it however you want.*
Hazlo como te dijeron.	*Do it how you were told.*

INTERROGATIVES FOR RELATIVE PRONOUNS

After verbs of perception and understanding a relative pronoun is replaced in Spanish by an interrogative pronoun.

No sé cómo hacerlo.	*I don't know how to do it.*
No sé qué decirle.	*I don't know what to tell her.*
No veo por dónde se pueda salir.	*I don't see how to get out of here.*
No comprendo qué significa.	*I don't understand what it means.*

RELATIVE PRONOUNS BEFORE INFINITIVES

In some cases in Spanish relative pronouns may occur before infinitives instead of full clauses. An auxiliary such as **deber** or **poder** may be considered as implicitly given. In English the infinitive is also used but the relative pronoun may be omitted.

No tiene nada que (pueda) ponerse.	*She has nothing to wear.*
No hay nada que (debes) temer.	*There is nothing to fear.*
Buscaba lugar donde (podía) esconderse.	*He was looking for a place to hide.*
No encontró forma como (podía) resolverlo.	*He did not find a way to solve it.*
No había lugar donde (podía) descansar.	*There was no place to rest.*

These same constructions may occur without an expressed antecedent when the antecedent refers to a person, a thing, a place, manner, or time. In English the antecedent must be supplied, with either an infinitive or a clause following it.

No tengo (nadie) en quien confiar.	*I have no one that I can trust.*
No tenía (cosa) que ponerse.	*She had nothing to wear.*
Buscaba (lugar) donde esconderse.	*He was looking for a place to hide.*
No encontró (forma) como resolverlo.	*He did not find a way to solve it.*
Pensaba (en la hora en que podía o debía) en cuando salir.	*He was thinking about the time he would have to (or should) leave.*

The use of a relative preceding an infinitive (which functions as a modifier) must be differentiated from the relator **que** in the auxiliaries **tener que** and **haber que**. With these two verbs the following infinitive is a direct object and not a modifier.

Tengo que trabajar.	*I have to work.*
Hay que callar.	*One must be silent.*

If **tener** and **haber** occur with an antecedent, the **que** is not only a relator but a relative pronoun, and the infinitive a modifier.

Hay mucho que ver aquí.	*There is much to be seen here.*
Tengo muchas cosas que decirte.	*I have many things to tell you.*
No tiene tiempo que perder.	*She has no time to waste.*
¿Hay algo que te guste?	*Is there something you like?*
Esto no tiene nada que ver con lo que dije.	*This has nothing to do with what I said.*

Spanish and English Relative Pronouns Contrasted

RELATIVE PRONOUNS

Spanish	*English*

FUNCTION

Relative pronouns connect two clauses which have a noun, noun phrase, pronoun, or whole clause in common. The relative pronoun not only relates the second clause to the first but reproduces a noun, noun phrase, etc., mentioned in the first. The noun, noun phrase, etc., which the pronoun refers back to is called its antecedent.

Conozco las ambiciones que tiene Pedro.	*I know the ambitions (that) Pedro has.*
Pedro tiene ambiciones. Conozco las ambiciones de Pedro.	*Pedro has ambitions. I know Pedro's ambitions.*

Since sentences containing relative clauses can be considered recasts of two independent sentences, the function of a relative pronoun, in its own clause, may be totally independent of the function of the noun which the relative pronoun reproduces.

Conozco las ambiciones que tiene Pedro. (**las ambiciones** = direct object of **conozco, que** = direct object of **tiene**)	*I know the ambitions (that) Pedro has.*
La casa en que vivo es muy húmeda. (**la casa** = subject of sentence, **que** = adverbial of **vivo**)	*The house (that) I live in is very humid.*

TYPES OF CLAUSES

Relative clauses may be restrictive and non-restrictive. Restrictive clauses identify which one of the possible items of a given class is being referred to.

La película que vimos anoche es muy original.	*The film that we saw last night was very original.*
El hombre que vive al lado es médico.	*The man who lives next door is a physician.*

Non-restrictive clauses provide additional information for things already identified.

María, quien llegó exhausta, se retiró enseguida.	*Maria, who arrived exhausted, retired immediately.*
Mi amigo, que vive al lado, es médico.	*My friend, who lives next door, is a physician.*

CLAUSE FORMATION

When a relative pronoun occurs with a preposition:

1. The preposition must occur before the clause.

La persona de quien te hablé no es de fiar.
La mujer de quien está enamorado es mayor que él.

2. Relative pronouns cannot be omitted.

La novela que escribió es muy buena.
Las conferencias que dió eran muy aburridas.

1. The preposition is placed at the end of a clause when the relative pronoun is omitted and in set phrases; *long for, aim at,* etc.

The person I spoke of is not to be trusted.

The woman he is in love with is older than he.

2. Relative pronoun may be omitted.

The novel (that) he wrote is very good.
The lectures (that) he gave were very boring.

USAGE OF FORMS

Que: Invariable in form. Used for persons and things. Occurs as subject and direct object. May be object of a preposition if the antecedent is a thing. Only form that occurs in restrictive clauses, the most common in Spanish.

El libro que me diste . . .
La carta que espero . . .
La mujer que entró a su casa . . .
María, quien llegó exhausta, . . .
La mujer que vi . . .

Equivalents = *that, who.* When the antecedent is object of preposition and a thing, the equivalent is *which.*

The book (that) you gave me . . .
The letter which I am waiting for . . .
The woman that went into his house . . .
Maria, who arrived exhausted, . . .
The woman (that) I saw . . .

Quien: Limited to human nouns or inanimate nouns when these are personified. Inflected for number. Must be used instead of **que** when relative is object of a preposition and indirect object. As subject it can only be used in non-restrictive clauses.

Equivalents = *whom, that, who.*

No recuerdo a quien se lo di.

I don't recall to whom I gave it.
I don't recall the person that I gave it to.

El hombre con quien hablaba es su jefe.

The man that she was talking with (with whom she was talking) is her boss.

María, quien llegó exhausta, se retiró.

Maria, who arrived exhausted, retired.

El cual, el que: Inflected for number. Co-occur with article in the masculine or feminine, depending upon antecedent. Used when a precise identification of the antecedent is necessary, such as when the antecedent occurs at some distance from the relative.

Equivalents = *which, who.*

Los apuntes de la clase de historia, los cuales me fueron muy útiles, me los prestó María.

Maria lent me her history class notes, which were very useful to me.

It occurs after prepositions of two or more syllables and prepositional phrases: **antes de, dentro de, cerca de**, etc. **El cual** also occurs after **sin, por**, and **tras**.

El cajón dentro del cual había guardado todas sus joyas estaba vacío.

The drawer in which she had put all of her jewels was empty.

It occurs when possible ambiguity exists as to which the antecedent is.

El marido de mi hermana, el cual . . .
(**quien** could either refer to **marido** or **hermana**)

My sister's husband, who (refers to him) . . .

Cuyo: Inflected for number and for gender. Agrees with the thing possessed and not the possessor. Restricted to literary style.

Equivalent = *whose.*

Quería visitar Italia, cuyos tesoros artísti-.cos conocía a través de sus lecturas.

She wanted to visit Italy, whose artistic treasures she knew through readings.

When the thing possessed is a body part, item of clothing or personal belonging, **quien** with an indirect object form occurs instead.

El soldado a quien le apuntaron la pierna está muy deprimido.	*The soldier whose leg was amputated is very depressed.*
La niña, a quien se le ensució el vestido, está llorando.	*The child, whose dress got dirty, is crying.*

Lo cual, **lo que**: neuter form. The antecedent is a whole clause.	Equivalent = *which*.
Supe que habían renunciado, lo cual me sorprendió enormemente.	*I found out that they had resigned, which surprised me enormously.*

Relative forms may occur with or without an expressed antecedent. The antecedent is omitted when the referent is indefinite, or implicity understood by the speaker. In either case the relative form can only refer to a member of a particular class.

Quien: person.	*whoever, whomever, anyone who, the one who, who, whom, etc.*
Quien te lo dijo te miente.	*Whoever has told you that is lying.*
No recuerdo a quienes se lo dije.	*I don't remember to whom I have said it.*
Quienes la conocen no lo pueden creer.	*Those who know her cannot believe it.*

El (la) que, **los (las) que**: person.	*the one (ones) who, whoever*
Los que no trabajan no comen.	*The ones who do not work do not eat.*
Las que estudien pasarán.	*The ones who study will pass.*

Lo que: thing.	*what, whatever*
Te daré lo que me pidas.	*I will give you whatever you ask for.*
Te di lo que me pediste.	*I gave you what you asked for.*

Cuanto (-s), **cuanta (-s)**: person or thing, plus quantifier.	*whatever (all that), whoever (all those that), as much as*
Cuanto occure es culpa tuya.	*Whatever is happening is your fault.*
Cuantos vengan serán bienvenidos.	*Whoever might come will be welcome.*
Te daré cuanto necesites.	*I will give you as much as you need.*

Donde: place, location, destination, source, origin, etc.	*where, wherever*
A donde iba él, iba ella.	*Wherever he went, she sent.*
No quiero vivir donde vive ella.	*I don't want to live where she lives.*

Cuando: time, hour, day, month, etc.	*when, whenever*
Te avisaré cuando llegue.	*I will let you know when he arrives.*
Despiértame cuando venga.	*Wake me up whenever he arrives.*

Como: manner.	*how, however*
Hazlo como quieras.	*Do it however you want.*
Hazlo como te dijeron.	*Do it how you were told.*

9

INTERROGATIVES AND EXCLAMATIVES

Interrogatives

INFORMATION QUESTIONS

Information questions involve the use of interrogative words in order to elicit concrete information about someone or something. An interrogative word is either an adverb, a limiting adjective, or a pronoun used to ask a question. Most of

Interrogative	Function	Form	Usage: Ask about	English Equivalent
¿cuándo?			Time	*when?*
¿cuánto?			Quantity	*how much?*
¿cómo? **¿qué tal?**	Adverbial	Invariable	Description Condition Manner	*how?* *what . . . like?*
¿dónde?			Location	*where?*
¿qué?	Adjectival or Pronominal	Invariable	Identity or description of animate or inanimate objects	*what / which?*

Interrogative	Function	Form	Usage: Ask About	English Equivalent
¿cuál? ¿cuáles?	Adjectival or Pronominal	Invariable for gender	Choice / selection among animate or inanimate objects	what? / which one(s)?
¿cuánto? ¿cuánta? ¿cuántos? ¿cuántas?		Agreement in gender and number	Quantity of animate or inanimate objects	how much? how many?
¿quién? ¿quiénes? ¿a quién(es)?	Pronominal	Agreement in number but not in gender	Identity of animate objects	who? whom?
¿de quién(es)?			Possession	whom? whose?

these words have the same correspondence in the two languages; they function more or less the same way and have the same word order; they normally open an interrogative statement. But in Spanish questions with interrogatives, the subject follows the verb. The intonational pattern in these questions is very similar in both languages: normally the pitch falls at the end of such questions. All interrogative words in Spanish carry a written accent.

USE OF ADVERBIAL INTERROGATIVES

¿cuándo? = *when?*

The interrogative adverb **¿cuándo?** is invariable in form. Since it refers to time, questions with **¿cuándo?** are derived from statements containing an adverb of time or a temporal expression.

Vienen mañana.	*They are coming tomorrow.*
el próximo año	*next year*
la semana entrante	*the coming week*
dentro de poco	*shortly*
etc.	*etc.*
¿Cuándo vienen?	*When are they coming?*

If the temporal expression includes a preposition, it will precede the interrogative word in the question.

Se quedará aquí hasta tarde.	¿Hasta cuándo se quedará aquí?
He'll stay here til late.	*For how long will he stay here?*
Estaban aquí desde ayer.	¿Desde cuándo estaban aquí?
They have been here since yesterday.	*Since when have they been here?*
Llegarán para las cuatro.	¿Para cuándo llegarán?
They will arrive by four o'clock.	*By when will they arrive?*

¿Para cuándo? implies that the speaker is asking the "approximate time" at which an event will take place. A verb such as **creer, pensar, esperer,** or **suponer** and/or an expression like **más o menos** or **aproximadamente** furthers this idea of imprecision in formulating the question.

Creo que estará listo para mañana, más o menos.	¿Para cuándo crees que estará listo, más o menos?
I think that it will be ready by tomorrow more or less.	*By when do you suppose it will be ready more or less?*
Espero enviarlo para la semana entrante aproximadamente.	¿Para cuándo esperas mandarlo aproximadamente?
I expect to send it by next week approximately.	*By when do you expect to send it approximately?*
Supongo que llegarán para las 8.	¿Para cuándo supones que llegarán?
I suppose that they will arrive by 8 o'clock.	*By when do you suppose they will arrive?*

¿cuánto? = *how much? | how?*

¿Cuánto? as an adverb is invariable in form. Since it refers to quantity, questions with **¿cuánto?** are derived from statements that contain an expression of quantity, either a numeral (**tres, dos, tercios,** etc.) or an indefinite (**varios, mucho, pocos,** etc.).

Requiere dos tercios.	¿Cuánto requiere?
It requires two thirds.	*How much does it require?*
Hace falta mucho.	¿Cuánto hace falta?
A lot is needed.	*How much is needed?*
Es cuatro millas de largo.	¿Cuánto es de largo?
It is four miles long.	*How long is it?*

In the literary language **¿cuánto?** has a shortened form **¿cuán?** which occurs before attributive adjectives.

¿Cuánto es de largo?⎱	
¿Cuán largo es?　 ⎰	*How long is it?*

But in everyday speech the predicative construction **¿cuánto + ser + de . . . ?** is preferred.

¿Como? may substitute **¿cuánto?** in this predicative construction:

¿Cuánto es de largo?

¿Cómo . . .

How long is it?

If the expression of quantity includes a preposition, it will precede the interrogative word in the question.

Hoy estamos a cinco de Mayo.
Today is May 5th.

¿A cuánto estamos hoy?
What day is it today?

La yarda de alambre se vende a (por) un dólar.
A yard of wire sells for one dollar.

¿A cuánto se vende la yarda de alambre?
¿Por cuánto . . .?
How much does a yard of wire sell for?

Compraron ese Picasso a (por) un millón de dólares.
They bought that Picasso for a million dollars.

¿A cuánto (por cuánto) compraron ese Picasso?
For how much did they buy that Picasso?

Los pagó a 65 centavos la docena.
He paid them at 65 cents the dozen.

¿A cuánto los pagó?
How much did he pay them for?

Pueden pagar hasta medio millón.
They can pay up to a million dollars.

¿Hasta cuánto pueden pagar?
How much can they pay?

¿A cómo? may replace **¿a cuánto?**

¿A cómo estamos hoy?
¿A cómo se vende?
¿A cómo lo compraron?
¿A cómo la pagaste?

What day is it today?
How much does it sell for?
How much did they buy it for?
How much did you pay for it?

In English, if the preposition is included in the interrogative statement it normally goes at the end. In Spanish it goes at the beginning.

¿cómo? = *how?* / *what is . . . like?*

The interrogative adverb **¿cómo?** is invariable in form. It refers to either a condition, state, description, or manner in which someone or something behaves or is found. Thus, questions with **¿cómo?** are derived from statements containing either a predicate adjective or an adverb of manner.

El Presidente está enfermo.
The President is sick.

¿Cómo está el Presidente?
How is the President?

El Presidente es joven.
The President is young.

¿Cómo es el Presidente?
How is the President?[1]

La criada salió enojada.
The maid left angry.

¿Cómo salió la criada?
How did the maid leave?

Los estudiantes viajaron por avión.
The students travelled by airplane.

¿Cómo viajaron los estudiantes?
How did the students travel?

Lo hizo con mucho cuidado.
He did it with care.

¿Cómo lo hizo?
How did he do it?

La invitó por carta.
He invited her by mail.

¿Cómo la invitó?
How did he invite her?

¿Cómo? is also used in other contexts:

1. If the speaker has not understood a previous statement and wishes clarification:

Necesito que me traiga los otros
documentos.
—¿Cómo (dijo)?

*I need you to bring me the other
documents.*
—What did you say?

2. If the speaker considers a previous statement to be wrong or if he wants to show surprise for what has been said:

Usted no tiene derecho a más de dos
semanas de pago.
—¿Cómo?

You are only entitled to two weeks pay.

—What?

In both contexts English uses *what?* instead.

Since Spanish **¿cómo?** is always followed by a verb phrase, English questions with *how* + adjective or *how* + adverb correspond in Spanish to a different word order or are asked with a different interrogative.

How wide is it?	¿Cómo es de ancho? ¿Cuánto es de ancho? ¿Cuán ancho es? ¿Qué anchura tiene?
How heavy is it?	¿Cómo es de pesado? ¿Cuánto es de pesado? ¿Cuán pesado es?
How fast did they sell the house?	¿Con qué rapidez vendieron la casa? ¿Cuán rápido vendieron la casa? ¿Con cuánta rapidez vendieron la casa?

---

[1] Since English lacks the **ser/estar** contrast, the equivalents to Spanish **¿cómo?** are different with either verb: **¿cómo + estar . . .?** = *how is someone (or something)* and **¿cómo + ser . . .?** = *what is someone (or something) like.*

¿Cómo estuvo el examen? *How was the exam?* BUT: ¿Cómo fue el examen? *What was the exam like?*

How early did he leave?	¿Cuán temprano salió?
How late is it?	⎰¿Cuán tarde es? ⎱OR SIMPLY: ¿Qué hora es?[1]

¿Qué tal? as an alternate to ¿cómo?

¿Qué tal? is frequently used instead of **¿cómo?**

1. As a common greeting:

¿Qué tal (están) Uds.?[2]	*How are you?*
¿Qué tal, Pedro?	*How are you, Pedro?*

2. To elicit one's opinion or evaluation about someone or something:

¿Qué tal (está) tu mujer? —Se siente muy pesimista con . . .	*How is your wife?* *She is feeling very pessimistic about . . .*
¿Qué tal (está) el café? —Está muy frío.	*How is the coffee?* *—It is very cold.*
¿Qué tal (fueron) las vacaciones? —¡Estupendas!	*How did your vacation go?* *—Great!*
¿Qué tal (es) tu prima? —Es rubia y de ojos verdes.	*What does your cousin look like?* *—She is blonde with green eyes.*
¿Qué tal lo hizo? —Muy bien. Obtuvo una A.	*How did she do?* *—Very well. She got an A.*

In certain contexts **¿cómo?** and **¿qué tal?** are not interchangeable, but one or the other must be used in order to avoid ambiguities:

1. **¿Cómo . . . ?** = to elicit the way in which something is done, prepared, or carried out.

¿Cómo te gusta el café? —Me gusta negro, sin azúcar.	*How do you like your coffee?* *—I like it black without sugar.*
¿Cómo viajaron? —Viajaron por avión.	*How did they travel?* *—They traveled by plane.*
¿Cómo lo cosieron? —Lo cosieron a mano.	*How did they sew it?* *—They sewed it by hand.*

---

[1] The interrogative **¿qué?** does not occur with the adverb **tarde** to inquire about clock-time. **Hora** must be used instead.

[2] With **¿qué tal?** if the verb is **ser**, **estar**, or **ir**, it may be omitted.

2. **¿Qué tal . . . ?** = to elicit an opinion or evaluation about someone or something.

¿Qué tal el café?
—Me gusta mucho.

How is the coffee?
—I like it very much.

¿Qué tal viajaron?
—Viajaron sin problemas.

How did they travel?
—They traveled without problems.

¿Qué tal escribe?
—Escribe rápido y sin cometer errores.

How does he write?
—He writes fast and without making mistakes.

3. **¿Qué tal** + noun . . . ? = *what kind of (a) +noun . . . ?*

¿Qué tal persona es?
(= ¿Qué clase de persona es?)
—Excelente.

What kind of (a) person is she?

—Excellent.

¿Qué tal recibimiento te dio?
(=¿Qué clase de recibimiento te dio?)
—Muy cordial.

What kind of reception did he give you?
—Very cordial.

¿Qué tal estadía tuvieron?
(=¿Qué clase de estadía tuvieron?)
—¡Maravillosa!

What kind of a stay did you have?

—A wonderful stay!

¿Qué tal+noun . . . ? (=**¿qué clase de**+noun . . . ?) is normally used to elicit an evaluation or opinion, but if a simple description is expected, then **¿qué clase de**+noun is used:

¿Qué clase de instrumentos son esos?
—Son unos instrumentos de navegación.

What kind of instruments are these?
—They are navigating instruments.

¿dónde? = *where?*

The interrogative adverb **¿dónde?** is invariable in form and it refers to place or location. Questions with **¿dónde?** are derived from statements containing a locative complement.

Vive muy cerca de aquí.
en casa de sus padres.
al otro lado del río.
etc.
¿Dónde vive?

He lives nearby.
at his parent's house.
on the other side of the river.
etc.
Where does he live?

Since the source of **¿dónde?** is a locative complement, with verbs of motion the interrogative is introduced by a directional preposition: **de, desde, a, para, hacia, por, hasta**, etc.

Interrogative	Meaning	English Equivalent
¿de dónde? **¿desde dónde?**	Source	*where . . . from?*
¿a dónde? **¿adónde?** **¿para dónde?**	Destination, in which direction	*where . . . (to)?*
¿por dónde? **¿hacia dónde?**	Means Proximity or destination	*how (through where) . . .?* *whereabouts . . .?* *where to . . .?* *where . . . for?*
¿hasta dónde?	Limit in destination	*how far . . .?*

Este avión viene de Lima.
This plane comes from Lima.

¿De dónde viene este avión?
Where does this plane come from?

Te llamó desde París.
He called you from Paris.

¿Desde dónde te llamó?
Where did he call you from?

Va a (para) la biblioteca.
He is going to the library.

¿Dónde va?
¿A dónde va?
¿Adónde va?
¿Para dónde va?
Where is he going (to)?

Se llega allí por el parque.
One gets there through the park.

¿Por dónde se llega allí?
How (through where) does one get there?

Le gusta pasearse por la Quinta Avenida.
He likes to walk along Fifth Avenue.

¿Por dónde le gusta pasearse?

Whereabouts does he like to walk?

Ahora nos dirijimos hacia la catedral.
We are now heading towards the cathedral.

¿Hacia dónde nos dirijimos ahora?

Where are we heading for now?

Lograron llegar hasta México.
They managed to go as far as Mexico.

¿Hasta dónde lograron llegar?
How far did they manage to go?
(= *Up to where . . .?*)

¿A dónde? (or **¿adónde?**) and **¿para dónde?** are practically interchangeable with **¿dónde?**, although **¿dónde?** simply refers to the location of the subject (**¿Dónde vives?**), whereas the forms with prepositions used with verbs of motion imply to which place, in which direction the subject is moving. **¿Hacia**

dónde? can also be used in this sense, although rather than exact destination it implies whereabouts, "around where."

¿en dónde? = *in what place?*
where exactly?

Questions with **¿dónde?** which are derived from statements containing the preposition **en** may delete the **en**. However, if emphasis is desired as to the exact source of location the preposition may be retained.

Lo compré en el nuevo almacén.

{¿Dónde lo compraste?
{¿En dónde . . .?

I bought it in the new store.

{*Where did you buy it?*
{*In what place . . .?*
{*Where exactly . . .?*

USE OF ADJECTIVAL AND PRONOMINAL INTERROGATIVES

¿qué? / **¿cuál(es)?** = *what?* / *which?* / *which one(s)?*

The interrogatives **¿qué?** and **¿cuál (es)?** function either as adjectives or pronouns. **¿Qué?** is invariable in form, **¿cuál?** has a plural **¿cuáles?** and both refer to either gender.

As a general rule **¿cuál (es)?** is derived from statements that imply a choice or selection among a certain number of alternatives.

Quiere el traje azul (no el verde).
She wants the blue dress.

¿Cuál traje quiere?
Which dress does she want?

Quiere los rojos.
She wants the red ones.

¿Cuáles quiere?
Which ones does she want?

But questions with **¿qué?** and even **¿quién (es)?** may also be derived from these statements.

Quiere el traje azul.

¿Qué traje quiere?
Which . . .?

De los dos, Pedro es el más inteligente.

¿Quién es el más inteligente de los dos?
¿Cuál . . .?
Who is the most intelligent of the two?
Which one . . .?

The English interrogatives also alternate in usage. However, the distribution is not the same in the two languages, so the following rules must be observed:

1. When the interrogatives **¿qué?** and **¿cuál (es)?** function as limiting adjectives, there is practically no difference in meaning—whether a choice or selection is implied or not—so either form may occur, just as the English interrogatives *what?/which?* are sometimes interchangeable in this context.

¿Qué ⎫ instrumento tocas?   *What* ⎫ *instrument do you play?*
¿Cuál ⎭   *Which* ⎭

¿Qué   ⎫ carteras prefieres?   *What* ⎫ *purses do you prefer?*
¿Cuáles ⎭   *Which* ⎭

2. When the interrogative pronouns **¿qué?** and **¿cuál (es)?** are objects of a verb, they function just as their English counterparts *what?* and *which one (s)?*, respectively.

¿Qué vas a pintar?   *What are you going to paint?*
¿Cuál vas a pintar?   *Which one are you going to paint?*
¿Qué llevaste tú?   *What did you take?*
¿Cuáles llevaste tú?   *Which one(s) did you take?*

A selection or choice seems to underline here the use of **¿cuál (es)?**.

3. When the interrogative pronouns **¿qué?** and **¿cuál (es)?** function as subjects of **ser**, they are not interchangeable.

a. **¿Qué?** is used if one asks for a definition or an explanation about some person or thing.

¿Qué es lingüística?   *What is linguistics?*
—Es el estudio científico del   —*It is the scientific study of language.*
  lenguaje.

¿Qué es un huracán?   *What is a hurricane?*
—Es una tormenta tropical.   —*It is a tropical storm.*

¿Qué es un problema matemático?   *What is a mathematical problem?*
—Es un cálculo numérico.   —*It is a numerical calculation.*

b. **¿Cuál (es)?** is used if one asks a question which implies a choice or selection among a number of things, regardless of the English equivalent.

¿Cuál es la rama de la lingüística   *What (or which) branch of linguistics*
  que estudia los sonidos?   *studies sounds?*
—La fonética.   —*Phonetics.*

¿Cuál fue el último huracán que   *Which was the last hurricane to hit*
  azotó la costa?   *the coast?*
—Fue el huracán Celia.   —*It was hurricane Celia.*

¿Cuáles son los problemas matemáticos que no comprendes?	*Which are the mathematical problems that you don't understand?*
—Los de la página 50.	*—Those on page 50.*

The use of **¿cuál (es)?** always implies a choice or selection. When it occurs with a phrase describing the choice, the phrase must be introduced by **de**.

Aquí tengo varias herramientas.	*Here I have several tools.*
¿Cuáles de estas necesitas?	*Which ones of these do you need?*

¿Cuál (es)?, however, may occur without an overt phrase expressing choice, the latter being implicitly understood from the context.

Aquí están todos mis libros de historia.	*Here are all my history books.*
¿Cuáles (de ellos) necesitas?	*Which ones (of them) do you need?*

¿Quién (es)? as an alternate to ¿cuál (es)?

If the selection or choice involves animate objects, **¿quién (es)?** is frequently used instead of **¿cuál (es)?**, just as English *who* or *whom* may replace *which one?*

¿Quién es más capaz, él o ella?	*Who is more capable, he or she?*
¿Cuáles son los más responsables?⎫ ¿Quiénes . . .? ⎬	*Which ones are the most responsible?*

In questions with **¿qué?** and **¿cuál (es)?** derived from statements in which the complement is introduced by either a preposition or a relative, these precede the interrogative in the question.

Me refiero al caso Dreyfus.	¿A qué caso te refieres?[1] ¿A cuál . . .?
I am referring to the Dreyfus case.	*To what case are you referring? To which . . .?*
Abrieron la puerta con un cuchillo. *They opened the door with a knife.*	¿Con qué abrieron la puerta? *With what did they open the door?*
Esa mujer cree en los espíritus. *That woman believes in ghosts.*	¿En qué cree esa mujer? *In what does that woman believe?*
De sus hijos prefiere al menor. *Of all her children she prefers the youngest.*	¿A cuál de sus hijos prefiere? *Which one of her children does she prefer?*
Se decidió por el más barato. *She decided for the cheaper one.*	¿Por cuál se decidió? *Which one did she decide on?*

---

1 There is very little difference in meaning whether a choice is involved or not, so either **¿a qué?** or **¿a cuál?** is possible.

Esta pastilla es para el dolor de cabeza. *This pill is for headaches.*	¿Para qué es esta pastilla? *What is this pill for?*
Le perdonó porque no tenía la culpa. *He forgave her because she was not guilty.*	¿Por qué le perdonó? *Why did he forgive her?*

¿Para qué? versus ¿por qué?

¿Para qué? always inquiries to what end, for what purpose. **¿Por qué?** inquires about the reason. Both may be rendered by *why?*, but **¿para qué?** always implies *what for?*

Why did she leave?

¿Para qué salió? —*In order to get something to eat.* —Para buscar algo de comer.	**¿Por qué** salió? —*Because she was furious.* —Porque estaba furiosa.

¿cuánto,-a? = *how much?*
¿cuántos,-as? = *how many?*

As an adjective or pronoun, **¿cuánto?** varies its ending according to the gender and number of the noun that it modifies or substitutes.

Llegaron tres policías. *Three policemen arrived.*	¿Cuántos policías llegaron? *How many policemen arrived?*
Lo han confirmado varias personas. *Several persons have confirmed it.*	¿Cuántas personas lo han confirmado? *How many persons have confirmed it?*
Algunos de ellos faltaban. *Some of them were missing.*	¿Cuántos de ellos faltaban? *How many of them were missing?*
Necesita mucho dinero. *He needs a lot of money.*	¿Cuánto dinero necesita? *How much money does he need?*
Hay poca (agua). *There is little (water).*	¿Cuánta hay? (agua) *How much is there? (water)*

If the expression of quantity includes a preposition, it will precede the interrogative word in the question.

Invitó a varias personas. *He invited several persons.*	¿A cuántas personas invitó? *How many persons did he invite?*
Recibí respuesta de cinco. *I got an answer from five people.*	¿De cuántos recibiste respuesta? *From how many did you get an answer?*
Lo hizo en poco tiempo. *She did it in a short time.*	¿En cuánto tiempo lo hizo? *How long did it take her to do it?* (= *in how long . . .?*)

Preparó comida para cien invitados.
She prepared food for a hundred guests.

¿Para cuántos invitados preparó comida?
For how many guests did she prepare food?

Se sacrifica por muy pocos.
He inconveniences himself for very few people.

¿Por cuántos se sacrifica?
For how many does he inconvenience himself?

¿**quién(es)**? (subject)   = *who?*
¿**a quién(es)**? (object of verb) = *whom?*

¿**Quién**? has a plural ¿**quiénes**? and both apply to either gender. This interrogative refers only to human beings and always functions as a pronoun: it replaces a human noun either in subject position or as object of a verb.

1. In subject position, ¿**quién (es)**? stands alone and corresponds to the English *who?*

Llamó Roberto.
Roberto called.

¿Quién llamó?
Who called?

Las enfermeras llegaron.
The nurses arrived.

¿Quiénes llegaron?
Who arrived?

2. As object of a verb, ¿**quién (es)**? must be introduced by a preposition; it corresponds to the English *whom?* or preposition + *whom?*

Roberto llamó a su primo.
Roberto called his cousin.

¿A quién llamó Roberto?
Whom did Roberto call?

Este regalo es para ellos.
This gift is for them.

¿Para quiénes es este regalo?
For whom is this gift?

Pasaba mucho tiempo con su madre.
She used to spend a lot of time with her mother.

¿Con quién pasaba mucho tiempo?
With whom did she spend a lot of time?

Creía en Dios.
She believed in God.

¿En quién creía?
In whom did she believe?

THE INTERROGATIVE OF POSSESSION

Spanish does not have an interrogative of possession that corresponds exactly to English *whose?* To inquire about possession Spanish has two resources:

---

1.   ¿**de quién (es)**? + **ser** + Noun   *whose?* + Noun + *to be*

¿De quién es esta pluma?
¿De quién son estos papeles?

Whose pen is this?
Whose papers are these?

¿De quiénes son estos libros?	*Whose books are these?*
¿De quién era la casa en que te quedaste?	*Literally: Whose was the house in which you stayed?*

---

2. ¿Preposition + **qué** ...?	Preposition + *whose* ...?

Con qué dinero lo compraste, ¿con el mio?	*With whose money did you buy it, with mine?*
A qué oficina te han mandado, ¿a la de ella?	*To whose office have they sent you, to hers?*
En qué casa te quedaste, ¿en la de ellos?	*In whose house did you stay, in theirs?*

There is, however, a slight semantic difference between the two patterns:

¿De quién era la casa en que te quedaste?	(*Emphasizes the possessor.*)
¿En qué casa te quedaste?	(*Emphasizes the selection of a house among a group.*)

YES/NO QUESTIONS

Yes/no questions elicit a simple affirmative or negative answer. A yes/no question in Spanish is derived from statements by one of the following rules:

1. Inversion of word order and intonation:

Statement	Question
Subject + Verb + Complement	Verb + Subject + Complement
Este joven es brillante. ↓ *This fellow is brillant.* ↓	¿Es este joven brillante? ↑ *Is this fellow brilliant?* ↑
Los empleados ganan buenos sueldos. ↓ *The employees earn good salaries.* ↓	¿Ganan los empleados buenos sueldos? ↑ *Do the employees earn good salaries?* ↑
Los empleados van a ir de huelga. ↓ *The employees are going on strike.* ↓	¿Van a ir los empleados de huelga? ↑ *Are the employees going on strike?* ↑
Los representantes llegarán mañana. ↓ *The representatives will arrive tomorrow.* ↓	¿Llegarán los representantes mañana? ↑ *Will the representatives arrive tomorrow?* ↑

El Senado ha concluído sus sesiones. ↓
The Senate has concluded its sessions. ↓

¿Ha concluído el Senado sus
sesiones? ↑
Has the Senate concluded its sessions? ↑

This rule calls for an inversion of the word order (the verb precedes the subject) and also for an inversion of the intonation (the voice rises at the end instead of falling).

English also uses this pattern for yes/no questions, except that the subject is sometimes preceded either by the helping verb *do* or by the auxiliary in the verb phrase. Spanish has no equivalent for this English *do* and the entire verb phrase is inverted: **¿Ha llegado José?** = *Has Jose arrived?* Both languages invert the intonation.

In Spanish the word order of the subject and complement may also be inverted depending on the emphasis.[1]

¿Es este joven **brillante**? ↑
¿Es brillante **este joven**? ↑
¿Ganan los empleados **buenos
sueldos**? ↑
¿Ganan buenos sueldos **los
empleados**? ↑

Is this fellow brilliant? ↑
Is this fellow brilliant? ↑
Do the employees earn good salaries? ↑

Do the employees earn good
salaries? ↑

2. By inversion of intonation only:

Statement	Question
Subject + Verb + Complement ↓	Subject + Verb + Complement ↓

Este joven es brillante. ↓ *This fellow is brilliant.* ↓	¿Este joven es brillante? ↑ *Is this fellow brilliant?* ↑
Los empleados ganan buenos sueldos. ↓ *The employees earn good salaries.* ↓	¿Los empleados ganan buenos sueldos? ↑ *The employees earn good salaries?* ↑
Salieron temprano. ↓ *They left early.* ↓	¿Salieron temprano? ↑ *Did they leave early?* ↑
Tienen razón. ↓ *They are right.* ↓	¿Tienen razón? ↑ *Are they right?* ↑

This rule calls for an inversion of the intonational pattern: the voice rises at the end instead of falling.

Since Spanish omits the subject pronouns (except to avoid ambiguities) it is

---

[1] English emphasizes a word by the use of stress. Spanish uses stress or word order, or both. As a general rule, the item in final position carries more emphasis.

important that the correct pattern of intonation be observed, otherwise the question might be interpreted as a simple statement.

A variation of this rule consists of separating the subject from the rest of the sentence by a pause, with the voice still rising at the end.

Este joven ‖ ¿es brillante?↑   *This fellow ‖ is he brilliant?↑*
Los empleados ‖ ¿ganan buenos   *The employees ‖ do they earn good*
  sueldos?↑   *salaries?↑*

TAG QUESTIONS

Spanish like English uses tag questions at the end of statements in order to ask for confirmation of the statement. Tag questions in Spanish are usually one or two words which remain invariable regardless of tense, number, or person. The only restriction is that with negative statements tag questions with **no** are not used.

English tag questions agree in tense, have inverted word order, and must be in the affirmative with negative statements and vice versa.

Hace calor, **¿verdad?**[1]   *It is hot, isn't it?*
     ¿no es verdad?
Vienes pronto, **¿no?**   *You are coming soon, aren't you?*
Este es el tuyo, **¿no es cierto?**   *This one is yours, isn't it?*
Es la amante de Francisco, **¿sabes?**   *She is Francisco's lover, don't you know?*
Mándame esta carta, **¿quieres?**   *Mail this letter for me, will you?*
Lo haremos mañana, **¿de acuerdo?**[2]   *We'll do it tomorrow, ok?*
No es tarde, **¿verdad?**   *It is not late, is it?*

Indirect discourse and questions

As in English, yes/no questions and information questions may be asked in indirect discourse.[3] Questions in indirect discourse are normally introduced by **preguntar** or an equivalent verb in the preterit. The other verbs are either in the imperfect, conditional, preterit, or past perfect in order to state what was originally asked in the present, future, and preterit, respectively.

Me preguntó:—¿Regresas mañana?   Me preguntó si regresaba mañana.
He asked me: Are you coming back   *He asked me if I was coming back*
  tomorrow?   *tomorrow.*

Le pregunté:—¿Cuánto tiempo   Le pregunté cuánto tiempo
  necesitarás?   necesitaría.
I asked her: How much time will you   *I asked her how much time she would*
  need?   *need.*

---

[1] In colloquial speech **¿eh?** is very common: **No es tarde, ¿eh?**
[2] **¿De acuerdo?** is a shortened version of **¿estamos de acuerdo?** The tag question can also be **¿estamos?**
[3] In indirect discourse one reports what someone else has said or thought. The written accent is kept on interrogative words.

Me preguntó:—¿Fuiste ayer?
He asked me: Did you go yesterday?

Me preguntó si fui ayer (había ido ayer).
He asked me if I went yesterday (had gone yesterday).

The main verb may also be in the present tense. The tenses in indirect discourse will in this case correspond to the tenses of the original questions.

Me pregunta:—¿Vas ahora?
—¿Irás mañana?
—¿Fuiste ayer?
—¿Irías mañana?
He asks me: Are you going now?
Will you go tomorrow?
etc.

Me pregunta si voy ahora.
si iré mañana.
si fui ayer.
si iría mañana.
He asks me if I am going now.
if I will go tomorrow.
etc.

Interrogative words are also used in statements when in the speaker's mind a question is implied, particularly after verbs of perception and understanding.[1]

No me has dicho cuál quieres.
Dime de dónde viene.
No se quién es ni qué quiere.

You haven't told me which one you want.
Tell me where it comes from.
I don't know who he is nor what he wants.

Exclamatives

INTERROGATIVES AS EXCLAMATIVES

Most interrogative words may function as exclamatives as follows:

| ¡**Qué** + Verb Phrase . . .! | *What* + Verb Phrase . . .! |

¡Qué cosas dices!
¡Qué vas a hacer!

What (The) things you say!
What are you going to do!

| ¡**Qué** + Noun Phrase . . .! | *What (a)* + Noun Phrase . . .! |

¡Qué suerte!
¡Qué mujer!
¡Qué día precioso!⎫
¡Qué precioso día!⎭
¡Qué grupo{tan / más} increíble!

What luck!
What a woman!
What a beautiful day!
What an incredible bunch!

---

[1] See Interrogatives for Relative Pronouns, page 124.

When **tan** or **más** appears in the noun phrase, the noun always precedes the adjective. In this context **más** and **tan** have no equivalents in English.

In colloquial speech, ¡**vaya**! (+ indefinite article) may be used with the same meaning of ¡**que**!=¡**Vaya un día precioso**! or ¡**Vaya día precioso**! The indefinite article is optional. Further modification with **tan** or **más** is omitted.

¡**Qué** + Adjective or ...! Adverb	*How* + Adjective or ...! Adverb

¡Qué espantoso!	*How horrible!*
¡Qué lindo baila!	*How pretty she dances!*
¡Qué fácilmente nada!	*How easily he swims.*

¡**Qué de** + Noun Phrase ...!	*How many* / *What a lot of* } + Noun Phrase ...! etc.

¡Qué de cosas lindas compró!	*How many beautiful things she bought!*
¡Qué de tonterías dijo!	*What a lot of nonsense he said!*

¡**Cómo** + Verb Phrase ...!	*How (much)* + Verb Phrase ...!

¡Cómo escribe!	*How he writes!*
¡Cómo lo detesto!	*How I hate him!*

¡**Cómo**! may be replaced in this context by either the invariable form ¡**cuánto**! or ¡**lo que**!

¡Cómo miente! ¡Cuánto ...! ¡Lo qué ...! }	*How (much) he lies!*

¡**Cómo** + Verb + **de** + Adjective or ...! Adverb	*How* + Adjective or ...! Adverb

¡Cómo es de peligrosa!	*How dangerous (she is)!*
¡Cómo enseña de mal!	*How poorly she teaches!*

| ¡**Cuánto** + Verb Phrase ...! | *How (much) + Verb Phrase ...!* |

| ¡Cuánto quisiera verla! | *How I would love to see her!* |
| ¡Cuánto sabe! | *How (much) he knows!* |

| ¡**Cuánto** + Noun Phrase ...! | *How much* ⎫ *+ Noun Phrase ...!* |
| | *How many* ⎭ |

¡Cuánto dinero recibe!	*How much money he gets!*
¡Cuánta suerte tiene!	*How lucky she is!*
¡Cuántas cosas han ocurrido!	*How many things have happened!*

	Adjective			Adjective	
¡**Cuán** +	or	...!	*How +*	or	*...!*
	Adverb			Adverb	

¡Cuán sagaz!	*How clever!*
¡Cuán elegante es!	*How elegant she is!*
¡Cuán rápido corre!	*How fast he runs!*
¡Cuán poco estudia!	*How little he studies!*
¡Cuán tarde llega siempre!	*How late he always arrives.*

In literary style ¡**cuánto**! shortens to ¡**cuán**! before an adjective or adverb. In everyday speech, however, the same idea is rendered by either ¡**qué**! or ¡**cómo** + verb + **de**! ¡**Cuánto**! and ¡**cuán**! are generally confined to the written language.

| ¡Qué sagaz! ⎫ | |
| ¡Cómo es de sagaz! ⎭ | *How clever!* |

| ¡Qué rápido corre! ⎫ | |
| ¡Cómo corre de rápido! ⎭ | *How fast he runs!* |

| ¡**Quién** + Verb in **-ra** | ⎧ *How I wish ...!* |
| (imperfect subjunctive) ...! | ⎩ *If only I could ...!* |

| ¡Quién pudiera convencerla! | *If only I could convince her!* |
| ¡Quién supiera la verdad! | *How I wish I knew the truth!* |

The exclamative ¡**quién**! in this context has the same meaning of **ojalá**. Otherwise the exclamative ¡**quién**! corresponds to the English *who.*

| ¡Quién lo diría! | *Who would have said so!* |

OTHER EXCLAMATIVE EXPRESSIONS

The spoken language uses a number of other exclamative expressions depending on the geographical area, the social strata, and the psychological context. The following are some of these expressions:

¡Ándale!	*Come on! Off with you!*
¡Cómo no!	*Of course! Sure!*
¡Cuidado!	*Be careful! Watch out!*
¡Dale!	*Keep at it! There you go again!*
¡Dios mío!	*My gosh! Good heavens!*
¡Eso es!	*That's it!*
¡Ojalá!	*Don't I wish! I hope so!*
¡Ojo!	*Look out! Be careful!*
¡Olvídate!	*Forget it!*
¡Oye! ¡Oiga!	*Hey! Listen!*
¡No faltaba más! ¡No faltaría más!	*What a nerve!*
¡No me digas!	*Don't tell me! Don't say!*
¡Qué va!	*Of course not! Come on!*

10

THE SUBJUNCTIVE TENSES:
CORRESPONDENCE WITH
THE INDICATIVE TENSES

The Subjunctive versus Indicative Tenses

The subjunctive mood has four tenses only: the present, the imperfect, the past perfect, and the past pluperfect. The traditional labels that designate these tenses are misleading insofar as all the subjunctive tenses not only refer to a temporal dimension co-existent with the present and the past but to a temporal dimension of subsequence, futurity, as well. For this reason the subjunctive tenses correspond not only to their indicative equivalents but also to the indicative tenses which express subsequence in relation to a given temporal perspective, present or past.

The following parallels between the indicative and subjunctive forms are valid as far as tense and aspect are concerned. The differences in meaning that these forms signal and the governing notions that determine the use of either mood are discussed separately.

Indicative	Subjunctive
Present: co-existent or subsequent actions in relation to the present.	
	Present
Future: subsequent actions in relation to the present.	

Indicative	*Subjunctive*
Es evidente que la quiere.	Es dudoso que la quiera.
It is evident that he loves her.	*It is doubtful that he loves her.*
Sé que estudiará medicina.	Dudo que estudie medicina.
I know he will study medicine.	*I doubt he will study medicine.*

Indicative	*Subjunctive*
Present perfect: completed actions in relation to the present.	
Future perfect: completed future actions in relation to the present	**Present perfect**
Afirma que lo ha escrito.	Niega que lo haya escrito.
He affirms that he has written it.	*He denies that he has written it.*
Es seguro que para mañana habrán terminado.	Es imposible que para mañana hayan terminado.
It is certain that by tomorrow they will have finished.	*It is impossible that they will have finished by tomorrow.*

Indicative	*Subjunctive*
Imperfect: co-existent or subsequent actions in relation to the grammatical past.	
Conditional: subsequent actions in relation to the grammatical past.	**Imperfect**
Estaba seguro de que era comprensiva.	Estaba emocionado de que fuera tan comprensiva.
He was certain that she was understanding.	*He was touched by the fact that she was so understanding.*
Se decía que pronto renunciaría.	Era posible que pronto renunciase.
There were rumours that he would resign soon.	*It was possible that he would resign soon.*

Indicative	*Subjunctive*
Past perfect: completed actions which are anterior to another past action or an adverbial of past time.	
Conditional perfect: completed subsequent actions in relation to the grammatical past.	**Past perfect**
Supe que había sido un administrador muy hábil.	No podía creer que hubiera sido un administrador muy hábil.
I learned he had been a very able administrator.	*I could not believe he had been a very able administrator.*
Era seguro que para el día siguiente habrían terminado.	Era improbable que para el día siguiente hubieran terminado.
It was certain that by the next day they would have finished.	*It was improbable that by the next day they would have finished.*

The Tenses of the Subjunctive

PRESENT SUBJUNCTIVE

1. The present subjunctive like the present indicative can refer to an action which co-exists with the actual or extended present. As such, it can be used for actual ongoing events at the time of the utterance, repeated or habitual events, states of being and conditions—short or long lasting—and future time.

Indicative	*Subjunctive*
ONGOING EVENTS	
No voy a entrar, sé que duerme. *I won't go in, I know he is sleeping.*	Voy a entrar, no creo que duerma. *I will go in, I don't think he is sleeping.*
REPEATED OR HABITUAL EVENTS	
Almuerzan juntos todos los días. *They have lunch together every day.*	¿Será posible que almuercen juntos todos los días? *Could it be true that they have lunch together every day?*
STATES OF BEING AND CONDITIONS	
El Perú está muy lejos de los Estados Unidos. *Peru is very far from the United States.*	¡Qué lástima que el Perú esté tan lejos de los Estados Unidos! *What a pity that Peru should be so far from the United States!*
FUTURE TIME OR INTENT	
Necesito verte mañana. *I have to see you tomorrow.*	Es necesario que te vea mañana. *It is necessary that I see you tomorrow.*

2. While the present indicative may refer to subsequent or future time with a limited number of verbs (emotion, need, desire, and volition), the present subjunctive can imply subsequence with any verb whose meaning permits it. For this reason it is equivalent to the present and future indicative as well.

Vive en Madrid. *He lives in Madrid.* Vivirá en Madrid. *He will live in Madrid.*	Es posible que viva en Madrid. *It is possible that he lives in Madrid.* *It is possible that he will live in Madrid.*

Whether or not the present subjunctive refers to a co-existent or subsequent action depends upon the intrinsic nature of the event itself, and the linguistic or extra-linguistic context in which it occurs.

When the meaning of the verb refers to a non-conclusive, durative event (**vivir, estudiar, querer, comprender, trabajar**, etc.), either co-existence or subsequence is signaled. When the meaning of the verb refers to a conclusive action, one that must be terminated in order to be completed (**ir, despedir, entregar, expulsar, contratar**, etc.), ongoingness or subsequence is conveyed. The governing notion in the main clause further determines what reading is possible. Implied commands always refer to subsequent events. Doubt or emotion can be expressed in relation to ongoing or subsequent actions.[1]

No quiero que vivas sola. (command, refers to subsequent time)	*I don't want you to live alone.*
No me gusta la idea de que vivas sola. (personal inclination, could refer to co-existent and/or subsequent time)	*I don't like the idea of your living alone.*
Es dudoso que lo echen. (subsequence)	*It is doubtful that he will be fired.*
Parece mentira que estos días despidan a tanta gente. (repeated events, extended into the future as well)	*It is incredible that these days so many people should be laid off (are being laid off).*

3. Since the present tense, indicative and subjunctive, occurs in relation to present time, it can occur subordinate to one of the following tenses: the present, the present perfect, the future, the conditional, or the imperative.

Le digo que viene. (information) *I am telling you that he is coming.*	Le digo que venga. (implied command) *I am telling you to come.*
Le he dicho que ella regresa. *I have told him that she is returning.*	Le he dicho que regrese. *I have told her to return.*
Le diré que ella se queda. *I will tell him that she is staying.*	Le diré que se quede. *I will tell her to stay.*
Yo le diría que ella viene pero no me atrevo. *I would tell him that she is coming but I don't dare to.*	Sería mejor que no le digas que viene. *It would be better not to tell him that she is coming.*
Dile que ella vuelve. *Tell him that she is returning.*	Dile que vuelva. *Tell her to return.*

4. The present subjunctive may also occur after a preterit verb if the main verb or governing notion is one of volition. In this case the subjunctive can only refer to subsequent time since what is ordered, suggested, or requested is always

---

[1] For other clauses governing the subjunctive see chapters 11 and 12.

subsequent to the act of speech. In other than commands, the usage of the preterit in the main clause is rare. The present subjunctive when subordinated to the preterit can only refer to subsequence in relation to the present or the future—but not in relation to the past.

Le sugerí que le escriba hoy.	*I suggested that she write to him today.*
Le dije que venga esta tarde.	*I told him to come this afternoon.*
Le aconsejó que deje de fumar lo más pronto posible.	*He has advised her to quit smoking as soon as possible.*

If subsequence within a past dimension is referred to, then the imperfect subjunctive must be used. The imperfect subjunctive may refer to future time in any temporal dimension—present, past, and future.

Le sugerí que le escribiera (hoy mismo, en aquel momento, la semana entrante).	*I suggested that she write to him (today, at that time, next week).*
Le aconsejó que dejara de fumar (lo más pronto posible, el año pasado, hoy mismo).	*He advised her to quit smoking (as soon as possible, last year, today).*

5. When the main verb implies future time, in which case either the present or the future is used, the present subjunctive can only refer to another future event.

Salgo después que él llegue. ⎫ Saldré después que él llegue. ⎭	*I will leave after he arrives.*
Busco quien te cuide.	*I am looking for someone to take care of you.*
Buscaré quien te cuide.	*I will look for someone to take care of you.*
Lo hago cuando pueda. ⎫ Lo haré cuando pueda. ⎭	*I will do it when I can.*

IMPERFECT SUBJUNCTIVE

1. The imperfect subjunctive, as well as the imperfect indicative, is equivalent to a retrospective or backshifted present. As such it has all the functions of the present subjunctive, but in relation to the grammatical past.

Indicative	*Subjunctive*
ONGOING EVENTS	
No iba a entrar, sabía que dormía. *I would not go in, I knew he was sleeping.*	Iba a entrar, no pensaba que durmiera. *I was going to go in, I did not think he was sleeping.*

REPEATED OR HABITUAL EVENTS

Almorzaban juntos todos los días.
*They would have lunch together
every day.*

¿Sería posible que almorzaran
juntos todos los días?
*Could it have been true that they had
lunch together every day?*

STATES OF BEING AND CONDITIONS

Era muy dedicado a su familia.
He was very devoted to his family.

Era admirable que fuera tan dedicado
a su familia.
*It was admirable that he should have
been so devoted to his family.*

FUTURE TIME OR INTENT

Necesitaba verme al día siguiente.
He had to see me the next day.

Era necesario que me viera al día
siguiente.
*It was necessary that he see me the
next day.*

2. The imperfect subjunctive, as opposed to the imperfect indicative which can refer to subsequence with a limited number of verbs, may refer to future time with any verb whose meaning permits it. For this reason it is equivalent to the imperfect and conditional as well.

Vivía en Madrid.
He lived (used to live) in Madrid.

Viviría en Madrid.
He would live in Madrid.

Era posible que viviera en Madrid.
*It was possible that he lived in Madrid.
It was possible that he would live in
Madrid.*

Whether the imperfect subjunctive refers to a co-existent or subsequent action depends, as with the present subjunctive, upon the intrinsic nature of the event itself and the linguistic or extra-linguistic context in which the event occurs.

No quería que viviera sola.
(command, refers to subsequent
time)

I did not want her to live alone.

No me gustaba la idea de que
viviera sola.
(co-existent and/or subsequent time)

*I did not like the idea of her living
alone.*

Era dudoso que lo echaran.
(subsequence)

It was doubtful that he would be fired.

Parecía mentira que en esos días
despidieran a tanta gente.
(repeated events, extended into the
future as well)

*It was incredible that in those days so
many people were being laid off.*

3. The imperfect subjunctive, as well as the imperfect indicative, can occur subordinated to any past tense, to the conditional, or to the present.

Temí que se ofendiera. ⎫
Temía que se ofendiera.⎭   *I feared she would get offended.*

He temido más de una vez que se ofendiera.   *I have feared more than once that she would get offended.*
Había temido más de una vez que se ofendiera.   *I had feared more than once that she would get offended.*

Lo haría cuando tuviera tiempo.   *She would do it when she had time.*
Es improbable que llegara ayer.   *It was improbable that he arrived yesterday.*

4. When the imperfect subjunctive occurs subordinated to a verb in the present tense, it describes an event as anterior to it. Whether the event itself is terminated or not depends upon the conclusive or non-conclusive nature of the event and the total context.

No creo que saliera tan temprano.
(conclusive event, terminated)   *I don't think he went out that early.*

No creo que salieron juntos tanto.
(conclusive event, repeated)   ⎧*I don't think they went out together that often.*
    ⎩(*I don't think they were going out together that often.*)

Es una tragedia que muriera tan
 joven.
(conclusive event, terminated)   *It is a tragedy that he should have died so young.*

Es natural que quisieran casarse.
(non-conclusive event, may be
 terminated or continued within the
 present itself)   ⎧*It is natural that they should have wanted to get married.*
    ⎩*It is natural that they should want to get married.*

Es posible que prefiriese vivir sola.   ⎧*It is possible that she might have preferred to live alone.*
    ⎩*It is possible that she might prefer to live alone.*

Es lógico que necesitara compañía.   ⎧*It is logical that he should have needed company.*
    ⎩*It is logical that he should need company.*

5. When the main verb implies future time, the imperfect subjunctive can only refer to another future event.

Salía después que él llegara. ⎫
Saldría después que él llegara.⎭   *She would leave after he arrived.*

Buscaría quien lo cuidara.

She would look for someone to take care of him.

Dijo que lo hacía cuando pudiera.
Dijo que lo haría cuando pudiera.

She said she would do it when she could.

6. Since the imperfect subjunctive (as well as the imperfect indicative) has imperfective aspect, it cannot be used to describe a terminated event when the subordinating verb is a past tense. The past perfect subjunctive must be used instead since the imperfect would describe a co-existent event.

Era probable que su audacia hubiera sido el factor más importante en su éxito. (completed, terminated)

It was probable that his audacity had been the most important factor in his success.

Era probable que su audacia fuera el factor más importante en su éxito. (co-existent, continued)

It was probable that his audacity was the most important factor in his success.

Pocos reconocían que hubiera sido un administrador efectivo.

Few admitted that he had been an effective administrator.

Pocos reconocían que era un administrador efectivo.

Few admitted that he was an effective administrator.

PRESENT PERFECT SUBJUNCTIVE

1. The present perfect subjunctive, as its indicative equivalent, describes a completed event as anterior to the grammatical present of the speaker.

Indicative	*Subjunctive*
No ha dormido ni comido en una semana.	Es imposible creer que no haya comido ni dormido en una semana.
He has neither slept nor eaten in a week.	*It is impossible to believe that he has neither slept nor eaten in a week.*
Nunca le ha faltado nada.	¿Será posible que nunca le haya faltado nada?
He has never lacked anything.	*Is it possible that he has never lacked anything?*

2. The present perfect subjunctive can also be used to describe a subsequent event as completed before another future event or an adverb of future time. When used to express subsequence it is equivalent to the future perfect.

Me aseguran que para mañana habrán terminado.

They assure me that by tomorrow they will have finished.

Es dudoso que para mañana hayan terminado.

It is doubtful that they will have finished by tomorrow.

Tú llegas el viernes. Para entonces él se habrá ido.

You arrive on Friday. By then he will have left.

Para cuando tú llegues es probable que él se haya ido ya.

By the time you arrive it is probable that he will have left already.

3. Since the present perfect subjunctive is used in relation to the present of the speaker, it can only occur subordinate to a verb in the present or the future.

Es una vergüenza que haya dejado a su familia sin un centavo.	*It is disgraceful that he should have left his family without a cent.*
¿Será verdad que haya dejado a su familia sin un centavo?	*Could it be true that he has left his family without a cent?*
Busca una secretaria que haya tenido experiencia.	*He is looking for a secretary who has had experience.*
Partirán cuando hayan recibido permiso.	*They will leave once they have received permission.*

PAST PERFECT SUBJUNCTIVE

1. The past perfect subjunctive, as its indicative equivalent, describes a completed event as anterior to another past event, or an adverbial of past time.

Indicative	*Subjunctive*
Me confesó que todos se habían negado a ayudarle.	Yo no podía creer que todos se hubieran negado a ayudarle.
He admitted to me that everyone had refused to help him.	*I could not believe that everyone had refused to help him.*
Entonces supo que había fracasado.	Entonces temió que hubiera fracasado.
Then he knew he had failed.	*Then he feared he had failed.*

2. The past perfect subjunctive can also be used to describe a subsequent event as completed before another past event or an adverb of past time. When used to express subsequence it is equivalent to the conditional perfect.

Me dijeron que para el día siguiente habrían regresado.	Era dudoso que para el día siguiente hubieran podido regresar.
They told me that they would have returned by the following day.	*It was doubtful that they could have returned by the following day.*
Nos informaron que para cuando tú llegaras él se había ido ya.	Era posible que para cuando tú llegaras él se hubiera ido.
They informed us that by the time you arrived he would have left already.	*It was possible that by the time you arrived he had left already.*

3. Since the past perfect subjunctive is always used in relation to the grammatical past, it occurs subordinated to a past tense or the conditional.

Era muy triste ⎫ Fue muy triste ⎪ que hubiera dejado No había sabido ⎨ a su mujer. Sería muy triste ⎭	*It was very sad* ⎫ *It was very sad* ⎪ *that he had left his* *I had not learned* ⎬ *wife.* *It would be very sad if he had left his wife.*

THE PRETERIT AND ITS SUBJUNCTIVE EQUIVALENTS

The preterit indicative always describes an event as completed, perfected, whether initiative or terminative aspect is referred to.[1] The subjunctive mood does not have a single form that is equivalent to it. The imperfect subjunctive, as previously described, is equivalent to the imperfect indicative. It describes an event as a continuum in time with no indication of the event's completion or termination. Only when the verb refers to non-durative and instantaneous action can the imperfect subjunctive refer to a completed and terminated event, and be equivalent to the preterit.

Indicative	*Subjunctive*
Creo que llegó a tiempo. *I think he arrived on time.*	No creo que llegara a tiempo. *I do not think he arrived on time.*
Sabemos que lo contrataron. *We know he was hired.*	Qué suerte que lo contrataran. *It was so fortunate that they gave him a contract.*
No se aprobó su propuesta. *His proposal was not approved.*	Era una lástima que no aprobaran su propuesta. *It was a shame that his proposal was not approved.*

In all other cases a perfect subjunctive tense must be used for the preterit.

1. If the main verb is in the present, the present perfect subjunctive occurs.

Dicen que se distanciaron mucho. *They say they have grown very distant.*	Es muy triste que se hayan distanciado tanto. *It is very sad that they should have grown so distant.*
Mantienen algunos que fue un gran presidente. *Some claim that he had been a great president.*	Yo niego que haya sido un gran presidente. *I deny that he has been a great president.*
Sé que estuvo muy enfermo. *I know he had been very sick.*	Dudo que haya estado muy enfermo. *I doubt that he has been very sick.*

2. If the main verb is a past tense, the past perfect subjunctive occurs instead.

Me enteré que se distanciaron mucho. *I learned that they had grown very distant.*	Era muy triste que se hubieran distanciado tanto. *It was very sad that they had grown so distant.*

---

[1] See Chapter 5, The Preterit.

Mantenían algunos que fue un gran presidente.
Some claimed that he had been a great president.

Supe que estuvo enfermo.
I learned he had been very sick.

Yo negaba que hubiera sido un gran presidente.
I denied that he had been a great president.

No supe que hubiera estado muy enfermo.
I did not hear that he had been very sick.

11

SUBJUNCTIVE AND INDICATIVE IN NOMINAL CLAUSES

Nominal Clauses

Subordinate clauses which can have the same functions as nouns are called nominal. Nominal clauses can, therefore, occur as:

SUBJECTS

Tu actitud me sorprende.
El que tu actúes así me sorprende.

Your attitude surprises me.
That you should act in such a manner surprises me.

DIRECT OBJECTS

Quiero renunciar.
Quiero **que él renuncie**.

I want to resign.
I want him to resign.

OBJECT OF A PREPOSITION, AS COMPLEMENT

Duda de su integridad.
Duda de **que sea una persona íntegra**.

He doubts his integrity.
He doubts that he is a trustworthy person.

ADVERBIALS

Iré después de cenar.
Iré después **que ellos cenen**.

I will go after dinner.
I will go after they have dinner.

CLAUSE FORMATION

Clauses in Spanish and in English are formed in the same way. The only significant difference is that the relator **que** is not omitted in Spanish as it may be done in English.

Sugiero **que** se levante la sesión.	*I suggest (that) the meeting be adjourned.*

The relator **que** must be differentiated from the relative **que** which replaces a noun in a subordinate sentence. The relator **que** replaces nothing; it merely serves to introduce a subordinate clause.

Necesito una persona que sea de confianza.	*I need a person that can be trusted.*

When a nominal clause functions as subject and it occurs in initial position (which is not frequent), **el que** may be used instead of **que**.

El que sea tan hipócrita es difícil de creer.	*That he should be so hypocritical is difficult to believe.*
Es difícil de creer que sea tan hipócrita. (more frequent usage)	*It is difficult to believe that he should be so hypocritical.*

Clauses versus Verb + INF

In Spanish, with exception of a small class of verbs which take an infinitive with a different subject from the conjugated verb, all others take clauses. If there is no change of subject and the verb is not one of communication, an infinitive occurs instead of a clause.[1] In English, on the other hand, clauses may occur with a different or the same subject as the main verb.

Dudo que pueda acompañarte María.	*I doubt that Maria can accompany you.*
Dudo poder acompañarte.	*I doubt that I can accompany you.*
Niega que su hijo lo haya hecho.	*He denies that his son has done it.*
Niega haberlo hecho.	*He denies that he has done it.*
Me alegro de que puedas venir.	*I am happy that you can come.*
Me alegro de poder venir.	*I am happy that I can come.*

However, clauses are less frequent in English than in Spanish because infinitive and *-ing* complements may occur with different subjects. When taking a different subject from the verb, these should be rendered as clauses in Spanish.

He *asked* you *to go.*	Te pidió que fueras.
He *said* for you *to go.*	Dijo que fueras.
I *am appalled* at your *going.*	Me desconcierta que vayas.
He *is opposed* to your *going.*	Se opone a que vayas.
He *disapproves* of your *going.*	No está de acuerdo con que vayas.

---

[1] See Verb + INF, page 93, and Verb + Clause instead of INF, page 98.

When a verb takes a preposition before a noun or infinitive, that preposition is usually retained when a clause occurs instead. In English the preposition is deleted before nominal clauses unless a factitive nominal (*the fact . . .*) precedes it.

Insisto en ir.	*I insist on going.*
Insisto en que vayas.	*{I insist that you go.* *{I insist on your going.*
Se queja de tu ingratitud.	*She is complaining about your* *ingratitude.*
Se queja de que seas tan ingrato.	*She is complaining about the fact that* *you are so ungrateful.*

Subjunctive versus Indicative

1. VOLITION OR DESIRE: RESULT HYPOTHETICAL → SUBJUNCTIVE

The subjunctive must be used in Spanish when the governing notion is one of causation of behavior, that is, when an attempt is made to cause or influence the behavior of a given subject or to attain a desired result. This may be achieved by various constructions: implied commands; more politely worded statements such as suggestions or requests; indirect commands; exclamatory wishes; or the description of an event as necessary.

The event that one attempts to bring about is subsequent, future in relation to the act of speech. Therefore, the result is hypothetical; nothing is ascertained whether it will or will not be achieved. In all types of commands—direct, implied, or indirect—there must be a change of subject, since no one can exert his influence if there is no subject to be influenced. If there is no change of subject there can be no implied command, but only an expression of the person's will insofar as his own behavior is concerned. If the latter is the case, only a noun or infinitive will follow the verb, but not a clause with a conjugated verb in the indicative or subjunctive.

Insisto en ir.	*I insist on going.*
Insisto en que vayan.	*I insist that they go.*
Exijo saber la verdad.	*I demand to know the truth.*
Exijo que se sepa la verdad.	*I demand that the truth be known (by* *everyone).*

NOTE: Some verbs such as **conseguir**, **lograr**, **alcanzar**, **obtener**, **aprobar**, **desaprobar**, and **esperar**, which imply volition on the subject's part, not only take the subjunctive for subsequent, future events but also for events which were completed in a past dimension.

Conseguiré que lo elijan presidente.	*I will succeed in having him elected* *president.*

Consiguió que lo eligieran presidente.	*He succeeded in having him elected president.*
Obtuve que lo echaran.	*I succeeded in having him fired.*
Obtendré que lo echen.	*I will succeed in having him fired.*

Implied commands

Implied commands may be worded in any one of the following ways:

ORDERS

Ordeno que no dejes entrar a nadie.	*I order that no one be permitted to enter.*
Le mandó que se examinara con un especialista.	*He ordered her to see a specialist.*

PROHIBITIONS

Les prohibió que se vieran.	*He forbade them to see each other.*
Les impidió que hicieran justicia.	*He prevented them from doing justice.*
Se opuso a que se casaran.	*He opposed their getting married.*

REQUESTS

Les suplico que lo hagan.	*I beg of you to do it.*
Nos pidió que regresáramos temprano.	*He asked that we return early.* *He asked us to return early.*
Quisiera que nos acompañes.	*I would like you to come along with us.*

SUGGESTIONS

Propongo que se apruebe la moción.	*I propose that the motion be approved.*
Sugiere que se levante la sesión.	*He suggests that the meeting be adjourned.*
Aconsejo que lo discutamos otro día.	*I advise that it be discussed another day.*

APPROVALS/DISAPPROVALS

No estamos de acuerdo con que se eliminen todos los prerequisitos.	*We do not agree that all prerequisites should be abolished.*
Preferimos que el asunto se estudie cuidadosamente.	*We prefer that the issue be studied carefully.*

DESIRES

No quisiéramos que se case con un extranjero y se vaya a vivir lejos de nosotros.	*We would not want her to marry a foreigner and live far away from us.*
Espero que seas más conciliatorio en el futuro.	*I expect you to be more conciliatory in the future.*
Espero que te mejores pronto.	*I hope you will get better soon.*

Indirect commands

When an implied command is not addressed to the listener but to a third party (indirect command), it may occur without a subordinating verb. The clause still must be introduced by **que** since the subordinating verb is always implicitly understood.

(Quiero) Que no me moleste nadie esta tarde.	*Let no one bother me this afternoon.*
(Quiero) Que entren ahora mismo.	*Have them come in right away.*
Que les sirva la comida y los acueste.	*Have her feed them and put them to bed.*

Wishes

When volition is expressed as an exclamatory wish the main verb may be omitted, but the **que** is retained in all cases except in some stereotyped expressions.

(Espero) que te mejores pronto.	*I hope you will get better soon.*
Que tengas mucha suerte.	*Good luck!*
¡Que Dios te bendiga!	*(May) God bless you!*
¡Que se vaya al diablo!	*I hope he drops dead! (or some equivalent expression)*
¡(Queremos) que cante Juan!	*Let John sing!*
¡Que hable él!	*Let him speak!*

BUT

¡Viva la libertad!	*Long live liberty!*
¡Mueran los opresores!	*Death to the oppressors!*

Clauses + predicate nominative

Behavior can be caused or influenced not only through commands—direct, indirect, or implied. An event may be described through a predicate nominative—**ser** + adjective—as necessary, desirable, indispensable, and so forth, thus causing pressure upon a given subject to act. The noun clause, functioning here as subject, will always be in the subjunctive since it refers to a subsequent, future event. The clause may either precede or follow the predicate.

Es necesario que vayas.	*It is necessary that you go (for you . . .).*
Necesito que vayas.	*I must have you go.*
Es preferible que no digas nada.	*It is preferable that you say nothing.*
Prefiero que no digas nada.	*I prefer that you say nothing.*
Es conveniente que explores esa posibilidad.	*It is best that you explore that possibility.*
Conviene que explores esa posibilidad.	*It is best that you explore that possibility.*
Es urgente que vuelvas.	*It is urgent that you return.*
Sería mejor que se dedicara a otra cosa más lucrativa.	*It would be better if he devoted himself to something more lucrative.*

2. BELIEF OR KNOWLEDGE: EVENT AFFIRMED → INDICATIVE

When the governing notion of a sentence is one of conveying information, whether the information be factual, true, or false, referring to past, present, or future events, the clause always takes the indicative.

Sé que él es bueno.	*I know that he is good.*
Presiento que va a pasar algo.	*I feel that something is going to happen.*
Creía que era un gran pintor.	*He thought he was a great painter.*
Oí que lo habían tomado preso.	*I heard he had been caught.*
Deduzco que no te interesa el asunto.	*I conclude that the issue does not interest you.*

NOTE: In Spanish after verbs of communication the clause stating the action may be omitted when it is implicitly understood. Confirmation or denial of the event may be rendered by verb + **que** + **sí (no)**. No equivalent structure exists for it in English. A clause with an auxiliary must be used instead.

Dijo que sí (podría ir).	*She said she could (go).*
Dijo que no (quería ir).	*She said she did not want to (go).*

3. INFORMATION VERSUS VOLITION

Verbs of communication, **decir, avisar, mencionar, escribir**, etc., may be used to convey information or to express implied commands. If the governing idea is one of information, the indicative is used. If, however, an implied command is expressed, only the subjunctive can occur.

Information → Indicative	*Implied command → Subjunctive*
Me dice que Juan viene mañana. *He tells me that John is coming tomorrow.*	Me dice que yo vaya. *He tells me to go.*
Nos comunicó que no lo aceptará. *He has informed us that he will not accept it.*	Nos comunicó que no lo aceptáramos. *He has informed us not to accept it.*
Le avisó que ella iría. *He has let him know that he would go.*	Le avisó que no fuera. *He has let him know that he should not go.*
Le ha escrito que Pedro le pagaría pronto. *He has written stating that Pedro would pay him soon.*	Le ha escrito que le pagara pronto. *He has written requesting that he pay him soon.*

4. DOUBT, CONJECTURE, DENIAL: EVENT HYPOTHETICAL OR DENIED → SUBJUNCTIVE

When the governing notion is one of doubt, conjecture, or denial with regards to the action of another subject, a clause in the subjunctive occurs. If the subject is the same, a verb + INF occurs instead. The hypothetical or denied event may refer to a co-existent, subsequent, or anterior action in relation to the subordinating verb.

No creo ser la persona indicada para juzgarlo.	*I don't think I am the right person to judge him.*
No creo que ella sea la persona indicada para juzgarlo.	*I don't think she is the right person to judge him.*

Doubt and denial

Since there is only one verb for doubt, **dudar**, and one for denial, **negar**, some verbs of belief and knowledge are used negatively in the main clause to convey the same notions: **no creer, no pensar, no considerar, no recordar, no sospechar**, etc.

Dudo que él pueda completar ese trabajo.	*I doubt that he can complete that work.*
Niego que él haya dicho eso.	*I deny that he has said that.*
No pienso que ese proyecto pueda realizarse.	*I don't think that project can be completed.*
No recuerdo que él haya dicho tal cosa.	*I don't remember that he has said such a thing.*
No considera que este sea un momento oportuno para hablarle de negocios.	*He does not think that this is an opportune moment to approach him about business matters.*
No sospechábamos que él fuera tan arbitrario.	*We did not suspect that he was so arbitrary.*
Niega que ella hubiera sabido algo de antemano.	*He denies that she knew anything beforehand.*

Conjecture

Conjecture may be expressed through declarative and interrogative sentences. **Creer, pensar, considerar, sospechar**, etc., are used in interrogative sentences without a negative marker to imply conjecture. **Saber** and **recordar** do not occur in this case, as they would function as information verbs and as such would take the indicative. However, **suponer**, which does imply conjecture, takes the indicative.

No estamos seguros de que haya recibido la carta.	*We are not sure (uncertain) that he has received our letter.*
¿Cree Ud. que sea prudente decirle algo ahora?	*Do you believe that it would be wise to tell him something now?*
¿Considera Ud. que esta oferta represente una buena oportunidad para progresar?	*Do you believe that this offer represents a good chance to progress?*

¿Piensa Ud. que ellos puedan ponerse
  de acuerdo?
Temo que ése no sea el caso.

*Do you believe that they could reach
  an agreement?*
I don't think that is the case.

BUT:

Supongo que lo verás.
Supongo que lo habrás visto.

I suppose that you will see him.
I suppose that you (will) have seen him.

Clause + predicate nominative

An event can also be described as hypothetical through a predicate nominative.
The noun clause functioning as subject will be in the subjunctive when the predicate expresses doubt, conjecture, probability, or denial.

Es dudoso que se pueda trabajar
  bajo esas condiciones.
Es improbable que nos veamos
  mañana.
Es difícil que la situación se resuelva
  favorablemente.
Hay pocas probabilidades de que se
  aumenten los salarios.
Es raro que no nos hubiera dicho
  nada.
No es improbable que él se haya
  enterado del caso.
No es cierto que yo haya dicho eso.
No es posible que él haya
  renunciado.

*It is doubtful that one could work under
  those conditions.*
*It is unlikely that we will see each·
  other tomorrow.*
*It is unlikely that the situation will be
  resolved favorably.*
*There is little probability that salaries
  will be increased.*
*It is strange that he should have failed
  to mention anything to us.*
*It is not improbable that he should have
  found out about the case.*
It is not true that I have said that.
It is not possible that he has resigned.

5. BELIEF: EVENT AFFIRMED → INDICATIVE

1. If an event is not conceived as hypothetical but is known or believed to be a
   fact, the clause will be in the indicative. This applies to declarative and interrogative sentences as well. Interrogatives in this case ask for confirmation of
   facts, or what are believed to be facts by the speaker.

No dudo que él te es fiel.

I don't doubt that he is faithful to you.
(no doubt = belief)

No niega que su hijo es responsable
  de lo sucedido.

*He does not deny that his son is
  responsible for what has happened.*
(no denial = affirmation)

Piensa que ella sería capaz de cualquier
  cosa si su posición peligrara.

*He believes she would be capable of
  anything if her position were in
  danger.*
(information)

¿No sabía Ud. que él estaba muy enfermo?	*Did you not know that he was very sick?* (speaker knew, is asking for information)
¿No considera Ud. que ésta es una gran oportunidad?	*Don't you think that this is a great opportunity?* (speaker thinks it is, asking for confirmation of his opinion)
¿No recuerdas que te lo mencionó ayer?	*Don't you remember he mentioned it to you yesterday?*

2. When the predicate nominative describes an event as a fact or affirms it as such, the clause is in the indicative in both declarative and interrogative sentences. In interrogatives, in this case, the speaker asks for confirmation of facts or what are believed to be facts.

Es indiscutible que él tiene razón y no tú.	*It is indisputable that he is right and not you.*
Es indudable que la crisis económica es severa.	*There is no doubt that the economic crisis is severe.*
Es obvio que los precios seguirán subiendo.	*It is obvious that prices will continue to rise.*
Es verdad que hay una crisis.	*It is true that there is a crisis.*
¿Es verdad que hay una crisis?	*Is it true that there is a crisis?*
Es seguro que ha renunciado.	*It is certain that he has resigned.*
¿Es seguro que ha renunciado?	*Is it certain that he has resigned?*

6. EMOTION AND PERSONAL INCLINATION: → SUBJUNCTIVE

The subjunctive is always used in Spanish when the governing notion is a causative of emotion or when it describes personal inclination. Thus, verbs which convey anger, pleasure, displeasure, surprise, regret, pardon, hope, fear, etc., always take the subjunctive when a clause is used.

Clauses which function as causatives of emotion may refer to subsequent, co-existent and anterior events in relation to the governing notion.

Me horroriza la idea de que te cases con ese hombre.	*The idea that you might (will) marry that man horrifies me.*
Siento que no estés de acuerdo conmigo.	*I regret that you should not agree with me.*
El que le hubieras ocultado la verdad es imperdonable.	*The fact that you should have hidden the truth from him is inexcusable.*

The fact that subjunctive clauses governed by verbs of emotion or personal inclination can refer to completed, future, or ongoing events is perhaps better understood if two things are considered. First, the completed or ongoing event may or may not be a fact; the speaker may assume that it is, but its confirmation

or denial depends upon extra-linguistic circumstances. Second, emotional responses to events are highly subjective, personal experiences. The same event that
affects one person may not ellicit any response at all in another; or it may even
trigger a completely different reaction. As such, causatives of emotion have little
objectivity outside of the subject who experiences them. It is perhaps for these
two reasons that clauses functioning as causatives of emotion always take the
subjunctive. This applies to affirmative and negative clauses as well.

1. The most common occurrence of the subjunctive as a causative of emotion is
   in subject clauses. The clause occurs with verbs that belong to the **gustar** class.
   The logical subject of the sentence is signaled by an indirect object form. The
   grammatical subjects in sentences with **gustar**-like verbs do not assume subject
   but object position.

Me interesa el arte moderno.	*I am interested in modern art.*
Le fascina Picasso.	*He is fascinated by Picasso.*

The same word order applies to complex sentences as well. Indirect object
forms occupy subject position while clauses tend to occur in object position.

Me preocupa que no puedas venir a la reunión. (object position)	*It worries me that you should not be able to come to the meeting.*
El que no puedas venir a la reunión me preocupa. (subject position, less frequent)	*The fact that you should not be able to come to the meeting worries me.*

A clause instead of an infinitive is used with **gustar**-like verbs when the subject
of an action is not the same person as the one signaled by the indirect object form.

Le molesta que mientan.	*It bothers him that people should lie.*
Le molesta mentir.	*It bothers him to lie.*
La posibilidad de que algo le pase me aterra.	*The possibility that something might happen to him frightens me.*
El que no me tengas confianza me duele.	*The fact that you do not trust me hurts me.*
Le indigna que no le hubieran consultado antes de proceder.	*It makes him indignant that they should not have consulted with him before proceeding.*
El hecho de que salga sin decir a donde va, nos irrita.	*The fact that he should go out without saying where he is going irritates us.*
Les da envidia que tengas tanto éxito.	*It makes them envious that you should be so successful.*
No les inquieta que su hijo tenga amigos tan poco serios.	*It does not upset them that their son has such flighty friends.*

2. Clauses as complements occur mainly with reflexive verbs and **estar** + adjectives, which convey essentially the same notions. However, if the complement
   has the same subject as the main verb, then an infinitive is used instead.

Se jacta de que lo hayan escogido a él.	*He is boasting about the fact that he has been chosen.*

Se jacta de haberlo escogido él.	He is boasting about the fact that he has chosen it.
Está triste de que tengas que irte.	She is sad because you have to leave.
Está triste de tener que irse.	She is sad because she has to leave.
Se lamenta de que no la hubieran atendido como esperaba.	She complains that she was not treated as she expected.
Se preocupa de que no estén bien de salud.	He is worried by the fact of their poor health.
	He is worried that they might be in poor health.
Está feliz de que le hayan aumentado el sueldo.	He is happy that they have given him a raise.
Están emocionados de que hayas ido a saludarlos.	They are touched because you have gone to greet them.

3. Clauses as direct objects occur mainly with verbs of hope, understanding, regret, pardon, fear, etc. If the direct object has the same subject as the main verb, an infinitive is used instead of a clause.

Espero que hayas tenido éxito.	I hope you have been successful.
Espero haber tenido éxito.	I hope I have been successful.
Comprende que no quieras verlo después de lo que pasó.	He understands that you should not want to see him after what has happened.
Confía que todo se haya resuelto a su favor.	He trusts that everything has been resolved in your favor.
No puedo perdonar que la hayas abandonado.	I cannot forgive you for having abandoned her.
Lamenta que no puedas ver nuestro punto de vista.	He regrets that you should not be able to see our point of view.
Siento que tengas que volver a hacerlo.	I am sorry that you have to do it all over.
Temo que todo haya sido en vano.	I fear everything has been in vain.

A noun clause functioning as subject will also be in the subjunctive if the predicate nominative describes emotion or personal inclination.

Es de preocuparse que diga eso.	That he should say that is cause for concern.
Me preocupa que diga eso.	It worries me that he should say that.
Es lamentable que estés enfermo.	It is regrettable that you should be sick.
Lamento que estés enfermo.	I regret that you are sick.
Era de esperar que renunciase.	It was to be expected that he would resign.
Es triste que no pueda ver a sus hijos.	It is sad that he should not be able to see his children.

No es sorprendente que se hubieran peleado.

It is not surprising that they should have had a falling out.

Que lo hayan despedido a él es una injusticia.

That they should have fired him is an injustice.

Es de temer que intente algún disparate.

It is to be feared that he might attempt something foolish.

Era vergonzoso que nadie la hubiera socorrido.

It is shameful that no one should have helped her.

TEMPORAL CLAUSES

Temporal clause $\Big\{$ ***Future Time or Subsequence → Subjunctive***
Present or Past Time → Indicative

Nominal clauses used as adverbials of time describe the temporal sequence between events. The relationship may be one of anteriority, co-existence, or subsequence.

The choice between the subjunctive and the indicative in temporal clauses depends upon the factual or hypothetical nature of the event or events. When the main verb refers to present or past habitual events, the temporal clause takes the indicative. When the main clause refers to an extended present, which includes future time, or to the future itself, the temporal clause takes the subjunctive. This also applies to future time within the past.

Temporal clauses, as well as other nominal clauses, are introduced by **que**, except for **mientras**, which may occur without it. Temporal clauses are used after one of the following relators:

a medida		*as*
después (de)[1]		*after*
hasta		*until*
antes (de)	+ **que**	*before*
luego		*after, when*
mientras		*while, for as long as*
desde		*since*

Después de, **hasta**, and **antes de** may take an infinitive or a clause with the same or a different subject from the main clause.

Iré después de cenar.

I will go after I eat.

Iremos después de que acabemos con estas tareas.

We will go after we finish these chores.

---

[1] After **después de** and **antes de**, the preposition may be deleted when a clause follows. It must, of course, be retained if a noun or infinitive follows.

Tomaré la medicina hasta que me sienta mejor.	*I will take the medicine until I feel better.*
No saldré antes de llamarla.	*I won't go out before calling her.*
No saldré antes de que la llame.	*I won't go out before I call her.*

When these relators introduce clauses with a different subject from the main verb, the clause is obligatory.

Iré después que tú cenes (hayas cenado).	*I will go after you have eaten.*
Tome Ud. la medicina hasta que se sienta mejor.	*Take the medicine until you feel better.*
No te vayas antes de que ella llame.	*Don't leave before she calls.*

All the other relators, **luego, mientras, desde, a medida**, always take clauses, regardless of whether the clauses have the same or a different subject.

Saldremos luego que tú llegues.	*We will leave after you arrive.*
Saldré luego que termine.	*I will leave after I finish.*
Te acompañaré mientras estés enfermo.	*I will keep you company for as long as you are sick.*
Escucharé música mientras escriba cartas.	*I will listen to music while I write letters.*
Desde que se fue no he tenido paz.	*Ever since he left I have had no peace.*
Desde que yo llegué no he tenido paz.	*Ever since I arrived I have had no peace.*
Corrijo los exámenes a medida que me los entregan.	*I correct the exams as they hand them in to me.*
La estimo más y más a medida que la voy conociendo mejor.	*I esteem her more and more as I get to know her better.*

Después de, luego, hasta:

All of these relators describe an event as posterior to another event. **Hasta** has the additional meaning of duration.

Subsequence, futurity within the actual or retrospective present	*Succession of events in the present or the past*
Deje Ud. de tomar la medicina después que se sienta mejor.	Deja de tomar la medicina después que se siente mejor.
Deje Ud. de tomar la medicina luego que se sienta mejor.	Deja de tomar la medicina luego que se siente mejor.
Discontinue the medicine after you feel better.	*She discontinues the medicine after she feels better.*
	Dejó de tomar la medicina después que se sintió mejor.
	Dejó de tomar la medicina luego que se sintió mejor.
	She discontinued the medicine after she felt better.

Tome la medicina hasta que se sienta mejor.	Toma la medicina hasta que se siente mejor.
Take the medicine until you feel better.	*She takes the medicine until she feels better.*
Le aconsejó que tomara la medicina hasta que se sintiera mejor.	Tomó la medicina hasta que se sintió mejor.
He advised her to take the medicine until she felt better.	*She took the medicine until she felt better.*
Tomaría la medicina hasta que se sintiera mejor.	Tomaba la medicina hasta que se sentía mejor.
She would take the medicine until she felt better.	*She used to take the medicine until she would feel better.*

Mientras:

It is used to introduce events which are co-existent with another event. When co-existence refers to present or past time, the indicative occurs. If co-existence refers to future time, within the present or the past, the subjunctive occurs instead.

Co-existence within the actual or retrospective future	*Co-existence within the present or the past*
Me quedaré contigo mientras me necesites.	Se queda con él mientras él la necesita.
I will stay with you for as long as you need me.	*She stays with him while he needs her.*
Se quedaría con él mientras la necesitara.	Se quedaba con él mientras él la necesitaba.
She would stay with him for as long as he needed her.	*She used to stay with him while he needed her.*
Escucharé música mientras lea el manuscrito.	Escucho música mientras leo el manuscrito.
I will listen to music while I read the manuscript.	*I listen to music while I read the manuscript.*
Escucharía música mientras leyera el manuscrito.	Escuché música mientras leí el manuscrito.
She would listen to music while she read the manuscript.	*I listened to music while I read the manuscript.*

A medida:

Introduces a clause which describes progression. When progression within the present and the past are described, the indicative is used. If progression refers to future time, within the present or the past, the subjunctive occurs instead.

Progression within the actual or retrospective future	*Progression within the present or the past*
Corregiré las pruebas a medida que me las entreguen.	Corrijo las pruebas a medida que me las entregan.
I will correct the galley proofs as they hand them in to me.	*I correct the galley proofs as they hand them in to me.*
Nos informó que corregiría las pruebas a medida que se las entregáramos.	Corregía las pruebas a medida que se las entregaban.
He informed us that he would correct the galley proofs as they handed them in to him.	*He used to correct the galley proofs as they handed them in to him.*

Antes de:

Introduces an event which is anterior to another event. The temporal clause always takes the subjunctive because the second event is always future in relation to the first, and was or was not completed when the first event occurred.

Tendré que irme antes de que lleguen.	*I will have to leave before they arrive.*
Tuve que irme antes de que llegaran.	*I had to leave before they arrived.*
Lo supe antes de que me notificaran oficialmente.	*I found out before I was officially informed.*

Desde:

Introduces clauses which describe the duration of a given event without indication of the event's completion. Since it refers to what has been ongoing, and as such to facts, **desde** only takes the indicative.

Desde que se casó su hija se ha sentido muy sola.	*Since her daughter got married she has been feeling very lonely.*
Desde que están divorciados no los he vuelto a ver.	*Since they have been divorced I have not seen them.*

GOAL OR FINALITY OF AN EVENT: RESULT HYPOTHETICAL OR NEGATIVE → SUBJUNCTIVE

When two events are set in relation to each other and one of them describes the goal or finality of the other, either an infinitive or a clause with the verb in the subjunctive occurs, depending upon the subjects involved.

If the two events are performed by one and the same subject, an infinitive is used.

He venido para pagarte.	*I have come (in order) to pay you.*
He venido a fin de aclarar este malentendido.	*I have come in order to clear up this misunderstanding.*
Me fui sin pagarle.	*I left without paying him.*

If the two events are performed by different subjects, a clause introduced by **que**, with the verb in the subjunctive, occurs instead. The clause may occur after the following relators:

para		*so (that), (in order) to*
a fin de } + **que**		*so (that), (in order) to*
sin		*without*

Clauses expressing the goal of an action take the subjunctive because the result is hypothetical. Nothing is ascertained whether the goal was achieved or not.

He venido para que me pagues.	*I have come so that you would pay me.*
He venido para que nos viéramos.	*I have come so we could see each other.*
Hemos escrito la carta a fin de que nos dieran más detalles.	*We have written the letter so that they would give us further details.*

When the goal is not or was not achieved, the negative formulation of the above sentences is rendered by the relator **sin**.

Me fui sin que me pagaran.	*I left without their paying me.*
Me fui sin que nos viéramos.	*I left without us having seen each other.*
Han contestado sin que nos dieran más detalles.	*They have answered without giving us further details.*

Other uses of **sin**

Sin has other functions besides being equivalent to contrary or opposite paraphrases of **para** + clause and **para** + INF. **Sin** may be used:

1. To describe the inevitable result or co-occurrence of an event:

No puedes decirle nada sin que se ofenda.	*You cannot tell her anything without her getting offended.*
Era imposible escuchar el relato sin que uno llorara.	*It was impossible to listen to the story without crying.*
No podía levantarse sin que alguien le ayudara.	*She could not get up without someone helping her.*

2. To describe the occurrence of an event without the expected co-occurrence of another action:

Salió sin que me dijera a donde iba.	*He left without telling me where he was going.*
Se fue sin que se despidiera de nosotros.	*He left without saying good-bye to us.*
Salió sin que yo me diera cuenta.	*He left without my realizing it.*

In all instances, however, a clause introduced by **sin que** always takes the subjunctive.

Spanish and English Nominal Clauses Contrasted

NOMINAL CLAUSES

Spanish	*English*

CLAUSE FORMATION

Essentially the same for both languages, except:

1. Relator **que** is not omitted.	1. *That* may be omitted.

Supongo que vendrá. Me aseguró que había ido.	*I suppose (that) he will come.* *He assured me (that) he had gone.*

2. Clauses have a different subject from the main verb, excepting those subordinated to a verb of communication, which may have the same subject.	2. May have the *same* or a *different* subject.

El me aseguró que había ido. Nos contó que había estado enfermo.	*He assured me he had gone.* *He told us he had been sick.*

BUT:

Niego que él lo haya hecho. Niego haberlo hecho.	*I deny that he has done it.* *I deny that I have done it.*
Me alegro de que hayas conseguido beca. Me alegro de haber conseguido beca.	*I am glad you have received a scholarship.* *I am glad I have received a scholarship.*

3. Although verbs of persuasion, perception, and observation can take an infinitive with a different subject, all other verbs must take a clause.	3. Infinitive and *-ing* forms with a different subject are more frequent than clauses.

La hizo estudiar. La oyó llorar. La vió salir.	*He made her study.* *He heard her crying.* *He saw her going out.*

BUT:

Dijo que lo hicieras tú. Te pidió que lo hicieras. Se opone a que te cases con él.	*He said for you to do it.* *He asked you to do it.* *He is opposed to your marrying him.*

MOOD: GOVERNING NOTIONS

COMMUNICATION

When information is conveyed, whether it be factual, intuitive, true or false, the clause takes:

Indicative

Soñé que habías llegado.
No sabía que estaba enfermo.
Me imagino que estarás exhausto.
Dijo que regresaría pronto.

Indicative

I dreamt you had come.
He did not know he was sick.
I imagine you must be exhausted.
He said he would return soon.

VOLITION

When a command is implied, whether it be expressed as an order, a request, a proposal, or a suggestion:

Subjunctive

Excepting a few verbs, *to propose, to demand, to move, to suggest*, etc., which take subjunctive clauses, others take the indicative, an infinitive, or an -*ing* form as complements.

Exigimos que renuncies.
Sugerimos que se le expulse.
Propongo que salgamos a cenar.

We demand that you resign.
We suggest that he be expelled.
I propose that we go out for dinner.

Confío que no le digas nada.
Desea que te mejores pronto.

I trust you will say nothing to him.
He hopes you will get better soon.

Dijo que te fueras.
Les impidió que hicieran justica.
Me opongo a que lo nombren.

He said for you to go.
He prevented them from doing justice.
I am opposed to his being appointed.

DOUBT, CONJECTURE, DENIAL

When doubt or conjecture is expressed either through a verb of doubt, a negative verb phrase, or an interrogative sentence:

Subjunctive

Dudo que su situación económica mejore.

No cree que se pueda arreglar este auto.
¿Crees tú que pueda arreglarse?
¿Sospechas que te haya mentido?

Indicative

I doubt that his financial situation will improve.
He does not think this car can be fixed.
Do you believe it can be fixed?
Do you suspect he has lied to you?

Affirmative verb phrases, declaratives with the same verbs, and interrogatives which ask for confirmation take:

Indicative	Indicative
No dudo que es un caballero.	*I don't doubt that he is a gentleman.*
No creo que este auto puede arreglarse.	*I don't think this car can be fixed.*
No sospecha que le ha mentido, lo sabe.	*She does not suspect he has lied to her, she knows it.*
¿No crees que debemos visitarle?	*Don't you think we ought to visit him?*

EMOTION AND PERSONAL INCLINATION

When an event is a causative of emotion, or of personal inclination, negative or affirmative:

Subjunctive	Indicative. Closest equivalent a modal auxiliary, or the "emotional" *should* which is used in passing judgment on occurrences which may or may not be facts.
Me molesta que me interrumpas a cada rato.	*It bothers me that you should interrupt me every few minutes.*
La idea de que algo le haya sucedido nos aterra.	*The mere idea that something might have happened to him terrifies us.*
El que se comporte de ese modo nos inquieta.	*That she should act in such a way worries us (is cause for concern).*
No me irrita que salgas, sino que no digas a donde vas.	*It does not bother me that you should go out, but that you do not say where you are going.*

SUBJECT CLAUSES + PREDICATE NOMINATIVE

When the predicate nominative describes an event as necessary, indispensable, good, bad, etc., thus causing pressure upon a given subject to act:

Subjunctive	Excepting a few which take a subjunctive clause, most take an infinitive.
Es necessario que vayas.	*It is necessary that you go.*
Es indispensable que vayas.	*It is indispensable that you go.*
No es bueno que comas tan mal.	*It is not good for you to eat that poorly.*
Es malo que fumes tanto.	*It is bad for you to smoke that much.*

When the predicate nominative describes an event as hypothetical, possible, probable, or when it denies it:

Subjunctive	Indicative
Es dudoso que venga.	*It is doubtful that he will come.*
Es difícil que él cambie de opinión.	*It is unlikely that he will change his mind.*
Es imposible que haya renunciado.	*It is impossible that he has resigned.*

No es posible que haya renunciado.	*It is not possible that he has resigned.*
No es difícil que cambie de opinión.	*It is not unlikely that he will change his mind.*
No es verdad que él te haya acusado.	*It is not true that he has accused you.*

When the predicate nominative describes an event as a causative of emotion, or expresses personal inclination:

Subjunctive	Indicative
Es muy triste que haya acabado así.	*It is very sad that it should have ended like this.*
Es una vergüenza que esos hermanos peleen tanto.	*It is shameful that those brothers should fight like that.*
Es lamentable que no se hubiera operado antes.	*It is regrettable that he should not have been operated on before.*

When the predicate nominative describes an event as a fact, affirms it:

Indicative	Indicative
Es seguro que viene.	*It is certain that he is coming.*
No cabe duda que es una persona magnífica.	*There is no doubt that he is a great person.*
Es verdad que nos vimos ayer.	*It is true that we saw each other yesterday.*
Es un hecho que él es malo.	*It is a fact that he is bad.*

TEMPORAL CLAUSES

When two events are set in a temporal sequence, and the main verb refers to future time within the actual or retrospective present, a temporal clause referring to subsequence takes:

Subjunctive	Indicative
Te esperaré mientras viva.	*I will wait for you as long as I live.*
Lo esperaría mientras viviera.	*She would wait for him for as long as she lived.*
No nos casaremos hasta que él no se reciba.	*We won't get married until he graduates.*
No se casarían hasta que él no se recibiera.	*They would not get married until he graduated.*
Iremos luego que tú llegues.	*We will go after you arrive.*

BUT:

Fuimos luego que tú llegaste.	*We went after you arrived.*

After **después de**, **antes de**, and **hasta,** an infinitive may be used if there is only one subject. The other relators only take clauses, regardless of subjects.

Iré después de acabar.	*I will go after I finish.*
No saldré antes de terminar.	*I won't go until after I finish.*
No saldré hasta no terminar.	*I won't go til I finish.*

Spanish	*English*

GOAL: RESULT HYPOTHETICAL OR NEGATIVE

When two actions with a different subject are set in relation to each other and one of them describes the goal of an action, the clause must take:

Subjunctive	Indicative; *-ing* after *without*.
He venido para que me aclares la situación.	*I have come so that you would clarify the situation to me.*
Me fui sin que me aclarara la situación.	*I left without him clarifying the situation to me.*
If the subject is the same an infinitive occurs instead:	Infinitive + *-ing* after *without*:
He venido para pagarte.	*I have come to pay you.*
Me fui sin pagarle.	*I left without paying her.*

12

SUBJUNCTIVE AND INDICATIVE IN CONDITIONAL, RELATIVE, AND INDEPENDENT CLAUSES

Subjunctive and Indicative in Condition-Effect Relationships

CONDITIONAL CLAUSES

Condition hypothetical: Effect contingent → Subjunctive

When the realization of one event is contingent upon the realization of another event they stand in a condition-effect relationship. Since all conditions are intrinsically hypothetical, and it is not ascertained whether or not a condition was fulfilled, all conditional clauses—excepting *if* clauses—always take the subjunctive. While all the relators of conditional clauses share the basic meaning of uncertainty described, they can be further subcategorized according to the shades of meaning they convey.

PROVISO:

con tal de que	*provided that*
a condición de que	*on condition that*
siempre que	*as long as*
mientras que	*as long as*

Le prometió un viaje a Europa con tal de que terminara sus estudios.	*He promised him a trip to Europe provided that he finished his studies.*
Repararía la casa a condición de que se la compraran.	*He would repair the house on condition that they buy it.*
Mientras que haya hecho lo que era justo no tiene de que preocuparse.	*As long as he did what was just he has nothing to fear.*
Mientras que él estudiara no le importaba pagar los gastos.	*As long as he was studying he did not mind paying for his expenses.*
Siempre que su padre estuviera de acuerdo, ella no se opondría.	*As long as her father was in agreement with it, she would not oppose it.*

EXCEPTION:

a no ser que	*unless*
a menos que	*unless*
salvo que	*unless*

Terminaremos hoy a menos que venga alguien a interrumpirnos.	*We will finish today unless someone should interrupt us.*
Todo saldrá bien a no ser que alguien haya divulgado nuestros planes.	*Everything will turn out fine unless someone should have divulged our plans.*
No podré ir salvo que tú me lleves.	*I won't be able to go unless you take me with you.*
No iba a ningún lado a menos que su marido la acompañara.	*She did not go anywhere unless her husband accompanied her.*
Salvo que renuncie ahora estará perdido.	*Unless he resigns now he will be lost.*

SUPPOSITION:

en caso de que	*in case*
suponiendo que	*supposing that*
como	*should*

En caso de que se haya ido ya, tendremos que conseguir su dirección.	*In case she should have left already, we would have to get her address.*
Suponiendo que hubieran decidido casarse, ¿se opondría Ud.?	*Supposing that they should have decided to get married, would you be opposed?*
En caso de que venga antes tendremos que posponer el viaje.	*In case he arrives earlier (should arrive), we will have to postpone the trip.*
Como se haya enterado de tu situación, no te prestará el dinero.	*Should he have found out about your situation, he will not lend you the money.*

"If"-clauses

If-clauses differ from the preceding conditional clauses insofar as they can refer not only to hypothetical but also to contrary-to-fact suppositions. Furthermore, they take either the subjunctive or the indicative.[1]

1. When an event will take place provided that the condition is fulfilled, the *if*-clause may take either the subjunctive or the indicative. The subjunctive is used instead of the indicative if the condition is less likely to be fulfilled, and the effect therefore less likely to occur.

Si no te paga lo que te debe, lo denunciaremos.	*If he does not pay you what he owes you, we will denounce him.*
Si no te pagara lo que te debe, lo denunciaríamos.	*If he should not pay you what he owes you, we would denounce him.*

2. When an event took place or would have taken place if a condition had not been fulfilled, only the indicative is used.

Si no pagaban la renta, los expulsaban.	*If they did not pay their rent, they were evicted.*
Si no trabajaba, no comía.	*If he did not work, he did not eat.*

3. When an event *cannot* or *could not* take place because the condition is not hypothetical, but *implicitly* denied, the imperfect or past perfect subjunctive is then used. In this case the reference is not to subsequent, future time (in relation to the present or past), but to the present and the past, respectively.

Si tuviera tiempo (ahora), iría. (Como no tengo tiempo, no voy.)	*If I had the time (now), I would go. (Since I don't have the time, I am not going.)*
Si no hubiera salido, la habría visto. (Como salío, no la vió.)	*If he had not gone out, he would have seen her. (Since he went out, he did not see her.)*

4. When both clauses are explicitly denied, that is, both contain a negative, only the imperfect or pluperfect subjunctive occurs. Although the two negative sentences cancel each other out, implying that the condition is a fact and that the effect was achieved, the negative form still requires the subjunctive. The imperfect is used for reference to the present, and the pluperfect for reference to the past.

Si no trabajara tanto, no tendría éxito. (Como trabaja tanto, tiene tanto éxito.)	*If he did not work as hard, he would not be as successful. (Since he works so hard he is so successful.)*

---

[1] NOTE: In addition to introducing hypothetical clauses, the conjunction **si** may be used to express alternatives. When it expresses alternatives it takes the indicative, and it is rendered in English by *whether*.

No está seguro si va aceptar o no.   *He is not sure whether he will accept or not.*

Si no hubieras ido, no te habrías enterado de nada.	*If you had not gone, you would not have found anything.*
(Como fuiste, te enteraste de algo.)	*(Since you went, you found out something.)*

"As if"-clauses

Comparative *if*-clauses, introduced by **como si**, always refer to hypothetical suppositions, and therefore occur only with the subjunctive: the imperfect to denote co-existent action, the pluperfect to denote anteriority. The clause stating the effect is not explicitly given but understood.

Me trata como (me trataría) si fuera su hijo.	*He treats me as (he would treat me) if I were his son.*
La miró como (la habría mirado) si no hubiera entendido nada.	*He looked at her as (he would look) if he had not understood a word.*

CONCESSIVE CLAUSES

When an event occurs in spite of an adverse situation or fails to materialize even though a favorable situation prevailed, the clause describing the situation is called *concessive*. The choice between the indicative and the subjunctive depends upon the factual or hypothetical nature of the situation. The clause can be introduced by one of the following relators:

a pesar de que	*in spite of, even though*
aunque	*even though, even if, although*
aún cuando	*even though, even if*
por más que	*even though, in spite of the fact*
por mucho que	*even though, no matter how*

1. When the clause refers to a factual situation the indicative is used. The main event may refer to present, past, or subsequent time.

Aunque trabaja mucho, gana poco.	*Even though he works a lot, he earns little.*
Aunque llueve, saldremos.	*Even though it is raining, we will be going out.*
Por más que intentó verla, no lo logró.	*Even though he tried to see her, he failed.*
Por mucho que estudió no pasó el examen.	*Even though he studied a lot, he failed the exam.*
A pesar de que sus padres se oponían, se casaron.	*Even though their parents were opposed to it, they got married.*

2. When the concessive clause refers to a hypothetical condition, a probable event (past, present, or future), or a contrary-to-fact situation, the subjunctive

is used instead. The main event refers to present or subsequent time only (future within the past or in relation to the present).

Voy a salir aunque llueva.	*I am going out even if it should rain.*
Irá a trabajar aún cuando esté enferma.	*She will go to work even if she should be sick.*
Iría a trabajar aunque estuviera muriéndose.	*She would go to work even if she were dying.*
Aún cuando me hubiera mentido, le perdonaría.	*Even if he had lied to me, I would forgive him.*
Por mucho que lo hubiera intentado, no lo habría logrado.	*No matter how hard she might have tried, she would not have succeeded.*

3. The subjunctive may, however, be used when the concessive clause refers to a factual situation *in spite of which* an event will occur or has occurred.

Aunque seas mi hijo, tengo que castigarte.	*In spite of the fact that you are my son, I will have to punish you.*
Aunque fuera tarde, tenía que hablarle.	*In spite of the fact that it was late, he had to speak to her.*
Se casaron aunque sus padres se hubieran opuesto.	*They got married in spite of the fact that their parents had been opposed to it.*
Podrías haber venido por más que lloviera.	*You could have come in spite of the fact that it was raining.*

Concessive relationships may also be expressed by some idiomatic formulas which always take the subjunctive.

sea lo que sea	*come what may*
venga lo que venga	*come what may*
cueste lo que cueste	*no matter how much it may cost*
etc.	
quieras o no (quieras)	*whether you be willing or not*
vengas o no (vengas)	*whether you come or not*
puedas o no (puedas)	*whether you can or not*
etc.	
Tendrás que ir, quieras o no.	*You will have to go, whether you are willing or not.*
Lo hizo, viniera lo que viniera.	*He did it, come what may.*

CAUSAL CLAUSES

Condition fulfilled: Effect achieved → Indicative

When two events are set in relation to each other, and one is viewed as the cause of the other, only the indicative occurs. They can be also considered as condition-effect relationships in which the condition is or was fulfilled, and the effect is or was achieved. Cause-effect relationships are introduced by one of the following relators:

en vista de que	in view of
ya que	since
puesto que	since
como	since
porque	because

Ya que no me necesitan me voy. *Since I am not needed, I am leaving.*
Puesto que él no me quiso ayudar a *Since he did not want to help me, now*
mí, ahora tampoco le voy a ayudar *I won't help him either.*
yo a él.

Como tú no puedes salir, no saldré *Since you cannot go out, I won't go*
tampoco yo. *out either.*
Le regaló un auto porque había *He gave him a car because he had*
cumplido con su promesa. *lived up to his promise.*

The cause-effect relationship can be inverted, one event then being described as a consequence or result of the other. Since results always refer to facts, only the indicative is used.

por lo tanto	therefore
así que	therefore
de modo que	therefore

No me necesitan, por lo tanto me *You don't need me; therefore, I am*
voy. *leaving.*
El no me quiso ayudar a mí, así que *He did not want to help me; therefore,*
ahora tampoco le voy a ayudar a él. *I won't help him now either.*
Tú no puedes salir, de modo que *You cannot go out; therefore, I won't*
tampoco saldré yo. *go out either.*

When a given cause is denied, and the expected result will not take place, a cause-effect relationship is not fulfilled. The subjunctive is therefore used. The only relator which takes the subjunctive under these conditions is **porque**.

Me quedo porque me necesitan. *I am staying because I am needed.*
No porque me necesiten voy a *Not because I am needed will I stay.*
quedarme.

Es la mayor, por lo tanto hace lo *She is the oldest and therefore does as*
que quiere. *she pleases.*
No porque sea la mayor hará lo que *Not because she is the oldest can (will)*
quiera. *she do as she pleases.*

Puesto que él está aquí no digo nada. *Since he is here, I won't say anything.*
No porque él esté aquí voy a *Not because he is here will I refrain*
callarme. *from speaking my mind.*

Occasionally the past perfect subjunctive is used after cause-effect relators. These subjunctive clauses, however, are to be interpreted as part of condition-effect sentences in which the clause stating the condition is implicitly given or understood.

No contesté porque (de haber
contestado) lo hubiera ofendido.

*I did not answer because (had I
answered) I would have offended him.*

Me fui porque (de haberme quedado)
me hubiera puesto a llorar.

*I left because (if I had stayed) I would
have started crying.*

Como (de haberme quedado) no
hubiera podido contenerme, decidí
salir del cuarto.

*Since I would not have been able to
control myself (if I had stayed) I
decided to leave the room.*

Subjunctive and Indicative in Relative Clauses

RELATIVE CLAUSES

Relative clauses are those which are introduced by relative pronouns. Relative pronouns connect two clauses and refer back to a noun mentioned in the subordinating clause. The noun which the pronoun refers back to is called its antecedent. Relative clauses fulfill the same function in the main sentence as noun modifiers.

Conozco a un muchacho **bilingüe**.
I know a bilingual boy.

Conozco a un muchacho **que es
bilingüe**.
I know a boy who is bilingual.

Te contaré una historia **de amor**.
I will tell you a love story.

Te contaré una historia **que trata de
amor**.
I will tell you a story that is about love.

No me gustan los días **sin sol**.
I don't like days without sunshine.

No me gustan los días **que no
tienen sol**.
*I don't like days when there is no
sunshine.*

Relative clauses are formed in Spanish and English essentially in the same way, except in Spanish the relative pronoun cannot be omitted; if a preposition occurs with it, it must precede the clause.[1]

Ya no era la misma persona **que**
conocía.

*He no longer was the same person
I used to know.*

La persona **para quien** trabaja . . .

The person he works for . . .

La ciudad **por la cual** pelearon . . .

The city they fought for . . .

---

[1] For a full discussion of relative clause formation see Chapter 8, "Relative Pronouns."

Some relative clauses, just as simple noun modifiers, may not only modify a noun but also a verb, thus describing the general circumstances under which the action is carried out.

El niño duerme **tranquilo**.
El niño está tranquilo y duerme tranquilamente.
The child sleeps peacefully.
The child is peaceful and he sleeps peacefully.

Viene los días **en que está libre**.
Está libre ciertos días y viene los días libres.
He comes on the days that he is off.
He is off on certain days and comes on his free days.

Lo hace **de buena fe**.
Tiene buena fé y lo hace con buena fe.
He does it in good faith.
He has good faith and does it in good faith.

Iremos a un restorán **en el que se come bien**.
Iremos a un restorán bueno y comeremos bien.
We will go to a restaurant where one eats well.
We will go to a good restaurant and we will eat well.

Relative clauses may be restrictive and non-restrictive. Restrictive clauses identify which one of the possible referents of a given class is being referred to. Non-restrictive clauses provide additional information about things previously identified.

Restrictive	*Non-restrictive*
El hombre que tiene dinero piensa que puede comprarlo todo. (El hombre **con** dinero piensa que puede comprarlo todo, pero no el hombre **sin** dinero.) *The man who has money thinks he can buy everything.*	El hombre, que tenía mucho dinero, era muy avaro. (El hombre tenía mucho dinero y era muy avaro.) *The man, who was very rich, was very stingy.*

Relative clauses, just as descriptive adjectives, may be nominalized by noun deletion.

Dame el traje **verde**.
Dame el verde.
Give me the green dress.
Give me the green one.

Dame el traje **que compré ayer**.
Dame el que compré ayer.
Give me the dress I bought yesterday.
Give me the one I bought yesterday.

Preséntame a la **mujer guapa**.
Preséntame a la guapa.
Introduce me to the good-looking woman.
Introduce me to the good-looking one.

Se lo daremos a la mujer **que más lo necesita**.
Se lo daremos a la que (a aquella que) más lo necesita.
We will give it to the woman who needs it the most.
We will give it to the one who needs it the most.

Relative clauses may occur without overt antecedents. The antecedent is omitted when it is indefinite—refers to any one member of a specific class—and when there is no ambiguity because it is implicitly understood by the speakers. The following relative forms may occur without expressed antecedents:[1]

Quien te lo dijo te miente.	*Whoever told you that is lying.*
La persona que te lo dijo, te miente.	*The person who told you that is lying.*
Cuantos vengan serán bienvenidos.	*Whoever might come is welcome.*
Todos los que vengan serán bienvenidos.	*All those that might come will be welcome.*
A donde va se porta como un caballero.	*Wherever he goes he behaves as a gentleman.*
Al lugar que va se porta como un caballero.	*Any place he goes he behaves as a gentleman.*
Lo hace **como** le enseñaste.	*He does it how you taught him.*
Lo hace en la forma que le enseñaste.	*He does it in the manner you taught him.*
Nos iremos **cuando** llegues.	*We will leave when you arrive.*
Nos iremos el día (mes, hora, minuto, etc.) que tú llegues.	*We will leave the day (month, hour, minute) that you arrive.*

Indicative versus subjunctive

The choice between the indicative and the subjunctive in relative clauses depends essentially upon the same notions as other clauses which take the subjunctive.

1. When the relative clause refers to a factual antecedent, one that refers to a specific person or thing, the indicative is used. Indicative relative clauses affirm the quality or condition of an antecedent as existing, in the present or the past. They affirm the existence of the antecedent itself. When the relative clause refers to present or past events, which in themselves are factual, the indicative is also used. Indicative relative clauses may either be restrictive or non-restrictive.

2. When the relative clause refers to a hypothetical antecedent, one that is non-specific or uncertain, the subjunctive occurs. Subjunctive relative clauses do not affirm the existence of a quality or condition of an antecedent; they describe it as contingent, as a condition that a given subject should fulfill. They do not assert the existence of an antecedent; they doubt, question, or negate it. When the relative clause refers to a subsequent event, the clause takes the subjunctive since all future events are hypothetical. Subjunctive clauses can only be restrictive since the antecedent has not been previously identified. In English there is no contrast between the indicative and subjunctive in relative clauses. Two

---

[1] For a full discussion on the topic see Chapter 8, "Relative Pronouns."

contrasting sentences in Spanish may therefore be rendered in English as one and the same sentence. Occasionally the difference in Spanish may be signaled in English by the presence of the definite or indefinite article, by a modal auxiliary, or by another word. However, since the English equivalents are of little use in understanding the differences in meaning involved, it is more helpful to take into account some of the possible recasts that each group of clauses admits in Spanish itself.

The Indicative versus the Subjunctive in Relative Clauses

RELATIVE CLAUSES

Indicative	*Subjunctive*

NON-RESTRICTIVE CLAUSES

Non-restrictive clauses provide additional information for previously identified referents.

1. The relative clause describes a condition which was fulfilled; the main clause, an effect which was achieved. The subordinate clause may be recast as a causal clause.

   El hombre, que había advertido el peligro, huyó.
   (El hombre huyó porque había advertido el peligro.)
   The man, who had noticed the danger, fled.
   (*The man fled because he had noticed the danger.*)

   Habla de modo tan persuasivo que engaña a muchos.
   (Como habla de modo tan persuasivo, él engaña a muchos.)
   He speaks in such a persuasive manner that he deceives many people.
   (*Since he speaks in such a persuasive manner, he deceives many people.*)

2. The relative clause describes a condition that was fulfilled, in spite of which a

given result followed. The clause may
be recast as a concessive clause.

Mis estudiantes, que habían estudiado
  mucho, tampoco pasaron el examen.
(Mis estudiantes, aunque habían
  estudiado mucho, tampoco pasaron
  el examen.)
My students, who had studied a lot, did
not pass the exam either.
(Even though they had studied a lot,
  my students did not pass the exam
  either.)

Juan, que no es tonto, se dejó
  engatusar por esa mujer.
(Juan, aunque no es tonto, se dejó
  engatusar por esa mujer.)
John, who is not a fool, let himself be
  taken by that woman.
(Even though he is not a fool, John let
  himself be taken by that woman.)

RESTRICTIVE CLAUSES

Restrictive clauses single out one of the possible referents of a given class.

Indicative	*Subjunctive*
1. The relative clause describes the quality of a subject as a fact, and the effect as certain to follow. The clause may be recast as an attributive noun phrase.	1. The relative clause describes the quality of a subject as hypothetical, and the effect as contingent upon its fulfillment. The clause may be rewritten as an *if*-clause.
El hombre que tiene voluntad, triunfa. (El hombre con voluntad, triunfa.) *The man who has willpower succeeds.* (*The man with willpower succeeds.*)	El hombre que tenga voluntad triunfará. (Si el hombre tiene voluntad, triunfa.) *The man who has willpower will succeed.* (*If a man has willpower, he succeeds.*)
El hombre que tiene perseverancia logra lo que se propone. (El hombre con perseverancia logra lo que se propone.) *The man who has perseverance attains what he aims at.* (*The man with perseverance attains what he aims at.*)	El hombre que tenga perseverancia, logrará lo que se propone. (Si el hombre tiene perseverancia, logrará lo que se propone.) *The man who has perseverance will attain what he aims at.* (*If a man has perseverance, he will attain what he aims at.*)

Indicative	*Subjunctive*

2. The relative clause describes the quality or condition of the subject as existing. The clause is a recast of a declarative sentence conveying information.

2. The relative clause describes a quality or condition as necessary, a subject must fulfill it. The clause is a recast of a sentence with a predicate nominative which describes the quality or condition as necessary.

Necesito la secretaria que habla español.
(Necesito la secretaria. La secretaria habla español.)
I need the secretary who speaks Spanish.
(*I need the secretary. The secretary speaks Spanish.*)

Necesito una secretaria que hable español.
(Necesito una secretaria. Es necesario que la secretaria hable español.)
I need a secretary who speaks Spanish.
(*I need a secretary. It is necessary that the secretary speak Spanish.*)

Vamos a un restorán donde sirven comida española.
(Vamos a un restorán. En el restorán sirven comida española.)
We go to a restaurant where Spanish food is served.
(*We go to a restaurant. In the restaurant Spanish food is served.*)

Vamos a un restorán donde sirvan comida española.
(Vamos a un restorán. Es necesario que sirvan comida española en el restorán.)
Let us go to a restaurant where Spanish food is served.
(*Let us go to a restaurant. It is necessary that Spanish food be served in the restaurant.*)

3. The relative clause describes a result as achieved; it affirms it as existing. The clause is a recast of a declarative sentence conveying information.

3. The relative clause describes the goal of an event, the result of which is hypothetical. It may or may not take place. The clause may be rewritten as one describing the finality of an event.

Toma una medicina que lo alivia.
(Toma una medicina. La medicina lo alivia.)
He takes a medicine that gives him relief.
(*He takes a medicine. The medicine gives him relief.*)

Toma una medicina que te alivie.
(Toma una medicina para que te alivies.)
Take some medicine that will (might) bring you relief.
(*Take some medicine to bring yourself relief.*)

Le di un libro que la distrajo.
(Le di un libro. El libro la distrajo.)
I gave her a book that entertained her.
(*I gave her a book. The book entertained her.*)

Te daré un libro que te distraiga.
(Te daré un libro para que te distraigas.)
I will give you a book that will (might) entertain you.
(*I will give you a book to entertain you.*)

Lo arregló de tal modo que quedó
perfecto.
(Lo arregló. Quedó perfecto.)
He fixed it in such a manner that it
came out perfect.
(He fixed it. It came out perfect.)

Arréglalo de tal modo que quede
perfecto.
(Arréglalo para que quede perfecto.)
Fix it in such a way that it comes out
perfect.
(Fix it so that it comes out perfect.)

4. The existence of an antecedent is
affirmed.

4. The existence of an antecedent is
negated, denied.

Encontró algo que le gustó.
He found something that he likes.

No encontró nada que le gustara.
He did not find anything that he liked.

Era capaz de dedicarse a todas aquellas
cosas que requieren disciplina.
He was capable of devoting himself to all
those things that require self-discipline.

Era incapaz de dedicarse a algo que
fuera serio. (No era capaz de
dedicarse a nada que fuera serio.)
He was incapable of devoting himself to
anything that was serious.

La cosa que más me interesa es tu
bienestar.
The thing that interests me the most is
your well-being.

No hay cosa que me interese más
que tu bienestar.
There is nothing that interests me more
than your well-being. (all other
things denied as uninteresting)

Lo único que le gusta es escribir.
The only thing he likes is writing.

No hay nada que le guste que no sea
escribir.
There is nothing that he likes except
writing.

5. The antecedent is known to the
speaker or assumed to be a certainty.

5. The antecedent is unknown to the
speaker or doubtful.

Te agradezco lo que hiciste.
I thank you for what you did.

Te agradezco lo que hayas hecho.
I thank you for whatever you did
(might have done).

Dame lo que te sobró.
Give me what was left over.

Dame lo que te haya sobrado.
Give me whatever you have (might
have) left over.

Muéstrame lo que has escrito.
Show me what you have written.

Muéstrame lo que hayas escrito.
Show me whatever you have (might
have) written.

6. The existence of an antecedent is
questioned. Affirmative answer
expected.

6. Negative answer expected.

¿Encontraste algo que te gustó?
Did you find something you liked?

¿Encontraste algo que te gustara?
Did you find anything you liked?

¿Hay alguien que quiere ir?
Is there someone who wants to go?

¿Hay alguien que quiera ir?
Is there anyone who wants to go?

Indicative	*Subjunctive*
¿Hay algo que es barato? *Is there something inexpensive?*	¿Hay algo que sea barato? *Is there anything inexpensive?*
7. The verb in the relative clause refers to a present or past event. As such it describes a specified, previously identified thing, time, manner, place, or person. The verb in the main clause refers to present, past, or subsequent events.	7. The verb in the relative clause refers to a subsequent event in relation to the present or past. As such, the thing, time, manner, place, or person is *yet to be specified*. The verb in the main clause refers to subsequent also.
Le da lo que le pide. *He gives him what he asks for.*	Le dará lo que le pida. *He will give him whatever he asks for.* (*thing* yet to be specified)
Le dará lo que le pide. *He will give him what he is asking for.*	Le daría lo que le pidiera. *He would give him what he asked for.* (*thing* yet to be specified)
Le dió lo que le pidió. *He gave him what he asked for.*	
Le daba lo que le pedía. *He used to give him what he would ask for.*	
Vendrá cuando le dijiste. *He will come when you told him to.*	Vendrá cuando le digas. *He will come whenever you tell him to.* (*time* yet to be specified)
Lo hace como le dices. *He does it the way you told him to.*	Lo hará como le digas. *He will do it the way you tell him to.* (*how* yet to be specified)
Iba a donde le decían. *He went (used to go) where he was told to go.*	Iría a donde le dijeran. *He would go wherever he was told to go.* (*where* yet to be specified)
Te agradezco lo que haces por él. *I thank you for what you do (are doing) for him.*	Te agradeceré lo que hagas por él. *I will thank you for whatever you (might) do for him.*
Le agradeció lo que hizo por él. *He thanked him for what he had done for him.*	Le agradecería lo que hiciera por él. *He would thank him for what he did (might do) for him.*
Hizo lo que quiso ella, y no lo que él le dijo. *She did what she wanted, and not what he said.*	Haré lo que quiera, y no lo que tú digas. *I'll do what I please, and not what you (might) say.* (his saying something is yet to take place)
Cuantos vienen, son bienvenidos. *All those who come, are welcome.*	Cuantos vengan, serán bienvenidos. *Whoever might come, will be welcome.*

The Subjunctive in Independent Clauses

USES OF THE SUBJUNCTIVE IN INDEPENDENT CLAUSES

The use of the subjunctive in independent clauses corresponds essentially to the same conditions as its occurrence in subordinate clauses. It is used to express volition in commands; it occurs after adverbs of probability to talk about hypothetical events; it is employed after **ojalá** to speak about desired events; and it occurs in polite assertions.

1. Commands

Excepting the affirmative command forms of **tú** and **vosotros**, which have special forms, all other commands take the parallel subjunctive forms.

a. Negative **tú** and **vosotros** forms:

No te vayas.	*Don't leave.*
(No quiero que te vayas).	*(I don't want you to leave.)*
No volváis hoy.	*Don't return today.*
(No es necesario que volváis hoy.)	*(It is not necessary that you return today.)*

b. Negative/affirmative **Ud., Uds.** forms:

Venga Ud. esta tarde.	*Come this afternoon.*
(Exijo que Ud. venga esta tarde.)	*(I demand that you come this afternoon.)*
No venga Ud. esta tarde.	*Don't come this afternoon.*
Váyanse Uds.	*Leave.*
(Es necesario que Uds. se vayan.)	*(It is necessary that you leave.)*
No se vayan Uds.	*Don't leave.*

c. Negative/affirmative **nosotros** forms:

Salgamos ya.	*Let us leave.*
(Es mejor que salgamos ya.)	*(It is advisable that we leave.)*
No lo discutamos más.	*Let's not discuss it any longer.*
(Es mejor que no lo discutamos más.)	*(It is better that we do not discuss it any longer.)*

In affirmative **nosotros** commands, **ir** + INF in the present tense can be used instead of the subjunctive.

Vamos a bailar.	*Let us dance.*
Vamos a comer afuera.	*Let us eat out.*

d. Impersonal command forms used in giving instructions or directions:

Tómese con leche.	*Take with milk.*
Guárdese bien tapado.	*Keep well covered.*
Manténgase al fresco.	*Store in cool place.*

2. Hypothetical events

The subjunctive is used after adverbs of probability, **tal vez, quizás, acaso, a lo mejor**, etc., to speak about hypothetical events. It may be employed to refer to past, present, or future hypothetical actions.

Tal vez haya venido ayer.	*She might have arrived yesterday.*
Quizás llegue mañana.	*She might arrive tomorrow.*
Acaso esté durmiendo ahora.	*She might be sleeping now.*
A lo mejor se haya ofendido.	*She might have gotten offended.*

These adverbs of probability may also be followed by the indicative when less uncertainty is implied.

3. Desired events

The subjunctive occurs after **ojalá** when probable or contrary-to-fact situations are spoken of. **Ojalá** may occur with or without the relator **que**. The relator is generally omitted when contrary-to-fact-situations are expressed.

Ojalá (que) te mejores pronto.	*I hope you get well soon.*
Ojalá (que) le haya avisado.	*I hope she has let him know.*
Ojalá (que) venga hoy.	*I hope he will come today.*
Ojalá hubieras estado aquí.	*I wish you had been here.*
Ojalá pudiera ir yo también.	*I wish I could go myself.*

When a wish is impossible, contrary-to-fact, and it refers to the first person, **quién** + imperfect subjunctive may also be used.

¡Quién fuera rico!	*I wish I were rich!*
¡Quién fuera ella!	*I wish I were she!*

4. Polite assertions

The **–ra** form of the imperfect subjunctive is used mostly with **querer** and **deber** to convey a polite tone to statements or requests.

Quisiera saber si puedes acompañarme esta tarde.	*I would like to know if you can come with me this afternoon.*
Debieras seguir sus consejos.	*It would be wise on your part to follow his advice.*

Subjunctive and Indicative Contrasted: Condition-Effect Relationships

CONDITIONAL CLAUSES

Spanish	*English*

Condition hypothetical, effect contingent upon the fulfillment of condition. Nothing is said whether the condition is or will be fulfilled. Excepting *if*-clauses, all others always take:

Subjunctive	Indicative
No iré a menos que me lleves en coche.	*I won't go unless you give me a ride.*
Saldré siempre que tú vengas conmigo.	*I will go provided that you come with me.*
No saldré a menos que tú vengas conmigo.	*I will not go out unless you come with me.*

If-CLAUSES

When the fulfillment of the condition is probable:

Indicative

Si vienes temprano, iremos al cine.	*If you come early, we will go to the movies.*
Si estudias, pasarás el examen.	*If you study you will pass the exam.*

When the fulfillment of the condition is improbable or implicitly denied:

Subjunctive	Indicative/Subjunctive
Si estudiaras, pasarías el examen.	*If you studied, you would pass the exam.*
Si viniera más temprano, dile que regreso enseguida.	$\begin{cases} \textit{If he arrives earlier, tell him I'll be right back.} \\ \textit{If he were to arrive earlier . . .} \\ \textit{If he should arrive earlier . . .} \end{cases}$
Si yo fuera tú, no lo haría.	*If I were you, I wouldn't do it.*

As *if*-CLAUSES

Subjunctive	Subjunctive or Indicative
Te quiere como si fuera tu hermano.	*He loves you as if he were your brother.*
Te mira como si no hubiera entendido nada.	*She is looking at you as if she had not understood a word.*

CONCESSIVE CLAUSES

Spanish	*English*

When the clause refers to a factual situation or condition:

Indicative	Indicative
Aunque fui a verla, no quiso recibirme.	*Even though I went to see her, she would not receive me.*

Spanish	*English*
Aunque estudia mucho, saca malas notas.	*Even though he studies a lot, he gets poor grades.*

When the clause refers to a hypothetical situation or condition:

Subjunctive

Aunque fueras a verla, no te recibiría.	*Even if you went to see her, she would not receive you.*
Aunque estudiaras mucho, sacarías malas notas.	*Even if you studied a lot, you would get poor grades.*

When the clause refers to a factual situation in spite of which a given event takes place:

Indicative/Subjunctive	Indicative
Aunque eres (seas) mi hijo, te desheredaré.	*In spite of the fact that you are my son, I shall disinherit you.*
Aunque eres (seas) muy inteligente, no puedes saberlo todo.	*In spite of the fact that you are very smart, you cannot know everything.*

CAUSAL CLAUSES

Spanish	*English*

A condition is fulfilled, and the effect is achieved:

Indicative	Indicative
Como me contaste todo, te confiaré algo.	*Since you have told me everything, I will confide in you.*
Tú me contaste todo, por lo tanto te confiaré algo.	*You told me everything; therefore, I will confide in you.*

RELATIVE CLAUSES

Spanish	*English*

CLAUSE FORMATION

Essentially the same for both languages, excepting:

Relative pronouns, like the relator **que** cannot be omitted:	Pronouns may be omitted:
La casa que compré ...	*The house (that) I bought ...*
La mujer a quien quiere ...	*The woman (that) he loves ...*
La carrera que escogió ...	*The career (that) he chose ...*

When a relative clause occurs with a preposition, the preposition occurs:

Before the clause:	At the end of the clause:
La persona de quien te hablo ...	*The person I speak of ...*
La mujer por quien se desvive ...	*The woman he longs for ...*
Las cosas de las que te quejas ...	*The things you complain about ...*

MOOD

Indicative and Subjunctive

Indicative. Two contrasting Spanish sentences may therefore be rendered in English as one and the same sentence. The difference can occasionally be signaled by the definite/indefinite article, by a modal auxiliary, or by another word.

INDICATIVE

1. Antecedent *factual*: specific person or thing.

Mi vecino, que es rico, es avaro.	*My neighbor, who is rich, is very stingy.*
El libro que me diste es muy interesante.	*The book you gave me is very interesting.*

2. Quality or condition a *fact*: the subject possesses the quality or condition.

Tiene una novia que es guapísima.	*He has a girl friend who is very beautiful.*
El hombre que tiene voluntad triunfa en la vida.	*The man who has willpower, succeeds in life.*
Quien se queja, sus males aleja.	*He who complains, his troubles dissipates.*

3. Existence of the antecedent *affirmed*, known by speaker, or assumed to be a certainty.

Encontró algo que le gustó.	*He found something that he liked.*
Muéstrame lo que has escrito.	*Show me what you have written.*
Te agradezco lo que hiciste.	*I thank you for what you have done.*

4. Main verb: past, present or future. Clause: present or past; specific things, time, place, manner and person.

Le pedirá lo que le hace falta.	*He will ask him for the things he needs.*
Vendrá a la hora que dijiste.	*He will come at the time you told him to.*
Vino a la hora que dijiste.	*He came at the time you told him to.*
Viene a la hora que tú dices.	*He comes at the time you tell him to.*

Spanish	*English*
Irá a donde dices.	*He will go where you say. (are saying)*
Irá a donde dijiste.	*He will go where you said.*
Fue a donde dijiste.	*He went where you said.*
Lo hace como le enseñaron.	*He does it the way he was taught.*
Lo hará como le enseñaron.	*He will do it the way he was taught.*
Lo hará como le enseñan.	*He will do it the way he is being taught.*
Cuantos lo conocen, lo estiman.	*All those who know him think highly of him.*

SUBJUNCTIVE

1. Antecedent *non-specific*: any one member of a given class. Quality or condition *hypothetical*.

Quien se queje, será despedido.	*Anyone complaining will be fired.*
El que bien te quiera, te dirá la verdad.	*He (the person) who loves you well, will tell you the truth.*

2. Quality or condition *necessary*: a subject must have it.

Quiero una casa que tenga diez cuartos.	*I want a house that has ten rooms.*
Se busca una persona que sea bilingüe.	*They are looking for a person who is bilingual.*

3. Existence of the antecedent *negated, denied*.

No hay nada que pueda ayudarte.	*There is nothing that can help you.*
No hay quien pueda aguantar a ese hombre.	*There is no one who can put up with that man.*

4. Existence of the antecedent *questioned, negative* answer expected.

¿Hay algo que te guste?	*Is there anything you like?*
¿Hay alguna manera de hacerlo que sea más económica?	*Is there another way of doing it that might be more economical?*

5. Antecedent *unknown* to speaker or *doubtful*.

Te agradezco lo que hayas hecho.	*I thank you for whatever you might have done.*
Cuéntame todo lo que te haya pasado desde que te vi por última vez.	*Tell me whatever might have happened to you since I last saw you.*

Main verb: subsequence.
Clause: subsequence; thing, time, place, manner and person as yet unspecified.

Te daré todo lo que mi pidas.	*I will give you whatever you (might) ask for.*
Iría cuando tú dijeras.	*She would go whenever you wanted her to go.* (*when*, yet to be specified)
Viviremos donde tú digas.	*We will live wherever you decide.* (*where*, yet to be specified)
Lo haré como sea más económico.	*I will do it whichever way it might be more economical.* (*manner* yet to be specified)
Quien lo conozca, lo estimará.	*Anyone who gets to know him will think highly of him.*

13

NOUNS AND NOMINALIZATIONS

Gender of Nouns

Spanish nouns are inherently masculine or feminine. Thus all word classes which either determine or modify nouns, such as articles and adjectives (including possessives, demonstratives, indefinites, and interrogatives), will almost invariably agree with the noun in gender. The gender distinction in Spanish is purely arbitrary. Excepting a few animate nouns, there is no natural system of gender whereby biological differences account for gender distinction.

el hijo	*the son*	la hija	*the daughter*
el muchacho	*the boy*	la muchacha	*the girl*
el abuelo	*the grandfather*	la abuela	*the grandmother*
el maestro	*the teacher*	la maestra	*the teacher*
el abogado	*the lawyer*	la abogada	*the lawyer*
el gato	*the cat*	la gata	*the female cat*
el león	*the lion*	la leona	*the lioness*
el manzano	*the apple tree*	la manzana	*the apple*
el cerezo	*the cherry tree*	la cereza	*the cherry*

Spanish nouns are not morphologically marked for gender:

1. In some cases the feminine counterpart of certain animate masculine nouns is an entirely different form.

el hombre	*the man*	la mujer	*the woman*
el padre	*the father*	la madre	*the mother*
el yerno	*the son-in-law*	la nuera	*the daughter-in-law*
el toro	*the bull*	la vaca	*the cow*

el caballo	*the horse*	la yegua	*the mare*
el rey	*the king*	la reina	*the queen*
el czar	*the czar*	la czarina	*the czarina*
el poeta	*the poet*	la poetisa	*the poetess*
el peral	*the pear tree*	la pera	*the pear*
el jabalí	*the wild boar*	la jabalina	*the javaline*

2. A few nouns which have grammatical gender and are modified accordingly may refer to either masculine or feminine subjects.

Su hermano es una buena persona.	*Her brother is a good person.*
Su hermana . . .	*Her sister . . .*
Este chico tiene un tipo espléndido.	*This boy is a splendid type.*
Esta chica . . .	*This girl . . .*
Su marido es un ángel.	*Her husband is an angel.*
Su mujer . . .	*His wife . . .*
Este señor es la víctima.	*This man is the victim.*
Esta señora . . .	*This woman . . .*

With certain nouns referring to animals the words **macho** (= *male*) and **hembra** (= *female*) are sometimes used to indicate the gender: **la pantera macho** = *the male panther.*

3. A few nouns regardless of their form may take either grammatical gender.

el artista or la artista	*the (male) artist or the (female) artist*
. . . periodista	*the journalist*
. . . pianista	*the pianist*
. . . estudiante	*the student*
. . . cantante	*the singer*
. . . mártir	*the martyr*
. . . testigo	*the witness*
. . . reo	*the prisoner*
. . . modelo	*the model*
. . . consorte	*the spouse (consort)*
. . . cónyuge	*the spouse*

4. A few nouns which have the same form vary their meaning according to differences in gender.

el Papa	*the Pope*	la papa	*potato*
el clave	*clef, musical instrument*	la clave	*code*
el capital	*capital, money*	la capital	*capital city*
el corte	*cut, edge*	la corte	*court*
el frente	*front, battlefront*	la frente	*forehead*
el parte	*judicial announcement, dispatch*	la parte	*a portion*

el pendiente	*earrings*	la pendiente	*hill*
el dote	*talent*	la dote	*dowry, endowment*
el guía	*guide*	la guía	*guidebook or a female guide*
el orden	*order, in the sense of arrangement, class, category, formation, peace, quiet*	la orden	*order, in the sense of command; fraternal, political, religious, etc. organization*
el moral	*mulberry tree*	la moral	*morals*
el Génesis	*book of the Bible*	la génesis	*origin*
el doblez	*fold, crease*	la doblez	*duplicity, double dealing*
el delta	*of a river*	la delta	*Greek letter*
el cura	*priest*	la cura	*cure*
el radio	*radio set*	la radio	*network*
el cometa	*comet*	la cometa	*kite*
el calavera	*libertine, a reckless fellow*	la calavera	*skull*

DETERMINING GENDER

A noun's gender is almost as important as its meaning since in every case we are dealing with different words, and not just variations of the same word. Although there are no morphological markers or definite semantic categories that determine a noun's gender, some useful guidelines do exist.

According to their morphological shape, and as a general rule:

1. Nouns ending in **-o** are usually masculine: **el libro, el vestido, el edificio**; but with many exceptions: **la mano, la dínamo, la foto, la soprano**, which are feminine.

2. Nouns ending in **-a** are usually feminine: **la casa, la carta, la mesa**, etc.; but with many exceptions: **el día, el mapa, el tema, el problema, el planeta**, and many other words of Greek origin ending in **-a** which are masculine.

3. Other common endings for feminine nouns are **-dad, -ción, -xión, -sión, -sis**:

la cantidad	la caridad	la amabilidad
la canción	la nación	la constitución
la conexión	la reflexión	la genuflexión
la excursión	la ocasión	la oclusión
la tesis	la crisis	la dosis

BUT: el análisis, el énfasis

According to their meaning, and as a general rule, the following are of the masculine gender:

1. Nouns which refer to males' occupations: **el orfebre, el pintor, el albañil, el ingeniero, el químico, el presidente.** In modern Spanish when the same occupation applies to a woman, either another noun may be created (**la ingeniera, la presidenta, la pintora**) or the definite article indicates the gender: **la ingeniero, la presidente, la químico.**

2. The proper names of rivers, seas, lakes, mountains, and volcanoes:

    el Orinoco, el Amazonas, el Mississippi
    el Titicaca
    el Atlántico, el Pacífico, el Caribe
    el Vesubio
    el Monte Blanco, el Aconcagua

3. Cardinal numbers (**el dos, el tres**); the cardinal points (**el norte, el sur, el este, el oeste**); the days of the week (**el lunes, el martes,** etc.); the months of the year (**el lluvioso abril**); the musical notes (**el do, el mi,** etc.).

4. The names of most fruit trees: **el naranjo** (*orange tree*); **el duraznero** (*peach tree*); **el manzano** (*apple tree*); etc.

Nouns which denote the following meanings are usually feminine:

1. Nouns which refer to females' occupations: **la modelo, la enfermera, la modista,** etc. In modern Spanish when the same occupation applies to males, either a new noun is created (**el enfermero, el modisto**) or the masculine form of the definite article indicates the gender: **el modelo.**

2. The names of some countries, cities, and towns ending in **-a**: **la Roma antigua, la Argentina revolucionaria, la Lima colonial.**

3. The names of the alphabet letters: **la efe, la ene, la ese,** etc.

Number: Plural and Singular Nouns

In contrast with the gender category Spanish nouns are with few exceptions marked for number. Thus Spanish nouns, as English nouns, are either singular or plural. In Spanish, however, noun modifiers must agree not only in gender but also in number with the noun. The plural form of nouns is obtained by adding either **-s** or **-es** to the singular form according to the following rules:

1. **-s** is added to nouns ending in unstressed vowels, to diphthongs, and to nouns with more than two syllables which end in stressed /é/:

casa	casas	*houses*
calle	calles	*streets*
metrópoli	metrópolis	*metropolis*
tribu	tribus	*tribes*

pie	pies	*feet*
café	cafés	*coffee*
corsé	corsés	*corsets*
canapé	canapés	*canapes, daybeds*

2. **-es** is added to:

a. Nouns ending in stressed vowels /á/, /í/, /ó/, /ú/:

sofá	sofáes	*sofas*
jabalí	jabalíes	*wild boars*
dominó	dominóes	*dominoes*
canesú	canesús	*guimpes*

Some exceptions to this rule are

papá	papás	*fathers*
mamá	mamás	*mothers*

In many cases, particularly with nouns ending in stressed /í/ or /ú/, there is no definite rule governing the selection of **-es** or **-s** to form the plural. Normally, both forms are accepted.

maravedí	maravedíes	OR	maravedís	*Arabic coin*
alelí	alelíes		alelís	*gilly flowers*
rubí	rubíes		rubís	*rubies*
bisturí	bisturíes		bisturís	*bistouries*
tabú	tabúes		tabús	*taboos*
menú	menúes		menús	*menues*
sofá	sofáes		sofás	*sofas*
dominó	dominóes		dominós	*dominoes*

b. Nouns ending in /y/:

buey	bueyes	*steers*
ley	leyes	*laws*
rey	reyes	*kings*
carey	careyes	*tortoise shells*

c. Nouns ending in a consonant other than /s/, except one syllable words ending in /s/:

papel	papeles	*papers*
león	leones	*lions*
flor	flores	*flowers*
verdad	verdades	*truths*
mes	meses	*months*
res	reses	*cattle heads*
Dios	dioses	*gods*

Those words ending in **z** change their spelling to **c** in the plural.

raíz	raíces	*roots*
perdíz	perdices	*partridges*
vez	veces	*times*

NOUNS INVARIABLE FOR NUMBER

Some nouns do not have a special form for the plural. The same form is used for both singular and plural and the distinction is made by the plural form of the article. The following are invariable for number:

1. Nouns with final unstressed syllable ending in /s/:

dosis	oásis	fénix
crisis	brindis	tórax
análisis	atlas	ántrax
paréntesis	tesis	etc.

Included here are the days of the week: **lunes, martes, miércoles, jueves, viernes.** Most of these are loan words of Greek origin.

2. Most family names, particularly those ending in /z/ or /s/:

los Fernández	los García	los Bazán
los Díaz	los Calvo	los Cortés
los Garcés	los Espinosa	los Pascual

THE PLURAL OF LOAN WORDS

Modern Spanish has incorporated many foreign words which end in a consonant. To form the plural of these loan words, native speakers do not always follow the rule of adding **–es** but choose some other alternatives:

1. Drop the final consonant and add either **–s** or **–es** accordingly:

cabaret	cabaré	cabarés
chalet	chalé	chalés
hipérbaton	hipérbato	hipérbatos
lord	lor	lores

2. Alternate both plural endings **–s** and **–es** (in spite of the fact that with **–s** unusual final consonant clusters are formed):

cóctel	cóctels OR	cocteles
suéter	suéters	suéteres
gol	gols	goles
film	films	filmes

3. Add **-s** in spite of the creation of unusual final consonant clusters:

club	clubs
coñac	coñacs
frac	fracs
kindergarten	kindergartens

THE PLURAL OF COMPOUND NOUNS

Compound nouns are nouns which consist of two words linked together in a single one, or two words in apposition which function as a single lexical unit. The plural of these compounds is formed as follows:

1. Compound words formed by a verb + plural noun are invariable; the number is determined by the accompanying article.

el apagavelas	los apagavelas	*snuffers*
el tocadiscos	etc.	*record player*
el sacapuntas		*pencil sharpener*
el sacacorchos		*corkscrew*
el portamonedas		*pocketbook*
el paraguas		*umbrella*
el portaplumas		*penholder*
el abrelatas		*can opener*

2. Most other compound nouns form their plural by adding **-s** or **-es** accordingly, at the very end.

NOUN + ADJECTIVE:	aguardiente	aguardientes	*spirituous liquor*
	aguamala	aguamalas	*jelly fish*
ADJECTIVE + NOUN:	altavoz	altavoces	*loudspeaker*
	bajorelieve	bajorelieves	*bas-relief*
	minifalda	minifaldas	*miniskirt*
NOUN + NOUN:	ferrocarril	ferrocarriles	*railroad*
	bocacalle	bocacalles	*street intersection*
	puntapié	puntapiés	*kickout*
	compraventa	compraventas	*buying and selling transaction*
PREPOSITION + NOUN:	traspié	traspiés	*stumble, slip*
	sinrazón	sinrazones	*injustice*
VERB + VERB:	vaivén	vaivenes	*unsteadiness, inconstancy*
	correveidile	correveidiles	*go-between, mischiefmaker*
	subibaja	subibajas	*seesaw*

3. The following compounds add the plural marker at the end of the first element:

NOUN+PRONOUN:	hijodalgo	hijosdalgo	*noble, illustrious*
PRONOUN+VERB:	cualquiera	cualesquiera	*just anyone*
	quienquiera	quienesquiera	*whoever*

4. Compounds which are formed by two nouns in apposition form their plural by adding the number marker to the first element.

día perro	días perro	*a terrible day*
hombre rana	hombres rana	*frog man*
noticia bomba	noticias bomba	*bombshell news*
coche cama	coches cama	*sleeper*
casa cuna	casas cuna	*day-care center*

5. Compounds which are formed by a noun + adjective form their plural by adding the number marker to both elements.

platillo volador	platillos voladores	*flying saucer*
nave espacial	naves espaciales	*space ship*
reactor atómico	reactores atómicos	*atomic reactor*

Mass Nouns and Count Nouns

An important classification of nouns is that of mass and count nouns. Mass nouns express a material substance or an abstract concept considered as a whole rather than in its parts. For this reason, mass nouns normally appear in the singular form, but imply in meaning a mass quantity.

la leche	*milk*
la arena	*sand*
el azúcar	*sugar*
la paciencia	*patience*
la honestidad	*honesty*
la justicia	*justice*

Whenever it is possible to indicate parts of this whole, a quantitative expression precedes the singular form.

un vaso de leche	*a glass of milk*
un balde de arena	*a bucket of sand*
dos libras de azúcar	*two pounds of sugar*
un poco de paciencia	*a little bit of patience*

Count nouns, on the other hand, may express the individual parts of a class in their plural form. They occur with numerals to express a specific number of individual units, or they may occur with articles or indefinite quantifiers to express plurality without being specific in the number.

dos plumas	*two pens*
cinco hombres	*five men*
las libertades humanas	*the human liberties*
los pueblos del orbe	*the peoples of the world*
algunas joyas	*some jewels*

This classification of mass versus count nouns is not as critical in Spanish as it is in English, since in Spanish a great deal more crossing between the two classes exists. In other words, most nouns in Spanish may occur in either a count or mass construction, so the distinction between the two categories is not as clear cut as it is in English.

MASS NOUNS	COUNT NOUNS
El avión cruza por el aire. *The plane cruises through the air.*	El avión cruza por los aires.
No resisto el frío invernal. *I cannot stand the winter's chilliness.*	No resisto los fríos invernales.
Prefiero el calor de verano. *I prefer the summer heat.*	Prefiero los calores de verano.
El Brazil produce café. *Brazil produces coffee.*	Nos tomamos dos cafés. *We drank two coffees.*

But since there are some Spanish nouns that can only occur in mass constructions the distinction is justified.

la justicia	*justice*
la gratitud	*gratitude*
la prudencia	*prudence*
el oro	*gold*
la plata	*silver*
el petróleo	*petroleum*

CLASSIFICATION OF MASS VS. COUNT NOUNS

One useful way of classifying mass and count nouns in Spanish is by examining whether the singular or plural form follows the quantitative expression. If the singular form occurs, the noun is classified as a mass noun; if the plural form occurs, it is classified as a count noun.

MASS NOUNS	COUNT NOUNS
una lata de arena *a can of sand*	una lata de frijoles *a can of beans*

una libra de arroz	una libra de uvas
a pound of rice	*a pound of grapes*
una taza de té	una taza de nueces
a cup of tea	*a cup of nuts*
una fuente de sopa	una fuente de frutas
a bowl of soup	*a bowl of fruits*

In dealing with mass and count nouns the main difficulty between Spanish and English consists in the differences of classification of nouns which are equivalent in meaning.

1. A few nouns which in Spanish are classified as count nouns function in English as mass nouns only.

COUNT NOUNS		MASS NOUNS	
Singular	*Plural*	*With quantitative expression*	
una noticia	noticias	a piece of news	*news*
un mueble	muebles	a piece of furniture	*furniture*
un helado	helados	a dish of ice cream	*ice cream*
un dulce	dulces	a piece of candy	*candy*
un consejo	consejos	a bit of advice	*advice*
una tostada	tostadas	a piece of toast	*toast*
una tontería	tonterías	a bit of nonsense	*nonsense*
un chisme	chismes	a bit of gossip	*gossip*
una cana	canas	a strand of white hair	*white hair*

These Spanish count nouns occur in the singular and can be counted in the plural with a numeral: **una noticia, dos noticias, tres muebles, cinco canas,** etc. In English, as mass nouns they always occur in the singular and are counted with a quantitative expression: *one piece of news, two pieces of news, three pieces of furniture, five strands of white hair,* etc.

2. Many Spanish mass nouns can easily be used in count constructions also, whereas their English equivalents occur in mass constructions only.

MASS NOUNS	COUNT NOUNS	ENGLISH MASS NOUNS
dos pedazos de gaza	dos gazas	*two pieces of gauze*
dos cabezas de ajo	dos ajos	*two cloves of garlic*
dos motas de algodón	dos algodones	*two wads of cotton*
dos cabezas de repollo	dos repollos	*two heads of cabbage*
dos panes de jabón	dos jabones	*two bars of soap*
dos trozos de madera	dos maderas	*two pieces of wood*

The other important difference between the two languages is the use of the article with mass and count nouns when they are used as subjects and objects.

1. Spanish mass nouns as subjects occur with the definite article.

La leche es la mejor fuente de calcio.   *Milk is the best source for calcium.*
La libertad es un derecho humano.   *Freedom is a human right.*

2. The occurrence of the definite article with a mass noun as object has a specifying function in Spanish.

El niño quiere la leche.   *The child wants the milk.*
Los esclavos quieren la libertad.   *The slaves want freedom.*

But if an indefinite quantity is meant, the article is omitted.

El niño quiere leche.   *The child wants milk.*

3. A Spanish noun as object when preceded by the indefinite article functions as a count noun.

Ricardo consiguió un trabajo en   *Ricardo found a job in New York.*
   Nueva York.
¿Tienes una pluma?   *Do you have a pen?*

But if the article is omitted it functions as a mass noun.

¿Conseguiste trabajo?   *Did you find a job?*
¿Tienes pluma?   *Do you have a pen?*

Noun Functions

Nouns may function (1) as subjects; (2) as predicate nominatives after **ser**; (3) as verbal objects (direct and indirect); (4) as adverbials; (5) as adjectival complements; and (6) as nominal modifiers.

NOUNS AS SUBJECTS: SUBJECT-VERB AGREEMENT

The function of subject is essentially a nominal one. Only nouns and words or clauses that can function as nouns occur as subjects. In Spanish the subject determines the agreement of its verb, which is marked for person (first, second, and third) and number (singular and plural).

El profesor con sus alumnos harán   *The professor with his students will*
   una excursión.   *take a trip.*
Tú y el profesor saldrán temprano.   *You and the professor will leave early.*
El resto de la clase y yo seguiremos   *The rest of the class and I will follow*
   después.[1]   *later.*

---

[1] If a first person pronoun is part of a compound subject, the verb takes the agreement in the first person plural.

There are, however, some special cases of subject-verb agreement:

1. Subjects with singular nouns indicating "quantity," such as the following, may take a verb in the plural:

multitud	*multitude*
infinidad	*infinity*
caterva	*a throng*
montón	*a bunch of*
millar	*a thousand*
centenar	*a hundred, hundreds of*
muchedumbre	*a crowd*
un tercio	*a third of*
una parte	*a part of*
una porción	*a portion of*
una cantidad	*a quantity*
el resto	*the rest*

Una multitud corrían desesperados.	*A multitude of people was running desperately.*
Un montón invadieron las oficinas.	*A bunch of people invaded the offices.*
Una cantidad enorme se perdieron.	*An enormous amount got lost.*

This type of agreement is more frequent when the noun expressing quantity is followed by **de** + plural noun.

Una porción de amigos suyos lo defienden.	*A portion of his friends defend him.*
Un millar de pájaros emigran cada año.	*A thousand birds emigrate each year.*
Infinidad de personas quedaron sin trabajo.	*A large number of persons found themselves without a job.*

It is also possible with collective nouns, **gente**, **pueblo** (= *people*), **tropa** (= *troop*), **regimento** (= *regiment*), etc., especially with a second verb removed from the subject:

La gente se reunió en la plaza, pero al comenzar a llover se dispersaron.	*The people gathered in the park, but as it began to rain, they scattered away.*

This type of subject-verb agreement is governed by the meaning of these quantitative nouns which imply plurality. A purely grammatical agreement calls for a verb in the singular in all of these cases.

2. Subjects with two or more singular nouns expressing related ideas that may constitute a single unit may take a verb in the singular:

Su inteligencia, capacidad y persistencia contribuyó a su éxito profesional.	*His intelligence, capabilities, and persistence contributed to his professional success.*

El hambre, las enfermedades y la
pobreza cundían por todo el país
después de la guerra.

*Hunger, illness, and poverty were all
over the country after the war.*

3. Subjects connected by **ni** which imply a single idea may take a singular verb:

Ni el alojamiento ni la comida le
gusta.

He doesn't like the room or board.

This type of subject-type agreement is also governed by the meaning of these
coordinated noun constructions which imply singularity. A purely grammatical
agreement calls for the verb in the plural.

NOUNS AS PREDICATE NOMINATIVES

Nouns as predicate nominatives occur only in phrases linked by the copulative
verb **ser**. The agreement for number between subject and predicate is observed as
in English. The agreement for gender is observed where nouns of different genders
exist or through noun modifiers (articles, demonstratives, etc.).

Sus amigos son **personas** amables.
Sus amigas son **personas** amables.

His friends are kind people.

El niño es mi **hijo.**
La niña es mi **hija.**

The child is my son.
The child is my daughter.

Mi hermano es **profesor.**
Mi hermana es **profesora.**

My brother is a professor.
My sister is a professor.

Este hombre es **periodista.**
Esta mujer es **periodista.**

This man is a journalist.
This woman is a journalist.

NOUNS AS VERB OBJECTS

A very important function of nouns is that of verbal objects, direct and indirect.
In fact, the object of a verb is always a nominal. Only nouns and words or clauses
that function as nouns occur as verbal objects.

Subject	Verb	Direct Object	Indirect Object
El gobierno *The government*	deportó *deported*	a los **criminales.** *the criminals.*	
(El) *He*	Aprendió *learned*	muchas **cosas** útiles. *many useful things.*	
El comité *The committee*	envió *sent*	la **recomendación** *the recommendation*	al **Senado.** *to the Senate.*

Nouns as verbal objects function almost the same way in both languages, excepting differences in word order, the use of the personal **a** to introduce certain classes of direct object nouns, and the use of object pronouns.[1]

NOUNS AS ADVERBIAL COMPLEMENTS

Nouns introduced by prepositions may function as adverbials. Adverbials describe the general circumstances under which the action is carried out. They may refer to:

PLACE: (Source and destination)

Lo llamaremos **desde mi CASA**.
We will call him from my HOUSE.

Llegaremos **hasta la PLAZA**.
We will get up to the PARK.

TIME: Conocí a mi novia **hacia fines de PRIMAVERA**.
I met my girl friend towards the end of SPRING.

MANNER: Escribiré la carta **con gran PLACER**.
I will write the letter with great PLEASURE.

MEANS: Viajaremos a los Estados Unidos **por AVION**.
We will travel to the United States by AIRPLANE.

AGENT: Abrimos la puerta **con un CUCHILLO**.
We opened the door with a KNIFE.

etc.

NOUNS AS ADJECTIVAL COMPLEMENTS

Nouns introduced by prepositions may also occur as adjectival complements. The main function of noun phrases in this context is to restrict the adjective's meaning. In a sentence such as **Las vitaminas son buenas** = *Vitamins are good*, the adjective **buenas** modifies **vitaminas** in a general sense. However, in an expanded version of the same sentence such as **Las vitaminas son buenas para la salud** = *Vitamins are good for your health*, the meaning of the adjective **buenas** has been restricted by the noun **salud**. Thus:

Esta muchacha es muy amable.
This girl is very kind.

Esta muchacha es muy amable con
  los niños.
This girl is very kind with children.

---

[1] See Chapter 3, Personal Pronouns, page 22.

Es una persona muy capaz.
She is a very capable person.

Es una persona muy capaz para el
trabajo y el estudio.
She is a very capable person for
work and study.

The adjective always agrees with the main noun, not with the noun serving as adjectival complement.

Es una mujer delgada.
She is a slender woman.

Es una mujer delgada de cuerpo.
She is a woman with a slender body.

However, in a prepositional phrase with **de** a change of word order allows a different agreement.

Es una mujer de cuerpo delgado.
(= Es una mujer delgada de cuerpo.)

In spite of the differences in agreement, the restrictive function of the noun as adjectival complement remains unchanged.

Es un hombre gordo.

He is a fat man.

Es un hombre gordo de cara.
(= Es un hombre de cara gorda)
He is a man with a fat face.

The infinitive may also function as an adjectival complement.[1]

Raúl está cansado.
Raul is tired.

Raúl está cansado de trabajar y
luchar.
Raul is tired of working and fighting.

NOUNS AS NOMINAL MODIFIERS

As nominal modifiers nouns occur either in appositional or prepositional phrases. An appositional phrase consists of two nouns in a juxtaposed sequence, the second noun complementing the first one either by reaffirming its contents or by further modifying it. Both Spanish and English have similar patterns of apposition.

Alejandro El Magno . . .
Juan Carlos, Rey de España . . .
los montes Himalayas . . .
Erasmo, el célebre humanista
europeo, nació en Rotterdam.
Mi hermano, ingeniero químico, vive
en Panamá.

Alexander the Great . . .
Juan Carlos, King of Spain . . .
the Himalaya mountains . . .
Erasmus, the famous European humanist,
was born in Rotterdam.
My brother, a chemical engineer, lives
in Panama.

---

[1] For a complete discussion of the infinitive as a verbal noun see Chapter 7.

There are, however, some differences between the two languages with regards to the uses of the definite article and word-order restrictions:

1. If the apposition is merely explanatory, Spanish omits the article, while English uses it:[1]

Washington, capital de los Estados Unidos, es una ciudad preciosa.	*Washington, the capital of the United States, is a gorgeous city.*

2. If a noun is in apposition with a preceding plural pronoun, Spanish uses the definite article, while English omits it:

Ustedes los católicos . . .	*You Catholics . . .*
Para nosotras la mujeres . . .	*For us women . . .*
Nosotros los extranjeros . . .	*We foreigners . . .*

3. In the enumeration with nouns, the numeral follows the noun in Spanish, while in English it precedes it:

El caballo número ocho ganó la carrera.	*Horse number eight won the race.*

4. The titles **señor**, **señora**, keep their position before proper names even if they mean *gentleman, lady*:

ese señor Fernández (= ese caballero Fernández)	*that Fernandez gentleman*
la señora Ramírez (= la dama Ramírez)	*that Ramirez lady*

In English, as opposed to Spanish, a noun can be directly modified by another noun without a preposition. In Spanish, excepting appositional phrases and some set expressions, nouns as modifiers must always be introduced by prepositions.

un banquete de estado	*a state dinner*
un vuelo sin escalas	*a non-stop flight*
un libro de cuentos	*a story book*
un viaje en tren	*a train trip*
una travesía por mar	*a sea cruise*
una manifestación de estudiantes	*a student demonstration*
una copa para vino	*a wine glass*

The usage of prepositional phrases as nominal modifiers is, of course, also common in English:[2]

a school for the blind	una escuela para ciegos
a room with private bath	una habitación con baño privado

---

[1] See The Definite Article in Appositional Constructions, page 282.

[2] In some cases the prepositional phrase is required to solve ambiguities: *a beer glass* = **un vaso para cerveza** vs. *a glass of beer* = **un vaso de cerveza**. In Spanish, the preposition used establishes the contrast.

a tree without leaves	un árbol sin hojas
a box of cookies	una caja de galletas
the bottom of the sea	el fondo del mar

In many instances, a modifying noun in Spanish has a corresponding adjective. In such cases the usage of the adjective is preferred to the prepositional phrase.

milk products	productos lácteos (= de leche)
meat industries	industrias cárnicas (= de carne)
a doctor's appointment	una cita médica (= con el médico)
state employee	empleado estatal (= del estado)
government decisions	decisiones gubernamentales (= del gobierno)

A few nominal prepositional phrases have become single lexical units.

punto de vista	point of view
cabello de ángel	angel's hair
juego de manos	sleight of hand

Nominalization

Nominalization is the syntactical process by which a part of speech or phrase takes up any of the functions normally fulfilled by nouns. Of all word classes adjectives are probably the most frequently nominalized words. Nominalization of descriptive adjectives in Spanish is achieved by noun deletion or by the addition of the neuter form **lo** before the adjective's singular form.

NOMINALIZATION OF DESCRIPTIVE ADJECTIVES BY NOUN DELETION

This is the most common type of adjective nominalization. By deleting the noun it modifies, an adjective will take up a nominal function. In English this type of nominalization usually requires the addition of one(s).

Los hombres pusilánimes no tienen ambición.
Pusillanimous men have no ambition.

Los pusilánimes no tienen ambición.
The pusillanimous have no ambition.

Esa chica rubia es mi hermana.
That blonde girl is my sister.

Esa rubia es mi hermana.
That blonde one is my sister.

¿Cuáles zapatos negros quieres?
Which black shoes do you want?

¿Cuáles negros quieres?
Which black ones do you want?

He comprado algunos productos importados.
I have bought some imported products.

He comprado algunos importados.
I have bought some imported ones.

Se casó con una chica alemana.
He married a German girl.

Se casó con una alemana.
He married a German.

No hay ningún buen médico en la
ciudad.
There is not a good doctor in the city.

No hay ninguno bueno en la ciudad.
There is not a good one in the city.

The noun determiners (articles, demonstratives, indefinites, the interrogative **¿cuál?**) are kept in their original form, thus acting as nominalizing agents. In fact, the definite and indefinite articles have an important nominalizing function when they immediately precede an adjective.[1]

Hizo el ridículo.
He made a fool of himself.

¡Es de un cursi!
It is so pretentious!

¡Andaba de un contento!
He was so happy.

un español . . .
a Spaniard . . .

el ambicioso . . .
the ambitious . . .

el absurdo . . .
the absurd . . .

The nominal function of these forms is fully appreciated when they occur with a modifier.

Es de un cursi increíble.
It is incredibly flashy.

Conocí a un español protestante.
I met a protestant Spaniard.

An adjectival modifying clause may also be nominalized by noun deletion.

Los heridos que enviaron al hospital
estaban muy graves.
*The wounded that were sent to the
hospital were in very critical condition.*

Los que enviaron al hospital estaban
muy graves.
*The ones sent to the hospital were in
very critical condition.*

La mujer que conocí anoche es
sumamente interesante.
*The woman I met last night is
extremely interesting.*

La que conocí anoche es sumamente
interesante.
*The one I met last night is extremely
interesting.*

Note that by deleting the noun **mujer**, the clause **que conocí anoche** is no longer an adjectival modifying clause but a nominal clause which functions as the entire subject rather than just a noun modifier.

Nominalization by noun deletion is widely used in both Spanish and English to avoid repetition of the same noun.

El vestido amarillo y el verde . . .
The yellow dress and the green one . . .

Un muchacho americano y uno
francés . . .
An American boy and a French one . . .

---

[1] This explains why there are so many forms which can be either nouns or adjectives: **El género humano es débil = Los humanos son débiles; El hombre conservador (radical, católico, español, blanco, etc.) = El conservador, el radical, etc.; Son personas mayores y merecen respeto = Los mayores merecen respeto,** etc.

Esta casa nueva y esa vieja . . .	*This new house and that old one . . .*
La ropa de los niños y la de ustedes . . .	*The children's clothes and yours . . .*
El hombre que vino ayer y el que vino esta mañana . . .	*The man who came yesterday and the one who came this morning . . .*

NOMINALIZATION OF DESCRIPTIVE ADJECTIVES WITH *LO*[1]

A descriptive adjective in its masculine singular form preceded by the neuter form **lo** is nominalized and functions as an abstract noun. Nominalizations with **lo** correspond in English to a variety of different constructions: *the* + noun; *what . . .*; *the* + abstract nouns ending in *-ness, -ity*; *the . . . thing (part, side, aspect,* etc.) *about.* There is no exact equivalent for the Spanish neuter form **lo**.

No hay que menospreciar lo sublime. (= las cosas sublimes)	*One should not underestimate the sublime.* (= *the things sublime*)
En lo profundo de su corazón sabía que le mentía. (= la parte profunda de su corazón)	*At the bottom of her heart she knew he was lying.*
Lo importado es siempre más caro. (= las cosas importadas)	*Imported things are always more expensive.*
Prefiere siempre lo caro. (= las cosas caras)	*He always prefers what is expensive.* (= *the expensive things*)
Lo bueno de esta universidad es la biblioteca. (= la cosa buena de)	*What is good about this university is the library.* (= *the good thing*)
Lo terrible de las ciudades grandes es el problema del crimen. (= la parte terrible de)	*The terrible thing (aspect, etc.) about large cities is the crime problem.*

Nominalized adjectives with **lo** correspond in many instances to abstract nouns already existing in the language.

En lo profundo de su corazón . . . En la profundidad . . .	Lo difícil del problema consiste en . . . La dificultad del problema . . .
Lo útil de esta explicación . . . La utilidad . . .	Lo inmoral de su conducta . . . La inmoralidad . . .
Lo ridículo de su conducta . . . La ridiculez . . .	Lo estúpido de esa decisión . . . La estupidez . . .

[1] See Chapter 16, The Neuter **lo**, page 294; Chapter 7, The Past Participle: Nominal Usage, page 109.

NOMINALIZATION OF OTHER WORD CLASSES

Other word classes may also serve a nominal function.

1. The infinitive form of a verb when not used with a true auxiliary always functions as a noun:[1]

(El) nadar es buen ejercicio.	*Swimming is good exercise.*
Comer bien y dormir mucho es esencial para la salud.	*To eat well and sleep a lot is essential to one's health.*
Ese perenne batallar suyo es admirable.	*That constant striving of hers is admirable.*

2. Adverbs preceded by the neuter form **lo**:

Me preocupa que estudie poco. *It worries me that he studies so little.*	Lo poco que estudia me preocupa. *The little he studies worries me.* (= *It worries me how little he studies.*)
Me sorprende que piense lento. *It surprises me that he should think (so) slowly.*	Lo lento que piensa me sorprende. *His slow thinking surprises me.* (= *It surprises me how slowly he thinks.*)
No puede hacer menos cosa que felicitarte. *He can do nothing but congratulate you.*	Lo menos que puede hacer es felicitarte. *The least he can do is to congratulate you.*

3. A few limiting adjectives may nominalize with **lo**:

   a. the masculine stressed form of the possessives and its alternate construction with **de**:

Dale lo mío ...	*Give him what is mine ...*
lo tuyo ...	*yours ...*
lo suyo ...	*hers ...*
lo de ustedes ...	*yours ...*
lo de ellos ...	*theirs ...*
etc.	*etc.*

   b. the masculine form of the ordinal numbers:

Lo primero que dijo ...	*The first thing he said ...*
Lo tercero que pidió ...	*The third thing he asked ...*

   c. the masculine singular form of the indefinites **otro, demás, suficiente**:

Dame lo otro.	*Give me the other thing.*
Dame lo demás.	*Give me the rest.*
Dame lo suficiente.	*Give me enough.*

---

[1] See Chapter 7, The Infinitive.

4. In many cases, the nominalized word or phrase has produced a permanent noun:

Hay que pensar en el **mañana**.	*One must think of tomorrow.*
Se encontró en la **nada**.	*He found himself in nothingness.*
Es un **cualquiera**.	*He is a non-entity.*
Esa **doña nadie** . . .	*That nobody . . .*
Tiene un **no se que**.	*She has that little something.*
No le hagas caso al **que dirán**.	*Don't pay attention to wagging tongues.*
Andaba en un **ir y venir**.	*She was in a tizzy.*

This is especially true with many infinitives and past participles.[1]

El **poder** trastorna a los hombres.	*Power makes man lose his head.*
Este es un **hecho** inevitable.	*This is an inevitable fact.*

NOMINALIZATION OF LIMITING ADJECTIVES: PRONOMINALIZATION

Limiting adjectives are also nominalized by deleting the noun, but in this case the resulting form is a pronoun rather than a noun. This process is called pronominalization. Thus, limiting adjectives can function either as noun modifiers or as noun substitutes (i. e., pronominal possessives, demonstratives, indefinites, etc.). As noun substitutes, they may occur as subject and/or verb objects.[2]

Possessives

Te vendo mi auto.	Te vendo el auto mío.	Te vendo el mío.
I sell you my car.		*I sell you mine.*
Necesito su pluma.	Necesito la pluma suya.	Necesito la suya.
I need her pen.	de ella.	de ella.
		I need hers.

Only the stressed possessives can be pronominalized, so the first step is substitution of the unstressed form for the stressed form and then deletion of the noun. A prepositional phrase with **de** is used in case of ambiguity with a third person possessor: **de él, de ellos, de ella (s), de usted (es)**.

Demonstratives

Recibí estas cartas.	Recibí éstas.
I received these letters.	*I received these ones.*

---

[1] See Permanently Nominalized Infinitives, page 99; Past Participle, Nominal Usage, page 109.
[2] See Pronominal Possessives, page 305; Pronominal Demonstratives, page 311; Chapter 20, for the pronominal function of numerals, indefinites and negatives; Chapter 9, for the pronominal function of interrogative words.

Mandaron aquel paquete.   Mandaron aquél.
They sent that package.   *They sent that one.*

Pronominal demonstratives carry a written accent mark.

Numerals

Préstame un dólar.   Préstame uno.
Lend me one dollar.   *Lend me one.*

Se encuentra en el primer piso.   Se encuentra en el primero.
It is on the first floor.   *It is on the first one.*

Es la segunda casa a la derecha.   Es la segunda a la derecha.
It is the second house on the right.   *It is the second one on the right.*

Pásame los tres primeros capítulos.   Pásame los tres primeros.
Pass me the first three chapters.   *Pass me the first three.*

The numerals **un**, **primer**, and **tercer** become **uno**, **primero**, and **tercero** respectively when pronominalized.

Indefinites

Vinieron algunas personas.   Vinieron algunas.
Some persons came.   *Some came.*

Mandarán a algún representante.   Mandarán a alguno.
They will send some representative.   *They will send someone.*

No mandaron a ningún   No mandaron a ninguno.
  representante.   *They didn't send any.*
They didn't send any representative.

The masculine singular **algún** and **ningún** have special pronominal forms: **alguno**, **ninguno**.

Compró muchos regalos.   Compró muchos.
He bought many gifts.   *He bought many.*

Compró las demás camisas.   Compró las demás.
He bought the rest of the shirts.   *He bought the rest.*

Other indefinites that are pronominalized in the same way are **poco**, **demasiado**, **otro**, **más**, **menos**, **bastante**, **suficiente**, **varios**, and **ambos**.

Todo pronominalizes as other indefinites but the definite article is also deleted, unless the noun is modified by an adjective or a clause.

Compró todos los vestidos.   Compró todos.
He bought all of the dresses.   *He bought all of them.*

Todas las casas se quemaron.
All of the houses burned down.

Todas se quemaron.
All burned down.

Todas las casas nuevas se quemaron.
All of the new houses burned down.

Todas las nuevas se quemaron.
All of the new ones burned down.

Todas las casas que construyó se
  quemaron.
*All of the houses that he built burned
  down.*

Todas las que construyó se quemaron.
All of the ones he built burned down.

Cualquier becomes **cualquiera** when used as a pronominal indefinite.

Dame cualquier ejemplo.
Give me just any example.

Dame cualquiera.
Give me just anyone.

Cada requires the addition of **uno/una** when used as a pronominal indefinite.

Cada hombre tiene su misión.
Each man has his own mission.

Cada uno tiene su misión.
Each one has his own mission.

Cada mujer tiene sus frivolidades.
Each woman has her own frivolities.

Cada una tiene sus frivolidades.
Each one has her own frivolities.

Interrogatives

¿Cuál chica te gusta más?
Which girl do you like the best?

¿Cuál te gusta más?
Which one do you like the best?

¿Cuánto dinero necesitas?
How much money do you need?

¿Cuánto necesitas?
How much do you need?

¿Qué cosa te dijo?
What thing did he tell you?

¿Qué te dijo?
What did he tell you?

14

ADJECTIVES

Function of Adjectives

The main function of adjectives is to describe and determine nouns in some way. Thus adjectives are classified into two main categories: descriptive and limiting adjectives. Descriptive adjectives describe something about the nature of the noun they modify, i.e., its color, size, shape, origin, condition, qualities, and so forth. Limiting adjectives modify a noun by relating it to its environment. They may state its possessor (possessives); indicate the noun's position with respect to time and space (demonstratives); indicate its quantity (numerals or indefinites); or may inquire for some information (interrogatives).

Descriptive adjectives may be modified by intensifiers to form adjective phrases: **es un estudiante muy bueno** ...; ... **bastante bueno**; ... **tan bueno**, etc. Their function is mainly lexical and as such they are an open class of words; i.e., together with nouns and verbs, descriptive adjectives make up the continuously increasing lexicon. Limiting adjectives, on the other hand, are not normally modified by intensifiers. Their function is mainly grammatical. As such they are a closed class of words; i. e., they are limited in number, usually come in sets or systems, and it is rather unlikely that new ones will be added.

The Morphology of Adjectives

GENDER AND NUMBER

Spanish adjectives must agree in form with the noun to which they refer. Since Spanish nouns have inherent gender, Spanish adjectives need to be inflected not only for number but also for gender.

Masculine		Feminine	
Singular	*Plural*	*Singular*	*Plural*
-o	**-s**	**-a**	**-s**
un chico guapo	guapos	una chica guapa	guapas
un chico bueno	buenos	una chica buena	buenas
BUT:			
un buen chico	buenos	una buena chica	buenas
ø	**-es**	**-a**	**-s**
un chico trabajador	trabajadores	una chica trabajadora	trabajadoras
llorón		llorona	
holgazán		holgazana	
bailarín		bailarina	
francés		francesa	
ø	**-es**	**ø**	**-es**
un chico feliz	felices	una chica feliz	felices
leal		leal	
familiar		familiar	
	-s		**-s**
un chico comunista	comunistas	una chica comunista	comunistas
cursi		cursi	
grande		grande	
BUT:			
un gran chico	grandes chicos	una gran chica	grandes

All Spanish adjectives have at least two forms: one singular and one plural. Most also show agreement according to their gender and thus have four endings: **-o, -a, -os, -as**. In the formation of the plural the same rules for nouns apply to adjectives: **-s** after vowel; **-es** after consonant ending forms. In the formation of gender not all adjectives follow the **-o/-a** opposition.

1. Many adjectives with a masculine form ending in **-dor, -ón, -án,** or **-ín** make

their feminine form by adding **-a**: **hablador/habladora** = *jabber mouth*; **comilón/comilona** = *big eater*; **holgazán/holgazana** = *lazy bum*; **bailarín/bailarina** = *dancer*.

Adjectives of nationality that end in a consonant also add **-a** to make the feminine: **francés** → **francesa**; **español** → **española**; **alemán** → **alemana**.

2. Many adjectives are invariable in form for both genders. They modify either a masculine or a feminine noun, such as:

a. certain adjectives ending in consonant:

un chico cortés	*a courteous boy*
una chica cortés	*a courteous girl*
un hombre feliz	*a happy man*
una mujer feliz	*a happy woman*
un amigo leal ⎱	
una amiga leal ⎰	*a loyal friend*

b. adjectives ending in **-e, -ista, -ita**:

un vestido verde	*a green dress*
una camisa verde	*a green shirt*
un criterio nacionalista	*a nationalistic criterion*
una decisión nacionalista	*a nationalistic decision*
un sistema capitalista	*a capitalistic system*
una economía capitalista	*a capitalistic economy*
un partido comunista	*a communist party*
una organización comunista	*a communist organization*
un sector cosmopolita	*a cosmopolitan sector*
una ciudad cosmopolita	*a cosmopolitan city*

c. adjectives ending in **-or** which have a comparative value such as **mejor, peor, mayor, menor, exterior, interior, inferior, superior, anterior, posterior, ulterior**:

el mejor alumno ⎱	
la mejor alumna ⎰	*the best student*
el hermano mayor	*the oldest brother*
la hermana mayor	*the oldest sister*

However, when these adjectives take suffixes they show gender inflection: **azul** → **azulito, azulita**; **verde** → **verdoso, verdosa**; **mejor** → **mejorcito, mejorcita**, etc.

SHORTENING OF ADJECTIVES (APOCOPE)

The following adjectives have a shortened form when occurring before certain nouns. Shortening is done by dropping the final **-o** or the final syllable.

1. bueno	buen		buen amigo
malo	mal		mal estudiante
primero	primer		primer día
tercero	tercer	Before masculine	tercer mes
postrero	postrer	singular nouns.	postrer año
uno	un		un hombre
alguno	algún		algún niño
ninguno	ningún		ningún libro
2. ciento	cien	Before all nouns and before **mil, millón.**	cien hombres cien mujeres cien mil casas cien millones
3. Santo	San	Before all masculine names, except **Tomás, Toribio, Domingo.**	San Angel San Carlos San Esteban San Pedro
4. grande	gran	Before singular nouns.	un gran señor una gran dama
cualquiera	cualquier		cualquier hombre cualquier mujer

Alguna and **ninguna** are frequently shortened to **algún, ningún** before nouns beginning with stressed **á** sound: **¿hay algún aula libre?** = *is there an empty classroom?*; **ningún alma viviente** = *no living soul.*

When **santo** means *holy* and is not used as the title *Saint* it is never shortened: **el Santo Padre** = *the Holy Father*; **el santo sacramento** = *the holy sacrament*; **el Santo Sepulcro** = *the Holy Sepulcher.*

The shortened form **cualquier** may alternate with **cualquiera** before feminine nouns: **cualquier mujer** or **cualquiera mujer.** The plurals **cualesquiera** and **cualesquier** are rarely used. Shortening also affects the possessive form.[1]

The addition of other adjectives does not normally affect shortening:

Vendrá algún buen día.　　　　　　　*She will come some fine day.*
Es el primer mal consejo que te da.　　*It is the first poor advice that he gives you.*

---

[1] See Chapter 17, Possessives, page 299.

Note that shortening does not occur when adjectives are linked through a conjunction.

Es un bueno y generoso padre.	*He is a good and loving father.*
Es malo e irresponsable empleado.	*He is a poor and irresponsible employee.*
Es grande y poderoso presidente.	*He is a great and powerful president.*

AGREEMENT

The general rule is that adjectives agree with nouns in gender and number. However, since it is possible that one adjective may modify more than one noun, the following rules of agreement must be observed:

1. When two nouns of the same gender are modified by one adjective, the adjective takes the plural of that gender:

Tiene camisas y corbatas finas.	*He has fine shirts and ties.*
Trajo testimonios y documentos nuevos.	*He brought forth new testimonies and documents.*

2. When two nouns of different gender are modified by one adjective, the adjective usually takes the masculine plural:

Compró casa y auto nuevos.	*He bought a new house and car.*

3. When two nouns are so closely related in meaning that the speaker considers them as one single unit of thought, the modifying adjective is then in the singular and takes the gender of the nearest noun:

Estudia lengua y literatura francesa.	*He studies French language and literature.*
No le interesaba ni la investigación ni el estudio intensivo.	*He did not care for intensive study or research.*
Hacía un calor y una humedad espantosa.	*The heat and humidity were horrible.*

If the nouns are considered as separate units, the adjective then takes the plural, and the gender according to 1 and 2:

Estudia lengua y literatura francesas.	*He studies French language and literature.*
Hacía una humedad y un calor espantosos.	*The humidity and heat were horrible.*

4. When the modifying adjective precedes the nouns, it is in the singular and takes the gender of the nearest noun:

Admiraba su tranquila disposición y talento.	*I admired his peaceful disposition and talent.*

5. With certain titles and forms of address the adjective agrees with the person addressed—not with the title:

Su Majestad (el Rey) está preocupado.	*His Majesty (the King) is concerned.*
Su Majestad (la Reina) está preocupada.	*Her Majesty (the Queen) is concerned.*
Su Santidad está enfermo.	*His Holyness is sick.*
Su Excelencia parece satisfecho.	*His Excellency seems satisfied.*

6. Adjectives modifying a collective noun may take the plural form if the adjective is not attached to the collective noun but to a prepositional phrase that qualifies it.

Una multitud de mujeres atemorizadas . . .	*A swarm of frightened women . . .*

BUT:

Una multitud atemorizada de mujeres . . .	

7. Adjectives that refer to a neuter form take the masculine singular:

Eso es malo.	*That's bad.*
Aquello es bonito.	*That's pretty.*

Position of Descriptive Adjectives

Spanish descriptive adjectives may modify a noun in two ways: in a predicate construction linked to the noun by a copula (predicate adjectives) or simply by being attached to the noun (attributive adjectives). Predicate adjectives present no major problem as a similar pattern of modification exists in English.[1]

La criada es magnífica.	*The maid is great.*
Es magnífica la criada.	*The maid is great.*
El niño está cansado.	*The boy is tired.*
Está cansado el niño.	*The boy is tired.*
El hombre me parece culto.	*The man seems knowledgeable to me.*
Me parece culto el hombre.	*The man seems knowledgeable to me.*

Attributive adjectives, however, are problematic insofar as in English they are placed before the noun, while in Spanish they have no fixed position: an adjective

---

[1] Note that Spanish may invert the word order and achieve different emphasis, while English uses stress. For a discussion of these constructions see **Ser** and **estar** with Adjectivals, page 253.

may either precede or follow the noun.[1] In many instances, this change of position may alter the meaning of a sentence in some way. The adjective may acquire a different connotation or a different emphasis may be placed either on the quality or on the thing described, although this may not always be the case. In English such adjectival modification may be expressed through different stress patterns.

Roughly speaking the contrast would be established as follows:

Spanish	*English*
Pre-nominal position	*Heavy stress on noun*

EMPHASIS ON THING DESCRIBED:

Es una linda **casa**.	*It is a beautiful* house.
Post-nominal position	*Heavy stress on adjective*

EMPHASIS ON THE QUALITY:

Es una casa **linda**.	*It is a* beautiful *house*.

However, in the sentences **¡Un día LINDO!** and **¡Un LINDO día!** with the stress on **lindo** in both cases, adjective position has not altered the meaning, nor has the emphasis shifted. Both correspond to: *A BEAUTIFUL day!* The emphasis has been placed on the quality through stress regardless of position. In **Es una linda CASA** = *It is a beautiful HOUSE*, although the emphasis is on the thing described as determined here by adjective position, the speaker may shift it to the quality without altering the position, but with a different stress pattern: **Es una LINDA casa**. Thus Spanish may use either word order or stress or both to convey different connotations, while English can only count on stress.

The position of descriptive adjectives in attributive constructions is then much more flexible. It cannot be predicted by a set of governing rules. The most that can be said is that there are certain considerations which may help to explain one usage or the other. But note that even these considerations may often be overridden by emphasis, stress, or stylistic and poetic effects. Ultimately, adjective position in Spanish is determined by the semantic contents of the two elements combined together: the noun (thing described) and the adjective (the quality it describes).

ADJECTIVES IN POST-NOMINAL POSITION

This is perhaps the most common position of adjectives in Spanish. Post-nominal adjectives usually restrict, clarify, or specify the meaning of the modified noun by adding an idea not expressed by the noun.

Leí un libro interesante.	*I read an interesting book.*
Vi una película sueca.	*I saw a Swedish film.*
Es el médico privado del presidente.	*He is the president's private doctor.*

[1] There is a class of adjectives in attributive constructions called *limiting adjectives* (demonstratives, possessives, numerals, indefinites), which normally precede the noun with very few exceptions. See Chapters 9, 17, and 20.

"To be interesting," "to be Swedish," "to be private," are not inherent character-istics included in the concepts expressed by "books," "film," "doctor," respectively. Instead, the quality seems to distinguish the noun from others of its kind.

Certain adjectives which express an inherent characteristic—those that merely describe and not specify—would normally precede: **la blanca nieve** = *the white snow*; **los feroces leones** = *the ferocious lions*; **las mansas ovejas** = *the meek sheep*. But for purely stylistic and poetic reasons the adjective could very well be placed after the noun: ... **y la nieve blanca continuaba cayendo** ... = ... *and the white snow kept on falling ...*.

On the other hand, not all adjectives in post-nominal position are used in a distinguishing, restricting sense. Depending upon the adjective/noun semantic relationship there are instances when a post-nominal adjective simply describes: **Me encantan sus ojos verdes** = *I love her green eyes* (she only has two eyes, so there is no referent from which to distinguish it); **Conocí a su madre viuda** = *I met his widowed mother* (he only has one mother who happens to be a widow).

It seems that from the point of view of the speaker the quality is the primary target when the adjective follows the noun. Adjectives in post-nominal position not only describe but by and large also serve to distinguish the modified noun from all others by classifying, characterizing, contrasting, and specifying it.

There are important categories of adjectives which because of their meanings are used in a distinguishing sense, and thus normally follow the noun, such as:

1. Adjectives expressing nationality, religion, political affiliation, status:

una mujer africana	*an African woman*
un joven argentino	*a young Argentinian*
un sacerdote católico	*a Catholic priest*
una ceremonia judía	*a Jewish ceremony*
un senador liberal	*a liberal senator*
un partido comunista	*a communist party*
un político adinerado	*a wealthy politician*
una familia aristocrática	*an aristocratic family*

2. Adjectives expressing color, shape, matter, condition:

una camisa blanca	*a white shirt*
un diseño triangular	*a triangular design*
una mesa plástica	*a plastic table*
una imagen clara	*a clear image*

Most past participles used as adjectives would fall under this category, so they would normally follow:

una ventana rota	*a broken window*
una puerta abierta	*an open door*
un asunto complicado	*a complicated matter*

Some of these forms may precede if a purely subjective appreciation of the quality is expressed:

Le rindieron un sentido homenaje.	*They paid him heartfelt homage.*
Contemplaba su esbelta figura de mujer.	*He admired her graceful feminine figure.*

3. Adjectives expressing scientific, technical, and classificatory concepts:

un problema matemático	*a mathematical problem*
un ataque cardíaco	*a heart attack*
un viaje espacial	*a space trip*
un género literario	*a literary genre*
una comedia musical	*a musical comedy*
un estudio sociológico	*a sociological study*
un criterio histórico	*a historical criterion*

4. Adjectives modified by adverbs (or intensifiers) are more apt to differentiate, so they too would normally follow:

Es el autor más leído.	*He is the most read author.*
Fue un pintor menos importante.	*He was a less important painter.*
Cantó una canción muy triste.	*He sang a very sad song.*
¡Qué mujer tan interesante!	*What an interesting woman!*
Es persona bastante astuta.	*She is a rather shrewd person.*

ADJECTIVES IN PRE-NOMINAL POSITION

Adjectives in pre-nominal position usually describe a quality which seems characteristic of the noun they modify, without necessarily adding anything new to its idea or restricting or specifying its meaning. Consequently, adjectives which express a typical, inherent characteristic quality; adjectives which enhance or express value judgments; or adjectives which stress a subjective attitude on the part of the speaker precede the noun.

Vimos al anciano profesor.	*We saw the elderly professor.*
Conocí a un famoso violinista.	*I met a famous violinist.*
Vivían en una pequeña ciudad.	*They lived in a small city.*
Le escribí una larga carta.	*I wrote her a long letter.*

The irregular comparatives and superlatives (**mejor, peor, mayor, menor**) normally precede, since they imply a value judgement.

Es el mejor estudiante de la clase.	*He is the best student in the class.*
No tiene mayor interés.	*He doesn't have much interest.*

In exclamatory sentences with **qué**, the adjective would normally be placed before the noun.

¡Qué linda mujer!	*What a beautiful woman!*
¡Qué precioso día!	*What a gorgeous day!*

In all of these examples the adjective either explains a characteristic quality of the noun or enhances it through a value judgement. It seems then that from the point of view of the speaker—apart from stress patterns—the noun is the primary focus of interest when the adjective precedes.

It should be pointed out, however, that these adjectives may also follow if the intent is one of specifying or contrasting.

Vimos al profesor anciano. (no vimos al joven)	*We saw the elderly professor. (not the young one)*
Vivían en una ciudad pequeña. (no en una grande)	*They lived in a small city. (not in a large one)*
Era un violinista famoso. (no era uno desconocido)	*He was a famous violinist. (not an unknown one)*
Le escribí una carta larga. (no una corta)	*I wrote her a long letter. (not a short one)*
Es el estudiante mejor de la clase. (no es cualquier estudiante)	*He is the best student in the class. (not just any student)*

Spanish adjective position could be related to the position of adverbs in English —and Spanish adverbs also—insofar as the item in final position seems to be the one that carries more emphasis or gives more information. In *They easily carried it* = **Fácilmente lo llevaron**, more emphasis is placed on the action, thus the verb is in final position and the adverb precedes it. But in *They carried it easily (with ease)* = **Lo llevaron fácilmente (con facilidad)**, the emphasis is on the manner in which the action was accomplished; thus the adverb follows the verb. This verb/ adverb relationship parallels the noun/adjective situation: **Es fiel compañero** = more emphasis on "companionship" and **Es compañero fiel** = more emphasis on the quality, "faithfulness."

ADJECTIVE POSITION AND ADJECTIVAL CLAUSES

Since a vast number of adjectives can be placed either before or after the noun, connoting enhancement or contrast, accordingly, one helpful way of determining the choice is to see whether there is a relationship between adjective position and these two types of clauses: restrictive versus non-restrictive adjectival clauses.

Restrictive adjectival clauses → Post-nominal adjectives

Restrictive adjectival clauses identify which one of the possible items of a given class is being referred to by supplying the necessary information. Thus, post-nominal adjectives would fit into this type of clause:

Esta mañana vimos al profesor **que es anciano**.	Esta mañana vimos al profesor **anciano**.
This morning we saw the professor who is old.	*This morning we saw the elderly professor.*
Conocí a un violinista **que es famoso** en casa de unos amigos.	Conocí a un violinista **famoso** en casa de unos amigos.

I met a violinist who is famous at
the house of some friends.

I met a famous *violinist at the house of
some friends.*

Le escribí una carta **que era larga**
pero nunca la contestó.
*I wrote him a letter that was long
but he never answered it.*

Le escribí una carta **larga** pero
nunca la contestó.
I wrote him a long *letter but he never
answered it.*

Non-restrictive adjectival clauses → Pre-nominal adjectives

Non-restrictive adjectival clauses provide supplementary information about items
already identified, but without attempting to contrast them with other items of
the same kind. In oral speech these clauses are signaled by the use of pauses, and in
writing by the use of commas. Thus, pre-nominal adjectives would fit into this
type of clause:

Vimos al profesor, **que es anciano**,
esta mañana.
*We saw the professor, who happens
to be old, this morning.*

Vimos al **anciano** profesor esta
mañana.
We saw the elderly professor *this
morning.*

Conocí a un violinista, **que es
famoso**, en casa de unos amigos.
*I met a violinist, who happens to be
famous, at the house of some friends.*

Conocí a un **famoso** violinista en
casa de unos amigos.
I met a famous violinista *at the house
of some friends.*

Le escribí una carta, **que era larga**,
pero nunca la contestó.
*I wrote him a letter, which happened to
be long, but he never answered it.*

Le escribí una **larga** carta pero nunca
la contestó.
I wrote him a long *letter but he never
answered it.*

ADJECTIVE POSITION AND MEANING

Many Spanish adjectives may acquire a different meaning depending upon whether
they occur in pre-nominal or post-nominal position.[1] There are a few cases in
which this variation in meaning is significant, but in most instances it is simply
a matter of difference in connotation. Furthermore, this variation in meaning
depends not only on adjective position but also upon the semantic contents
of the noun modified, the context itself, or stress. For instance, although **único**
could mean "only" or "sole" in pre-nominal position (**Era la única novela** = *It
was the only novel*,) and "unique" in post-nominal position (**Era una novela
única** = *It was a unique novel*), such a difference is not made in **Era el único hijo**
or **Era el hijo único**. Both sentences translate as *He was the only (sole) child*. It
should not be taken for granted then that adjective position automatically conveys
a different meaning.

---

[1] For the differences in meaning of adjectives in predicative constructions joined by **ser** and **estar**, see
Usage and Meaning of Some Adjectivals, page 255.

The following are some of the most common adjectives that may vary their meaning within certain contexts:

Adjective	Pre-nominal position	Post-nominal position
grande	'great' Kennedy fue un gran hombre. *Kennedy was a great man.*	'big' Era un hombre grande. *He was a big man.*
pobre	'pitiable,' 'pitiful' Es un pobre hombre. *He is a pitiful man.*	'not rich' Es un hombre pobre. *He is a poor man.*
cierto	'few,' 'certain' Me dijo ciertas cosas. *He told me certain things.*	'certain', 'true' Me dijo cosas ciertas. *The things he told me were certain (true).*
alto	'high' Desempeña un alto cargo. *He fulfills a high position.*	'tall' Es un hombre alto. *He is a tall man.*
viejo[1]	'long standing,' 'former' ¿ Viste a la vieja criada? *Did you see the old (former) maid?*	'elderly' ¿ Viste a la criada vieja? *Did you see the old (elderly) maid?*
dichoso[2]	'disagreeable' Allí viene esa dichosa mujer. *There comes that darned woman.*	'lucky' Allí viene esa mujer dichosa. *There comes that lucky woman.*
diferente	'various' Había diferentes clases de plantas. *There were various kinds of plants.*	'different, dissimilar' Había clases diferentes de plantas. *There were different kinds of plants.*
nuevo	'another' Compró un nuevo auto. *He bought a new (another) car.*	'new' Compró un auto nuevo. *He bought a new car.*
puro	'just nothing but,' 'sheer' Habla puros disparates. *He talks pure (sheer) nonsense.*	'pure' Toma café puro. *He drinks pure coffee.*

[1] Context may give the same meaning in both positions: **¿Viste a la vieja criada?** or **¿Viste a la criada vieja?** could both mean *Did you see the former (old) maid?*

[2] This is another instance where adjective position does not predict automatically a different connotation. Both meanings, "disagreeable" and "lucky," could be attributed to **dichoso**, depending not only on position but on the context itself. With another noun, only one meaning would be possible: **no llega el dichoso autobús, ... el autobús dichoso** = *the darned bus doesn't arrive.*

simple	*'mere'* Es una simple ama de casa. *She is a mere housewife.*	*'simple minded'* Es una persona simple. *She is a simple person.*
triste	*'without status'* Es un triste personaje. *He is a sad character (without any status or ambition).*	*'sad,' 'melancholic'* Tenía una personalidad triste. *He had a sad personality.*
alguno	*indefinite 'some'* ¿Llamó alguna persona? *Did someone call?*	*emphatic negative* No llamó persona alguna. *Absolutely no one called.*
cualquier	*'any whatsoever'* Dame cualquier libro. *Give me any book.*	*'any old'* Dame un libro cualquiera. *Give me just any old book.*
ese	*demonstrative form* Ese hombre nos sigue. *That man is following us.*	*demonstrative used in a derogatory sense* El hombre ese . . . *That darned man . . .*
medio	*'half'* Es medio chino. *He is half Chinese.*	*'average'* Es un hombre medio. *He is an average man.*
mismo	*'same'* Llamó la misma persona. *The same person called.*	*'oneself'* Llamó la persona misma. *The person herself called.*
primer	*'first'* Hoy es el primer día de vacaciones. *Today is the first day of vacation.*	*'first' referring to date* Vienen el día primero del mes. *They are coming on the first of the month.*
propio	*'own'* Fue su propia decisión. *It was his own decision.*	*'just,' 'appropriate'* Fue una decisión propia. *It was an appropriate decision.*
semejante	*'such a'* Nunca oí semejante cosa. *I never heard such a thing.*	*'similar'* Nunca oí cosa semejante. *I never heard such a (similar) thing.*
único	*'only,' 'sole'* Comer es su único vicio. *Eating is his only vice.*	*'unique'* Tiene un apetito único. *He has a unique appetite.*
varios	*'several'* Allí se venden varios artículos. *They sell several articles there.*	*'miscellaneous'* Allí se venden artículos varios. *They sell miscellaneous articles there.*

IDIOMATIC EXPRESSIONS

There are a few adjectives which have a fixed position with respect to certain nouns and which form a number of idiomatic expressions.

IN PRE-NOMINAL POSITION:

¡Qué **mala suerte**!	*What bad luck!*
Me dijo la **pura verdad**.	*He told me the real truth.*
Viene a vernos en **raras ocasiones**.	*She comes to see us on rare occasions.*
Merece el castigo por el **mero hecho** de mentir.	*He deserves the punishment for the mere fact of lying.*
Es sólo una **mera opinión** que no merece considerarse.	*It is just a mere opinion that doesn't deserve to be considered.*
Con su **negra suerte** es posible que le nieguen el trabajo.	*With her horrible luck it is possible that they might deny her the job.*

IN POST-NOMINAL POSITION:

No la contradigas cuando tiene una **idea fija**.	*Don't contradict her when she has a fixed idea.*
No hay duda de que llevan una **vida fácil**.	*There is no doubt that they lead an easy life.*

All of these stereotyped expressions are actually nominals which in some cases have been nominalized permanently and have formed compound nouns, as in:

Descartes era un libre pensador.	Descartes era un **librepensador**.
Descartes was a free thinker.	*Descartes was a freethinker.*

PLACEMENT OF TWO OR MORE DESCRIPTIVE ADJECTIVES

When two or more descriptive adjectives modify a noun in Spanish, they are placed according to the following patterns:

1. Both adjectives may follow the noun if they are used in a distinguishing, classificatory sense. The adjective more restrictive in meaning takes the last position.

Estudia arte moderno **español**.	*He studies* Spanish *modern art.*
Estudia arte español **moderno**.	*He studies* modern *Spanish art.*

In the first example the adjective in last position, **español**, rather than **moderno** restricts even more the concept **arte**. The adjective **español** actually modified a whole unit: **arte moderno**. English achieves this contrast by inverting the order in some cases or by using a different stress pattern.

Es un escritor contemporáneo **realista**.	*He is a* realistic *contemporary writer.* *He is a contemporary* realistic *writer.*

BUT:

Es un escritor realista **contemporáneo**.   *He is a* contemporary *realistic writer.*

2. One adjective may precede the noun and one or two may follow it. Usually the more subjective and enhancing adjective would precede; the more informative and restrictive in meaning would follow accordingly.

la estupenda pintura impresionista francesa	*the stupendous* French *impressionistic painting*
la estupenda pintura francesa impresionista	*the stupendous* impressionistic *French painting*
un gran escritor mexicano moderno	*a great* modern *Mexican writer*
un gran escritor moderno mexicano	*a great* Mexican *modern writer*

3. Adjectives that have the same value are either joined by the relator **y** (**e**) or by commas. If their value is a restrictive, classificatory one, they would normally follow the noun. If they are subjective or enhancing, or if a poetic and dramatic effect is intended, they would precede.

Era un hombre alto y delgado.	*He was a tall and slim man.*
Tiene una mujer guapa, rica e inteligente.	*He has a handsome, rich, and intelligent wife.*
Es un investigador excelente, serio, dedicado.	*He is a serious, excellent, and dedicated scholar.*
Poseía un vocabulario rico y abundante.	*He had a rich and abundant vocabulary.*

BUT:

Su delgada y alta figura se distinguía entre la muchedumbre.	*Her slim and tall figure stood out in the crowd.*
Es un excelente, serio y dedicado investigador.	*He is an excellent, serious, and dedicated scholar.*
Poseía un rico y abundante vocabulario.	*He had a rich and abundant vocabulary.*
Se arrastraba por el largo, oscuro, penoso sendero de una existencia infeliz.	*He struggled along the long, bleak, arduous path of a sad existence.*

4. While in English a noun could be modified by several adjectives without the need of commas or a relator, in Spanish when more than two modifying adjectives occur, they are either joined by commas or relators, or they are arranged in both pre- and post-nominal positions.

He is a good wholesome rich American boy . . .
Es un chico americano, bueno, rico y sano . . .

OR:

Es un buen chico americano, sano y rico . . .

Other Functions of Adjectives

ADJECTIVES AS ADVERBIALS[1]

Some adjectives in Spanish may function as adverbials. This can best be seen in cases when the adverbial adjective refers to the subject by describing its state or condition while performing the action, thus showing agreement in gender and number. But at the same time it may describe the manner in which the action is performed. This type of usage occurs especially with stative and intransitive verbs.

Los niños duermen tranquilos.   *The children sleep peacefully.*
(= Los niños están tranquilos.
    Los niños duermen
    tranquilamente.)

La niña duerme tranquila.   *The girl sleeps peacefully.*
(= La niña está tranquila.
    La niña duerme tranquilamente.)

La mujer entró callada.   *The woman came in quietly.*
(= La mujer estaba callada.
    La mujer entró calladamente.)

La familia vive feliz.   *The family lives happily.*
(= La familia es feliz.
    La familia vive felizmente.)

If reference is made only to the manner in which the action is performed, de-emphasizing the state or condition of the subject, the adverbial form in **-mente** is preferred to an adverbial adjective.

Los niños duermen tranquilamente.
                    con tranquilidad.
La familia vive felizmente.
                con felicidad.

A few adjectives with adverbial function can only refer to the manner in which the action is performed and thus are in the masculine singular form.

El orador habló claro.   *The speaker spoke clearly.*
                claramente.   *with clarity.*
                con claridad.   .
La anciana caminaba lento.   *The old woman walked slowly.*
                    lentamente.
                    con lentitud.
Las secretarias escriben rápido.   *Secretaries write fast.*
                        rápidamente.
                        con rapidez.

---

[1] See Adverbs, page 349.

Not all of these forms have an equivalent adverb in **-mente**.

La tortuga camina despacio.	*The turtle walks slowly.*
Las mujeres hablan alto.	*Women speak loudly.*
La artista canta bonito.	*The actress sings beautifully.*

Idiomatic adverbial phrases

There are a few stereotyped adverbial phrases which have been formed by preposition + adjective:

El hombre caminaba **a ciegas**.	*The man walked blindly.*
La casa se encontraba **a oscuras**.	*The house was dark.*
La asamblea fue convocada **de nuevo**.	*The assembly was convoked again.*
Mis invitaciones llegaron **de último**.	*My invitations came last.*

ADJECTIVES AS NOMINALS

Spanish descriptive adjectives may function as nouns when nominalized. Nominalization is achieved by noun deletion or by addition of the neuter **lo** before the adjective's singular form.[1]

Sólo he enviado las cartas certificadas.	Sólo he enviado las certificadas.
I have only sent the registered letters.	*I have only sent the registered ones.*
Admiro las cosas bellas.	Admiro lo bello.
I admire beautiful things.	*I admire what is beautiful.*

Some limiting adjectives may also function as nouns when the neuter **lo** occurs before the masculine singular form with the following:

1. the stressed possessives and the alternate **de** constructions:

Quiero las cosas tuyas.	Quiero lo tuyo.
I want your things.	*I want what is yours.*
Dale las cosas nuestras.	Dale lo nuestro.
. . . de nosotros.	. . . lo de nosotros.
Give him our things.	*Give him what is ours.*

2. the ordinal numerals:

La primera cosa que hay que hacer es . . .	Lo primero que hay que hacer es . . .
The first thing that one has to do is . . .	*The first thing that one has to do is . . .*

---

[1] See Nominalization, page 218; The Neuter Form **lo**, page 294.

3. certain indefinites:

Envía las otras cosas.   Envía lo otro.
Send the other things.   *Send the other (things).*

But in general, limiting adjectives nominalize by noun deletion. This process is called pronominalization since the resulting is a pronominal form. Limiting adjectives may then function as noun substitutes.[1]

MODIFYING SUFFIXES INSTEAD OF ADJECTIVES

Spanish often attaches diminutive and augmentative suffixes to nouns (and also to adjectives) in order to convey the idea of size (smallness or bigness) or to express favorable or unfavorable impressions (endearment, derision). Since these modificative suffixes modify or somehow change the meaning of the noun to which they are attached, the need for further modification is usually unnecessary.

The presence or absence of a modifying adjective will depend on how much the speaker wishes to intensify the quality of the noun, although it may give a redundant effect: **Vive en una casita** = *He lives in a small house* versus **Vive en una casita pequeña** = *He lives in a small little house.* Since most of these modifying suffixes can also be added to adjectives,[2] the speaker may intensify the quality even further by adding the suffix to both the noun and the adjective: **Vive en una casita pequeña** = *He lives in a small little house* versus **Vive en una casita pequeñita** = *He lives in a tiny little house.*

Ultimately, of course, these choices are governed by stylistic considerations: the semantic relation between the noun/adjective combination; to what extent the redundant effect is stylistically acceptable; the forms of language, written and spoken; and within the spoken language, the dialectal and social preferences. Some of these noun derivations have acquired permanent lexical status: **chiquillo** = *kid*; **casucha** *shack.*

Diminutive suffixes

Diminutive suffixes are mostly a characteristic of the spoken familiar language, although they are also used in writing (in literary texts rather than in journalistic, official, or technical writings).

In addition to the main connotation of smallness and depending on the meaning of the noun to which they are added, these suffixes may express:

1. smallness and endearment simultaneously:

2. only endearment with no connotation in size;

3. derision ranging from insignificance, contempt to irony and sarcasm.

---

[1] See Nominalization of Limiting Adjectives, page 222; Pronominal Possessives, page 305; Pronominal Demonstratives, page 311, and chapters 9 and 20 for the pronominal function of interrogatives, indefinites and negatives.

[2] See Chapter 19, Comparatives, Modifying Suffixes.

English has a few diminutive suffixes, i.e., *-let, -ny, -y, -ie*, but on the whole, English conveys the effect of suffixation by using adjectives (one, two, or more preferably) or by using an entirely different word.

The following are the most common and productive diminutives in Spanish. They take gender and number forms according to the noun to which they are added.

Suffix	Meaning	Examples	
-ito Added to nouns ending in **-o**, **-a**, **-l**.	Smallness.	**un puerquito** *a piglet* **un gatito** *a kitten* **un perrito** *a doggy*	
	Smallness and endearment.	Me encanta su casita. *I love his cute little house.* Atiende a la niñita. *Take care of the little girl.*	
	Endearment only.	mi muchachito	*my dear loving child*
		mi querida abuela mi abuelita	*my dear grandmother* *my granny*
	Irony, sarcasm.	¡ No es más que una niñita!	*She is nothing but a girlie!*
ALTERNATE FORMS:			
-cito Added to nouns with endings other than **-o, -a, -l**. **-ico** Used instead of **-ito, -cito**, in many areas of Spanish America.	The same range of meanings covered by **-ito**.	un hombrecito una mesica un animalico unos libricos	*a cute little man* *a tiny little table* *a cute little animal* *some cute little books*
-illo	Smallness and endearment. Endearment only. Sarcasm, insignificance.	un chiquillo una casilla un vinillo un periodiquillo	*a cute little boy* *a nice little house* *a nice tasty wine* *a cheap unimportant newspaper*
ALTERNATE FORMS:			
-cillo	Same range of meanings as **-illo**.		

Suffix	Meaning	Examples	
	Sarcasm, insignificance.	un autorcillo un profesorcillo	a would-be author an insignificant, lousy professor
-uco	Most pejorative: ugliness, insignificance.	una mujeruca un frailuco	a wretched woman a most insignificant friar
-ucho	Most pejorative: ugliness.	Vive en una casucha.	He lives in a tumbled-down house.
		Vive en un cuartucho.	He lives in a shack.
-uelo	Most pejorative: contempt, scorn, insignificance.	No es más que un doctorzuelo.	He is no more than just a lousy doctor.
		No es más que una mujerzuela.	She is no more than just a low-class vulgar woman.

Augmentative suffixes

Augmentative suffixes are not as common as diminutives, but are, nevertheless, used extensively. They are primarily part of the familiar and popular spoken language, with some use in writing—particularly in literary texts that reflect this speech. Besides the main connotation of bigness and depending on the meaning of the noun to which they are added, these suffixes may express:

1. bigness and derogatory connotations simultaneously;

2. derogatory connotations ranging from ugliness, grotesqueness, coarseness, wretchedness to bothersome or comic qualities;

3. in a few cases they may express bigness with a connotation of "impressiveness," "grandeur."

Augmentive suffixes have no counterpart in English. Instead, the equivalent for these forms is a construction with adjectives (one, two or more preferably) or the use of adverbial intensifiers.

The following are the most common and productive augmentatives in Spanish. Their gender and number forms depend on the noun to which they are added.

Suffix	Meaning	Examples	
-aco	Bigness with derogatory connotations: ugly, wretched, bothersome.	Tráeme ese libraco.	Bring me that huge cumbersome book.
	Derogatory without necessarily referring to size. Ugly, grotesque.	Saca ese pajarraco de aquí.	Get that horrible looking bird out of here.

-azo	Bigness with possible derogatory connotations: grotesque, cumbersome.	¿Viste a ese hombrazo?	*Did you see that big husky fellow?*
	Size with connotations of impressiveness, grandeur.	Se compró un carrazo.	*He bought himself quite a car. (a nice, big, luxurious car)*
		¡Qué perrazo!	*What an impressive looking dog!*
-ón	Bigness with connotations of impressiveness.	Se han construído un caserón.	*They have built themselves quite a house. (an impressive, huge house)*
		El nuevo gerente es un hombrón.	*The new manager is a giant of a man. (impressive looking)*
	Could be derogatory, especially in the feminine referring to persons.	La nueva criada es una mujerona.	*The new maid is an enormous woman.*
-ote	Bigness and usually derogatory: ugly, grotesque, vulgar.	Es un hombrote.	*He is a brutish man.*
		Se construyeron una casota.	*They built themselves an enormous, ugly-looking house.*
	Derogatory without reference to size.	No digas palabrotas.	*Don't say dirty words.*

Spanish and English Adjectives Contrasted

ADJECTIVES	
Spanish	*English*

FUNCTION

Adjectives describe and determine nouns in some way. The two main categories, descriptive and limiting (possessives, demonstratives, numerals, indefinites), exist in the two languages.

MORPHOLOGY

Special markers for gender and number depending on the noun modified. Four basic forms: **-o, -a, -os, -as.**	Invariable in form.
A few shortened forms in pre-nominal position, their distribution depending on the gender and number of the modified noun.	Invariable in form.

Spanish	*English*

AGREEMENT

Basic rule: Adjectives agree with nouns in gender and number. Since one adjective may modify more than one noun, special rules of agreement apply.	Since adjectives are invariable in form, such special rules of agreement do not apply.
Compró una casa nueva.	*He bought a new house.*
Compró casa y auto nuevos.	*He bought a new house and car.*
Su Majestad (el Rey) está enfermo.	*His Majesty (the King) is sick.*

POSITION

PREDICATE ADJECTIVES

Adjectives in a predicate construction linked to the noun by a copula present no major problem. Similar patterns exist in both languages.

El niño está cansado.	*The child is sick.*
La criada es magnífica.	*The maid is great.*

ATTRIBUTIVE ADJECTIVES

May occur in pre-nominal or post-nominal position. There is no set of governing rules to predict position, only a few guidelines, but there are also stylistic considerations.	Occur only in pre-nominal position.

Post-nominal position:

1. Roughly speaking it is the most common position.

2. In general, adjectives in this position restrict, clarify, specify the meaning of the modified noun. They contrast and distinguish it from others of its kind.

Vi una película sueca (no una americana).	*I saw a Swedish film (not an American one).*

3. The emphasis seems to be on the quality.

	Since position is fixed, heavy stress is used to bring out the quality.
Llegó una mujer hermosa.	*A beautiful woman arrived.*

4. There are important categories of nouns which because of their meaning are used in a distinguishing sense. Therefore, adjectives expressing

nationality, religion, political affiliation, status, color, shape, matter, condition, or scientific, technical, and classificatory concepts normally follow.

una estudiante alemana	*A German student*
un concepto católico	*a Catholic concept*
una mesa redonda	*a round table*
una solución matemática	*a mathematical solution*

Past participles normally fit within this category.

una puerta abierta	*an open door*
una ventana rota	*a broken window*

Adjectives modified by adverbs are more apt to distinguish, so they would normally follow.

es un edificio muy alto	*it is a very high building*

5. Post-nominal adjectives are related to restrictive adjectival clauses.

Conocí a un violinista **que es famoso** en casa de unos amigos.	*I met a violinist who is famous at some friends' house.*
Conocí a un violinista **famoso** en casa de unos amigos.	*I met a famous violinist at some friends' house.*

Pre-nominal position:

1. Generally describe inherent, characteristic qualities of the noun, without necessarily contrasting it from others of its kind.

It is the normal position of attributive adjectives.

2. The following categories would normally precede:

a. adjectives that express typical, characteristic qualities:

la blanca nieve	*the white snow*

b. adjectives which enhance:

Conveyed by heavy stress on noun.

Es una hermosa mujer.	*She is a beautiful woman.*

c. adjectives which express value judgement:

Son malos estudiantes.	*They are poor students.*

d. adjectives which stress a subjective attitude:

¡Qué inútil persona!	*What a useless person!*

Spanish	*English*

3. Pre-nominal adjectives are related to non-restrictive adjectival clauses.

Conocí un violinista, que es famoso, en casa de unos amigos.	*I met a violinist, who happens to be famous, at the house of some friends.*
Conocí a un famoso violinista en casa de unos amigos.	*I met a famous violinist at the house of some friends.*

ADJECTIVE POSITION AND MEANING

A few adjectives may alter their meaning or connotation depending on their position within certain contexts.	These variations in meaning and connotation are conveyed either by different stress patterns or by using different adjectives.

Es un pobre hombre.	*He is a pitiable man.*
Es un hombre pobre.	*He is a poor man (not rich).*

Both languages have certain commonly used expressions, the difference being word order in some cases.

mala suerte	*bad luck*
por el mero hecho	*by the mere fact*
una idea fija	*a fixed idea*

PLACEMENT OF TWO OR MORE DESCRIPTIVE ADJECTIVES

The placement of two or more descriptive adjectives follows the basic guidelines for single modifying adjectives: whether they classify, distinguish, or whether they enhance, express value judgements. But with two or more adjectives there are several possibilities: both adjectives could precede or follow depending on their sense; one may precede, the other(s) may follow (the more informative usually in the last position); or they may be joined by relators or commas.	Sometimes the order of the modifying adjectives may be inverted; or different stress patterns may show the contrast in the emphasis of the quality. Adjectives may also be joined by relators or commas, or both.

Estudia arte moderno español.	*He studies* Spanish *modern art.*
Estudia arte español moderno.	*He studies* modern *Spanish art.*
un gran escritor mexicano moderno	*a great* modern *Mexican writer*
un gran escritor moderno mexicano	*a great* Mexican *modern writer*
un novelista contemporáneo realista	*a realistic* contemporary *novelist* / *a contemporary* realistic *novelist*

un novelista realista contemporáneo
la estupenda pintura italiana renacentista
Tiene una mujer guapa, rica e inteligente.

a contemporary *realistic novelist*
the stupendous Renaissance *Italian painting*
*He has a rich, handsome, and intelligent
wife.*

When more than two modifying adjectives occur, they are either joined by
relators or commas, or arranged in both
pre- and post-nominal positions.

A noun could be modified by several
adjectives without the need of commas
or relators.

Es un chico americano, bueno, rico y sano.
Es un buen chico americano, sano y rico.

He is a good wholesome rich American boy.

ADJECTIVES AS ADVERBIALS

Particularly true with stative and intransitive verbs; the adverbial may refer to the
subject and/or to the manner in which
action is performed.

The adverbial ending *-ly* is preferred, or
any other adverbial construction. There
are very few adjectives that function as
adverbials.

La niña duerme tranquila.
    duerme estando tranquila.
    AND/OR:
    duerme de una manera tranquila
    (tranquilamente).

The girl sleeps peacefully.

El orador habló claro.
Las secretarias escriben rápido.
La tortuga camina despacio.

The speaker spoke clearly.
Secretaries write fast.
The turtle walks slow (or slowly).

MODIFYING SUFFIXES INSTEAD OF ADJECTIVES

The use of modifying suffixes (diminutives
and augmentatives) creates new nouns
that express qualities—size, favorable or
unfavorable impressions—and often may
cancel the need for adjectives.

With the exception of a few diminutive
suffixes, modification with one, two, or
more adjectives and the use of intensifiers
is preferred.

Vive en una casucha.
Mira el perrito.
Saca ese pajarraco de aquí.
Se compró un carrazo.

He lives in a tumbled down house.
Look at the doggy.
Get that horrible looking bird out of here.
He bought himself quite a car

15

SER AND ESTAR

Usage of *Ser* versus *Estar*

There are two verbs in Spanish that correspond to the English verb *to be*: **ser** and **estar**. They are not interchangeable. Each has its own characteristic usage. **Ser** occurs with nouns, noun phrases, and adverbs of time. **Estar** occurs with adverbs of place and of manner to express location and condition. **Ser**, on the other hand, takes adverbs of place to express origin and occurrence. Both **ser** and **estar** can co-occur with adjectivals. The meaning of the sentence, however, will be altered by the use of one verb or the other. **Ser** with adjectivals expresses a quality of the subject. **Estar** with adjectivals describes a state of being, but not a quality. **Ser** co-occurs with past participles to form passive constructions, while **estar** takes present participles to form progressive constructions.

SER WITH NOUNS AND NOUN PHRASES

1. **Ser** occurs with nouns and words that can function as nouns, such as pronouns, adjectives, infinitives, and past participles.

Es la verdad.	*It's the truth.*
Juan es abogado.	*Juan is a lawyer.*
Pedro es aquél.	*Pedro is that one.*
Este es el joven de quien te hable.	*This is the young man about whom I spoke to you.*
La vida es luchar y más luchar.	*Life is struggling and more struggling.*
Juan es el invitado de honor.	*Juan is the guest of honor.*

2. **Ser de** + noun phrase denotes:
   a. Possession:

La casa es de Juan.	*The house belongs to Juan.*
Eso no es de él.	*This is not his (does not belong to him).*

   b. The composition or material of a thing:

Es una casa de ladrillos.	*It's a brick house.*
El vestido es de encaje.	*It's a lace dress.*
Es un problema de muchas facetas.	*It's a multi-faceted problem.*

   c. The makeup of a person, physical or spiritual:

Juan es de estatura mediana.	*Juan is of medium height.*
Es un hombre de gran visión.	*He is a man of great vision.*
Era una mujer de gran audacia.	*She was a woman of great daring.*
Es un hombre de gran integridad.	*He is a man of great integrity.*

3. **Ser para** + noun phrase or an infinitive describes:
   a. The beneficiary of an action:

Los libros son para Juan.	*The books are for Juan.*
La criada es para María.	*The maid is for Maria.*

   b. The goal or destination of a thing or event:

Estos ejercicios son para adelgazar.	*These exercises are for reducing.*
El vino es para la cena del sábado.	*The wine is for the dinner on Saturday.*
Las fiestas son para descansar.	*Holidays are for relaxation.*

Ser versus estar de + noun phrase

The only occurrence of **estar** followed by a noun phrase is **estar de**, meaning **desempeñar una función** = *to occupy a position* or *to act as*. Only the context can clarify whether it is a permanent or temporary function or occupation. It is a construction of marginal importance.

Está de director del hospital.	*He is the hospital director.* *He is the acting hospital director.*
Está de payaso.	*He is a clown.* *He is acting like a clown.*

ESTAR WITH ADVERBIALS

Estar is used to express location. As such it is followed by adverbials of place. The adverb may be explicitly given or merely implied.

LOCATION

Juan está en Venezuela.	*Juan is in Venezuela.*
El no está (aquí).	*He is not here.*
Las montañas están lejos.	*The mountains are far away.*
Siempre están juntos (en todas partes).	*They are always together (everywhere).*
Estamos todos presentes (aquí).	*All of us are present (here).*
Mi oficina está cerca.	*My office is close by.*

Estar also occurs with adverbs of manner, **bien**, **mal**, **mejor**, **peor**, etc., to describe the *condition* of a person or thing.

¿Cómo estás?	*How are you?*
Estoy bien.	*I am well.*
Eso está mal.	*That is wrong.*
El no está mejor.	*He is not better.*
Está peor.	*He is worse.*

SER WITH ADVERBIALS

1. **Ser de** with adverbial phrases expresses the origin of a person or a thing.

El es de Venezuela.	*He is from Venezuela.*
Es de una familia distinguida.	*He comes from a distinguished family.*
Los azulejos son de México y las alfombras son de Portugal.	*The tiles are from Mexico and the rugs are from Portugal.*

2. When subject nouns referring to events occur with adverbs of location, **ser** is used to denote "occurrence." In this case, **ser** is equivalent to **tener lugar**, **ocurrir**, meaning *to take place, to happen.*

La clase es en el auditorio.	*The class is (takes place) in the auditorium.*
La reunión fue en su casa.	*The meeting was (took place) in his house.*
La revuelta fue en el centro.	*The riot happened downtown.*
El incidente fue en la esquina.	*The incident took place at the corner.*

3. **Ser** with adverbials of time conveys temporal relationships: time, dates, and seasons.

Es la una.	*It is one o'clock.*
Mi cita es el viernes.	*My appointment (date) is on Friday.*
Hoy es veinte de agosto.	*Today is August 20.*
La fiesta es mañana.	*The party is tomorrow.*
Es verano.	*It is summer.*
Es temprano.	*It is early.*
Es de noche.	*It is night-time.*

SER VERSUS *ESTAR* WITH ADVERBS OF LOCATION

Although **estar** normally occurs with adverbs of location, there is, however, a marginal construction of **ser** with these same adverbs which can be explained along the following lines:

Estar aquí	{ must be used to denote the location of things and persons.
Ser aquí	{ can be used to denote the existence— not location—of a place only. It is not used with other nouns.

María está aquí, con su madre.	*Maria is here, with her mother.*
No busques más, el libro está aquí.	*Don't look any further, the book is here.*
Puedes entrar, aquí es.	*You may come in, it is here (the place we were looking for).*
Debes tener la dirección equivocada, aquí no es.	*You must have the wrong address, it is not here (the place we are looking for).*

Estar cerca **Estar lejos**	{ must be used to denote the location of persons or things in terms of distance.
Ser cerca (de) **Ser lejos (de)**	{ can be used to denote the existence of a place in terms of its distance from some other point of reference. The latter may be expressed or merely implied.

Su mujer está lejos.	*His wife is far away.*
Mi oficina está cerca.	*My office is nearby.*
Vamos a pie, la iglesia es cerca (de aquí).	*Let's walk, the church is nearby.*
Debemos salir temprano, la playa es muy lejos de aquí.	*We have to leave early, the beach is far away from here.*

SER AND *ESTAR* WITH ADJECTIVALS

Most adjectivals, adjectives, and past participles functioning as adjectives may occur with both **ser** and **estar**. However, a limited number of adjectivals occurs exclusively with **ser** or **estar**, or has a different meaning when used with one verb or the other. Whether **ser** or **estar** co-occurs with an adjectival depends in part upon the range of meaning of the adjectival itself and, above all, upon the meaning intended by the speaker.

Ser with adjectivals

Ser is used whenever the speaker wishes to qualify or to characterize the subject in an atemporal way, that is, without consideration to the transitory or permanent nature of the quality expressed.

The usage of **ser** should not be then equated with inherent or permanent qualities exclusively. There is only a limited number of them, and even these may be altered by the circumstances. Man is inherently human, rational, and free; yet he is just as likely to be subhuman, irrational, and in bondage—literally or figuratively speaking. The usage of **ser** should be thought of as encompassing all adjectives and past participles that characterize, define, or describe a subject in an atemporal way.

Es venezolano, católico, liberal y soltero.	He is Venezuelan, a Catholic, a liberal, and a bachelor.
Era joven, inteligente y guapa.	She was young, intelligent, and good-looking.
Era un niño muy nervioso e inquieto.	He was a very nervous and restless child.
Es frío, calculador y altanero, pero muy capaz.	He is cold, calculating, and arrogant, but very capable.
Es una ciudad pequeña, pero muy agradable.	It is a small city but a very pleasant one.
El agua del lago es muy fría.	The water of the lake is very cold.
Los días de lluvia son muy tristes.	Rainy days are very gloomy.
El Brasil es el país más grande de Sud América.	Brasil is the largest country in South America.
La población es muy heterogénea.	The population is very heterogeneous.
Este gobierno es muy arbitrario.	This government is very arbitrary.

Estar with adjectivals

While **ser** + adjective denotes the existence of a quality, **estar** with the same attribute describes a state of being. The state of being is thought of as contrasting in quantity or degree with the same or opposite condition in a previous temporal dimension. The duration of the state itself is not of major importance. It may be short or long lasting. It may even be permanent and final, as in **está muerto** (which contrasts with **está vivo**). What is important is that **estar** + adjective implies a contrast with a previous condition in time.

Ella es nerviosa.	Ella está nerviosa.
She is a nervous person.	*She is nervous (now or these days).*
Es un niño intranquilo.	El niño está intranquilo.
He is a restless child.	*The child is restless (at the time in question and as compared to his usual behaviour).*
Es una persona enferma.	Está enfermo.
He is a sick person.	*He is ill (in a state of ill health).*
Es un niño sano.	Está vivo y sano.
He is a healthy child.	*He is alive and in good health.*

Here are additional possibilities of clarifying certain uses of **estar**:

1. When the English verb *to be* can be substituted for *to look, to seem, to feel*, or *to become*, **estar** must be used.

María es triste.
Maria is a sad person.

El agua del lago es fría, pero hoy
está cálida.

Las montañas son muy altas.
The mountains are very high.

Es muy guapa, pero ahora está más
 guapa que nunca.
*She is very beautiful, but now she
 looks more beautiful than ever.*

El niño es alto.
The child is tall.

Es viejo.
He is old.

María está triste.
Maria is (looks, seems) sad.

*The water of the lake is cold, but
 today it is (feels) warm.*

¡Qué altas están las montañas!
How high the mountains look!

El niño está alto.
The child has become tall.

Está viejo.
*He has become old (has aged unduly
 or acts old).*

2. When *to be* + adjective is equivalent to *to show oneself* or *to act*, or when *to be* occurs in the progressive, then **estar**, not **ser**, is used in Spanish.

*She has been (has shown herself, has
 acted) very cold and arrogant
 toward us.*
She is very cold and arrogant.

He is being (acting) very daring.
He is very daring.

He is being (acting) very liberal.
He is very liberal.

Ha estado muy fría y altanera con
 nosotros.

Es muy fría y altanera.

Está muy atrevido.
Es muy atrevido.

Está muy liberal.
Es muy liberal.

Usage and meaning of some adjectivals

1. Adjectives and past participles that signify a state of being or condition normally take **estar**. **Hallarse** and **encontrarse** may substitute in these cases for **estar**. If **ser**, on the other hand, is used with any of the following adjectivals, a habitual condition or quality is expressed:

Está borracho.   *He is drunk.*
Está enfermo.   *He is ill.*
Está aburrido.   *He is bored.*
Está divertido. *He is amused.*
Está entretenido. *He is occupied.*

Es borracho.   *He is a drunkard.*
Es enfermo.   *He is sickly.*
Es aburrido.   *He is boring.*
Es divertido. *He is amusing.*
Es entretenido. *He is entertaining.*

Está interesado.	*He is interested.*	Es interesado.	*He is mercenary.*
Está callado.	*He is silent.*	Es callado.	*He is quiet.*
Está despierto.	*He is awake.*	Es despierto.	*He is alert.*
Está desconocido.	*He is unrecognizable.*	Es desconocido.	*He is unknown.*

2. A limited number of adjectives change their meaning when constructed with **ser** or **estar**.

ser			**estar**
to be green	verde		*to be unripe, immature*
to be clever	vivo		*to be alive*
to be clever, smart	listo		*to be ready*
to be decent, honest	decente		*to be presentable, dressed*
to be rich	rico		*to taste good*
to be good	bueno		*to be in good health*
to be mean	malo		*to be in ill health*

3. Adjectives and past participles that occur only with **ser**:

eterno	*eternal*	comprometedor	*compromising*
efímero	*ephemeral*	asombroso	*astonishing*
crónico	*chronic*	lícito/ilícito	*licit/illicit*
contemporáneo	*contemporary*	legítimo/ilegítimo	*legitimate/illegitimate*
conocido	*well-known*	posible/imposible	*possible/impossible*
leído	*well-read*		
sufrido	*resistant (when said of things)*; *long-suffering (when said of people)*		

4. Adjectives and past participles that occur only with **estar**:

contento	*contented*	ausente	*absent*
muerto	*dead*	satisfecho	*satisfied*
lleno	*full*	resignado	*resigned*
descalzo	*barefoot*	vinculado	*to have good connections*
perplejo	*perplexed*	desarreglado	*to be in a state of disarray*
harto	*fed up*	emparentado	*to be related to someone*
presente	*present*		

5. The following past participles are normally constructed with **ser**. They qualify, describe the subject. If **estar** is used instead, a state of being, a way of acting, is conveyed.

considerado	*to be considerate*	porfiado	*to be stubborn or opinionated*
desconfiado	*to be distrustful*	precavido	*to be cautious*
moderado	*to be moderate*	recatado	*to be modest*
osado	*to be bold*	esforzado	*to be stout or brave*

Es muy atrevido.	*He is very daring.*
Está muy atrevido.	*He is being (acting or showing himself) very daring (or he has become so).*

Es osado.	*He is bold.*
Está osado.	*He is being (acting or showing himself) very bold (or he has become so).*

IDIOMATIC EXPRESSIONS WITH *ESTAR*

estar de moda	*to be fashionable*
estar a la moda	*to be dressed fashionably*
estar con ganas de (ir)	*to feel like (going)*
estar en lo cierto	*to be on the right track or to be right*
estar en blanco	*to have a mental blank*
estar de pie	*to be on foot, standing*
estar de mal humor	*to be in a bad mood*
estar de vacaciones	*to be on vacation*
estar de guardia	*to be on call, on duty*
estar de acuerdo	*to be in agreement with*

Ser and *Estar* with Participles

Ser is used with past participles to form the passive voice. The past participle agrees in number and in gender with the passive subject.[1]

Fue expulsado del club por el Comité.	*He was expelled from the club by the Committee.*
Fueron expulsados del club por el Comité.	*They were expelled from the club by the Committee.*

Whereas in English the same auxiliary is used with past participles for the actional passive and for the description of states of being, in Spanish **ser** occurs in passives, and **estar** in the description of states of being.

Era temido de todos.	*He was feared by everyone.*
Es respetado por los alumnos.	*He is respected by the students.*
La casa **está** rodeada de árboles.	*The house is surrounded by trees.*
La tierra **está** rodeada de mares.	*The earth is surrounded by seas.*
El hombre **está** cansado.	*The man is tired.*

---

[1] For usage of the passive voice in Spanish, see **Ser** Passives, page 258.

Estar is used with present participles to form progressive constructions.[1]

Está trabajando en México.	*He is working in Mexico.*
Los niños están jugando afuera.	*The children are playing outside.*

SER WITH PAST PARTICIPLES FOR THE ACTIONAL PASSIVE

Ser passives

Ser occurs with past participles to form the passive voice. In the passive voice the grammatical subject does not perform the action as it does in the active voice, but is acted upon by a specified or implied agent.

An active sentence is made passive by making the direct object of the verb the subject of the passive, and the subject of the active verb the agent. The agent is introduced by **por** or **de**. The past participle agrees in number and in gender with the passive subject.

Active	Passive
El fuego destruyó **la casa**.	**La casa** fue destruída **por el fuego**.
The fire destroyed the house.	*The house was destroyed by the fire.*
La ley castiga a **los delincuentes**.	**Los delincuentes** son castigados **por la ley**.
The law punishes delinquents.	*Delinquents are punished by the law.*

Although active and passive sentences convey the same information, they are not entirely synonymous because the focus of emphasis is different in each case. Generally, the person or thing that is emphasized is made the subject of the sentence; therefore, the verb is in some cases put in the active voice, in others in the passive, depending upon the speaker or the viewpoint. While the **ser** passive is formed essentially in the same way as the English *be* passive, its usage is very limited compared to the productivity of passive sentences in English. The sense of the English passive cannot always be rendered through the **ser** passive; it must be conveyed through reflexive constructions, passive reflexives, impersonal sentences, or **estar** + past participle. If a choice exists between an active construction and a **ser** passive, an active sentence is more idiomatic in Spanish. In the spoken language **ser** passives are rare; they are generally found in formal writing and newspapers only.

Restrictions and usage of the **ser** passive

PASSIVES WITH HUMAN SUBJECTS:

1. The passive with **ser** cannot be used in Spanish with human subjects when the meaning of the verb implies the subject's deliberate or non-deliberate involvement or participation in the action. As such the **ser** passive is ungrammatical

---

[1] See Progressive Constructions, page 42.

with all verbs of emotion, perception, change, motion, and memory. An active construction must be used for verbs of perception and a reflexive verb for the others.

Juan se conmovió con tu gesto.	*Juan was moved by your gesture.*
Se atormentaba por sentimientos de culpa.	*She was tormented by guilt feelings.*
Se preocupa por los exámenes.	*She is worried because of her exams.*
Todos se burlaban de él.⎫	
Todos se burlaron de él.⎭	*He was laughed at by everyone.*
La vieron sola.	*She was seen alone.*
No han oído de él desde que se fue.	*He has not been heard of since he left.*
Nos enseñaron la casa.	*The house was shown to us.*
Se transformó en otra persona.	*He was changed into a different person.*
Se sentó a su lado por sugerencia de la anfitriona.	*He was seated next to her by the hostess.*
La anfitriona lo hizo sentar a su lado.	
Uno se olvida fácilmente de nombres extranjeros.	*Foreign names are easily forgotten.*

2. Whereas in English a direct or an indirect object of an active verb can become a passive subject, in Spanish the indirect object cannot be passivized. English sentences containing passivized indirect objects and an agent must be rendered in Spanish through active sentences. The emphasis placed upon the passive subject in English is rendered in Spanish by using the emphatic prepositional form **a mí** ... with the indirect object in subject position.

The teacher gave me the book.	El profesor me dio el libro.
I *was given the book by the teacher.*	**A mí me** dio el profesor el libro.

Even if the direct object of the same sentence had been chosen as the passive subject, in Spanish an active construction would still be used since it is more idiomatic. The emphasis placed upon the subject in English is rendered in Spanish by putting the direct object in subject position.

The book *was given to me by the teacher.*	**El libro** me lo dio el profesor.

English sentences which have passivized indirect objects without agents are rendered in Spanish through impersonal constructions with **se** or with the verb in the third person plural. The latter variant for the impersonal sentence is somewhat less formal than its equivalent with **se**.[1]

We *were shown the house.*	Nos enseñaron la casa.
(*The house was shown to* us.)	**Se** nos enseñó la casa.
He *was asked to resign.*	Le pidieron que renunciara.
(*They asked* him *to resign.*)	**Se** le pidió que renunciara.

---

[1] See **Se** as an Impersonal Subject Reference, page 83.

She *was given the first prize.*	Le otorgaron el primer premio.
(*The first prize was given to* her.)	**Se** le otorgó el primer premio.

The same rule applies to passivized direct objects when they are human and no mention of an agent is made.

John is easily pleased.	⎰ **A Juan** lo complace uno fácilmente.
	⎱ **A Juan** se le complace fácilmente.
He is easily deceived.	⎰ **A él** uno lo engaña fácilmente.
	⎱ **A él** se le engaña fácilmente.

3. With verbs other than those previously mentioned in 1, the passive with human subjects is used in formal writings and speech when emphasis is put upon the action as it affects the passive subjects. It may occur with or without an agent. It is particularly productive when the agent is unknown to the speaker, is of no interest to the message, or is intentionally omitted.

Fue desterrado por el dictador.	*He was banished by the dictator.*
Ha sido atropellado por un auto.	*He was run over by a car.*
Fue herido mortalmente.	*He was mortally wounded.*
Era explotado cruelmente.	*He was being cruelly exploited.*
Ha sido acusado falsamente.	*He has been falsely accused.*

In informal speech an active construction would always be used instead of the **ser** passive. Therefore, whenever an English passive does not belong to a formal speech context, it should not be rendered in Spanish by the **ser** passive. If the sentence makes reference to an agent, an active sentence will be used in Spanish; if no mention of an agent is made, an impersonal sentence will be its equivalent.

I was not invited by them.	Ellos no me invitaron.
She was hated by everyone.	Todos la odiaban.
He was highly esteemed by his students.	Sus estudiantes lo estimaban mucho.
The doctor was not called on time.	⎰ No llamaron al médico a tiempo.
	⎱ No se llamó al médico a tiempo.
He was not informed.	⎰ No lo informaron.
	⎱ No se le informó.

PASSIVES WITH INANIMATE SUBJECTS:

1. The **ser** passive can be used with all inanimate subjects whenever a human agent is expressed or strongly implied. Even though it is more frequent than the passive with human subjects because inanimates can easily be passivized, in informal speech active constructions are more commonly employed.

El cuadro fue pintado por Goya.	*The picture was painted by Goya.*
Las clases fueron suspendidas.	*Classes were suspended.*
Su firma había sido falsificada.	*His signature had been forged.*
La cerradura ha sido forzada.	*The lock has been forced.*

2. If an agent is not implied or not specifiable, the passive reflexive or impersonal **se** are used instead of the **ser** passive—whether the speech context is formal or informal.[1]

Se vendió la casa.	*The house was sold.*
Se inundó la casa debido a las lluvias.	*The house was flooded due to the rains.*
Se abrió la sesión.	*The session was opened.*
Hoy se inician las negociaciones de paz.	*Peace negotiations will be initiated today.*
Se levanta la sesión.	*The meeting is adjourned.*
Se estima que el costo de vida subirá.	*It is estimated that the cost of living will rise.*
El problema económico se ha agravado.	*The economic problem has grown worse.*
El decano solicitó que se reconsiderara la resolución.	*The dean requested that the resolution be reconsidered.*
El presidente reiteró su exhortación para que se acentuara la unidad del mundo occidental.	*The president reiterated his exhortation that the unity of the Western World be fortified.*
El futuro de Gibraltar se decidirá mediante negociaciones.	*The future of Gibraltar will be determined by negotiations.*

Tenses in **ser** passives

The following tense restrictions apply to Spanish passive sentences.

1. The present and the imperfect tenses are used only when sustained or repeated action is implied by the meaning of the verb. If the action of the verb is conclusive, meaning that it has to be ended in order to be completed, the sense conveyed by the present and the imperfect will be one of repeated action in the present and in the past, respectively.

Sus cuentas son pagadas regularmente.	*His bills are paid regularly.*
Sus cuentas eras pagadas regularmente.	*His bills were paid regularly.*

If the action of the verb is non-conclusive, such as with verbs of inner life which do not have to come to an end in order to be complete, the sense conveyed by the same tenses will be one of sustained action.

Era temido por todos.	*He was feared by everyone.*
Es muy conocido.	*He is very well known.*

An English passive sentence with a conclusive verb in the present tense referring to a single action will have to be rendered in Spanish either through an active

---

[1] See Chapter 6, Reflexive Constructions.

sentence, if an agent is expressed, or through a passive reflexive, if no agent is mentioned.

This evening the orchestra is directed by Ormandy.	Ormandy dirige la orquesta esta noche.
Today the class is taught by my friend.	Mi amigo dicta la clase hoy.
Tonight the leading role is played by Geraldine Page.	Esta noche actúa en el papel principal Geraldine Page.
Peace negotiations are initiated today.	Hoy se inician las negociaciones de paz.
The treaty is signed tonight.	Esta noche se firma el tratado.
The proposal is debated this afternoon.	Esta tarde se debate la propuesta.

2. English passives in the present or the preterit, on the other hand, can either describe an action or a state of being. A sentence with a conclusive verb could either mean action, single or repeated, or the resulting state of an action.

(1) *His bills are paid.* ⎫ repeated action.   Sus cuentas son pagadas.
    His bills were paid. ⎭   Sus cuentas eran pagadas.

(2) *His bills are paid.* = ⎫   Sus cuentas **están** pagadas.
    He has paid his bills. ⎪ resultant *state* from
    His bills were paid. = ⎬ an action.
    He had paid his bills. ⎭   Sus cuentas **estaban** pagadas.

With non-conclusive verbs the passive could either describe sustained action or a state of being, with no thought of previous action.

(1) *The French were surrounded* ⎫ sustained action.   Los franceses eran asediados
    by the enemy. ⎭   por el enemigo.

(2) *The house is surrounded* ⎫   La casa **está** rodeada de
    by trees. ⎪   árboles.
    The moon is not inhabited. ⎬ state of being   La luna no **está** habitada.
    He was related to them. ⎭   **Estaba** emparentado con
                                            ellos.

Since in Spanish only **ser** is used for the actional passive and **estar** for states of being, whereas in English the same auxiliary is used for both, the English speaker will have to train himself to differentiate the actional passive from the same construction describing states. Occasionally, the two are formally differentiated in English.

He was awakened.	Lo despertaron.
He was awake.	Estaba despierto.
The door was opened.	⎧ Se abrió la puerta. ⎨ Abrieron la puerta. ⎩
The door was open.	La puerta estaba abierta.

However, in most instances the English speaker has to rely upon the meaning of the sentence and/or its total context in order to grasp the underlying structure.

The battle was lost.	La batalla estaba perdida.
The battle was lost (by the French).	Los franceses perdieron la batalla.
The door is shut at seven.	La puerta se cierra a las siete.
The door is (stands) shut.	La puerta está cerrada.
The magazine was edited by him.	La revista era editada por él.
The magazine was edited with care.	La revista estaba editaba con esmero.
The manuscript was finished (by him).	El manuscrito lo terminó él.
The manuscript was finished (ready).	El manuscrito estaba listo.

3. Progressive tenses are not used with **ser** passives. An English sentence in the progressive will be rendered by the simple tenses in Spanish.

Es perseguido por la policía.	*He is being persecuted by the police.*
Era perseguido por la policía.	*He was being persecuted by the police.*

If the **ser** passive is not admissible in Spanish, then the progressive may occur, provided that ongoing action at the time in question is being referred to.[1]

Lo está operando el Dr. Rivas.	*He is being operated on by Dr. Rivas.*
Se estaba atormentando con sentimientos de culpa.	*She was being tormented by guilt feelings.*
Todos se estaban riendo de él.	*He was being laughed at by everyone.*

ESTAR WITH PAST PARTICIPLES FOR STATES OF BEING

Estar is used with past participles to describe the location, position, state, or condition of a person or thing. The past participle functions here as an adjective; as such it agrees in number and gender with the noun it modifies. But since the past participle denotes either perfected or terminated action, when a noun is modified by the past participle, the state of being described may be the result of a previous or simultaneous action.

1. When the meaning of the past participle refers to conclusive, non-durative action, the state of being is the result of a previous action.

Resultant State	*Previous action*
La carta está escrita.	La carta ha sido escrita.
The letter is written.	*The letter has been written.*
El libro está impreso.	Se ha imprimido el libro.
The book is printed (in print).	*The book has been printed.*
Los documentos están firmados.	Los documentos han sido firmados.
The documents are signed.	*The documents have been signed.*

[1] See **Estar** + **-ndo**, page 42.

2. When the meaning of the past participle refers to non-conclusive, durative events, the state of being may be simultaneous with the action.

ATTAINED STATE SIMULTANEOUS WITH ACTION

Juan está entretenido.	Juan se entretiene.
Juan is amused.	*Juan is amusing himself.*
María está preocupada.	María se preocupa.
Maria is worried.	*Maria worries.*
El está aburrido.	El se aburre.
He is bored.	*He gets bored.*

3. With stative verbs, **estar** merely describes a state of being without reference to previous action.

STATE OF BEING

La industria está subdesarrollada.	*Industry is underdeveloped.*
Perú está situado en el hemisferio sur.	*Peru is located in the Southern hemisphere.*
El universo está compuesto de diversos planetas.	*The universe is made up of various planets.*
El pueblo está alejado del mar.	*The town is located far away from the sea.*
La luna no está habitada.	*The moon is not inhabited.*

The duration of the state described has no bearing upon the usage of **estar** + past participle. It may be durative:

La casa está rodeada de árboles.	*The house is surrounded by trees.*
El está aislado de todos.	*He is isolated from everyone.*

It may be transitory:

El está dormido.	*He is asleep.*
El está parado.	*He is standing up.*

Or it may be final and permanent:

El está muerto.	*He is dead.*
El cuadro está arruinado.	*The painting is ruined.*

The duration of a state depends upon the meaning of the past participle itself, as well as upon other elements in the sentence. In **La tierra está rodeada de mares** a permanent state is described; but in **El está rodeado de sus familiares** the state could either be transitory or durative, depending upon the actual life-situation.

Estar + past participle occurs with transitive verbs—those that require an object to complete their meaning—and with intransitive reflexives. With all

other intransitive verbs, except those denoting a change of state such as **cambiar,
decaer,** and **envejecer,** it does not occur. A few transitive verbs, **querer, amar,
saludar, besar,** do not occur in this construction because they cannot be thought
of as bringing about a state in the subject.

This construction is frequent with some verbs of motion which give place to
postures, **acostar-se, sentar-se, parar-se, levantar-se,** and those that give
place to situations, **encerrar-se, esconder-se,** etc.

Se acostó.	Está acostado.
He has lied down.	*He is lying down.*
Se encerró en su cuarto.	Está encerrado en su cuarto.
He has locked himself in his room.	*He is locked up in his room.*
Ha envejecido mucho.	Está muy envejecido.
He has aged very much.	*He looks much older.*

When **estar** + past participle occurs with a participle that refers to non-
conclusive, durative action (the state of being is simultaneous with the sustained
action), an agent may co-occur with the construction. The subject of the active
sentence becomes the agent in the stative sentence. The stative sentence is
rendered in English by the *be* passive.

Su sobrino administra la fábrica.	La fábrica está administrada por su
His nephew manages the factory.	sobrino.
	The factory is managed by his nephew.
El gobierno controla la prensa.	La prensa está controlada por el
The government controls the press.	gobierno.
	The press is controlled by the
	government.
El tirano oprime al pueblo.	El pueblo está oprimido por el
The tyrant oppresses the people.	tirano.
	The people are oppressed by the tyrant.
Un extranjero dirige el programa.	El programa está dirigido por un
A foreigner directs the program.	extranjero.
	The program is directed by a foreigner.

But if the verb refers to a conclusive event, **estar** + past participle does not
co-occur with an agent.

*Está condenado por el juez.	{ Está condenado.
	{ *He is condemned.*
*Está desterrado por el dictador.	{ Está desterrado.
	{ *He is banished.*
*Está expulsado por la junta	{ Está expulsado.
directiva.	{ *He is expelled.*

Tenses in **estar** + past participle constructions

Estar + past participle generally occurs in the present, the imperfect, or the preterit (when the state of being is terminated). It is used in the simple tenses, because the state or condition described is either the result of a previous action or co-exists with an action in the actual or retrospective present.

1. Resultant state from a previous action: the tense of the active sentence immediately precedes that of the stative sentence.

El hombre está encarcelado. *The man is imprisoned.*	El hombre ha sido encarcelado. *The man has been imprisoned.*
Los libros estaban esparcidos por toda la casa. *The books were scattered all over the house.*	Los libros habían sido esparcidos por toda la casa. *The books had been scattered all over the house.*
Estuvo separado de su mujer. *He was (had been) separated from his wife.*	El se había separado de su mujer. *He had separated himself from his wife.*

2. Attained state simultaneous with sustained action: the tense of **estar** corresponds to the tense of the active sentence.

Está divertido. *He is amused.*	Se divierte. *He is amusing himself.*
Estaba dedicado a su profesión. *He was dedicated to his profession.*	Se dedicaba a su profesión. *He dedicated himself to his profession.*
Estaba muy bien portado. *He was very well behaved.*	Se portaba muy bien. *He behaved very well.*

With stative verbs, those which cannot be thought of as resulting from a previous action, the tense depends upon the temporal perspective intended by the speaker. Since these verbs refer to events which exist within an actual or retrospective actual present, they are also generally restricted to the simple tenses.

La ocasión está perdida.	*The opportunity is lost.*
El estaba emparentado con los Molina.	*He was related to the Molinas.*
El estaba muy bien vinculado.	*He had very good connections.*

Ser Contrasted with *Estar*

Ser	Estar
+ NOUNS	
Occurs with nouns, parts of speech that can function as such, and noun phrases.	Does not occur with nouns, except in a few idiomatic phrases.

Ser de + noun describes:

1. possession:

   Es de María.
   It belongs to Maria.

2. composition of a thing:

   La casa es de ladrillos.
   It is a brick house.

3. the make up of a person:

   Es un hombre de gran visión.
   He is a man of great vision.

Ser para + noun describes:

1. the beneficiary of an action:

   Los libros son para Juan.
   The books are for John.

2. the goal of a thing or event:

   Las fiestas son para descansar.
   Holidays are for relaxation.

+ ADVERBIALS

1. Takes adverbials of place to express origin and occurrence of an event.

   Es de Venezuela.
   He is from Venezuela.

   La reunión es en el auditorio.
   The meeting takes place in the auditorium.

   Takes adverbials of place to describe location.

   Está en Venezuela.
   He is in Venezuela.

2. Takes adverbs of time to express temporal relationships.

   Son las siete.
   It is seven o'clock.

   Mi cita es a las cuatro.
   My appointment is at four.

   Takes adverbs of manner to describe condition.

   Juan está mejor.
   Juan is better.

   Está bien.
   It is fine.

+ ADJECTIVALS

Describes the existence of a quality. It qualifies, characterizes the subject in an atemporal way.

Describes a state of being, which contrasts with the same or opposite condition in a previous temporal dimension.

Ser	Estar
Es nervioso. *He is a nervous person.*	Está nervioso. *He is nervous (these days).*
Es impaciente. *He is an impatient person.*	Está impaciente. *He is being (acting) impatient.*
Es liberal. *He is a liberal person.*	Está más liberal. *He is (has become) more liberal now.*
Es joven. *She is young.*	Está joven. *She is (looks and acts) young.*

+ PAST PARTICIPLES

Forms the passive voice.	Describes the resultant state from a previous action or a state of being.
Fue expulsado del club. *He was expelled from the club.*	Está divorciado (resultant state from "se ha divorciado"). *He is divorced.*
	La tierra está rodeada de mares. *The earth is surrounded by seas.*

+ PRESENT PARTICIPLES

Does not occur with present participles.	Forms progressive constructions.
	Está cantando. *He is singing.*

The Spanish and English Passive Contrasted

PASSIVES

Spanish Ser	*English* Be

FORM

Ser + past participle ($\mp$ agent). The past participle agrees in number and in gender with the passive subject.	*Be* + past participle ($\mp$ agent).

The thing or person that is emphasized is made the subject of the sentence. Therefore, the verb is sometimes put in the active voice, sometimes in the passive.

César venció Pompeo.	*Ceasar defeated Pompeyus.*
Pompeo fue vencido por César.	*Pompeyus was defeated by Ceasar.*

RESTRICTIONS

An indirect object of an active verb cannot become a passive subject. An active sentence must be used. Even when a direct object is passivized in English, in Spanish an active sentence is more idiomatic. Direct and indirect objects may be emphasized by occurring in subject position.	Either a direct or an indirect object can become a passive subject.

El maestro **me** dio **el libro**.	*The teacher gave me the book.*
A mí me dio el libro el maestro.	*I was given the book by the teacher.*
El libro me lo dio el maestro.	*The book was given to me by the teacher.*

Found in formal writings and newspapers only. Active sentences are more idiomatic in the spoken language.	Highly productive. It occurs in oral and written contexts, formal and informal.

HUMAN SUBJECTS

Cannot be used with a human subject when the verb implies the subject's participation in the action: verbs of motion, change, emotion, perception, and memory. An active sentence or a reflexive construction must be used for the English passive.	

La vieron sola.	*She was seen alone.*
Todos se reían de él.	*He was laughed at by everyone.*
Se conmovió con tu reacción.	*She was moved by your reaction.*
Se ofendió por tu falta de cortesía.	*She was offended by your lack of courtesy.*
Todos se acordaban de él.	*He was remembered by everyone.*

INANIMATE SUBJECTS

With inanimate subjects when no agent is expressed or strongly implied, passive reflexive and impersonal **se** sentences are used instead of **ser** passives.	

Spanish **Ser**	English Be
La cerradura ha sido forzada.	*The lock has been forced.*
BUT:	
Se suspendieron las clases.	*Classes were suspended.*
Se vendió la casa.	*The house was sold.*
Se hundió la lancha.	*The boat sank.*

TENSES

Does not admit progressive tenses. A simple tense equivalent to the time expressed by the English progressive should be used instead.	
Es perseguido por la policía.	*He is being persecuted by the police.*
Era perseguido por la policía.	*He was being persecuted by the police.*

STATES OF BEING

Spanish	English
Estar + past participle. The past participle agrees in number and in gender with the noun it modifies.	*Be* + past participle.
	Whereas in Spanish a different auxiliary is used for the passive of action and for the description of states of being, in English *be* is used for both. The English speaker will have to rely upon the meaning of the sentence and/or its total context in order to decipher the underlying structure.
La batalla fue perdida por los franceses.	*The battle was lost by the French.* (= action)
La batalla estaba perdida.	*The battle was lost.* (Resultant state of a previous action).
El manuscrito fue editado	*The manuscript was edited.* (*edited by him*).
El manuscrito estaba editado.	*The manuscript was edited.*

The construction may either describe a resultant state from a previous action, a state of being that is simultaneous with the action, or a state of being without consideration of the action that might have brought it about.

La carta está escrita (= ha sido escrita).	*The letter is written (= has been written).*
El está preocupado (= él se preocupa).	*He is worried (= he worries).*
La tierra está rodeada de mares.	*The earth is surrounded by seas.*

The duration of the state in question has no bearing upon its usage. It may be short or long lasting, or permanent.

Está muy enamorado.	*He is very much in love.*
Está rodeado de sus hijos.	*He is surrounded by his sons.*
Los Andes siempre están cubiertos de nieve.	*The Andes are always covered with snow.*

The construction is used in the simple tenses because the state of affairs is viewed as either resulting from a previous or simultaneous action or as existing within the present or the past.

Está cansado (se ha cansado).	*He is tired (has gotten tired).*
Estaba casado (se había casado).	*He was married (had gotten married).*
Está situado en el centro.	*It is located downtown.*
Estaba situado en el centro.	*It was located downtown.*

16

ARTICLES: DEFINITE AND INDEFINITE: THE NEUTER **LO**

Definite Articles

FORMS OF THE DEFINITE ARTICLE

English	Spanish		
		Singular	Plural
	Masculine	**el libro**	**los libros**
the	Feminine	**la casa**; **(el) arpa**	**las casas**
	Neuter	**lo bueno**	

The form of the definite article in Spanish signals the gender and number of the noun to which it refers. In addition, Spanish has a neuter form as in "**Lo** bueno de este libro" = "*The* good thing about this book." All of these correspond to the English form *the*.

la → el before á-, há-

The singular form **el** must be used before singular feminine nouns that begin with a stressed **á** sound, excepting proper names.

el agua	*the water*	el ala	*the wing*
el arpa	*the harp*	el ancla	*the anchor*
el aya	*the governess*	el águila	*the eagle*

el aula	*the classroom*	el hambre	*the hunger*
el alma	*the soul*	el hacha	*the axe*

BUT: la Ana, la Angela
la a, la hache
la Haya

If the first syllable is not stressed, the feminine form is used: **la hacienda, la artista**. The use of the form **el** does not apply to adjectives of like form: **la alta torre, la ancha calle**, etc. It does not change by any means the gender of the noun, which is observed by the adjective agreement: **El agua en Madrid es muy buena** = *The water in Madrid is very good.*

Article + preposition

English	Spanish	
to the *from the*	$\begin{array}{l} \mathbf{a} \\ \mathbf{de} \end{array} + \mathbf{el}\Big\}$	**al** **del**

The masculine singular form **el** is contracted to **al**, **del**, when preceded by the prepositions **a**, **de**, respectively.

Vamos al teatro esta noche.	*We are going to the theater tonight.*
Vengo del cine.	*I am coming from the movies.*

However, when the article is part of a title of a book, play, etc., there is no contraction.

Compré varios ejemplares de *El siglo de las luces* de Carpentier.	*I bought several copies of Carpentier's "El siglo de las luces."*

In the following example the form **él** (with an accent mark) corresponds to the subject pronoun *he*; therefore, there is no contraction:

Este libro es de él.	*This book is his.*

Masculine plural

With plural nouns referring to both genders, the masculine plural form of the article is used.

Los hermanos (hermano y hermana) de Pepe.	*Pepe's brother and sister.*
Los suegros (suegro y suegra) de Ricardo.	*Ricardo's father and mother-in-law.*

USES OF THE DEFINITE ARTICLE

For specifying objects

The main function of the definite article in both Spanish and English is to specify or to limit animate or inanimate objects according to an identifying context previously known and understood by the speaker. In a sentence like **Pablo compró corbatas** = *Paul bought ties*, we don't know which ties he bought, nor how many, except that Paul did not buy all of the ties. If, however, we hear **Pablo compró las corbatas (que vió ayer)** = *Paul bought the ties (that he saw yesterday)*, we still may not know how many ties, but at least we know which specific ties he did buy, according to an identifying context understood by the speaker. Thus, as a general rule, both languages use the definite article to specify animate or inanimate objects and omit it to show the idea of "some," "a few," "any," or an indefinite mass.

Dame más arroz.	*Give me more rice.*
Dame el arroz.	*Give me the rice.*
El señor Pérez construye casas.	*Mr. Perez builds houses.*
El señor Pérez construye la casa en que viviremos.	*Mr. Perez is building the house in which we will live.*
El niño tiene ideas brillantes.	*The child has brilliant ideas.*
Las ideas que tiene el niño son brillantes.	*The ideas that the child has are brilliant.*
Venezuela tiene hierro y petróleo.	*Venezuela has oil and iron.*
Venezuela tiene el hierro y el petróleo necesarios para la industria.	*Venezuela has the oil and iron necessary for its industry.*

This function of the definite article of identifying, specifying, limiting items within a given context can be better understood if we substitute the definite article with one of the other determiners (demonstratives, possessives).

El señor Pérez construye **la** casa. (esta, esa, aquella casa; mi, tu, su, nuestra casa)	*Mr. Perez is building* the *house.* (*this, that house; my, your, his, our house*)

Definite articles, then, must be used when a noun is omitted, provided that the context is previously understood as in:

1. Article + **que** = *the one that, the one who, the ones who, she/he who, those who:*

Pedro tiene el libro.	*Peter has the book.*
Necesito **el que** tiene Pedro.	*I need the one that Peter has.*
La señora llamó esta mañana.	*The lady called this morning.*
La que llamó esta mañana no vino.	*The one who called this morning didn't come.*
	She who....
Los (hombres) **que** pintaron la casa no están aquí.	*The ones who painted the house are not here.*
	Those who ...

2. Article + **de** = *the one(s) with/of; that/those of, with; the . . . one*:

Hay una mujer con un traje verde.	*There is a woman with a green dress.*
¿Puedes ver **la del** traje verde?	*Can you see the one with the green dress?*
Las elecciones de este año son más difíciles que **las del** año pasado.	*This year's elections are more difficult than those of (the ones) of last year.*
No me gusta esta corbata, prefiero **la de** seda.	*I don't like this tie, I prefer the silk one.*

The identifying context which serves as the background for the specification or limitation of a given object may sometimes be provided by a unique idea or experience within the culture.

Spanish and English, therefore, differ insofar as Spanish consistently marks uniqueness by using the definite article, whereas English doesn't always do it.

El sol es caliente.	*The sun is hot.*
El infierno debe ser horrible.	*Hell must be horrible.*
Ha conquistado el cielo.	*He has conquered Heaven.*

In some instances, English labels the unique entity as a proper noun (*Hell, Heaven,* etc.).

With nouns used in a general or abstract sense

Definite articles are used in both Spanish and English to refer to all members of a whole class in general. Totality may be understood in terms of the "generic whole," the "whole class or species." The main difference between the two languages is that while Spanish consistently and systematically uses the definite articles to mark totality (i.e., to refer to all of something, to refer to an entire class or species in an abstract, general, or universal sense), English only does so rarely.

1. Thus, English like Spanish uses the definite article in the following constructions with singular nouns that refer to a whole class:

El diamante es una piedra cara.	*The diamond is an expensive stone.*
El camello es un animal doméstico.	*The camel is a domestic animal.*
El caballo es muy útil.	*The horse is very useful.*
El indio y el negro son un sector importante.	*The Indian and the Negro are an important sector.*

2. While Spanish always uses the article with plural nouns that refer to a whole class, English really tends to avoid it.

Los anglo-sajones son gente trabajadora.	*The Anglo-Saxons are hardworking people.*
Los Americanos son idealistas.	*Americans are idealistic.*
Los perros son animales domésticos.	*Dogs are domestic animals.*
Los caballos son animales útiles.	*Horses are useful animals.*
Me gustan los huevos.	*I like eggs.*

3. As a general rule Spanish always marks the generic whole by using the definite article while English does not.

El tiempo es valioso.	*Time is precious.*
La tecnología desarrolla la industria.	*Technology develops industry.*
Me interesa el arte moderno.	*I am interested in modern art.*
La leche es básica para la nutrición.	*Milk is basic for nutrition.*

Only context, then, can tell the English speaker the two possible meanings that a single sentence may have in Spanish:

El hombre es idealista.

Man is idealistic.
("Man" considered in general, as a whole class).
The man is idealistic.
(Referring to a specific "man" already mentioned, known or understood in the context: *this man, that man*.)

Los estudiantes son inteligentes.

Students are intelligent.
("Students" in a general sense).
The students are intelligent.
(The "students in my class, my students, these students.")

La leche es buena.

Milk is good.
("Milk" in general, as a whole.)
The milk is good.
(The "milk in this area, here, this milk," referring to something defined and specific.)

4. If the partitive idea of *some, any, every,* is implied or if only a portion of a substance or class is under consideration, then the article is omitted in Spanish as well as in English.

Me gusta el pan.

I like bread.
("Bread" refers to a whole class.)

Como pan en el desayuno.

I eat bread for breakfast.
("Bread" does not refer to the whole class, but the partitive idea is present: *some*.)

El dinero es necesario.
¿Tienes dinero?
Los españoles conquistaron el Nuevo Mundo.

Money (in general) is necessary.
Do you have (some) money?
The Spaniards conquered the New World.
(The "Spaniards" considered as a whole class of people).

| Españoles conquistaron el Nuevo Mundo. | *Spaniards conquered the New World. (The "Spaniards" considered as individuals, as part of a whole class of people.)* |

5. **Todo** + article and **todos**

When **todo** = *all, the entire*, means "the whole of a class," it contributes to the idea of generalization of the noun. As such it is followed by the article.

Todo el hombre es un ser íntegro.	*Man as a whole is an integral being.*
Todo el café se procesa aquí.	*All of the coffee is processed here.*
Toda la idea es interesante.	*The entire idea is interesting.*

This idea of generalization is more obvious and clear in the plural. **Todos, todas,** is always followed by the article.

| Todos los hombres son mortales. | *All men are mortal.* |
| Todas las mujeres son guapas. | *(All women are beautiful. (All of the women are beautiful.* |

But when **todo** means "each one, "everyone of," suggesting each one of a whole class, then the article is not used.

Todo hombre de este gobierno es honrado.	*Every man in this government is honest.*
Toda mujer aquí es inteligente.	*Every woman here is intelligent.*
Todo café es bueno.	*Any coffee is good.*
Toda idea merece atención.	*Every idea deserves attention.*

With proper names of persons

As a general rule the definite article is not used before singular unmodified proper names of persons, unless these are used as common nouns to describe the character of an individual or to denote his work.

Esteban llegó ayer.	*Stephen arrived yesterday.*
Jorge no está aquí.	*George is not here.*
Napoleón invadió Rusia.	*Napoleon invaded Russia.*
BUT: Traéme el Webster.	*Bring me the Webster.*
Compró el Velázquez.	*He bought the Velazquez.*
Quiere ser el Napoleón de América.	*He wants to be the Napoleon of America.*

In Spanish, however, the definite article occasionally accompanies an unmodified proper name.

1. In informal speech denoting contempt:

| Vi a la María. | *I saw that Mary.* |
| Llamó el Pérez. | *That Perez called.* |

In this context it is roughly equivalent to the use of the English demonstrative *that*.

2. In figurative speech. The article may be used here to refer to famous, unique, and well known personalities. Its presence, however, may also denote contempt, depending on the context, intonation, etc.:

La Taylor es la artista principal.	*Taylor is the main actress.*
¿Viste la foto de la Jackie?	*Did you see Jackie's picture?*
¡Qué persona más antipática es la Luisa!	*What an unpleasant person that Luisa is!*

3. In legal proceedings:

Y declaró el (dicho) Pérez que había visto a la María . . .	*And this (the said) Perez testified that he had seen the said Mary . . .*

The definite article is also used in Spanish in the following cases:

1. With modified proper names of persons:

Llamó la pobre Susana.	*Poor Susan called.*
¡La pobre Susana!	*Poor Susan!*

However, it may be omitted in exclamations. When omitted the statement is less emphatic.

¡Pobre Susana!	*Poor Susan!*

2. With all titles except **don, doña, san, santo/a, fray, sor,** when something is said about a person:

El señor García es el nuevo gerente.	*Mr. Garcia is the new manager.*
El doctor Fernández lo operó.	*Dr. Fernandez operated on him.*
BUT: Sor Juana fue una gran escritora.	*Sor Juana was a great writer.*
Hoy es el día de San Juan.	*Today is St. John's feast.*
Don Enrique no está aquí.	*Don Enrique is not here.*

It is also omitted in direct address as in English:

Hasta luego, Profesor Ayala.	*So long, Professor Ayala.*
Por favor, venga mañana, doctor García.	*Please come tomorrow, Doctor Garcia.*

3. In epithets or with nicknames immediately after the proper name as in English:

Iván, el Terrible.	*Ivan, the Terrible.*
Alejandro, el Magno.	*Alexander, the Great.*
Juanito, el travieso.	*Johnny, the rascal.*

With the cardinal or ordinal number that follows a royal title, Spanish omits the definite article.

El Emperador Carlos Quinto . . .	*The Emperor Charles the Fifth . . .*
El Papa Juan Veintitrés . . .	*Pope John the Twenty-third . . .*

With geographical and other proper names

1. The definite article is used with names of oceans, seas, rivers, mountains, volcanoes, and deserts.

el Atlántico, el Pacífico . . .	*the Atlantic, the Pacific . . .*
el Caribe, el Adriático . . .	*the Caribbean, the Adriatic . . .*
el Amazonas, el Potomac . . .	*the Amazon, the Potomac . .*
los Andes, los Rocosos . . .	*the Andes, the Rockies . . .*
el Gran Cañon, el Aconcagua . . .	*the Grand Canyon, the Aconcagua . . .*
el Vesubio . . .	*Vesuvius . . .*
el Sahara . . .	*the Sahara . . .*

Spanish also uses it with names of lakes.

el Titicaca	*Lake Titicaca*
el lago Superior	*Lake Superior*

2. The article is always used in Spanish with modified names of countries and cities.

Visitamos el México colonial.	*We visited Colonial Mexico.*
¿Qué le pareció el Nueva York financiero?	*What did you think of financial New York?*

3. As a general rule the definite article is not used in Spanish with most unmodified proper names of countries, cities, or geographical areas or regions.

He visitado España varias veces.	*I have visited Spain several times.*
Estuvimos en Alemania Oriental.	*We were in East Germany.*
Me encanta París.	*I love Paris.*
Latinoamérica tiene gran futuro.	*Latin America has great future.*

There are, however, certain instances where the definite article has been used with proper names of this type:

(la) Argentina	(los) Estados Unidos	(la) Siberia
(el) Brazil	(la) Gran Bretaña	(el) Asia Menor
(el) Camerón	(la) India	(la) Europa Occidental
(el) Canadá	(el) Japón	(la) América Latina
(la) China	(el) Paraguay	(la) América del Norte
(el) Congo	(el) Perú	(el) Asia
(el) Ecuador	(el) Uruguay	(el) Africa
(el) Vietnam del Norte	(la) Corea del Sur	(el) Medio Oriente

The trend today in newspaper and colloquial usage is towards omitting the article, particularly after prepositions.

Vive en Argentina.	*She lives in Argentina.*
Va para Estados Unidos.	*He is going to the United States.*

Nevertheless, the use of the article still persists in those instances where it has become part of the proper name, as in **El Salvador, La Habana, La Paz, El Cairo, El Havre, La Haya, La Mancha**; where it is still used as part of a descriptive name, as in **los Países Bajos, la Guayana Holandesa, la Unión Soviética, la Gran Bretaña, los Estados Unidos**; and where it is traditional with such geographic names as **la Patagonia, la Pampa, el Tirol, la Crimea**, etc.

4. Spanish like English uses the definite article with proper names of famous ships, airplanes, buildings.

el France	*the France*
el Cristóforo Colombo	*the Christopher Columbus*
el Espíritu de San Luis	*the Spirit of St. Louis*
el Espíritu de 1776	*the Spirit of 1776*
la Casa Blanca	*the White House*
el Capitolio	*the Capitol*
la Escala de Milán	*the Scala of Milan*
la Metropolitana	*the Metropolitan*
el Plaza	*the Plaza*
el Waldorf Astoria	*the Waldorf Astoria*

5. Spanish, however, goes farther in also using the definite article with other modified proper names as in:

La calle 34 es una de las más importantes.	*Thirty-fourth Street is one of the most important ones.*
¿Qué te parece la Quinta Avenida?	*What do you think about Fifth Avenue?*
Hemos cruzado el puente Washington.	*We have crossed Washington Bridge.*
El túnel Lincoln es impresionante.	*Lincoln Tunnel is impressive.*
El Centro Rockefeller queda cerca.	*Rockefeller Center is nearby.*
Vamos al Parque Central.	*We are going to Central Park.*

With names of languages

Definite articles are used in Spanish with names of languages.

El español es bastante fácil.	*Spanish is rather easy.*
Prefiero el francés al alemán.	*I prefer French to German.*
Es traducido del francés.	*It is translated from (the) French.*
Viene del sánskrito.	*It comes from Sanskrit.*
Existe en el latín clásico.	*It exists in Classical Latin.*

After certain verbs such as **aprender, comprender, enseñar, escribir, estudiar, hablar, leer, oír**, and **saber**, the article is generally omitted.

¿Prefieres aprender (el) francés?	*Do you prefer to learn French?*
¿Hablan Uds. (el) rumano?	*Do you speak Rumanian?*
¿Comprendes (el) griego?	*Do you understand Greek?*

When a name of a language describes a quality of the subject, the article is not used.

Este documento está escrito en italiano.	*This document is written in Italian.*
El señor García es profesor de portugués.	*Mr. Garcia is a professor of Portuguese.*
Esta novela está traducida al ruso.	*This novel is (has been) translated into Russian.*

With expressions of time

Definite articles are used in Spanish with expressions of time as in:

1. The equivalents of *last, next*:

Llegó el año pasado.	*He arrived last year.*
Viene el próximo mes.	*He comes next month.*
Hoy es el último domingo de mayo.	*Today is the last Sunday of May.*
El siguiente día de la semana es miércoles.	*The next day of the week is Wednesday.*

2. The hours of the day:

| La reunión comienza a la una. | *The meeting begins at one o'clock.* |
| Eran las dos y media. | *It was two thirty.* |

With exact hours, English has an expression "o'clock" which has no equivalent in Spanish.

3. The days of the week, seasons of the year:

El invierno es muy frío en el norte.	*Winter is very cold in the North.*
Prefiero mejor el otoño.	*I prefer the fall.*
Los lunes llego temprano.	*I arrive early on Mondays.*
¿Llamó el martes?	*Did she call on Tuesday?*
Viene todos los domingos.	⎰*He comes on Sundays.* ⎱*He comes every Sunday.*

The definite article is equivalent to the English preposition *on* in the preceding three examples.

When the days of the week and seasons of the year are modified by an adverbial clause of time (**ahora, mañana, ayer,** etc.), the article is then omitted.

La fiesta es el miércoles.	*The party is on Wednesday.*
Mañana es miércoles.	*Tomorrow is Wednesday.*
La fiesta es mañana miércoles.	*The party is tomorrow Wednesday.*

La reunión fue el jueves.	*The meeting was on Thursday.*
Ayer fue jueves.	*Yesterday it was Thursday.*
La reunión fue ayer jueves.	*The meeting was yesterday, Thursday.*

La primavera es la estación más linda del año.	*Spring is the most beautiful season of the year.*
Ahora es primavera.	*It is spring now.*

4. With dates of the month the use of the definite article is optional in Spanish; but after the expression **estar a** + DATE meaning "it is . . .," the article is omitted.

Es (el) primero de septiembre. *It is September the first.*	Estamos a primero de septiembre. *It is . . .*
Era (el) jueves tres de febrero. *It was Thursday, February the third.*	Estábamos a jueves tres de febrero. *It was . . .*

The article is used with modified names of months.

El precioso octubre . . .	*Beautiful October . . .*
El lluvioso abril . . .	*Rainy April . . .*

It is also used to refer to the meals of the day.

La invité para el almuerzo.	*I invited her for lunch.*
el desayuno.	*breakfast.*
la cena.	*dinner.*
el té.	*tea(time).*

The English expression "*at* + age" always calls for the use of the definite article in Spanish.

Aprendió a leer a los cuatro años.	*He learned to read at four.*

In appositional phrases

Since the definite article is used consistently in Spanish to mark totality, it occurs with a noun in apposition with a pronoun, because of the meaning of *all*:

Nosotros, los americanos, queremos justicia.	*We Americans want justice.*

In Spanish, the definite article is used with a noun in apposition with another noun when the purpose is to emphasize, identify, single out, or bring out some outstanding quality. If the apposition is merely explanatory, the article is omitted as in English.

Washington, capital de los Estados Unidos, está situada . . .	*Washington, capital of the United States, is located . .*
Washington, **la capital** de los Estados Unidos, está situada . . .	*Washington, the capital of the United States, is located . . .*

| El presidente del comité, Señor López . . . | The president of the committee, Mr. Lopez . . . |
| El presidente del comité, **el señor López** . . . | The president of the committee, Mr. Lopez . . . |

| Mi hermano, ingeniero de esta firma . . . | My brother, an engineer with this firm . . . |
| Mi hermano, **el ingeniero** de esta firma . . . | My brother, the engineer in this firm . . . |

Outstanding qualities are usually brought out by a superlative adjectival clause.

Madrid, la ciudad más importante de España . . .	Madrid, the most important city in Spain . . .
El perro, el animal más fiel al hombre . . .	The dog, the most faithful animal to man . . .
Mi hermano, el mejor ingeniero de esta firma . . .	My brother, the best engineer of this firm . . .

OTHER USES OF THE DEFINITE ARTICLE IN SPANISH

1. The definite article is used in Spanish to indicate rate, measure, or weight; but when an indefinite mass is under consideration, it is omitted.

Me cobraba diez dólares la visita.	He used to charge me ten dollars a visit.
Costó ochenta centavos la docena.	It cost eighty cents a dozen.
Pagué cinco dólares la yarda.	I payed five dollars a yard.
Cuesta veinticinco centavos la libra.	It costs twenty-five cents a pound.

BUT:

Los regala por docena.	He gives them away by the dozen.
Le paga por hora.	He pays her by the hour.
Los vende por libra.	He sells them by the pound.

2. Spanish uses the definite article instead of the possessive with body parts and personal belongings, unless the possessive is required for emphasis or to avoid possible ambiguities.

Me duele el estómago.	My stomach aches.
Tengo las manos sucias.	My hands are dirty.
Me quité la corbata.	I took off my tie.
No dejes el libro aquí.	Don't leave your book here.

3. The definite article must be used with the stressed possessive forms that follow the noun when the possessive is nominalized.

| Es mi **libro**. | It is my book. (Emphasis on the object possessed) |

BUT: Es **el** libro **mío**.	*It is my book.*
	(Emphasis on the possession)
Es el **mío**.	*It is mine.*
Ella tiene su libro, pero yo olvidé **el mío**.	*She has her book, but I forgot mine.*

The article is also used when possession is expressed by the preposition **de**.

Mi casa y **la de** Pablo están cerca.	*My house and Paul's are nearby.*

4. The definite article may occur with an infinitive functioning as a verbal noun in subject position. Only the masculine singular form can be used. This construction corresponds to the English *-ing* form or the infinitive.

(El) caminar es buen ejercicio.	*Walking is a good exercise.*
(El) viajar es siempre interesante.	*Traveling is always interesting.*
(El) ver es creer.	*To see is to believe.*

OMISSION OF THE DEFINITE ARTICLE IN SPANISH

Apart from the few instances already mentioned, the definite article is also omitted in Spanish as follows:

1. Where it is not part of a title of a book, movie, poem, newspaper, or magazine article, etc., it is omitted.

¿Viste la película *Sangre y Arena*?	*Did you see the movie "Sand and Blood?"*
¿Leíste *Alturas de Machu Picchu*?	*Did you read "Alturas de Machu Picchu?"*
¿Quién escribió *Respuesta a la leyenda negra*?	*Who wrote "Respuesta a la leyenda negra?"*

2. It is omitted before a noun which is merely a synonym or explanation of a preceding noun linked with the preposition **o** = *or*.

El vestíbulo o entrada de la casa ...	*The hall or entrance of the house ...*
BUT: El vestíbulo o la cocina de la casa ...	*The hall or kitchen of the house ...*

3. The article is omitted before a noun in many adverbial and prepositional phrases.

con motivo de mi partida	*on account of my departure*
en nombre del comité	*on behalf of the committee*
a orillas del Potomac	*on the banks of the Potomac*

But it may be retained for emphasis:

en el nombre de este comité ...
y con el motivo de mi partida ...

4. The article is usually omitted in enumerations.

Llegaron padre e hijo.	*Father and son arrived.*
Ya son marido y mujer.	*They are already husband and wife.*

5. With certain commonly used names such as **casa**, **clase**, **misa**, and **cama**, accompanied by the preposition **a**, **de**, or **en**, Spanish may omit the definite article.

Vamos a misa el domingo.	*We are going to mass on Sunday.*
¿Está María en casa?	*Is Mary home?*
¿Vienes de clase?	*Are you coming from class?*
¿Se quedó en cama hoy?	*She stayed in bed today?*

This use is purely idiomatic and is by no means as widespread in Spanish as it is in English (*I am going to work . . .; . . . to school; They sent him to prison . . .; . . . to jail; He is at sea . . .; Stay for supper . . .,* etc.). All of these have Spanish equivalents with the definite article. In Spanish the omission of the article is restricted to very few everyday set phrases in which the nouns refer to places where some activity is taking place and where the reference is as much to the activity as to the place. The difficulty is that this is not consistently applicable in the two languages and that in Spanish it varies from area to area, depending on the frequency and familiarity of a place name. Thus, some speakers may accept also: **Vamos a Palacio . . ., El niño ya va a colegio . . ., Lo llevaré a corte . . ..**

To avoid confusion, it is simply safer to learn the few set phrases as idiomatic expressions, and to use the article elsewhere.

6. The definite article is frequently omitted in proverbs and in other idiomatic expressions.

Dádivas quebrantan penas.	*Gifts move mountains.*
Pobreza no es vileza.	*Poverty is no crime.*
Vamos a levantar ancla.	*Let's raise anchor.*
Ya tiene que sentar cabeza.	*He has to settle down.*
Tiene ganas de ver mundo.	*He wants to see the world.*
La novia no lleva dote.	*The bride has no dowry.*
¿Ya han puesto casa?	*Have you set up house?*

7. In impersonal expressions with **ser**, the article is normally omitted. Sometimes it may be used to add emphasis.

Es costumbre de la Universidad.	*It is the custom of the university.*
Es **la** costumbre de la Universidad.	*It is the custom of the university.*
Es privilegio del Decano.	*It is the privilege of the Dean.*
Es **el** privilegio del Decano.	*It is the privilege of the Dean.*

Indefinite Articles

FORMS OF THE INDEFINITE ARTICLE

English	Spanish	
	Masculine	*Feminine*
Singular *a, an*	Tengo **un** libro	**una** casa; (**un**) arpa
Plural *some*	**unos** libros	**unas** casas

While in English the forms of the indefinite article only signal number, in Spanish the indefinite article signals the gender and number of the noun to which it refers.

una → un before á, há-

The singular form **un** must be used before singular feminine nouns that begin with a stressed form **á** sound.

un arpa	*an harp*	un aula	*a classroom*
un hada	*a fairy*	un alma	*a soul*

If the first syllable is not stressed, the feminine form is used: **una hacienda**, **una artista**, etc. The use of the form **un** does not apply to adjectives of like form: **una alta torre**, **una ancha calle**, etc. It never changes the gender of the noun, which is observed by the adjective agreement: **Es un aula magnífica**.

Un, una as numerals

Spanish in contrast with English does not have a different form for the indefinite article and the numeral. Therefore, Spanish **un** and **una** correspond not only to English *a, an*, but also to the number form *one*.

Tienen un hijo.

{ *They have a son.*
{ *They have one son.*

Tiene una tía.

{ *He has an aunt.*
{ *He has one aunt.*

To clarify such ambiguity Spanish may add an adverbial when **un** and **una** correspond to a numeral. Stress may also be added.

Tienen sólamente **un** hijo.	*They have only one son.*
Tiene únicamente **una** tía.	*He has only one aunt.*

Possible meanings of the indefinite forms

The forms **unos** and **unas** could also mean **algunos, -as** (*some*); **unos pocos, -as** (*a few*), **varios, -as** (*several*); **ciertos, -as** (*certain*); **alrededor de** (*about*, in the sense of approximately).

Dame **unas** peras.	*Give me* some *pears.*
algunas	some
unas pocas	a few
varias	several
Tiene **unos** diez mil dólares.	*He has* some *ten thousand dollars.*
alrededor de	about
Tiene **unos** gustos raros.	*He has* some *strange tastes.*
ciertos	certain

Although **unos, -as** and **algunos, -as** are both translated as "some," **unos** should be used if a more specific reference is desired. The same applies to the singular forms: **un, -a; algún, -a.**

Tendrá un buen amigo.	*He might have a good friend.*
Tendrá algún buen amigo.	*He might have a good friend.*

The singular forms **un** and **una** may also mean **cierto, -a** = *a certain.*

Llamó a un señor.	*He called a man.*
Llamó a cierta persona.	*He called a certain person.*

Cierto and **tal**, however, may refer to someone or something specific, in which case they are accompanied by the article.

Me dijo que llamó a un tal señor.	*He told me that he called a certain man.*
Me dijo que llamó a una cierta persona.	*He told me that he called a certain person.*

USES OF THE INDEFINITE ARTICLE

Both Spanish and English use the definite article to specify or to limit animate or inanimate objects according to an identifying context previously known and understood by the speaker. When such a context is not clear (known or understood) by the speaker, both languages use the indefinite article. In **Trae el libro** = *Bring the book*, the speaker knows and understands which particular book is being referred to. But in **Trae un libro** = *Bring a book*, the speaker does not have a particular book in mind; the object has not been previously identified. In both cases, however, the speaker directs his attention to things already considered to be in existence.

Me llamó la mujer. (que vino ayer)	*The woman called me.* (*the one who came yesterday*)
Me llamó una mujer.	*A woman called me.*
Está escribiendo la carta. (que tú pediste)	*He is writing the letter.* (*the one you asked for*)
Está escribiendo una carta.	*He is writing a letter.*

As a general rule, the indefinite article is omitted in Spanish if the speaker simply wishes to identify the noun (animate or inanimate), or if he just wants to point out the existence of someone or occurrence of something *versus* its non-existence or non-occurrence.

If in addition to identifying the noun the speaker also wishes to make it stand out, to individualize it, to single it out in opposition to the other members of the class, or to emphasize it, then he may use the indefinite article. Spanish has other resources such as stress and intonation to convey individualization, so the use of the indefinite article is not always obligatory in this case. Individualization can also be expressed by modification, emphatic constructions, and figurative speech.

In dealing with this problem Spanish and English very often differ. In fact, English tends to use the indefinite article much more than Spanish.

After verbs of identification

After verbs of identification like **ser**, **parecer**, **considerar(se)**, and **llamar(se)**, the use of the indefinite article depends on whether the speaker wishes to express mere identification or emphasis and individualization. If mere identification is expressed, the article is omitted. This is especially common with unmodified nouns that refer to profession, occupation, rank, nationality, or religious and political affiliations. Identification is expressed when answering the questions "What is he?" "What do you consider it?" etc.

¿Qué es María?	*What is Mary?*
María es peruana.	*Mary is (a) Peruvian.*
Raúl es católico.	*Raul is (a) Catholic.*
El Sr. López es profesor.	*Mr. Lopez is a professor.*
Parece lobo y no perro.	*It looks like a wolf, not a dog.*
¿Qué lo consideras, fruta o vegetal?	*What do you consider it, (a) fruit or (a) vegetable?*
Se llama mono y no gorila.	*It is called a monkey, not a gorilla.*

If emphasis or individualization is desired, then the indefinite article may be used.

¡El señor López es **un profesor**!	*Mr. Lopez is a professor!*

Here the speaker is not merely identifying (**El Sr. López es profesor**), but he is also individualizing him, singling him out in opposition to the other members of the class "professors" (i.e., a professor in the true sense of the word!). Nevertheless, the use of the indefinite article is not obligatory. Spanish can also make this contrast with intonation and stress.

El señor López es **profesor**.	(Mere identification.)
El señor López **es** profesor.	(Identification, but also individualization in opposition to the other members of the class.)

To express existence and occurrence

With verbs that refer fundamentally to existence and occurrence, such as **tener**, **haber**, **buscar**, **encontrar**, and **poseer**, the indefinite article is omitted.

¿No tienes reloj?	*Don't you have a watch?*
¿No hay secretaria aquí?	*Isn't there a secretary here?*
¿Buscan Uds. casa?	*Are you looking for a house?*
¿Encontró Ud. criada?	*Did you find a maid?*
¿Tuviste reunión ayer?	*Did you have a meeting yesterday?*
¿Hay examen mañana?	*Is there an exam tomorrow?*

All of these examples may take the indefinite article if emphasis or individualization is also conveyed.

¿Tuviste una reunión ayer?	*Did you have a meeting yesterday?*
¿Hay un examen mañana?	*Is there an exam tomorrow?*

In these cases the speaker has a particular individual event in mind—not just its occurrence.

While Spanish can make this contrast (identification: no article *versus* individualization: article) in both singular and plural forms, English only does it in the plural.

IDENTIFICATION:

¿Tuviste reunión ayer?	*Did you have a meeting yesterday?*
¿Tuviste reuniones ayer?	*Did you have meetings yesterday?*

IDENTIFICATION AND INDIVIDUALIZATION:

¿Tuviste una reunión ayer?	*Did you have a meeting yesterday?*
¿Tuviste unas reuniones ayer?	*Did you have some meetings yesterday?*

After the prepositions **sin** and **con**

When the concept of number is de-emphasized, the indefinite article is omitted.

Vine sin lápiz.	*I came without a pencil.*
Salió sin corbata.	*He left without a tie.*
Llegó con paraguas.	*He arrived with an umbrella.*

But if the concept of "number" or individualization is pointed out, then the indefinite article is used.

Vine sin un (solo) lápiz.	*I came without a (single) pencil.*
Llegó con unos (pocos) dólares.	*He arrived with some (a few) dollars.*

Only rarely does English omit the indefinite article in this context: *Write it in pencil.*

After negative constructions

When the concept of quantity is de-emphasized, the indefinite article is omitted.

No tengo camisa.	*I don't have a shirt.*
No dijo palabra.	*He didn't say a word.*

But if the concept of quantity is emphasized, then the indefinite article is used, often accompanied by some other word such as **solo, -a** or **ni**.

No tengo una (sola) camisa.	*I don't have a (single) shirt.*
No dijo (ni) una palabra.	*He didn't (even) say a word.*

With modified nouns

Since individualization may also be brought out by modification (with an adjective or with a modifying phrase), the indefinite article is normally used with modified nouns. This occurs more regularly in singular than in plural constructions.

¿Tienes un buen reloj?	*Do you have a good watch?*
¿Hay una secretaria bilingüe aquí?	*Is there a bilingual secretary here?*
Vine sin una buena pluma.	*I came without a good pen.*
No tiene una camisa limpia.	*He does not have a clean shirt.*
Ricardo es un excelente padre.	*Richard is an excellent father.*
El Sr. López es un hombre de familia distinguida.	*Mr. Lopez is a man from a distinguished family.*
Son unos arquitectos de mucha reputación.	*They are architects with much reputation.*
Nunca vi unos jardines tan lindos.	*I never saw such beautiful gardens.*

However, modification in itself does not necessarily imply individualization. Therefore, the article may also be omitted before a modified noun, thus expressing identification only.

¿Tienes un buen reloj?
¿No hay aquí una buena secretaria bilingüe?
No tengo camisa limpia.
Nunca vi jardines tan lindos.

In some instances a noun and an adjective occur so frequently together that the combination becomes a stereotyped expression without the article, and only identification is expressed.

Es fiel católico.	*He is a faithful Catholic.*
Es excelente orador.	*He is an excellent speaker.*
Es persona distinguida.	*He is a distinguished person.*
Es hombre de familia noble.	*He is a man of noble blood.*
Es mal estudiante.	*He is a poor student.*
Es buen amigo.	*He is a good friend.*

In plural constructions the article is even more easily omitted.

Son magníficos estudiantes.	*They are magnificent students.*
Son ingenieros expertos.	*They are expert engineers.*

In these cases the English usage coincides with Spanish.

With emphatic constructions

Occasionally, the indefinite article may be used as an emphatic device to bring out, point out a special characteristic or trait.

Necesito paciencia.	*I need patience.*
¡Necesito **una paciencia**!	*What patience I need!*
Tiene talento para mentir.	*He has a talent for lying.*
¡Tiene **un talento** para mentir!	*What a talent he has for lying!*

In figurative speech

Individualization can be expressed by certain stereotyped phrases used as figures of speech.

¡Es un ángel!	*He is an angel!*
¡Es un diablo!	*He is a devil!*
¡Son unos piratas!	*They are crooks!*
¡Es un Napoleón!	*He is a Napoleon!*

OTHER CASES OF OMISSION OF THE INDEFINITE ARTICLE

In Spanish the indefinite article is also omitted as follows:

1. After the prepositions **de** or **como** when they mean "as":

Trabaja aquí de vendedor.	*He works here as a salesman.*
Como consecuencia de su falta de paciencia . . .	*As a result of his lack of patience . . .*
Como resultado de su conversación . . .	*As a result of his conversation . . .*

In all of these constructions only identification or occurrence is pointed out.

2. In text titles:

Panorama de Historia Mundial	*A Panorama of World History*
Diccionario Ilustrado de la Lengua Española	*An Illustrated Dictionary of the Spanish Language*
Tratado de Física Experimental	*A Treatise of Experimental Physics*

3. After **otro, -a** = *another, one other*; **cien/ciento, -a** = *one hundred*; **mil** = *a, one*

thousand; **medio, -a** = *half a*; **¡qué!** (used as an exclamation: *what a!*). After **tal** = *such a*; **cierto, -a** = *a certain*, when these do not refer to anything specific:

Necesitamos otro documento.	{ *We need* another *document.* { *We need* one other *document.*
Pesa 125 libras.	*She weighs a hundred and twenty-five pounds.*
Dame media naranja.	*Give me half an orange.*
¡Qué precioso día!	*What a beautiful day!*
¡No digas tal cosa!	*Don't say such a thing!*
Trajo ciertos documentos.	*He brought certain documents.*

Tal and **cierto**, however, may take the article since they can express more than just identification; the speaker may have someone in mind.

Lo llamó un tal señor.	*A certain man called him.*
Lo llamó una tal persona.	*A certain person called him.*

Medio may take the article if quantity is emphasized.

Dame media naranja (solamente).	*Give me (just, only) half an orange.*
Dame una media naranja, más o menos.	*Give me half an orange, more or less.*
Lo terminé en medio día.	*I finished it in half a day.*
Lo terminé en un medio día, exactamente.	*I finished it in half a day, exactly.*

4. In appositive constructions when the noun is not modified:

Pasamos por Matamoros, población de la frontera.	*We went by Matamoros, a border town.*
Pasamos por Matamoros, una pequeña población de la frontera.	*We went by Matamoros, a small border town.*

REPETITION OF ARTICLES IN COMPOUND NOUN CONSTRUCTIONS

In both Spanish and English, articles may modify not only a single name, but they modify two or more nouns compounded with the conjunction **y** = *and*, particularly if they can be thought of as one unit. The devices are:

Article + Noun			Conjunction + Article + Noun		
Tengo	la	sal	y	la	pimienta.
I have	*the*	*salt*	*and*	*the*	*pepper.*
Tengo	un	hermano	y	una	hermana.
I have	*a*	*brother*	*and*	*a*	*sister.*

or it may be:

	Article	Noun + Conjunction + Noun		
Tengo	la	sal	y	pimienta.
I have	*the*	*salt*	*and*	*pepper.*
Tengo	un	hermano	y	hermana.
I have	*a*	*brother*	*and*	*sister.*

Although Spanish and English are similar in accepting these two constructions, the two languages contrast in their actual usage.

1. Spanish and English agree in using only one article in compound noun constructions when the names refer to the mental, abstract characteristics of a being or when several nouns refer to a single unit of thought.

La blancura, firmeza y porosidad de esta madera . . .	*The whiteness, hardness, and porosity of this wood . . .*
La energía, talento y devoción del general . . .	*The energy, talent, and devotion of the general . . .*
Los testimonios, documentos y cartas comprobaban que era culpable.	*The testimonies, documents, and letters proved that he was guilty.*
Los exámenes, composiciones y tareas son parte de la nota final.	*The exams, compositions, and homework are part of the final grade.*

In these examples, both languages may also repeat the article before each noun if the purpose is to be more emphatic about the qualities.

2. If the nouns refer to actual possessions of the subject, the article is usually repeated in both languages.

El sombrero, las botas y el abrigo del general . . .	*The hat, the boots and the coat of the general . . .*

3. As a general rule, however, English modifies more readily than Spanish two or more names with just one article.

Pásame la sal y (la) pimienta.	*Pass me the salt and pepper.*
Hay un niño y una niña afuera.	*There is a boy and (a) girl outside.*
Compré una casa y un carro.	*I bought a house and (a) car.*
Llegaron el padre y la madre.	*The father and (the) mother arrived.*

The Neuter *lo*

FUNCTION OF NEUTER *LO*

Spanish has a neuter form **lo** which does not refer to any specific gender or number. As such **lo** never occurs before concrete nouns. Instead, it is used as a nominalizing agent before adjectives and adverbs that describe some aspect or part of a noun, an idea, a situation, or an action. Thus, adjectives or adverbs preceded by **lo** function as abstract nouns. **Lo** also occurs in phrases and clauses that refer to an unspecified gender or number. In most cases the constructions with **lo** can be substituted by something else.

EQUIVALENTS OF NEUTER *LO* IN ENGLISH

There is no similar form for **lo** in English; instead there are a number of equivalents according to the different contexts in which **lo** occurs.

Lo + adjective or adverb

1. the . . . (thing), . . . part, (the) . . . way

Lo maravilloso es su talento.
(= la cosa maravillosa)

The wonderful thing is his talent.

Hizo lo imposible para no caer en desgracia.
(= la cosa imposible, el asunto imposible)

He did the impossible not to fall in disgrace.
(= the impossible thing)

Lo poco que escribió no sirve.
(=la poca cosa)

The little that he wrote is no good.
(=the few things)

Lo primero que debe hacer es callarse la boca.
(= la primera cosa)

The first thing he ought to do is to shut his mouth.

Cuéntame lo otro.
(=las otras cosas, el otro asunto)

Tell me the other thing.
(=the other things, the other matter)

Vivió lo mejor que pudo.
(= de la mejor manera)

He lived the best way he could.
(= the best he could)

Llegó lo más rápido posible.
(= de la manera más rápida)

He arrived the fastest way he could.
(as fast as . . .)

---

[1] See Nominalization of Descriptive Adjectives with **lo**, page 220.

En lo profundo de su alma sabía que
  mentía.
(=en la parte profunda)

Deep down in his heart he knew she
  was lying.
(=*in the depths of* . . .)

2. what is . . .; (the) . . . things

Le gusta lo caro.
(= las cosas caras)

He likes what is expensive.
(= *expensive things*)

Detesto lo barato.
(= las cosas baratas)

I hate what is cheap.
(= *cheap things*)

Te doy lo mío.
(= las cosas mías)

I give you what is mine.
(= *the things that are mine*)

3. the . . . thing (of, about)
     . . . aspect . . .
     . . . part . . .
     . . . side . . .

Lo bueno del profesor es su justicia.
(=la cosa buena del profesor es,
   el lado bueno)

The good thing about the professor is
his fairness.

Lo interesante de la película viene
  al final.
(=la parte interesante,
   el aspecto interesante)

The interesting part of the movie comes
  at the end.

Lo malo de su madre . . .
(=la cosa mala, el aspecto malo)

The bad aspect of her mother . . .

Lo mejor de su discurso . . .
(=el aspecto mejor, la parte mejor)

The best part of his speech . . .

Lo peor de su conducta . . .
(=el asunto peor, la cosa peor)

The worst part of his conduct . . .

4. Noun suffixes: -*ness*, -*ity*

Lo útil del experimento . . .
(= el aspecto útil
   la cosa útil
   la utilidad)

The usefulness of the experiment . . .

Lo práctico del arreglo . . .
(= el aspecto práctico
   la cosa práctica
   la practicalidad)

The practicality of the arrangement . . .

The phrases **la cosa** . . ., **la parte** . . ., **el aspecto** . . ., **el asunto** . . ., and **el
lado** . . . may be substituted with **lo** in the preceding constructions. In many
cases the Spanish adjective already has a corresponding abstract noun (**útil/utilidad**)
which can also substitute for **lo**: **La utilidad del experimento = Lo útil del
experimento** . . .

Lo de . . . and lo que . . .[1]

Lo also occurs before **de** phrases and **que** clauses in a neuter sense (in reference to some idea, concept, or action), without regard to gender or number.

Lo de . . .	*The business of (about)* . . .
	The affair of . . .
	The matter of . . .
	The part of . . .
	etc.
	—'s part (**de** as possessive)

Lo de los impuestos no es cierto. (= el asunto de)	*The affair about the taxes is not true.*
Lo de su accidente me preocupa. (= el asunto de) la parte de)	*The matter of his accident worries me.*
Lo de leer todo el manuscrito es una molestia. (= la cosa de)	*The business of reading the whole manuscript is a nuisance.*
Dame lo de José. (= las cosas de)	*Give me Jose's.* (= *Jose's*)
¿Recuerdas lo del (el negocio) otro día?	*Do you remember the affair of the other day?*

Lo de may be substituted by **el asunto de**, **el aspecto de**, **el negocio de**, **la cosa de**, or **la parte de**, which corresponds to the English equivalents of **lo de**.

Lo que . . .	*That which* . . .
	What . . .

Le interesa su dinero. *He is interested in her money.*	Lo que le interesa es su dinero. *That which interests him is her money.*
No quiero que se queje tanto. *I don't want him to complain so much.*	Lo que no quiero es que se queje tanto. *What I don't want him to do is to complain that much.*
Vale la pena conservar su amistad. *It is worthwhile to keep his friendship.*	Lo que vale la pena es conservar su amistad. *What is worthwhile is to keep his friendship.*

---

[1] See Neuter Relatives, page 119.

Me gusta comer y beber.
I like to eat and drink.

Lo que me gusta es comer y beber.
What I like is to eat and drink.

Adverbial phrase **a lo**

A lo may be used as a substitute for **como** or **tipo** in adverbial phrases of manner to express comparison or similarity. The English equivalents are *as a*, *like*.

Se comporta a lo gran dama.
   como
   tipo

She conducts herself as a grand lady.

Vive a lo millonario.
  como
  tipo

He lives as (like a) a millionaire.

Se disfrazó a lo fin de siglo.
   como
   tipo

She masqueraded in 1890s clothes.

Viste a lo antiguo.
  tipo

She dresses in an old-fashioned way.

Pronunció un discurso a lo Kennedy.
    tipo
    como

He gave a Kennedy-type speech.

Lo + adjective or adverb + **que**

Lo ... que used with adjectives or adverbs indicates degree or extent. The adjective may keep the agreement in gender and number with the noun it modifies. The English equivalent is *how* + adjective or adverb. **Lo ... que** may be substituted by **como** + verb + **de**, by **cuan**, or by the exclamatives **¡qué!**, **¡cómo!**, **¡cuán!**

No sabías lo complicado que era. ⎫
   como era de complicado. ⎬
   cuan complicado era. ⎭

You didn't know how complicated it was.

¡Lo buena que es su madre! ⎫
¡Cómo es de buena su madre! ⎬
¡Cuán buena es madre! ⎭

How good her mother is!

No comprendes lo difíciles que son
estos problemas. ⎫
... cómo son de difíciles estos ⎬
problemas.
... cuán difíciles son estos ⎭
problemas.

You don't understand how difficult these problems are.

Me sorprende lo mucho que come. ⎫
   cómo come de mucho. ⎭

I am surprised by how much he eats.

De lo + intensifier adverb

De lo + an intensifier adverb expresses degree or extent of a quality or an action in an almost superlative manner.

Es un buen abogado—de lo mejor que hay en el país.	*He is a good lawyer—about the best there is in the country.*
Lleva un traje de lo más fino.	*She is wearing a very fine dress.*
Este estudiante es de lo peor que hay.	*This student is among the worst you can find.*
Se comporta de lo más infantil.	*He behaves in quite an infantile fashion.*
Es de lo menos imaginativo.	*He is most unimaginative.*
Son de lo más estúpidas.	*They are quite (rather) stupid.*

Lo in idiomatic expressions

por lo general	*as a general rule*	por lo pronto	*for the time being*
por lo común	*usually*	por lo tanto	*therefore*
por lo menos	*at least*	a lo mejor	*possibly, maybe, perhaps*
por lo visto	*apparently*	a lo lejos	*in the distance*

17

POSSESSIVES AND DEMONSTRATIVES

Possessives

Possessives and demonstratives in Spanish are a group of noun modifiers that belong to a class of words called *limiting adjectives*. Limiting adjectives modify a noun in terms of different order of relations. They may state the possessor (possessives); indicate the noun's position with respect to time and space (demonstratives), indicate its quantity (numerals, indefinites), or inquire information (interrogatives).

The possessive forms modify the noun by stating its possessor, thus expressing a relationship of possession. There are two sets of possessives in Spanish: unstressed (short forms) and stressed (long forms).

UNSTRESSED POSSESSIVES

Unstressed possessives in Spanish agree in number (and some agree in gender also) with the object possessed, not with the subject possessor as in English. Hence, Spanish has many more forms: **su** auto, **sus** autos = *his car, his* cars; **nuestro** auto, **nuestra** casa, **nuestros** autos, **nuestras** casas = *our car, our* house, *our* cars, *our* houses.

The only forms that show agreement for gender (in addition to number) are **nuestro** and **vuestro** with their corresponding feminine forms **nuestra** and **vuestra**. **Vuestro** and its variants have been substituted by **su/sus** in most parts of the Hispanic world.

Possessor	*Masculine*			*Feminine*	
One possessor	*Singular*	*Plural*		*Singular*	*Plural*
yo	**mi** auto	**mis** autos	*my*	**mi** casa	**mis** casas
tú	**tu**	**tus**	*your*	**tu**	**tus**
él ⎫ ella ⎬ usted ⎭	**su**	**sus**	⎧ *his* ⎫ ⎨ *her* ⎬ ⎪ *your* ⎪ ⎩ *(its)* ⎭	**su**	**sus**
Several possessors					
nosotros, –as	**nuestro** auto	**nuestros** autos	*our*	**nuestra** casa	**nuestras** casas
vosotros, –as	**vuestro**	**vuestros**	*your*	**vuestra**	**vuestras**
ellos ⎫ ellas ⎬ ustedes ⎭	**su**	**sus**	⎧ *their* ⎫ ⎨ *your* ⎬	**su**	**sus**

Position of unstressed possessives

These forms always appear immediately before the noun. They are called unstressed possessives because normally the stress and emphasis are placed on the object possessed, not on the subject possessor. Thus, they function as the English possessives in phrases in which the noun carries the stress.

Voy para mi **casa**.   *I am going to my* house

| Unstressed Possessive | + | **propio,-a/-s** | + | Noun |

The unstressed possessives may be followed by the adjective **propio** = *own* and its variants, in order to bring out the relationship of possession.

Manejo mi propio auto.   *I drive my own car.*
Vivimos en nuestra propia casa.   *We live in our own house.*

STRESSED POSSESSIVES

Possessor	Masculine			Feminine	
One Possessor	Singular	Plural		Singular	Plural
	el auto	los autos		la casa	las casas
yo	**mío**	**míos**	my, of mine	**mía**	**mías**
tú	**tuyo**	**tuyos**	your, -s	**tuya**	**tuyas**
él ella usted	**suyo**	**suyos**	his/his her(s) your(s)	**suya**	**suyas**
Several Possessors					
nosotros, -as	**nuestro**	**nuestros**	our(s)	**nuestra**	**nuestras**
vosotros, -as	**vuestro**	**vuestros**	your(s)	**vuestra**	**vuestras**
ellos ellas ustedes	**suyo**	**suyos**	their(s) your(s)	**suya**	**suyas**

Stressed possessives show a complete set of forms in both gender and number to make the agreement with the object possessed.

Position of stressed possessives

These forms appear in all positions except before the noun. They are called stressed possessives because the stress and emphasis are placed on the subject possessor. Therefore, they appear in the usual positions of stress and function as follows:

1. When emphasis is on the subject possessor rather than on the object possessed:

Voy para la casa **mía**.   *I am going to my house.*
Compraron el auto **nuestro**.   *They bought our car.*

The emphasis could be due to contrast or it could be due to rhetorical effect. Note that in Spanish the definite article precedes the noun in these constructions.

2. In occasional emphatic expressions with stress on both object and possessor:

¡Por culpa tuya!   *On account of you!*
¡Por suerte suya!   *With your luck!*

It must be kept in mind that Spanish may also achieve the same effects by placing emphasis on the unstressed possessives.

3. In predicate constructions after the verb **ser**, for contrast of possessors, corresponding to the English forms *mine, yours, his,* etc.

La casa es **mía**.	*The house is* mine.
(no es de Enrique)	*(it's not Henry's)*
El auto es **suyo**.	*The car is* hers.
(no es mío)	*(it's not mine)*

4. In sentences with an indeterminate sense, corresponding to the English forms *of mine, of yours, of theirs,* etc.

Vino un amigo **suyo**.	*A friend* of hers *came.*
	of his
	of theirs
	of yours
Llamó a una hermana **mía**.	*He called a sister* of mine.
Son unas amigas **suyas**.	*They are some friends* of hers.
	of his.
	etc.

In constructions with **ser** the indefinite article may be omitted: **Son amigas suyas** = *They are friends of hers*; **Son buenos compañeros tuyos** = *They are good companions of yours.*

AMBIGUOUS POSSESSIVES

Possessives **su, suyo,** etc.

Since the possessive forms **su, sus, suyo,-a, suyos,-as,** may refer to different possessors (*his, her, its, your,* singular and plural, and *their*), in order to clarify the noun-possessor relationship, or to point out one possessor in contrast with another, these third person possessives are often substituted by the following alternate constructions with **de** + subject pronoun.

1. ¿Quién heredó **sus** casas?	*Who inherited his* houses?
las casas **suyas**?	his *houses?*
2. Me prestó **su** auto.	*He lent me his* car.
el auto **suyo**.	his *car.*

Definite Article	+	Noun	+	**de**	+	Subject Pronoun

1. ¿Quién heredó las casas de él?	*his*
ella?	*her*
usted?	*your*
ellos?	*their*
ellas?	*their*
ustedes?	*your*

2. Me prestó el auto de él.   *his*
                      ella.   *her*
                      usted.   *your*
                      etc.   *etc.*

Its which is used for inanimate and animate non-human nouns cannot be rendered by **de** + subject pronoun since these nouns are rarely pronominalized. It is rendered by either the possessives or **de** + noun: **La pata del perro** = *The dog's leg*; *its leg* = **Su pata** . . .; **El techo de la casa** = *The roof of the house*; *its roof* = **su techo**.

The construction with **de** + subject pronoun is actually very widely used in the sense of *his, her, its, their* (**de él, de ella, de ellos, de ellas**), without necessarily implying contrast or emphasis. **Su/suyo**, etc., are usually used instead in the sense of "your" (**de usted, de ustedes**): **Préstame la corbata de él** = *Lend me his tie*; **Préstame su corbata** = *Lend me your tie*. However, in sentences where both the subject and another possessor are of the third person, **su/suyo** usually refer to the subject and the other possessors are expressed by **de**: **María no tiene sus documentos, tiene los de usted.** = *Mary doesn't have her documents, she has yours.*

Nuestro, vuestro → de nosotros, de vosotros

Although there is no ambiguity with these forms, the construction with **de** + subject pronoun is also preferred with **nuestro, vuestro**, and their feminine and plural variants in most Spanish-speaking regions.

De vosotros, -as has been substituted by **de ustedes** in most parts.

FURTHER USES OF POSSESSIVE FORMS

1. In formal speech or writing, **nuestro, -a** may refer to the first person singular.

Nuestro propósito es llevar adelante   *Our purpose is to carry out the*
   la reforma . . .   *reform . . .*
                                              (the president speaking)

2. In direct address, the stressed forms of the first person possessives are used. If the noun is further modified, then either the unstressed or stressed forms are possible.

Hijo mío . . .   *My son . . .*
Amigos míos . . .   *Friends . . .*

BUT:

Mi querido hijo . . . ⎫
Querido hijo mío . . . ⎭   *My dear son . . .*

Nuestros queridos amigos . . . ⎫
Queridos amigos nuestros . . . ⎭   *Our dear friends . . .*

3. In Spanish the possessives are often used in constructions where English would use a prepositional object pronoun.

Ven aquí a mi lado.	*Come here next to me.*
. . . al lado **mío**.	
La policía fue en busca **suya**.	*The police went out in search of him (of her, etc).*
Isabel no ha recibido carta **nuestra**.	*Isabel has not received a letter from us.*
¿No fuiste a **su** encuentro?	*Didn't you go out to meet her?*
Lo hizo a fe **mía**.	*He did it out of faith in me.*
La llamó a pesar **suyo**.	*He called her in spite of him (her, you, them).*

4. With **alrededor, detrás, delante, enfrente**, Spanish normally uses the construction **de** + subject pronoun: **alrededor de mí** = *around me*. In colloquial and popular language, however, this construction is often replaced by a stressed possessive. Only **alrededor** can take either an unstressed or stressed form.

Estaba alrededor de mí.	
. . . alrededor mío.	*He was around me.*
. . . a mi alrededor.	
Estaba detrás de mí.	*He was behind me.*
. . . detrás mío.	
Lo vi delante de ti.	*I saw him in front of you.*
. . . tuyo.	
Está en frente de mí.	*He is in front of me.*
. . . frente mío.	

English doesn't use a possessive but rather a prepositional object pronoun.

Idiomatic expressions with possessives

Vamos **a casa tuya**.	*Let's go to your house.*
Lo logró **a costa mía**.	*He achieved it at my expense.*
Va a hacerlo **a instancias suyas**.	*She is going to do it on his entreaty.*
Estudiaba **a insistencia mía**.	*He studied at my insistence.*
Dígale que es **de parte nuestra**.	*Tell her that it is on our behalf.*
La llamó **a pesar tuyo**.	*He called her in spite of you.*

Repetition of possessive forms

The possessive forms are repeated before each noun, except when reference is made to the same person or object.

Mi amigo y su prima . . .	*My friend and his cousin . . .*
Su casa y su auto son nuevos.	*His house and his car are new.*

Mi amiga y mi compañera de cuarto . . .	*My friend and my roommate . . .* *(would refer to two different persons)*
Mi amiga y compañera de cuarto . . .	*My friend and roommate . . .* *(would refer to the same person)*

PRONOMINAL POSSESSIVES

Definite Article	+	Stressed Possessives
¿Cuáles son **las** (camisas) *Which are*		**mías**? *mine?*
¿Cuáles son **los** (zapatos) *Which are*		**suyos**? *his? hers?* etc.
¿Cuáles son **los** (zapatos) *Which are*		**de él**? *his?*

The stressed forms of the possessives and the alternate form with **de** (**de ellos, de Uds., de nosotros**, etc.) occur as noun substitutes when nominalized, thus functioning as pronominal possessives. Since possessives nominalize the same way as other adjectives (by deletion of the noun), the pronominal possessives keep the agreement for gender and number with the noun they stand for.

Occurrence of the pronominal possessives

The pronominal possessives occur as (1) subject, (2) predicate after **ser**, (3) object of a verb, or (4) they may occur alone. As such they parallel the English pronominal possessives *mine, yours, his, hers, ours, theirs.*

1. PRONOMINAL POSSESSIVES AS SUBJECT:

El (auto) suyo siempre funciona.	
El suyo siempre funciona.	*His* *Hers* }*always works.* *Yours*
El de él siempre funciona.	*His always works.*
El de ella siempre funciona.	*Hers always works.*

2. PRONOMINAL POSSESSIVES AFTER "SER":

Esta es la (casa) **mía**.	*This is* my *house.*
Esta es **la** **mía**.	*This is* mine.

Esta es la (habitación) **nuestra**.		*This is* our *room.*
Esta es la **de nosotros**.		

Esta es **la** **nuestra**.		*This is* ours.
Esta es **la** **de nosotros**.		

It is important to note that in predicate constructions with **ser** a difference in meaning exists between the possessive used as an adjective and its usage as a pronoun. As an adjective it simply signals possession; as a pronoun it points out the selection of one or more objects from a group, it responds to the question "which one?" or "which ones?"

As adjective—possession:

Esta casa es mía.	*This house is mine.*

As pronoun—selection among a group:

¿Cuál es tu casa?	*Which one is your house?*
—Esta casa es la **mía**.	—*That house is* mine.

3. PRONOMINAL POSSESSIVES AS OBJECTS OF A VERB:

Préstame el (libro) tuyo.	*Lend me your book.*
Préstame el tuyo.	*Lend me* yours.

4. PRONOMINAL POSSESSIVES OCCURRING ALONE:

Aquí hay dos plumas. ¿Cuál quieres?	*There are two pens here? Which one do you want?*
—La suya.	⎰*His.* ⎱*Hers.* *Yours.* *Theirs.*
—La de ella.	*Hers.*

Alternate construction with **de** + subject pronoun

The alternate construction with **de** is also used with the pronominal possessives to clarify any possible ambiguity with the third person possessors, or as an alternate for the second person plural.

Mis padres y los suyos.	*My parents and . . .*
los de él.	*his.*
los de ella.	*hers.*
los de usted.	*yours.*
los de ellos.	*theirs.*
etc.	*etc.*
Tus primos y los nuestros.	*Your cousins and ours.*
los de nosotros.	
Mis tíos y los vuestros.	*My uncles and yours.*
los de vosotros.	

The masculine plural forms of the pronominal possessives (**los míos**, **los tuyos**, **los suyos**, etc.), may be used to refer to relatives, close friends, servants, subordinates, and so forth.

Los nuestros ganaron el partido.	*Our men (team) won the game.*
Saludos a **los tuyos**.	*Give my regards to your family (folks).*
El general mandó que **los suyos** se retiraran.	*The general ordered his troops to withdraw.*

NOMINALIZATION OF POSSESSIVES WITH *LO*

	Spanish	English
	Stressed Possessives	Possessives + "part"
lo +	OR	OR
	Construction with **de**	*What is* *That which is* + Possessive

Quiero **lo mío**.	*I want my part.* *what is mine.* *that which is mine.*
Dame **lo suyo**.	*Give me her part.* *etc.*
Dale **lo de ella**.	*Give him her part.* *what is hers.*

Stressed possessives as well as the alternate constructions with **de** + subject pronoun may be nominalized with **lo** in order to express possession in an abstract sense. The equivalent in English corresponds to phrases such as *What is . . ., that which is . . ., . . . part.*

OTHER EXPRESSIONS OF POSSESSION

Besides using possessive forms Spanish also expresses possession through other means:

1. By a prepositional phrase with **de**:

Since Spanish nouns are not inflected for possession, there is no equivalent of the English expression of possession as in "the boy's parents." Instead, Spanish must use a prepositional phrase with **de**. This construction is not uncommon in English, which in fact uses it with most inanimate nouns.

the bottom of the sea	el fondo del mar
the dances of Spain	los bailes de España
the wheels of the car	las ruedas del auto

The prepositional phrase with **de** cannot be used to express possession related to the first and second persons singular. With these only the possessives can be used: **mi casa**, **la casa mía** = *my house*; **una casa mía** = *a house of mine*; **una casa tuya** = *a house of yours*; but never **una casa de mí** or **una casa de ti**.

2. With the verb **pertencer** = *to belong*, in the following noun constructions:

Indirect Object Pronoun	+ **pertencer**	
La casa me	pertenece.	
The house		*belongs to me*
. . . le	pertenece.	. . . *belongs to her.*
		to him.
		to you.

pertenecer a +	Prepositional Object Pronoun	
La casa pertenece a	mí.	. . . *belongs to me.*
	. . . ti.	. . . *belongs to you.*

3. With the definite article instead of a possessive adjective, to relate body parts, personal effects, and belongings to the possessor, whenever the possessor can be easily identified:

Le duele el estómago.	*His stomach aches.*
Quítate la camisa.	*Take off your shirt.*
Baja la cabeza.	*Lower your head.*
Levanta los pies.	*Lift up your feet.*

In most cases the possessor is already indicated by an indirect object pronoun (**le duele**) or by a reflexive (**quítate**). Whenever the possessor cannot be identified, then a possessive adjective must be used. This is usually the case when the body part or personal belonging is the subject of the verb. Observe the following:

Me duelen los pies.   *My feet hurt.*

The possessor is made clear by the indirect object pronoun **me**.

BUT:

Mis pies ya no dan más.   *My feet can't hold out any longer.*

If the article were used instead of the possessive **mis**, there would be no way of determining "whose feet hurt."

Me quité la corbata.	*I took off my tie.*

BUT:

Mi corbata me gusta más.	*I like my tie better.*

4. With the relative pronoun **cuyo** (**cuya**, **cuyos**, **cuyas**) = *whose* in relative constructions. (See Relative Pronouns, page 000.)

Este candidato, cuyos méritos aún no conocemos, merece consideración.	*This candidate, whose merits we still don't know, deserves to be considered.*
Su madre, cuyas virtudes admiro, es una mujer magnífica.	*His mother, whose virtues I admire, is a great woman.*

Demonstratives

FORMS AND USES

Relation		Singular		Plural	
Place	Time	Masculine	Feminine	Masculine	Feminine
		this		*these*	
Near speaker	Present	**este** hombre día	**esta** mujer horas	**estos** hombres días	**estas** mujeres horas
		that		*those*	
Removed from speaker	Near past or future	**ese**	**esa**	**esos**	**esas**
Farther removed	Remote past, remote future	**aquel**	**aquella**	**aquellos**	**aquellas**

Demonstrative adjectives modify a noun by relating it to the subject in terms of place and time. As noun modifiers they show agreement for gender and number with different forms. The masculine singular forms end in **-e**, instead of the usual **-o**.

The three sets of demonstratives point out an object (animate or inanimate) and relate it to the speaker in terms of time, space, or thought.

Este, **esta**, etc., indicate what is near and closely connected with the speaker.

Esta novela es fascinante.	*This novel is fascinating.*
Estuvo enferma esta mañana.	*She was sick this morning.*
¿Qué te parecen estos ejemplos?	*What do you think of these examples?*

Ese, **esa**, etc., indicate an object (animate or inanimate) not too far removed from the speaker, or near the person addressed and closely connected with this person.

¿Viste a ese chico?	*Did you see that boy?*
Ese ejemplo tuyo me gusta.	*I like that example of yours.*
Vinieron a verme esa tarde.	*They came to see me that afternoon.*

Aquel, **aquella**, etc., indicate what is further removed from the speaker in time, space, or thought, or indicate what is remote for both the speaker and the person addressed.

Mira aquel hombre allá.	*Look at that man over there.*
Durante aquellos años de guerra . . .	*During those war years . . .*
Fue en aquella reunión en que . . .	*It was at that meeting in which . . .*

The distinction between **ese** and **aquel** many times is not very clear, and in everyday speech, **ese** alternates with **aquel**, except when the speaker wants to express real remoteness; then **aquel** is used.

Word order

As limiting adjectives the demonstratives precede the nouns to which they refer. Occassionally they may follow, but then the definite article precedes the noun:

1. For stylistic purposes to add emphasis or to bring out the idea of remoteness in time or space:

Durante los años aquellos de guerra . . .	*During those war years . . .*
El cautivo, perdido por las selvas aquellas del Amazonas . . .	*The captive, lost in the midst of that Amazonian jungle . . .*

2. In everyday colloquial speech to express contempt or disdain:

No me gusta la mujer esa.	*I don't like that (silly, nasty, etc.) woman.*
Vinieron otra vez los niños esos.	*Those (mischievous, nasty) children came by again.*
El tonto aquel . . .	*That fool . . .*

Repetition of demonstrative forms

Demonstrative adjectives are normally repeated before each noun, particularly if the nouns to which they refer are of different genders.

Este hombre y esta mujer tuvieron un accidente.	*This man and this woman had an accident.*

Demonstratives as nominalizers

Demonstratives can nominalize an adjective if the accompanying noun is deleted. As such, they function as nominalizers but are considered demonstrative adjectives. In the examples that follow **esa** and **este** modify the nominalized adjectives **moderna** and **extranjero**, respectively. Spanish does not add **uno** in the nominalization process as English does in *that one.*

Me gusta **esa** casa moderna.
I like that *modern house.*

Me gusta **esa** moderna.
I like that *modern* one.

Prefiero **este** auto extranjero.
I prefer this *foreign car.*

Prefiero **este** extranjero.
I prefer this *foreign* one.

PRONOMINAL DEMONSTRATIVES

Demonstratives can stand in place of a noun (modified or unmodified). In this case they function as noun substitutes and are considered pronominal demonstratives, keeping the same form in gender and number of the noun they substitute. Pronominal demonstratives carry an accent mark. Spanish does not add **uno** in the pronominalization process as English adds *one.*

Me gusta esa **casa moderna**.
I like that *modern house.*

Me gusta **ésa**.
I like that modern one.

Prefiero este **auto**.
I prefer this *car.*

Prefiero **éste**.
I prefer this one.

Pronominal demonstratives are repeated in order to clarify the subject of a verb in a dependent clause.

La clase no quiere al profesor porque **éste** no responde bien.

The class doesn't like the teacher because he does not respond well.

Occurrence of pronominal demonstratives

1. As subject:

   Ese vestido es muy lindo.
   That dress is very pretty.

   Ese es muy lindo.
   That one is very pretty.

2. As object of a verb:

   Toma estos utensilios.
   Take these utensils.

   Toma **éstos**.
   Take these ones.

3. Alone in a response to a question:

   ¿Cuál te gusta más?
   —Esta.

   Which one do you like best?
   —*This one.*

Idiomatic uses of the pronominal demonstratives

1.

$$\textbf{ésta, ésa} \begin{cases} \textit{this city,} \\ \textit{your city, etc.} \end{cases}$$

In business and commercial correspondence, the feminine singular forms of the pronominal demonstratives may be used with the meaning of "this city," "your city," "this place," etc.

Todavía no hemos recibido en ésta el pedido que les hicimos.	*We still have not received here (in this city) the order that we placed with you.*
Se los enviaremos a ésa cuanto antes.	*We will send them to you (to that city, to that place) as soon as we can.*

Esta could also mean the letter being written.

Le escribo ésta para informarle que . . .	*I am writing this letter in order to inform you that . . .*

2.

$$\left. \begin{array}{l} \textbf{éste} \\ \textbf{ésta} \\ \textbf{éstos} \\ \textbf{éstas} \end{array} \right\} \textit{the latter} \qquad \left. \begin{array}{l} \textbf{aquél} \\ \textbf{aquélla} \\ \textbf{aquéllos} \\ \textbf{aquéllas} \end{array} \right\} \textit{the former}$$

The pronominal demonstratives **éste** and **aquél** — with their variants — correspond to *the latter* and *the former*, respectively, but the order of reference is precisely the opposite in English.

Kennedy y Johnson fueron dos presidentes demócratas. Aquél gobernó sólo tres años y éste cinco.	*Kennedy and Johnson were two democratic presidents. The former governed for only three years and the latter for five.*

Pronominal demonstratives in relative constructions[1]

Spanish pronominal demonstratives, especially **aquél**, are used as antecedents in relative constructions governed by a preposition. They correspond to the English *the one(s) whom . . ., this (one) whom . . ., that (one) whom . . ., those (ones) whom.*

---

[1] See Chapter 8, Relative Pronouns.

Demonstrative + Preposition + Relative				
Aquél	de	quien	te hablé.	*The one of whom . . .*
Ese	de	quien	te hablé.	*That one of whom . . .*
Aquéllos	con	quienes	hablamos.	*The ones with whom . . .*
Esos	con	quienes	hablamos.	*Those with whom . . .*
Este	con	quien	hablé.	*The one with whom . . .*
				This one with whom . . .
Aquél	a	quien	vi.	*The one whom . . .*
Esa	a	quien	vi.	*That one whom . . .*

NEUTER DEMONSTRATIVES

RELATION					
Place	*Time*				
Near speaker	Present	**Esto**	es lindo.	This	*is pretty.*
	Near past		ocurrió hoy.		*happened today.*
	Near Future		lo mandas luego.		*you will send later.*
Away from speaker		**Eso**	es feo.	That	*is ugly.*
	Far past		pasó ayer.		*happened yesterday*
	Far future		viene mañana.		*comes tomorrow.*
Farther away		**¡Aquello**	era hermoso!	That	*was beautiful!*
	Remote past		ocurrió hace muchos años.		*happened many years ago.*

The neuter forms of the demonstratives, **esto**, **eso**, **aquello**, only function as pronouns. These invariable forms refer to an abstract idea, to a situation or action, to things in a general sense, or to things unidentified. Since they never refer to a specific gender or number, they are written without an accent mark as are the other demonstrative pronouns.

1. Reference to an abstract idea:

    Esto es realmente hermoso.   *This is really beautiful.*

2. Reference to a situation:

    Eso no puede continuar.   *That cannot go on.*

3. Reference to an action:

    ¡No vuelvas a hacer eso!   *Don't ever do that again!*

4. Reference to generalities:

¿Has visto aquello?   *Have you seen that?*

5. Reference to an unidentified object:

¿Qué es eso que traes?   *What is that you are bringing?*

As with the other demonstratives, the neuter forms express the same relationship of time and space. In everyday language, **eso** and **aquello** are practically interchangeable.

Expressions with neuter demonstratives

1.

Neuter
Demonstratives + **de** + Object

Esto	de	estudiar . . .	*This business of studying . . .*
		ir a verlo . . .	*This idea of going to see him . . .*
Eso	de	mi hermano . . .	*That matter about my brother . . .*
Aquello	de	trabajar y ganar tanto dinero . . .	*That story about working and earning so much money . . .*

The neuter demonstrative followed by **de** is a commonly used construction in Spanish to refer to an action, situation, or state in an abstract and general way. It is equivalent to the neuter construction **lo de** . . .: **Esto de estudiar = Lo de estudiar**. Since there is no equivalent in English it can only be translated with such phrases as *that business of . . ., this question of . . .*, etc.

2.

$$\text{y eso que} \begin{cases} \textit{although} \\ \textit{even though} \end{cases}$$

No me pagó el dinero y eso que tenía suficiente.

She didn't pay me the money although she had enough.

Llegaron muy tarde y eso que les advertí.

They arrived very late even though I warned them.

18

RELATORS: PREPOSITIONS AND CONJUNCTIONS

Prepositions

Prepositions are invariable, uninflected forms which relate two grammatical units. The relationships they signal are varied and complex: from temporal and spatial orientation to many other abstract relations. Some prepositions may relate only phrases, while others may relate phrases and clauses (the latter of course must be introduced by **que**). The object of a preposition in Spanish can only be a nominal: nouns, pronouns, pronominal adverbs, infinitives, adjectives, or clauses functioning as nominals.

Bodas **de** plata . . .	*Silver anniversary . . .*
El libro **de** historia . . .	*History book . . .*
El libro **de** él . . .	*His book . . .*
Va **a** Madrid.	*He is going to Madrid.*
Van **para** las once.	*It is going on eleven.*
Ven **para** acá.	*Come over here.*
Entre ellos . . .	*Among them . . .*
Entre los mejores . . .	*Among the best . . .*
No sé **de** eso.	*I don't know about that.*
No sé **de que** me hablas.	*I don't know what you are talking about.*
Vengo **a** estudiar.	*I have come to study.*
Vengo **a que** me pagues.	*I have come so that you could pay me.*

Very few Spanish prepositions stand in a one-to-one correspondence with English prepositions. The majority has a semantic range which differs greatly from the English prepositions. In English, many prepositional relationships are rendered by other grammatical means (as seen above) and many simple forms are rendered by prepositional phrases (as will be seen later). For all of these reasons any translational equivalent may only be considered as one of the possible meanings of the Spanish form and not as an absolute equivalent which applies to the whole semantic range of the English form.

BASIC SIMPLE PREPOSITIONS

The basic simple prepositions are the following:

a	*to, at, in, for, upon, by*	excepto	*except*
ante	*before*	hacia	*toward*
bajo	*under*	hasta	*until, up to, as far as*
con	*with*	para	*for, to, on, around*
contra	*against*	por	*for, by, in, through, because of*
de	*of, from, to, about*	salvo	*except, save*
durante	*during*	según	*according to*
desde	*since, from*	sin	*without*
en	*in, into, at, on*	sobre	*on, about, over*
entre	*among, between*	tras	*after*

In Spanish, prepositions may combine with other prepositions, with adverbs, and with nouns to express more complex relations for which no simple form exists. These may correspond in English to simple prepositions or to prepositional phrases.

COMPOUND PREPOSITIONAL FORMS

The most commonly used compound prepositions and prepositional phrases are the following:

antes de	*before*	a causa de	*on account of*
después de	*after*	a fuerza de	*by dint of*
alrededor de	*around, about*	a pesar de	*in spite of*
arriba de	*above*	a través de	*through*
cerca de	*close to, near*	a excepción de	*with exception of*
debajo de	*below, underneath*		
delante de	*in front of, before*	en contra de	*against*
dentro de	*inside of*	en frente de	*in front of*
detrás de	*behind*	en vez de	*in place of*
encima de	*on top of, upon, above*	en lugar de	*instead of*
fuera de	*outside of*		
lejos de	*far from*	en cuanto a	*as for*
más allá de	*beyond*		
acerca de	*about*		
conforme a	*in accordance with*	respecto a	*with respect to*
frente a	*in front of*	igual a	*the same as*
junto a	*next to*	contrario a	*contrary to*

The following simple prepositions are closely related in meaning to compound prepositions. The basic difference between the two is that the compound forms in Spanish are restricted to describing spatial relationships only, whereas the simple forms may assume figurative meanings as well.

---

ante *before*	**delante de** *in front of, before*
Ante mis ojos se extendía el mar. *The sea spread out before my eyes.*	Delante de mis ojos se extendía el mar. *The sea spread out before my eyes.*
Ante la ley todos los hombres son iguales. *In the eyes of the law all men are equal.*	
Compareció ante el juez. *He appeared before the judge.*	

---

tras *after*	**detrás de** *behind*
El ladrón se escondía tras el biombo. *The burglar was hiding behind the screen.*	Detrás del biombo se escondía el ladrón. *The burglar was hiding behind the screen.*
Algo se encubre tras estos hechos. *There is something suspicious behind these facts.*	

---

bajo *under*	**debajo de** *under, below*
Bajo los apuntes debe estar la carta. *The letter must be under my notes.*	Debajo de los apuntes debe estar la carta. *The letter must be under my notes.*
Bajo la ley todos los hombres son iguales. *In the eyes of the law all men are equal.*	

---

sobre *on, upon, over, about*	**encima de** *on*
Los documentos estaban esparcidos sobre la mesa. *The documents were scattered on the table.*	Los documentos estaban esparcidos encima de la mesa. *The documents were scattered on the table.*
El condor vuela sobre las cumbres. *The condor flies over the mountains.*	
Sobre esta enfermedad poco se cabe. *Little is known about this disease.*	
Sobre la novela contemporánea mucho se ha escrito. *Much has been written on (about) the contemporary novel.*	

USAGE OF PREPOSITIONS

Uses of **a**

Dynamic relationships between two entities. Motion, direction, in space or in time.

1. Verbs of motion with adverbials of destination:

Llegó a Lima.	*He arrived in Lima.*
Se subió al techo.	*He climbed unto the roof.*
Se arrojó al piso.	*He threw himself on the floor.*
Volvió a París.	*He returned to Paris.*
Se acercó a nosotros.	*He approached us.*
Se fue a Europa.	*He left for Europe.*
Ponlo al sol.	*Put it in the sun.*
Ven a mi casa.	*Come to my house.*
Siéntate a la mesa.	*Sit down at the table.*

2. Location in relation to another point of reference:

La biblioteca está a mano derecha.	*The library is on the right-hand side.*
Está a unas dos cuadras de aquí.	*It is some two blocks away from here.*
Corpus Christi está a poca distancia (de aquí).	*Corpus Christi is at a short distance (from here).*
Está al nivel del mar.	*It is at sea level.*

3. Movement (figurative) toward the performance of some activity, or the attempt to move someone to act:

La invitó a bailar.	*He invited her to dance.*
Le enseñaré a hablar francés.	*I will teach her to speak French.*
Lo obligó a estudiar.	*He forced him to study.*
Se consagó a su profesión.	*He devoted himself to his profession.*
Uno se acostumbra a todo.	*One gets used to everything.*
Hay que limitarse a lo posible.	*One must limit oneself to what is possible.*
Se sometió a un régimen muy severo.	*She put herself on a very strict diet.*

4. Destination, purpose of an action:

¿A qué has venido?	*What have you come for?*
—A verte.	*To see you.*
¡A cenar que es tarde!	*Everybody to the table, it is late!*
Vine a que me pagues.	*I have come so that you could pay me.*

5. Point in time:

Salió a las ocho.	*He left at eight.*
Saldrá a la mãnana.	*He will leave in the morning.*
Saldrá al día siguiente.	*He will leave the next day.*
Al llegar, te llamaré.	*Upon arriving, I will call you.*

Al poco tiempo me enteré de la
  verdad.
Nos veíamos a diario.
Al principio nos llevábamos bien.

*Shortly thereafter I found out the
  truth.*
We saw each other daily.
At the beginning we got along well.

6. Manner:

Lo haré a mi gusto y antojo.
Vino a pie.
Vino a caballo.
Está hecho a máquina.
Está escrito a mano.
Lo hizo a la fuerza.

I will do it whichever way I please.
He came by foot.
He came on horseback.
It is machine-made (made by machine).
It is hand-written.
He did it because he was forced to do it.

7. Measures by unit:

El dólar está a 1000 pesos
  argentinos.
La casa se vende a 60,000 dólares.
La temperatura está a 90 grados.
Va a sesenta kilómetros por hora.

The dollar is at 1000 Argentine pesos.

The house is priced at 60,000 dollars.
The temperature is at 90 degrees.
He is traveling at 60 miles per hour.

8. Causal phrases:

A petición del público la función de
  esta noche se suspende.
A insistencia del juez la sentencia
  fue conmutada.

*By public demand the performance
  tonight is canceled.*
*At the judge's insistence the sentence
  was changed.*

9. Set phrases:

A veces estudia.
Lo hizo a escondidas.
A sabiendas de que era ilegal decidió
  proceder.

Sometimes he studies.
He did it behind their backs.
*Knowing that it was illegal he
  decided to proceed anyway.*

10. Distributive value:

Los invitados fueron llegando uno
  a uno.
Paso a paso se acercaba hacia
  nosotros.
Poco a poco se fue agotando mi
  paciencia.

The guests were arriving one by one.

*Step by step he was coming closer to
  us.*
*Little by little my patience was
  coming to an end.*

Uses of **de**

1. Origin or point of departure:

Es de Madrid.
Es de una familia distinguida.

He is from Madrid.
He comes from a distinguished family.

Salió de la oficina a las seis.	*He left the office at five. (He departed from the office at five.)*
De Austin a Dallas hay unas doscientas millas.	*From Austin to Dallas it is some 200 miles.*

2. Figurative analogue: origin of emotional states:

Me alegro de que hayas venido.	*I am happy that you have come.*
Se arrepintió de sus errores.	*He regretted his mistakes.*
Se admiraba de su elocuencia.	*She admired his eloquence.*
Tengo miedo de que nos oigan.	*I am afraid of their overhearing us.*

3. Possession, belongingness:

La iglesia de San Pedro es la más bella de todas.	*Saint Peter's Church is the most beautiful of all of them.*
Es el hijo de mi hermana.	*He is my sister's son.*
La secretaria de mi marido es excelente.	*My husband's secretary is excellent.*
El agua del Caribe es cristalina.	*The water in the Caribbean is crystal clear.*
La población de los Estados Unidos es heterogénea.	*The population of the United States is heterogeneous.*

4. Composition and content:

El reloj es de oro.	*It is a gold watch.*
Le regaló una cartera de cuero.	*He gave her a leather purse.*
Llena la jarra de agua.	*Fill the pitcher with water.*
Dame una taza de té.	*Give me a cup of tea.*
Escribe novelas de misterio.	*He writes mystery novels.*
Nos dio una lección de historia.	*He gave us a history lesson.*

5. Characteristic or condition:

¿Conoces al hombre de la barba?	*Do you know the man with the beard?*
Preséntame a la mujer del vestido rojo.	*Introduce me to the woman in the red dress.*
Me gusta la casa de la esquina.	*I like the house on the corner.*
Es el peor estudiante de la clase.	*He is the worst student in the class.*
Es pequeño de cuerpo pero grande de espíritu.	*He is small in body but great in spirit.*
Tenía las manos sucias de tinta.	*His hands were stained with ink.*
Es difícil de entender.	*It is difficult to understand.*
Está cansado de luchar.	*He is tired of fighting.*
Exhausto de trabajar, se quedó dormido.	*Exhausted from working, he fell asleep.*
Aburrida de estudiar no sabía qué hacer con su vida.	*Bored of studying she did not know what to do with her life.*

6. Use for which a thing is intended:

máquina de coser	*sewing machine*
máquina de escribir	*typewriter*
cuarto de baño	*bathroom*
casa de huéspedes	*guest house*
caña de pescar	*fishing rod*
perro de caza	*hunting dog*

7. Manner:

Llegó cubierto de polvo.	*He arrived covered with dust.*
Lo hizo de mala fe.	*He did it in bad faith.*
Cayó de rodillas.	*He fell on his knees.*
Ponte de pie.	*Stand up.*
La observaba de reojo.	*He was watching her out of the corner of his eye.*

8. Cause:

De tanto leer se le estropeó la vista.	*He ruined his eyes from so much reading.*
De tan poco dormir se enfermó.	*He got sick from getting so little sleep.*
Murió de cáncer.	*He died of cancer.*
Se desmayó del susto.	*She fainted from fright.*

9. Time:

Es de día.	*It is daytime.*
Es de noche.	*It is nighttime.*
Es de madrugada.	*It is dawn.*
Estudia de día y trabaja de noche.	*He studies during the day and works at night.*
Es hora de comer.	*It is time to eat.*

10. Partitive:

Dame un poco más de carne.	*Give me some more meat.*
Ella tiene de todo.	*She has everything.*
Necesito dos docenas de flores.	*I need two dozen flowers.*
Diez de los presentes votaron a favor.	*Ten of the people present voted in favor.*
No tiene nada de tonto.	*There is nothing stupid about him.*

11. Derisive descriptions of people:

El loco de Pedro se casó.	*That crazy Peter got married.*
El charlatán del abogado me engañó.	*That charlatan lawyer deceived me.*
La tonta de su mujer trató de consolarme.	*That silly wife of his tried to console me.*

12. Matter spoken of, verbal complements:

Habla de sus proyectos con gran entusiasmo.	He speaks about *his projects with great enthusiasm.*
Cada uno se queja de lo que más le molesta.	*Everyone complains about what bothers him most.*
Infórmame de lo sucedido.	*Inform me of what has happened.*
Se expresó muy bien de ti.	*He spoke very highly of you.*

Uses of **en**

Static relationship between two entities which can be surrounded, enclosed, or contained in other entities.

1. Location, with verbs which take locative adverbials:

No está en su casa.	*He is not at home.*
Se quedó en Madrid.	*He remained in Madrid.*
Se sentó en una silla.	*He sat down on a chair.*
Se acostó en el sofá.	*He laid down on a sofa.*
La comida está en la mesa.	*Dinner is on the table.*
Nos conocimos en una corrida de toros.	*We met at a bullfight.*
No puede atenderte porque está en una reunión.	*He cannot see you because he is in a meeting.*
El accidente ocurrió en la esquina.	*The accident took place at the corner.*
El ladrón logró meterse en la casa.	*The burglar succeeded in getting into the house.*
El niño se metió en la cama.	*The child got into bed.*

2. Figurative location, in idiomatic expressions of states of being:

Está metido en un lío.	*He is in a fix.*
Se encuentra en un apuro.	*He is in a bind.*
De la noche a la mañana se encontró en la calle.	*Overnight he found himself broke (jobless).*
Cayó en desgracia con su jefe.	*He fell into his boss' bad graces.*
Déjame en paz.	*Leave me in peace.*

3. Complements of predicate nominative:

Es sabio en jurisprudencia.	*He is an expert in law.*
Es ignorante en todo.	*He is ignorant in every field.*
Es muy conocido en su campo.	*He is very well known in his specialty.*
Es doctor en medicina.	*He is a medical doctor.*

4. Manner:

Nunca habla en serio.	*He never speaks in earnest.*
Me lo dijo en broma.	*He said it to me in jest.*
Lo intenté en vano.	*I tried it in vain.*

5. Means, instrument:

No se expresa bien en inglés.   *He does not express himself well in English.*

Viajamos en avión supersónico.   *We traveled in a supersonic jet.*
Llegó en un coche último modelo.   *He arrived in a brand new car.*

6. Extent of time:

Terminaré en dos días.   *I will finish in two days.*
Se graduará en un año.   *She will graduate in a year.*
En tan poco tiempo nada puede hacerse.   *In such a short time nothing can be done.*

Uses of **por**

1. Approximate location:

Estará por Europa ahora.   *He must be (some place) in Europe now.*

La tienda debe estar por aquí.   *The store must be some place around here.*

Por todas partes encuentra uno gente interesante.   *One finds interesting people everywhere.*

2. Place of transit:

Pasé por tu casa pero no te encontré.   *I went by your house but I did not find you there.*

De regreso pasaremos por Washington.   *On the way back we will go through Washington.*
Pasaron por el puente.   *They went over the bridge.*
Pasaron por debajo del puente.   *They went under the bridge.*
Debes pasar por Los Angeles.   *You must go via (through) Los Angeles.*

Esto no entra por la puerta.   *This cannot go in through the door.*
Paseaban por el zoológico.   *They were strolling around the zoo.*

3. Temporal expressions:

a. Approximate time.

Por diciembre hará frío.   *Around December it will be cold.*
Por esos años pasaba trabajo.   *Around those years he was having a hard time.*

b. Elapsed time during which an action took place, or space of time during which it continues or will take place:

Estuvo en el extranjero por un año.   *He was abroad for a year.*

Por muchos años vivió engañada.   *For many years she lived a delusion.*

Nos quedaremos aquí por cuatro días.	*We will stay here for four days.*
Por ahora no digo nada.	*For the time being I am saying nothing.*
Ven por la mañana.	*Come in the morning.*
Ven por la noche.	*Come in the evening.*

4. Correspondence:

Le pagarán por hora.	*He will be paid by the hour.*
Tienen seis materias por año.	*They have six subjects per year.*
Por docena es más barato.	*It is cheaper by the dozen.*

5. Exchange, substitution of one thing for the other, proxy:

Me dieron 300 dólares por el piano.	*They gave me 300 dollars for the piano.*
Pide demasiado por su casa.	*He is asking too much for his house.*
Tomó el insulto por cumplido.	*He mistook the insult for a compliment.*
Ve tú por mí.	*Go in my place (instead of me).*
Habla tú por él.	*Speak for him (instead of him).*

6. Cause, motive, inner compulsion, or moral obligation:

No pudo asistir a clase por estar enfermo.	*He could not attend class because he was sick.*
Perdona por la demora.	*Forgive me for the delay (because of the delay).*
Consiguió trabajo por ser quien es, pero no por lo que vale.	*He found a job because of who he is, but not because of what he is worth.*
¿Por qué (motivo) renunció?	*Why did he resign? (What was the motive for his resigning?)*
De no haber sido por él todo habría salido bien.	*Had it not been for him everything would have turned out fine.*
La ha hecho por ti.	*He has done it for your sake.*
No te niegues a hacerlo por mí.	*Don't refuse to do it for my sake (because of me).*
No me gusta por mentiroso.	*I don't like him because he is a liar.*
Se ha sacrificado por sus hijos.	*She has sacrificed her own life for her children's sake.*
No puedo hacerlo por el jefe.	*I cannot do it because of my boss.*

7. Finality:

Votaré por que se eliminen todos los prerequisitos.	*I shall vote for (in favor of) the abolition of all prerequisites.*
Votaré por el candidato oficial.	*I shall vote for the official candidate.*
¿Qué puedo hacer por Ud.?	*What can I do for you?*
Viaja por placer.	*He travels for pleasure.*
Viaja por razones de negocios.	*He travels for business reasons.*

| Lucha por forjarse una posición. | *He struggles in order to secure a position for himself.* |
| Haría cualquiera cosa por verte feliz. | *I would do anything (in order) to see you happy.* |

8. Manner, instrument:

Han llegado por barco.	*They have come by boat.*
Hablará por radio esta noche.	*He will speak on the radio tonight.*
Lo he conocido por medio de Pedro.	*I have met him through Pedro.*
Consiguió trabajo por él.	*He found a job through him.*
No se lo cuentes por teléfono.	*Don't say it over the phone.*

9. Agency:

| Fue nombrado por el presidente. | *He was appointed by the president.* |

10. Equivalent of **sin** when introducing an infinitive:

Tengo muchos exámenes por corregir.	*I have many exams that must be graded.*
Queda mucho por hacer.	*There is much to be done.*
Eso está por verse.	*That remains to be seen.*

11. Assertions, oath:

Te lo juro por lo que más quieras.	*I swear by whatever you hold dear.*
Déjame en paz, por favor.	*Leave me alone, please.*
Por Dios, ¡cómo puedes creer eso!	*For heaven's sake how can you believe that!*

12. Equivalent of **estar a punto de** + INF:

Estaba por salir cuando llegaron.	*I was about to leave when they arrived.*
Está por casarse.	*She is about to get married.*
Está por nevar.	*It is about to snow.*

Uses of **para**

Direction in space and in time:

1. With verbs of motion which take adverbials of direction:

Va para Madrid.	*He is going to (towards) Madrid.*
Viene para acá.	*He is coming over here.*
Vete para allá.	*Go over there.*
¿Para dónde vas?	*Where are you heading for?*

NOTE: **Para** cannot be used to introduce adverbials of final destination; **a** must be used instead.

| Llegó a Madrid. | *He arrived in Madrid.* |
| Se acercó a ella. | *He approached her.* |

2. Time expressions, approximate time and deadlines:

Va para las diez. ·	*It is going on ten.*
Lo dejaremos para la semana que viene.	*We will leave it for next week.*
Llegarán para las seis.	*They will be here around six (or by six).*
Para enero refrescará.	*By January it will cool off.*
Para el jueves se vence el plazo.	*By Thursday the term expires.*

3. Goal, purpose, suitability of an object or person:

Tengo dos cartas para Ud.	*I have two letters for you.*
Toma dos aspirinas para la fiebre.	*Take two aspirins for the fever.*
¿Para qué sirve ese aparato?	*What is this gadget for?*
El tiene mucho talento para la música.	*He has much talent for music.*
Ese hombre no sirve para nada.	*This man is good for nothing.*

estantes para libros	*bookcases*
agujas para máquinas de coser	*sewing-machine needles*
papel para forrar	*wrapping paper*

Quiero algo para comer.	*I want something to eat.*
Dale algo para leer.	*Give him something to read.*
Le dió una inyección para calmarla.	*He gave her a shot to clam her down.*
No tiene las aptitudes necesarias para descollar.	*He does not have the necessary qualities to excel.*

4. Goal or purpose of an action:

Lo hace para llamar la atención.	*He does it in order to attract attention.*
No se lo digo para que no se preocupe.	*I won't tell her anything so she won't worry.*
Me voy para no llegar tarde.	*I am leaving in order not to be late.*
Para dominar una lengua extranjera se requiere mucha tesón.	*To master a foreign language much endurance is required.*
Te lo he dicho para que te cuides de él.	*I have told you so that you would watch out for him.*

5. Comparisons:

Para ser tan joven tiene poca energía.	*Considering that he is so young he has little energy.*
Para lo poco que trabaja gana demasiado.	*For the little he works he earns too much.*
Para un extranjero habla muy bien el español.	*For a foreigner he speaks Spanish very well.*
Para mí esa persona no te comprende.	*In my opinion (as far as I am concerned) that person does not understand you.*

Para él no hay obstáculos que sean invencibles.	*For him there are no obstacles that cannot be overcome.*
Para playas no hay como el Caribe.	*As for beaches there is no place like the Carribean.*

CONTRASTIVE CHART

Para	*Por*
1. Place: Direction.	1. Place: Place of transit.
Voy para Madrid.	Pasaré por Madrid.
I am going to Madrid.	*I will stop in Madrid.*
	I will go through Madrid.
2. Time: Deadline.	2. Time: Approximate.
Para enero refresca.	Por enero refresca.
By January it cools off.	*Around January it cools off.*
Termínalo para la noche.	Termínalo por la noche.
Finish it by tonight.	*Finish it tonight.*
3. Extent:	
Estuvo en la India por diez años.	
He was in India for ten years.	
4. Goal, destination of an object, person or event:	3. Cause, motive:
He escrito la carta para el decano.	He escrito la carta porque quiero una respuesta definitiva.
I have written the letter for the dean (addressed to him).	*I have written the letter because I want a definitive answer.*
No tiene las aptitudes necesarias para ser médico.	Más ha logrado por tenaz que por inteligente.
He does not have the aptitude required to be a physician.	*He has achieved more because of his tenacity than his intelligence.*
Lo he hecho para complacerte.	Lo he hecho por complacerte.
I have done it to please you.	*I have done it to please you.*
	4. Exchange:
Este dinero me lo dieron para (comprar) el piano.	Este dinero me lo dieron por el piano.
This money was given to me for (in order to buy) the piano.	*This money was given to me for (in exchange of) the piano.*

Use of **con**

Accompaniment, people, things or abstract entities:

Llegó con varios amigos.	*He arrived with several friends.*
Le serví un whiskey con soda.	*I served him a whiskey* with *soda.*
Era una casa con todas las comodidades.	*It was a house with every imaginable comfort.*
Está con fuertes dolores.	*He is in severe pain.*
Está con gripe.	*He has the flu.*
Está con el ánimo muy decaído.	*He is in very low spirits.*

Uses of **hasta**

1. Terminus of motion in space:

Viajaremos en tren hasta Chicago.	*We will go by train* up to (*as far as*) *Chicago.*
Llegaron hasta Madrid.	*They went* as far as *Madrid.*
Hasta aquí leído.	*I have read* this *far.*

2. Terminus of motion in time:

¿Hasta qué hora estarás en tu oficina?	Until *what time will you be in your office?*
—Hasta las siete.	—*Until seven.*

3. Figuratively, "including":

Hasta las mujeres y niños pelearon.	*Even women and children fought.*
Hasta él, que es tan plácido, se indignó.	*Even he, who is so placid, became indignant.*

Uses of **desde**

1. Point in time from which an event has been ongoing:

No ha comido desde el lunes.	*He has not eaten* since *last Monday.*
Desde que volvió no hay paz.	*Since he returned there is no peace.*

2. Point in space from which a given distance is measured:

Desde aquí se ve mejor.	From *here one can see better.*
Caminamos desde el centro hasta la casa.	*We walked from downtown to our house.*

Use of **sin**

Lack of an entity or thing:

Es un hombre sin sentimientos.	*He is an unfeeling person.*
Dejó muchas cosas sin acabar.	*He left many things unfinished.*

La casa estaba decorada sin gusto.	*The house was furnished without taste (in a tasteless fashion).*
Es un pobre hombre sin recursos algunos.	*He is a helpless man without any resources.*
No puede vivir sin ti.	*He cannot live without you.*

Conjunctions

COORDINATING CONJUNCTIONS

There are two classes of conjunctions: coordinating and subordinating. Coordinating conjunctions are invariable, uninflected forms which join two or more phrases or clauses of equal grammatical status in a coordinate relationship. For other conjunctions and conjunctive phrases, coordinating and subordinating (those which subordinate a clause to a sentence), see Nominal and Conditional Clauses, pages 162 and 181.

Simple conjunctive forms :

y	*and*
Vinieron Juan y Pedro.	*Peter and John came.*
Dame papel y tinta.	*Give me some paper and ink.*
Es bueno y diligente.	*He is good and diligent.*
Lo hizo tarde y mal.	*She did it badly and too late.*
Estudia y trabaja.	*He works and studies.*
Dijo que no podía ir y que por lo tanto no lo esperásemos.	*He said he could not go and that therefore we should not wait for him.*

o . . . o	*either . . . or*
O me das lo que te pido o me voy.	*Either you give me what I am asking for or else I shall leave.*
O vienes tú o no voy yo.	*Either you come or I won't go.*
Que venga Pedro o María.	*Have either Peter or Mary come.*

ni . . . ni	*neither . . . nor* *not . . . nor*
No vinieron ni Juan ni Pedro.	*Neither John nor Peter came.*
Ni come ni duerme.	*He neither sleeps nor eats.*
No quiere ni trabajar ni estudiar.	*He neither wants to work nor study.*
No tiene ni padre ni madre.	*He does not have a father nor a mother.*

sino, pero	*but*
Tengo tres libros de él, pero ninguno tuyo.	*I have three books of his, but none of yours.*
No tengo ningún libro tuyo sino uno de él.	*I don't have any of your books but one of his.*

ya . . . ya	*now . . . now*
Ya llora ya canta.	*Now he cries now he sings.*
Ya me critica ya me alaba.	*Now he criticizes me now he praises me.*

NOTE:

1. When the conjunctions **y** and **o** occur before another homologous vowel, they change to **e** and **u**, respectively.

i + i > e	**o + o > u**
español e inglés	plata u oro
Spanish and English	*silver or gold*
desafiante e indignado	mujer u hombre
defiant and indignant	*woman or man*

No change occurs before **hie-** or **y**.

soda y hielo
soda and ice

carbón y hierro
coal and iron

ella y yo
she and I

2. The conjunctions **sino** and **pero** are synonymous. **Sino** is used before an affirmative phrase or clause in contrast to a preceding negative. In all other instances **pero** occurs instead.

Vino Juan pero no María.	*John came but not Maria.*
No vino María sino Juan.	*Maria did not come but John did.*
Trabaja pero no estudia.	*He works but he does not study.*
No estudia sino que trabaja.	*He does not study but he does work.*

19

COMPARATIVE CONSTRUCTIONS AND ADVERBS

Comparative Constructions

Comparative constructions are used to express different degrees of intensity in relating two or more objects (animate or inanimate), ideas, qualities, or actions. These degrees of intensity are in terms of equality, inequality (inferiority or superiority), or absolute inferiority or superiority.

COMPARISONS OF EQUALITY

Comparisons of equality in English always involve the formula "*as . . . as.*" Spanish uses different formulas depending on whether the point of comparison is an adjective, an adverb, or a noun.

I.

$$\textbf{tan} + \begin{Bmatrix} \text{Adjective} \\ \text{OR} \\ \text{Adverb} \end{Bmatrix} + \textbf{como} \qquad as + \begin{Bmatrix} \text{Adjective} \\ \text{OR} \\ \text{Adverb} \end{Bmatrix} + as$$

Es tan alta como él.	*She is as tall as he (is).*
Es tan guapa como inteligente.	*She is as handsome as she is intelligent.*
Habla tan bien como escribe.	*He speaks as well as he writes.*
Llegaba tan tarde como el jefe.	*He used to arrive as late as the boss (did).*

Occasionally in the literary language, **tan** may be omitted for stylistic effects.

Azul como el mar.	*Blue as the sea.*
Malo como el diablo.	*Evil as the devil.*

2.

$$\left.\begin{array}{l}\textbf{tanto(-a)}\\\textbf{tantos(-as)}\end{array}\right\} + \text{Noun} + \textbf{como} \qquad as + \left\{\begin{array}{l}much\\OR\\many\end{array}\right\} + Noun + as$$

Tengo tanto trabajo como Uds.	*I have as much work as you do.*
Te escribí tantas cartas como él.	*I wrote you as many letters as he wrote you.*

In these cases **tanto** functions as an adjective; therefore, it agrees in gender and number with the noun it refers to. If the noun is deleted, **tanto** then functions as a pronoun and the agreement is also observed.

Tengo tanto como Uds. (trabajo)	*I have as much as you do. (work)*
Te escribí tantas como él. (cartas)	*I wrote you as many as he did. (letters)*

As an adverb **tanto** is invariable.

No trabaja tanto como yo.	*He does not work as much as I do.*
Escribo tanto como él.	*I write as much as he does.*

Cuanto instead of como

When **tanto** is not immediately followed by an adjective, noun, or adverb, **cuanto** may be used instead of **como** for stylistic or literary effects:

Gana tanto dinero como quiere.⎫	
Gana tanto cuanto quiere. ⎭	*He earns as much money as he wants.*

COMPARISONS OF INEQUALITY

In English, comparisons of inequality may be formed by either using the words *more* and *less* with nouns, adjectives, pronouns, or adverbs or by adding the suffix *-er* to certain adjectives and adverbs. In Spanish, with the exception of a few irregular forms (**mayor, menor, mejor, peor**), comparisons of inequality are formed with **más** or **menos** followed by **que** or **de** as follows:

I.

$$\left.\begin{array}{l}\textbf{más}\\\textbf{menos}\end{array}\right\}\textbf{que} \qquad \left.\begin{array}{l}more\\less,\,fewer\end{array}\right\}than$$

Entiende más que tú.	*She understands more than you do.*
Tengo menos que la mujer.	*I have less (fewer) than the woman.*
Lee más que antes.	*He reads more than he used to read.*
Es él más que ella quien insiste en partir.	*It is he more than she who insists on leaving.*

2.

$$\left.\begin{array}{l}\textbf{más}\\\\\textbf{menos}\end{array}\right\} + \begin{array}{c}\text{Adjective}\\\text{OR}\\\text{Adverb}\end{array} + \textbf{que} \qquad \left.\begin{array}{l}\left\{\begin{array}{l}\textit{more} + \text{Adjective OR Adverb}\\\textit{er-} \text{ form}\end{array}\right.\\\\\left\{\begin{array}{c}\text{Adjective OR Adverb}\\\textit{less} + \qquad\text{OR}\\\textit{-er} \text{ form}\end{array}\right.\end{array}\right\} + \textit{than}$$

La salud es más importante que el dinero.	*Good health is more important than money.*
Su consejo es más sabio que sus acciones.	*His advice is wiser than his actions.*
Esta carta es menos comprometedora que la otra.	*This letter is less compromising than the other.*
Es menos listo que su amigo.	*He is less smart than his friend.*
Es menos joven que su prima.	*She is less young than her cousin.*
El habla más despacio que tú.	*He speaks more slowly than you do.*
Ella conduce más rápido que su marido.	*She drives faster than her husband.*
Caminan menos lento que los niños.	*They walk less slowly than the children.*
El anciano camina menos rápido que tú.	*The old man walks less fast than you do.*
Se comporta mejor que tú.[1]	*He behaves better than you do.*
peor.	*worse.*

3.

$$\left.\begin{array}{l}\textbf{más}\\\textbf{menos}\end{array}\right\} \text{Noun} + \textbf{que} \qquad \left.\begin{array}{l}\textit{more}\\\textit{less}\\\textit{fewer}\end{array}\right\} \text{Noun} + \textit{than}$$

Hay más problemas que soluciones.	*There are more problems than solutions.*
Quiere más a su padre que a mí.	*She loves her father more than she loves me.*
Te molesto menos a ti que a ella.[2]	*I bother you less than I bother her.*
Exigen menos documentos que antes.	*They demand fewer documents than before.*

---

[1] The forms **mejor** and **peor** are always used as adverbs instead of **más bien**, **más mal**, respectively.

[2] In Spanish one does not need to expand the second member of the comparison by repeating the verb or using an auxiliary, as is the case in English: **Tengo tanto trabajo como Uds.** = *I have as much work as you do.*

De instead of que

In affirmative statements **de** is used instead of **que** directly before numbers or before words that imply a given amount or quantity.

Necesito más de diez dólares.	*I need more than ten dollars.*
Le di más de la mitad.	*I gave him more than half.*
Pasamos menos de dos horas.	*We spent less than two hours.*
Le tocó menos de su cuota.	*He got less than his share.*

Even if the quantity is not specifically stated but implied, **de** is preferred over **que**.

Compraba más cosas de las necesarias. de las que eran necesarias.	*He used to buy more things than was necessary.*
(. . . más de la cantidad necesaria)	(. . . *more than the necessary amount*)
Tomó más cursos de los requeridos. de los que eran requeridos.	*He took more courses than the required ones.*
(. . . más del número requerido)	(. . . *more than the required number*)
La habitación era más grande de lo que yo pensaba. (. . . más grande que el tamaño que yo pensaba)	*The room was larger than what I thought.* (. . . *larger than the size that I thought it was*).
Estudia más de lo normal. de lo que es normal.	*He studies more than normal.* *than what is normal.*
(. . . más de la cantidad normal)	(. . . *more than the normal amount*)

If the point of comparison in the two clauses is a noun, **de** is followed by the corresponding form of the definite article. If the point of comparison is an adjective, adverb, or a whole idea, **de** is followed by the neuter form.

In negative statements either **que** or **de** may occur with numerals, but the meaning is different.

---

1.   Amount simply stated

---

no . . . más que = *but, only*

No necesito más que diez dólares. (=sólo necesito diez dólares)	*I don't need but ten dollars.* (=*I only need ten dollars.*)
No le di más que la mitad. (=sólo le di la mitad)	*I didn't give her but half.* (=*I only gave her half.*)

---

2.   Amount stated, but is the maximum allowed

---

no . . . más de = *not more than*   *up to*

No necesito más de diez dólares.	*I don't need more than ten dollars.*
(=necesito sólo diez dólares)	*(=I need only ten dollars)*

If two numerical expressions are compared, **que** and not **de** links the two members of the comparison.

Tres docenas cuestan más que dos.	*Three dozen cost more than two.*
Tres cuartos es más que tres octavos.	*Three fourths is more than three eighths.*

IRREGULAR COMPARATIVE FORMS OF ADJECTIVES

Adjective	Regular Comparative	Irregular Comparative	
bueno	**más bueno**	**mejor**[1]	*better, best*
malo	**más malo**	**peor**	*worse, worst*
grande **viejo**	**más grande** **más viejo**	**mayor**	*older, oldest* *(greater, greatest,* *bigger, biggest)*
pequeño **joven**	**más pequeño** **más joven**	**menor**	*younger, youngest* *(smaller, smallest,* *lesser, least)*

A few adjectives have an irregular comparative form ending in **-or**, which never occurs with **más** or **menos**. In most cases these irregular comparatives are interchangeable with their corresponding regular forms, but there are some restrictions.

1. The regular and irregular comparatives of **bueno** and **malo** co-occur with **más** if reference is made to the moral qualities of a person:

Es más mala (peor) que el diablo.	*She is worse than the devil.*
Es más bueno (mejor) que un santo.	*He is better than a saint.*

But the irregular forms must be used if reference is made to more general qualities or traits of animate or inanimate objects:

Rembrandt es mejor pintor que Cezanne.	*Rembrandt is a better painter than Cezanne.*
Este ensayo es mejor que aquél.	*This essay is a better one than that one.*
Su oficina es peor que la mía.	*His office is worse than mine.*

2. The irregular forms **mayor** and **menor** when used with human nouns normally refer to differences in age:

Su madre es mayor que la mía.	*Her mother is older than mine.*
Mi hermano es menor que yo.	*My brother is younger than I am.*

---

[1] The forms **mejor** and **peor** also function as adverbs. See Adverbs of Manner, page 355.

But when reference is made to the physical size of an object (animate or inanimate), **más grande** and **más pequeño** are used instead:

Mi hermano es más grande que yo.	*My brother is bigger than I am.*
Tu coche es más pequeño que el nuestro.	*Your car is smaller than ours.*

3. The regular comparatives **más viejo** and **más joven** when used with human nouns refer to age, particularly to imply that someone is "really old" or "really young":

Dale la silla a la señora, ¡no ves que es más vieja (mayor) que tú!	*Give the chair to the lady, don't you see that she is older than you are!*

Más viejo when used with inanimate objects cannot be replaced by **mayor**:

Este cuadro es más viejo que los otros.	*This painting is older than the other ones.*

The irregular comparatives **mejor**, **peor**, **mayor**, and **menor** usually precede the noun, except when **mayor** and **menor** refer to age:

Tiene mejores intenciones que Uds.	*He has better intentions than you.*
Tuve peores resultados que tú.	*I had worse results than you did.*
Esto tiene mayor importancia que otras cosas.	*This has greater importance than other things.*

BUT:

Ella es la hermana mayor (menor).	*She is the older sister (younger).*

Another way of making a comparison of inequality is to negate the corresponding comparison of equality, thus

No tiene tanto dinero como él.	*She doesn't have as much money as he does.*

means the same as:

Tiene menos dinero que él.	*She has less money than he does.*

Repetition of comparative forms

If several adjectives, adverbs, or nouns occur together in a comparison, the comparative forms **tan**, **más**, **menos**, accompany only the first of these items. But if emphasis is desired, then the comparatives may be repeated.

Es más competente, leal y discreto que el otro jefe.	*He is more competent, more loyal and more discreet than the other boss.*
Vive más solo y más triste que el resto de sus hermanos.	*He lives a lonelier and sadder life than the rest of his brothers.*

Further modification with comparatives of inequality

The comparatives of inequality may be further modified in order to intensify the degree of inequality.

Entiende mucho más que tú.
    bastante
    poco
    algo

He understands much more than you.
    a lot
    a little
    somewhat

La salud es mucho más importante
que el dinero.
    algo
    poco
    bastante
    aun
    considerablemente

Good health is much more important
than money.
    somewhat
    a little
    a lot
    even
    considerably

Rembrandt es mucho mejor pintor
que Cezanne.
    tanto
    considerablemente

Rembrandt is a much better painter than
Cezanne.
    so much
    considerably

Hay muchos más problemas que
soluciones.
    tantos
    aun
    considerablemente

There are many more problems than
solutions.
    so many
    even
    considerably

(Note that **mucho, tanto,** and **poco** refer here to **problemas,** so they function as adjectives and therefore agree with the noun: Hay **muchas (tantas)** más soluciones que problemas.)

Superlative Constructions

Superlatives express the highest or lowest degree of a quality in the comparison of objects (animate or inanimate) of the same kind.

SUPERLATIVE OF ADJECTIVES

Article OR Posses-sive	+ (Noun) +	**más** / **menos** } + Adjective OR Irregular Comparative	Article OR Posses-sive	+	Adjective + *-est* / *most* + Adjective / *least* + Adjective OR Irregular Comparative	+ (Noun)

Es la (chica) más lista de la clase.	*She is the smartest (girl) in the class.*
Elena es su hija más linda.	*Elena is her prettiest daughter.*
Díaz es el funcionario más importante del gobierno.	*Diaz is the most important official in the government.*
Es el concepto menos democrático de la Constitución.	*It is the least democratic concept in the Constitution.*
Nueva York, el centro financiero más importante de este país . . .	*New York, the most important financial center in this country . . .*
La peor solución de todas es la que tú propones.	*The worst solution of them all is the one you propose.*
El sacerdote es la persona mayor entre nosotros.	*The priest is the oldest person among us.*
Mi hermano menor llegó ayer.	*My younger brother arrived yesterday.*

Spanish does not have special comparative forms as English does (-*est* or *most*, *least*) to express the superlative notions. Instead, Spanish uses the definite article or a possessive with the noun before **más** or **menos**, or before one of the irregular comparatives.

To indicate the point of reference in the comparison, **de** rather than **en** is normally used. **Entre** is sometimes used: **el más docto entre los hombres** = *the most learned among men.*

Spanish does not make the distinction that English sometimes does in comparing two or more things:

Su coche es el más caro.	{ *His car is the more expensive.* { *His car is the most expensive.*
¿Quién es el más alto?	{ *Who is the taller?* { *Who is the tallest?*

Word order in superlative constructions

The word order in superlative constructions generally follows the same guidelines established for the position of descriptive adjectives (See Adjective Position, page 230). Normally, superlatives follow the noun to which they refer, with few exceptions in which case for stylistic purposes they might precede.

Esta novela ofrece la visión más clara de la Revolución Mexicana.	*This novel offers the* clearest *vision of the Mexican Revolution.*
Esta novela ofrece la más clara visión de la Revolución Mexicana.	*This novel offers the clearest* vision of *the Mexican Revolution.*
Es éste su problema mayor. Es éste su mayor problema.	*This is her* biggest *problem.* *This is her biggest* problem.

La pobreza es el enemigo peor del hombre.	*Poverty is the* worst *enemy of man.*
La pobreza es el peor enemigo del hombre.	*Poverty is the worst* enemy *of man.*

THE ABSOLUTE SUPERLATIVE

The absolute superlative expresses a very high degree or the highest possible degree of a quality or manner of an action without necessarily having a frame of reference for a comparison.

Absolute superlative of adjectives

I.

$$\text{Adjective} + \begin{cases} \textbf{-ísimo} \\ \textbf{-ísima} \\ \textbf{-ísimos} \\ \textbf{-ísimas} \end{cases} \quad \left. \begin{array}{l} \textit{very} \\ \textit{most} \\ \textit{extremely} \\ \textit{exceedingly} \\ \textit{absolutely} \\ \textit{terribly} \\ \textit{highly, etc.} \end{array} \right\} + \text{Adjective}$$

una tarea dificilísima	*a very difficult task*
una persona interesantísima	*a most interesting person*
un muchacho amabilísimo	*an extremely kind fellow*
una familia riquísima	*an exceedingly rich family*
una tormenta ferocísima	*an absolutely ferocious storm*
unas novelas larguísimas	*some terribly long novels*
unos funcionarios importantísimos	*some highly important officials*

One way of forming the absolute superlative of adjectives in Spanish is by adding the suffix **-ísimo** as follows:

a. The suffix is attached directly to adjectives ending in a consonant: **difícil/ dificilísimo; feliz/felicísimo** (note the orthographic change in this case, **z→c**);

b. Adjectives ending in a vowel or a diphthong drop the vowel before adding the suffix: **simple/simplísimo; limpio/limpísimo; sucio/sucísimo**;

c. After dropping the last vowel, some orthographic changes occur: **c→ qu-**: **ric-/riquísimo**; **g→gu-**: **larg-/larguísimo**;
d. Adjectives ending in **-ble** change it to **-bil**: **amable/amabilísimo**; **notable/ notabilísimo**;
e. In literary speech the diphthongs **-ué** and **-ié** of some adjectives become **-o** and **-e** respectively: **bueno/bonísimo**; **fuerte/fortísimo**; **ferviente/ ferventísimo**—although in everyday language, **buenísimo, fuertísimo, fervientísimo**, are totally acceptable.
f. In adding **-ísimo** the main stress always changes from the adjective to the first syllable of the suffix, which carries an accent mark.

English does not have a precise equivalent for **-ísimo**. Instead, English uses an adverb modifying the adjective, to render the idea of an absolute superlative.

In Spanish, absolute superlatives with **-ísimo** are quite common in everyday speech and in the literary language. The literary language also retains the original Latin forms of a few superlative adjectives ending in **-ísimo**; or the learned suffix **-érrimo**; or other special Latin forms.

Adjective	Popular Language	Literary Language		
amigo	amiguísimo	amicísimo		*friendly*
antiguo	antigüísimo	antiquísimo	*very*	*old, ancient*
fiel		fidelísimo	*extremely*	*faithful*
frío	friísimo	frigidísimo	*exceedingly*	*cold*
piadoso	piadosísimo	pientísimo	*excessively*	*devout*
sabio		sapientísimo		*wise*
sagrado	sagradísimo	sacratísimo		*sacred*
áspero	asperísimo	aspérrimo		*harsh*
célebre	celebrísimo	celebérrimo	*very*	*famous*
íntegro	integrísimo	integérrimo	*extremely*	*honest, wholesome*
libre	librísimo	libérrimo	*exceedingly*	*free*
mísero	miserísimo	misérrimo	*excessively*	*wretched*
pobre	pobrísimo	paupérrimo		*poor*
bueno	buenísimo	óptimo bonísimo		*optimus*
malo	malísimo	pésimo		*pessimus*
grande	grandísimo	máximo		*maximus*
pequeño	pequeñísimo	mínimo		*minimus*

2.

Adverbial Modifier	+	Adjective	Adverbial Modifier	+ Adjective
muy sumamente extremadamente en extremo altamente en alto grado excesivamente en exceso etc.		hermoso peligroso confidencial etc.	very terribly extremely highly excessively	beautiful dangerous confidential etc.

The absolute superlative of adjectives may also be formed by placing an adverbial modifier before the adjective, just as English does it.

Recibieron un regalo muy hermoso.	*They received a very beautiful gift.*
Le hicieron una operación sumamente peligrosa.	*They performed an exceedingly dangerous operation on him.*
Siempre tiene que hacer con asuntos extremadamente (en extremo) delicados.	*He always has to do with extremely delicate issues.*
Es un persona en alto grado reservada.	*He is an extremely reserved person.*
Lo supe de una fuente altamente confidencial.	*I found out through a highly confidential source.*
Las ceremonias judías son en extremo sagradas.	*Jewish ceremonies are extremely sacred.*

Modifying suffixes as intensifiers

In everyday colloquial speech Spanish often uses diminutive and augmentative suffixes attached to adjectives in order to express a high degree of the quality. These suffixes, however, also add other semantic connotations such as endearment, contempt, irony, grotesqueness, impressiveness, etc. (See Modifying Suffixes Instead of Adjectives, page 242). Some of the most widely used are:

1. **-ito** (and its variants **-cito**, **-ico**):

feo	un niño feíto (feíco)	*a rather ugly child*
bajo	una mujer bajita	*a rather short woman*
pequeño	unos niños pequeñitos	*some very small children*
	una casa pequeñita	*a very small house*
bueno	un niño buenecito	*a rather good child*
gracioso	un vestido graciosito	*a rather cute dress*

2. **-ón**:

alegre	un viejo alegrón	*a rather gay old man*

3. **-ote**:

guapo	un muchacho guapote	*a rather handsome fellow*
gordo	una mujer gordota	*a rather fat woman*
bueno	un chico buenote	*a rather kind fellow*
grande	una casa grandota	*a very large (cumbersome) house*

The reiterative prefixes **re-** and **requete-** are also used in colloquial speech to intensify the high degree of a quality.

La comida estaba rebuena.	*The meal was very, very good.*
Es una persona requete inteligente.	*She is an extremely intelligent person.*
Es requete ambicioso . . .	*He is most ambitious . . .*

ADVERBIAL SUPERLATIVE[1]

Spanish adverbs acquire a superlative meaning when they appear in the following constructions:

1.

$$\text{lo} \begin{Bmatrix} \textbf{más} \\ \textbf{menos} \end{Bmatrix} + \text{Adverb} + \begin{Bmatrix} \textbf{posible} \\ \text{OR} \\ \textbf{que} + \textbf{poder} \end{Bmatrix}$$

Llegó lo más temprano posible (que pudo).	*He arrived as early as possible (he could).*
Caminábamos lo más rápido posible (que podíamos).	*We walked as fast as possible (we could).*
Hablaré lo más claro posible (que pueda).	*I will talk as clearly as possible (I can).*
Escríbele lo más pronto posible (que puedas).	*Write to him as soon as possible (you can).*

2.

$$\text{lo} \begin{Bmatrix} \textbf{mejor} \\ \text{OR} \\ \textbf{peor} \end{Bmatrix} + \begin{Bmatrix} \textbf{posible} \\ \text{OR} \\ \textbf{que} + \textbf{poder} \end{Bmatrix}$$

[1] See **De lo** + Intensifier Adverb, page 298.

La traté lo mejor posible (que pude).   *I treated her the best possible way (I could).*

Lo hiciste lo peor posible (que pudiste).   *You did it the worst possible way (you could).*

In these constructions, the superlative meaning is actually more absolute than in comparatives. In the expression of possibility **que + poder**, the subject of the subordinated verb is identical to that of the main clause.

SUPERLATIVE OF ADVERBS

The superlative of adverbs involves the same forms used as comparatives or superlatives of adjectives. Only context may determine one usage over the other. With the superlative of adverbs the definite article is not used; the superlative simply follows the verb.

Ellos leen más.   *They read more.*
El necesita menos.   *He needs less.*
¿Quién pinta mejor?   *Who paints better?*
Ahora lo arreglaste peor.   *Now you made it worse.*

In order to emphasize and clarify the superlative idea, it may be necessary to expand the sentence further.

El necesita más que nadie.   *He needs more than anybody else.*
                que ninguno.

Ahora lo arreglaste peor que nunca.   *Now you made it worse than ever before.*

De todas sus virtudes admiro más su paciencia.   *Of all his virtues I admire his patience the most.*

De todas sus virtudes la que más admiro es su paciencia.   *Of all his virtues the one that I admire the most is his patience.*

Absolute superlative of adverbs

Adverbs form the absolute superlative the same way as adjectives: either by adding the superlative suffix **-ísimo** or by further adverbial modification with **muy, extremadamente, sumamente, excesivamente, terriblemente**, etc.

It should be pointed out that a few restrictions apply:

1. **Mucho** is never modified by **muy**, so its absolute superlative is **muchísimo**: **trabaja muchísimo** = *he works very much.*

2. **Bien** never takes the suffix **-ísimo**; it can only form the absolute superlative with further adverbial modification: **muy bien, extremadamente bien**.

3. The absolute superlative is occasionally used with adverbs ending in **–mente**. In these cases **–ísimo** becomes **–ísima** and precedes **–mente**: **rápidamente rapidísimamente**.

Adverb	–ísimo	Further Modification		
pronto	prontísimo	muy sumamente extremadamente ⎱ pronto		*soon*
tarde	tardísimo	muy sumamente extremadamente ⎱ tarde		*late*
lejos	lejísimo	muy sumamente extremadamente ⎱ lejos		*far*
cerca[1]	cerquísima	muy sumamente extremadamente ⎱ cerca		*near*
poco	poquísimo	muy sumamente extremadamente ⎱ poco	*very extremely*	*little*[2]
mucho	muchísimo	sumamente extremadamente ⎱ *mucho*		*much*
bien		muy sumamente extremadamente ⎱ bien		*well*
duro[3]		muy sumamente extremadamente ⎱ duro		*hard*
claro		muy sumamente extremadamente ⎱ claro		*clear*
claramente	clarísimamente			

[1] The ending **–a** in **cerquísima** is not a gender marker, but a transposition from the last vowel in **cerca**.
[2] Only *very* can occur with "little" and "much."
[3] It should be remembered that many adjectives function as adverbs.

Other Comparative Constructions

COMPARISONS OF EQUIVALENCE: *MISMO* AND *IGUAL*

Comparisons of equivalence involve two constructions. They do not differ so much in meaning — both express similarity and equivalence — as in grammatical restrictions and the classes of words they may compare.

1.

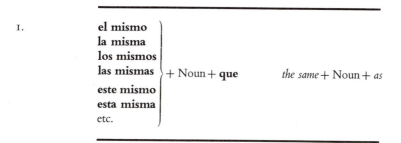

el mismo	
la misma	
los mismos	
las mismas } + Noun + **que**	*the same* + Noun + *as*
este mismo	
esta misma	
etc.	

To express identity between one and the same thing, **el mismo** + noun + **que** can be used. However, this construction may also be used to express equivalence or similarity between two or more entities of the same kind. **El mismo . . . que** occurs only with nouns. The noun always co-occurs with either the definite article or a demonstrative. **Mismo** precedes the noun it modifies and as any other adjective agrees in number and gender with it.

Ya no es el mismo hombre que yo conocía.	*He is no longer the same man I used to know.*
Dame el mismo vestido que me puse ayer.	*Give me the same dress I wore yesterday.*
Es la misma cosa que vimos antes.	*It is the same thing we saw before.*
El pobre merece el mismo respeto que el rico.	*A poor man deserves the same respect as a rich one.*
Aún teniendo la misma preparación, las mujeres no ganan los mismos sueldos que los hombres.	*Even with the same qualifications, women do not earn the same salaries as men.*
Tiene la misma fe que cuando era niño.	*He has the same faith as when he was a child.*

The term of comparison may be explicitly given or implied, being understood from the context by the speakers.

María ya no es la misma mujer (que yo conocía).	*Maria is no longer the same woman (I used to know).*
Dales el mismo examen (que les diste al año pasado).	*Give them the same exam (you gave them last year).*

Nominalization of **mismo**

Mismo may be nominalized through the neuter **lo**, the definite article, or a demonstrative. The term of comparison, as in the preceding sentences, may or may not be overtly present. When **mismo** is nominalized and occurs with a transitive verb, one that requires an object to complete its meaning, **mismo** functions as an object.

The equivalents in English are "the same thing" for **lo mismo**, "the same one" for **el mismo**, etc.

No quiero lo mismo que ayer.	*I don't want the same thing as yesterday.*
Préstame el mismo (libro).	*Lend me the same one.*
Préstame este mismo.	*Lend me this very same one.*
Pienso lo mismo (que tú).	*I think the same thing (as you).*

When **lo mismo** occurs with intransitive verbs, or transitive verbs with an object noun, **mismo** functions as an adverbial meaning "the same way." In this context it is equivalent to and replaceable by **igual que. Este mismo** or **el mismo, la misma**, etc., do not occur in this context. They never function as adverbials.

Está lo mismo que ayer.⎫	
Está igual que ayer. ⎭	*He remains the same way as yesterday.*
El pobre merece consideración lo⎫ mismo que el rico. .	*A poor man deserves consideration the*
El pobre merece consideración igual que el rico. ⎭	*same way as a rich man.*

But when **lo mismo** occurs with transitive verbs without an object, it always functions as an object of that verb. It corresponds to "the same thing" in English.

Hago lo mismo que ella.	*I do the same thing she does.*
Come lo mismo todos los días.	*He eats the same thing everyday.*

---

2.   Noun + **igual** + $\begin{cases} \textbf{que} \\ \textbf{a} \end{cases}$ Noun + (*just*) *like*
       Noun + *the same* + *as*

To express similarity or equivalence between two or more entities which are nouns this construction may also be used. The nouns, however, never take a definite article. They either occur with an indefinite article, an indefinite adjective, a demonstrative, or a numeral, if they are count nouns. With count nouns, **igual** always follows the noun and agrees in number with it.

Compró unas camisas iguales que las mías.	*He bought some shirts just like mine.*
Tiene un auto igual que el tuyo.	*He has a car just like yours.*
Necesito otro sobre igual que éste.	*I need another envelope like this one.*

When this construction is used with nouns that function as abstract mass nouns, those that do not take an indefinite article and occur in the singular, **igual** precedes the noun and occurs in the singular accordingly. The equivalent in English is "the same as."

El pobre merece igual respeto que el rico.	*A poor man deserves the same respect as a rich one.*
Tengo igual cantidad que tú.	*I have the same quantity as you.*
Tiene igual fe que cuando era niño.	*He has the same faith as when he was a child.*

Igual a for igual que

When the verb in the sentence is **ser**, or when an implied or expressed relative clause with **ser** is present, the preposition **a** is normally used instead of the relator **que**. **Igual** follows **ser** if it is the main verb or if the clause is explicitly given. It corresponds to the English "like."

Esta tela no es igual a la que vimos ayer.	*This fabric is not like the one we saw yesterday.*
Este hombre es igual a su padre.	*This man is just like his father.*
Tiene un auto (que es) igual al tuyo.	*He has a car (that is) just like yours.*
Dame un sobre (que sea) igual a éste.	*Give me an envelope (provided that it be) like this one.*

Igual que may also be used with indefinite nouns, which do not take articles or demonstratives. With indefinite nouns **igual** follows the noun if the relative clause is omitted. In this case, however, the term of comparison may be omitted in Spanish, being understood from the context by the speakers.

No hay nadie (que sea) igual a él.	*There is no one (that is) like he (is).*
No hay nada (que sea) igual a esto.	*There is nothing (that is) like it.*

Igual may be nominalized with the indefinite article, an indefinite adjective, or a numeral.

Quiero uno igual (a éste).	*I need one like this one.*
Dame otro igual (a éste).	*Give me another one like this one.*
Necesito cuatro iguales (a éstos).	*I need four like these.*

Igual que may also express equivalence between the manner of action of two events. As an adverbial it is invariable in form and occurs after the verb. The equivalent in English is "the same way (as)."

Está igual que ayer.	*He is the same way as yesterday.*
Piensa igual que tú.	*He thinks the same way you do.*
Se agotará de trabajo igual que su madre.	*She will kill herself with work the same way as her mother did.*
Tienes que hacerlo igual que ella (lo hace).	*You have to do it the same way she does it.*

Multiple comparisons

Spanish has only one way to express multiple comparisons, while in English these may be expressed by two different constructions.

Las avenidas son tres veces más anchas que las calles.

Avenues are three times as wide as streets.
Avenues are three times wider than streets.

Cumulative comparisons

cada vez más **cada vez menos**	*more and more* *-er and -er* *less and less*

Al acercarnos la montaña se veía cada vez más grande.
A medida que pasaba el tiempo se impacientaba cada vez más.
Hoy estudian cada vez menos.

As we came near the mountain it looked bigger and bigger.
As time went on, he got more and more impatient.
Today they study less and less.

In everyday speech, **más y más** and **menos y menos** are usually accepted.

Los niños a medida que crecen comen más y más.

As children grow older they eat more and more.

Proportionate comparisons

Tanto, cuanto, and **mientras** followed by a comparative form are used to express proportion or ratio between two persons, objects, or ideas. There are a number of possible combinations which would correspond to the English *the more ... the more; the -er ... the -er; the -ier ... the -ier; the less ... the less,* etc.

tanto cuanto mientras	+	más menos mejor peor etc.	+	Adjective Adverb Verb Noun	+	más menos mejor peor etc.	+	Adjective Adverb Verb Nounn

Tanto   \ más alta es una mujer
Mientras/ más guapa se ve.

The taller a woman is the prettier she looks.

Tanto más rápido (vayamos), más pronto llegaremos.	*The faster we go, the sooner we will arrive.*
Cuanto ⎫ Mientras⎭ más rápido menos seguro.	*The faster it is the less safer it is.*
Tanto más come más hambre le da.	*The more he eats, the hungrier he gets.*
Cuanto menos duerme más cansada está.	*The less she sleeps, the more tired she is.*
Mientras más lee menos entiende.	*The more she reads, the less she understands.*
Tanto más población más problemas surgen.	*The more people there are, the more problems develop.*
Cuanto más dolor, más drogas le daban.	*The more pain she had, the more drugs they gave her.*
Cuantas menos personas, vayan mejor.	*The fewer persons, the better.*
Mientras más ciudades visite, más experiencias recorgerá.	*The more cities he visits, the more experiences he will gather.*

Cuanto agrees in gender and number with the noun that it modifies. **Tanto** may accompany the second member of the comparison.

Tanto más difícil tanto más interesante.	*The more difficult it is, the more interesting.*
Cuanto más practica tanto más progresa.	*The more he practices, the more he progresses.*
Mientras menos trabaja tanto menos gana.	*The less he works, the less he earns.*

Adverbs

FUNCTION OF ADVERBS

Adverbs are uninflected, invariable words. Excepting the suffix **–mente**, which is used to derive adverbs from adjectives, no other adverbs have special endings. While the simple adverbs are few, the words and structures that can function as adverbials are many, and the relationships they signal complex. Adverbs modify verbs, adjectives, other adverbs, and whole sentences. Without being exhaustive, the function of adverbials may be correlated with the four interrogative adverbs of time: **¿cuándo?**, place: **¿dónde?**, manner: **¿cómo?**, and extent: **¿cuánto?** As seen in the preceding chapters different word classes other than adverbs may function as adverbials: noun phrases, clauses, adjectives, present participles, past participles and indefinites.[1]

---

[1] For more on adverbial usage see The Gerund, **–ndo** form, page 100; Past Participles, Adverbial Usage, page 108; Relative Adverbs for Relative Pronouns, page 121; Interrogatives, page 129; Nouns as Adverbial Complements, page 215; Adjectives as Adverbials, page 240; **Estar** with Adverbials, page 251; **Ser** with Adverbials, page 252; **Lo** + Adverb, page 294; Adverbial Phrase **a lo**, page 297; **Lo** + Adverb + **que**, page 297; **De lo** + Intensifier Adverb, page 294; Relators, Prepositions and Conjunctions, page 315; Comparative Constructions, page 331; Numerals as Adverbs, page 367; Indefinites, page 371; Affirmative and Negative Words, page 380.

Llegó ahora.	*He arrived just now.*
Llegó la semana pasada.	*He arrived last week.*
Llegó por la noche.	*He arrived at night.*
Llegó antes que yo.	*He arrived before I did.*
Llegó triste.	*He was sad when he arrived.*
Llegó corriendo.	*He came in running.*
Llegó cansado.	*He came in exhausted.*
No llegó nunca.	*He never arrived.*

ADVERB DERIVATION

The only adverbial suffix in Spanish is **-mente**; it corresponds to the suffix *-ly* in English. The suffix **-mente** is added to the feminine singular of adjectives or to the common form used for both genders.

Es lento.
He is slow.

Es lenta.
She is slow.

Habla lentamente.
He (she) speaks slowly.

El es feliz.
He is happy.

Ella es feliz.
She is happy.

Vive felizmente.
He (she) lives happily.

When more than one adverb ending in **-mente** modifies the same verb, only the last one takes the suffix.

Habla lenta y cuidadosamente.	*He speaks slowly and carefully.*
Trabaja rápida y eficientemente.	*She works quickly and efficiently.*

If the adverbs do not modify the same verb, then one of them is rendered by the alternate prepositional phrase **con** + noun.

Aunque estudiaba con diligencia progresaba lentamente.	*Even though he studied diligently he advanced slowly.*
La miró con cariño y le habló dulcemente.	*She looked at her with affection and spoke softly.*

All other simple adverbs are words which have no special suffixes and are not inflected for number or gender. Since this group constitutes a small class, they co-occur with other adverbs and prepositions to express more complex relationships.

ADVERBIAL FORMS

Demonstrative adverbs of place

aquí	*(right) here*	ahí	*there*	allí	*(right) over there*
acá	*here*	ahí	*there*	allá	*over there*

In most instances both sets of adverbs overlap in usage. **Aquí, ahí,** and **allí,** however, indicate a somewhat closer, more precise location in relation to the subject. For this reason, **acá** and **allá** may occur with prepositions and the intensifier **más** to denote a more exact identification.

Ponlo aquí.	*Put it right here.*
Tráelo más hacia acá.	*Bring it closer over here.*
Ponlo más para allá.	*Put it farther over there.*
Está más hacia allá.	*It is farther over there.*

Positional and directional adverbs

arriba	*up, upstairs*	afuera	*outside, out*
abajo	*down, downstairs*	adentro	*in, inside*
atrás	*back, in the back*	enfrente	*opposite, across from*
cerca	*close by*	lejos	*far away*

Excepting **cerca, lejos,** and **atrás,** which do not function as directional adverbs because they do not co-occur with verbs of motion, the others can either occur with verbs of motion, denoting direction, or with locative verbs denoting position or location.

Ven arriba.	*Come upstairs.*
Está arriba.	*He is upstairs.*
Vete abajo.	*Go downstairs.*
Sigue abajo.	*It remains downstairs.*

The directional suffix *-ward* has no equivalent in Spanish. It is rendered by **hacia** or **para** and a directional adverb.

upward	para/hacia arriba
downward	para/hacia abajo

The positional prefixes *up-, down-,* and *out-* are rendered by adverbial phrases.

uphill, downhill	cuesta arriba, abajo
upstream, downstream	río arriba, abajo
inland	tierra adentro
out to sea	mar adentro

The suffix *-where* is rendered in Spanish by the words **parte, sitio,** or **lugar** with an indefinite adjective.

somewhere	en algún lado, sitio
	en alguna parte
nowhere	en ningún lado, lugar
	en ninguna parte

Pronominal adverbs of place may co-occur with positional and directional adverbs. In Spanish the demonstrative adverb precedes positional and directional adverbs, as opposed to English where it follows.

aquí arriba	*up here*
allá abajo	*down there*
ahí afuera	*out there*
allí adelante	*up front*
ahí adentro	*in there*

Adverbs of time

antes	*before, earlier*	anoche	*last night*
después	*later*	enseguida	*right away*
luego	*later*	hoy	*today*
aún	*still, yet*	mañana	*tomorrow*
todavía	*still*	ya	*already*
tarde (más)	*late, later*	siempre	*always*
temprano (más)	*early, earlier*		

When **aún** occurs in affirmative sentences, it is equivalent to *still*; in negative sentences it is rendered by *yet*.

Aún la quiere.	*He still loves her.*
Aún no ha llegado.	*He has not arrived yet.*

When **ya** occurs in affirmative sentences it is equivalent to *already* or *now*; in negative sentences it is rendered by *no longer*.

Ya es demasiado tarde para lamentarse.	*It is already too late for regrets.*
¿Ya camina el niño?	*Does the child walk already?*
Ya no se hablan.	*They are no longer on speaking terms.*

Aún, ya, and **todavía** normally begin a sentence in Spanish, but they can also occur at the end of the verb phrase.

No le he dado la carta aún.⎫ Aún no le he dado la carta.⎭	*I have not given him the letter yet.*
Ya no la quiere.⎫ No la quiere ya.⎭	*He no longer loves her.*

Aún and **ya** do not occur between the auxiliary and the main verb as in English.

He is still studying.	Todavía está estudiando.
Is he still studying?	¿Está estudiando todavía?
I have not heard him say anything kind.	Todavía no le he oído decir nada amable.

Preposition + adverb

Demonstrative adverbs of place, positional and directional adverbs, interrogative adverbs, and adverbs of time, excepting **después**, **aún**, and **todavía**, occur with prepositions in Spanish to signal more complex relationships.

desde aquí, acá	*from over here*	desde antes	*from before*
ahí	*from over there*	hoy	*as of today*
allá, allí	*from over there*	ayer	*as of yesterday*
			since yesterday
desde cuándo	*since when*	desde temprano	*since the early morning,*
			since early childhood
desde luego	*of course*	por ahora	*for the time being*
por aquí, acá	*this way*	por adelante	*in, through the front*
ahí	*that way, someplace*	atrás	*in, through the back*
allá, allí	*that way, someplace*		
de dónde	*where from*	para dónde⎫ hacia ⎭	*where to*
para adentro	*(to the) inside*	para cuándo	⎰*by when* ⎱*when*
afuera	*(to the) outside*		
adelante	*(to the) front*		
atrás	*(to the) back*		
de adelante	*from the front*	de tarde	*in the afternoon(s)*
atrás	*from the back*		
a cuánto	*at what price, cost*	por cuánto	⎰*at what price* ⎱*for how much*
a cómo	*at what price for how much*		
de cerca	*from a close range*	de lejos	⎰*from a distance* ⎱*from afar*

Adverbs of extent or intensity

mucho (muy)	*much, a lot, very much*	menos	*less*
poco	*little, not much*	más	*more*
bastante	*enough, sufficiently, considerably*	tanto (tan)	*so (very much)*
demasiado	*too much*	suficiente	*enough, sufficiently*

1. **Mucho** is reduced to **muy** when it modifies adjectivals or adverbials other than **mayor**, **menor**, **peor**, **más**, **menos**, **antes**, and **después**.

Me saludó muy efusivamente.	*He greeted me very effusively.*
Es muy simpático.	*He is very pleasant.*

Es muy tarde.	*It is very late.*
Es muy mujer.	*She is very much of a woman.*

The full form **mucho** occurs when it modifies verbs, adjectivals, and adverbials not explicitly given but implied, such as in answers to questions.

¿Está muy triste?	*Is he very sad?*
—No mucho.	*—Not much.*
¿Está muy lejos de aquí?	*It is very far from here?*
—No mucho.	*—Not much.*
Come mucho y se mueve poco.	*He eats a lot and exercises little.*
Te respeta mucho.	*He respects you very much.*

While in English *very* can modify *much* and *little*, in Spanish **muy** cannot modify **mucho**; the absolute superlative in **-ísimo** is used instead: *very much* = **muchísimo**. Only **poco** can be modified by **muy**, although the absolute superlative may also be used in this case: *very little* = **poquísimo/muy poco** (See Absolute Superlative of Adverbs, page 339).

2. **Poco** + adjective is often used for English adjectives beginning with the prefix *un-* when no Spanish adjective beginning with **in-** exists.

Nos dieron una comida saludable pero poco apetitosa.	*They gave us a healthy but unappetizing meal.*
Es poco interesante.	*He is uninteresting.*

BUT:

Es muy infeliz.	*She is very unhappy.*

3. As an adjective modifier **muy** intensifies a given quality and may convey the meaning of "excessively," equivalent to the English *too*. In this context **muy** alternates with **demasiado**.

Es muy joven para casarse.	*She is too young to get married.*
Es demasiado torpe para entender.	*He is too dumb to understand.*

4. **Tanto**, like **mucho**, is reduced to **tan** when modifying adjectives other than **mayor**, **menor**, **mejor**, and **peor**, or adverbs.

¡Habló tan sagazmente!	*He spoke so astutely!*
¡Es tan altanero!	*He is so arrogant!*
¡Va tan de prisa!	*He is in such a hurry!*
¡Es tan tarde!	*It is so late!*

But the full form **tanto** occurs when it modifies verbs.

Trabaja tanto que se va a enfermar.	*He works so hard he will get sick.*

Tanto may co-occur with **un** and **algún** to form adverbial phrases equivalent to the English *somewhat* or *a little*.

Está un tanto cansada pero ya se repondrá pronto.	*She is somewhat tired but she will recuperate soon.*

5. The adverbs **más**, **menos**, and **tan** are used immediately before nouns functioning as adjectivals with the same value they have before adjectives. In English, *such* or *more/less* precedes the noun phrase which is introduced by *a* or *of a*, respectively.

Es tan hombre.	*He is such a man.*
Lo creía más caballero.	*I thought him more of a gentleman.*
Me la imaginaba menos mujer.	*I pictured her as less of a woman.*

Más occurs in Spanish with many adverbs of time, place, position, and location which do not take *more* in English but are rendered by different means.

más adelante	*later on*	más allá del pueblo	*beyond the town's limits*
más tarde	*later on*	más arriba	*higher up*
más temprano	*earlier*	más abajo	*lower*
más allá	*farther (over there), beyond*	más cerca, lejos	*closer, farther*

Adverbs of extent or intensity assume the same position in Spanish as in English. However, with **gustar**-like verbs which have infinitives as grammatical subjects, the intensifiers may either follow the verb or the infinitive, depending upon the message.

Le gusta poco estudiar.	*He does not like studying much.*
Le gusta mucho bailar.	*He likes dancing a lot.*
Me interesa poco verla.	*I am not very interested in seeing her.*

BUT:

Le gusta estudiar poco.	*He likes to study just a little (just enough).*
Le gusta bailar mucho.	*He likes to dance a lot (as opposed to just a few dances).*
Me interesa verla poco.	*I am interested in not seeing her very often.*

When **gustar**-like verbs occur with nouns instead of infinitives, the adverbs may follow either the verb or the noun without causing a change in meaning.

Le gusta mucho el arte.⎫ Le gusta el arte mucho.⎭	*He likes art very much.*
Me interesa poco la política.⎫ Me interesa la política poco.⎭	*Politics interests me very little.*

Adverbs of manner

bien	*well*	mejor	*better*
mal	*badly, poorly*	peor	*worse*
bajo	*low*		

Other adverbs of manner are formed from adjectives by adding **-mente**.

Except for the irregular comparatives **mejor** and **peor**, adverbials of manner may take the superlative in Spanish.

Está malísimo.	*It tastes terrible.* / *He is very ill.*
Está buenísimo.	*It tastes great.*
Habló bajísimo.	*He spoke in the lowest voice possible.*

Adverbs of manner generally follow the verb immediately in Spanish, unless the action itself is emphasized, in which case the adverb assumes initial position.

Muy bien he comido aquí.	*I have eaten very well here.*
Aquí se come muy bien.	*Here one eats very well.*
Nos atendió muy mal.	*He treated us very badly.*
Sigue mucho mejor gracias a la medicina.	*He is much better thanks to the medication.*

They cannot, however, occur between an auxiliary and the main verb as in English.

I had completely forgotten.	Se me había olvidado completamente.
He has repeatedly denied it.	Lo ha negado repetidas veces.
I will quickly go to her.	Iré inmediatamente a su lado.
I cannot honestly say so.	Honestamente no puedo decir eso.
	No puedo decir eso honestamente.

Sentence modifiers

Affirmative adverbs and adverbial phrases, **sí, por cierto, sin duda**, negatives, **no, nunca, jamás**, and dubitatives, **acaso, tal vez, quizás**, have no interrogative counterparts and do not modify individual words but sentences.

Sí may be used in Spanish to emphasize an assertion. As such it is equivalent to the English emphatic *do, indeed, by any means,* or other similar expressions.

Sí que lo hizo ella.	*She has indeed done it.* / *She did do it.*
Dijo que sí se haría.	*He said it would indeed be done.*
Eso sí que no lo acepto yo.	*By no means will I accept that. (Under no circumstances . . .)*

Sí and **no** are frequently used for emphasis in contrastive clauses. In English, which does not have an equivalent usage with *yes* and *no*, the emphatic *do* or a lexical word occurs in this case.

El no me vio pero yo sí (lo vi).	*He did not see me but I did see him.*
No estaba más gordo pero sí más avejentado.	*He was not any heavier but he did look considerably older.*
Se expresaba con firmeza sí, pero no sin cortesía.	*He expressed himself in no uncertain terms, indeed, but not without courtesy.*

As a negative, **no** must precede the verb phrase in Spanish. It cannot be placed, as in English, between the auxiliary and the main verb or after *be*.[1]

No lo he visto.	*I have not seen him.*
No puedo ir.	*I cannot go.*
No debo ir.	*I must (should) not go.*
Eso no es cierto.	*That is not true.*
Ella no está aquí.	*She is not here.*
No es el jefe.	*He is not the boss.*

---

[1] For further treatment of negation see page 390.

20

NUMERALS, INDEFINITES, AND NEGATIVES

Numerals

CARDINAL NUMERALS

One to ninety-nine

0 cero	10 diez	20 veinte
1 uno,-a; un	11 once	21 veintiuno
2 dos	12 doce	22 veintidós
3 tres	13 trece	23 veintitrés
4 cuatro	14 catorce	24 veinticuatro
5 cinco	15 quince	25 veinticinco
6 seis	16 dieciséis	26 veintiséis
7 siete	17 diecisiete	27 veintisiete
8 ocho	18 dieciocho	28 veintiocho
9 nueve	19 diecinueve	29 veintinueve

30 treinta	+ y + uno = 31	treinta y uno
40 cuarenta	+ y + dos = 42	cuarenta y dos
50 cincuenta	53	cincuenta y tres
60 sesenta	64	sesenta y cuatro
70 setenta	75	setenta y cinco
80 ochenta	86	ochenta y seis
90 noventa	99	noventa y nueve

The numeral **uno** has a feminine form **una** and a short variant **un**, depending on the noun it modifies. (See Morphological Changes, page 361.)

Compound numbers 16 to 29 are normally written as one word:[1] **dieciséis**, **veintiuno**, etc. Beyond 29, they are written separately, linked by the conjunction **y**: **treinta y uno**, **cuarenta y tres**, etc.

One hundred and multiples

100	cien, ciento	600	seiscientos(-as)
200	doscientos(-as)	700	setecientos(-as)
300	trescientos(-as)	800	ochocientos(-as)
400	cuatrocientos(-as)	900	novecientos(-as)
500	quinientos(-as)		

Cien is the equivalent for *one hundred*:

cien niños	*one hundred children*
cien personas	*one hundred persons*
cien técnicos de radio	*one hundred radio technicians*

Except for 500, 700, and 900, the other multiples of 100 are formed by the unit plus the ending **-cientos (-as)**.

Compound hundreds

	Units	101 ciento uno
		102 ciento dos
		203 doscientos tres
		504 quinientos cuatro
		etc.
Hundreds +	Tens	110 ciento diez
		620 seiscientos veinte
		730 setecientos treinta
		etc.
	Compound tens	121 ciento veintiuno
		842 ochocientos cuarenta y dos
		999 novecientos noventa y nueve

---

[1] These numbers can also be written separately: **diez y seis, veinte y cinco**, etc.

The compound numerals beyond 100 are formed by simply adding the smaller numbers directly to the hundreds. English uses *and* (*two hundred and twenty*), but Spanish does not use **y**: **doscientos veinte**. Inversely, Spanish uses **y** to form compound tens beyond 29 (**treinta y uno**), while English does not: *thirty one*.

Cien becomes **ciento** when a unit smaller than 100 is added: 100 + 3 = **ciento tres**; 100 + 99 = **ciento noventa y nueve**.

The ending **-cientos** has a feminine form **-cientas** (See Morphological Changes, page 361).

One thousand: multiples and compounds

1,000 and multiples[1] +	Units, tens, hundreds (single or compound)	Compound thousands
1.000 mil	1.001	mil uno
2.000 dos mil	2.010	dos mil diez
10.000 diez mil	10.500	diez mil quinientos
15.000 quince mil	15.100	quince mil cien
28.000 veintiocho mil	28.050	veintiocho mil cincuenta
100.000 cien mil	101.720	cien mil uno setecientos veinte
600.000 seiscientos mil	600.200	seiscientos mil doscientos
900.000 novecientos mil	920.605	novecientos veinte mil seiscientos cinco.

Mil is the equivalent for *one thousand*. The multiples are formed just as in English: the smaller unit + 1,000 (**cinco mil, cuarenta mil**, etc.). To form the compounds, smaller numbers are added to 1,000 and its multiples. Spanish does not use **y** for the compounds, while English uses *and*: *one thousand and twenty* = **mil veinte**.

Spanish cannot express thousands by multiples of hundreds as English does: *ten hundred* is the equivalent of *one thousand* = **mil**; *thirteen hundred* is the equivalent of **mil trecientos** (*one thousand and three hundred*); *twenty-five hundred* = **dos mil quinientos** (*two thousand and five hundred*), etc. Therefore, the year 1776 can only be expressed in Spanish as **mil setecientos setenta y seis**, *one thousand seven hundred and seventy-six*.

---

[1] In the punctuation of numerals, Spanish uses a period where English uses a comma. The comma is used as a decimal point, $2,50.

Morphological changes

1. Shortening (apocope):

$$uno \longrightarrow un$$
$$una \longrightarrow un$$

The numeral **uno** becomes **un** before singular masculine nouns, whether modified or not. Before feminine singular nouns which begin with stressed **á**, **una** becomes **un**.

Hay un hombre allí.	*There is one man there.*
Encontré sólo un buen estudiante.	*I found only one good student.*

BUT:

Hay sólamente uno.	*There is only one.*
Uno de ellos vino a verte.	*One of them came to see you.*
No había ni un alma allí.	*Not one soul was there.*

BUT:

No había ni una sola alma.	*There wasn't one single soul.*
Encontró una buena alma.	*He found one good soul.*
Encontró una, no dos.	*He found one, not two.*

The short form **un** occurs under the same circumstances with all numerals that add **uno**.

veintiún
treinta y un
ciento un   } hombres
quinientos un   almas
cuarenta y un mil

2. Feminine numeral forms:

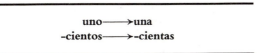

The only numerals that have a feminine form to show agreement with the nouns they modify are **uno/una** (including all compounds ending in "one") and the ending **-cientos/-cientas**.

una   hora

veintiuna ⎫
cuarenta y una ⎪
ciento una ⎬ horas
doscientas una ⎪
dos mil seiscientas ⎪
quinientas mil ⎭

Ciento in itself is invariable: **ciento veinte horas** = *120 hours*.

When a numeral ending in **uno** modifies **mil** rather than a noun, the feminine variant is not normally used.

treinta y un mil ⎫
doscientas un mil ⎬ libras

3. Plural numeral forms:

Since numeral adjectives express quantity, they are already pluralized (except for **uno**). The only ones that take a plural ending are the multiples of 100: **ciento**, but **doscientos**, **trescientos**, etc.

Mil and **ciento** can take a plural, **miles**, **cientos**, but then they function as collective nouns.

Había **miles** de personas.	*There were* thousands *of persons.*
Había **cientos** de personas.	*There were* hundreds *of persons.*

By the same token, any numeral form used as a noun can either occur in the singular or plural.

Me gusta el **dos.**	*I like number two.*
Se escribe con cuatro **unos.**	*It is written with four ones.*
Le salieron un par de **cincos.**	*He drew a pair of fives.*

Millón, billón:

Indefinite Article	+	millón billón	+	de Numeral	+ Noun	a one	+	million billion	+	Noun or Numeral
un		millón		de personas		a		million		persons
un		millón		quinientos mil		one		million		five hundred thousand

Multiples:

dos millones de dólares	*two million dollars*
tres millones doscientos mil	*three million two hundred thousand*

The numerals **millón** and **billón** are always nouns. Therefore, they take the indefinite article (except with multiples), are followed by the preposition **de** (unless another numeral is added), and their multiples are pluralized.

cuatro millones de refugiados	*four million refugees*
seis millones trescientos mil	*six million three hundred thousand*
cincuenta habitantes	*and fifty inhabitants*

Un billón in Spanish is a *million millions*, not a *thousand millions* as in English.

ORDINAL NUMBERS

Ordinals: 1st to 10th

1st	primer,-o,-a	*6th*	sexto,-a
2nd	segundo,-a	*7th*	séptimo,-a
3rd	tercer,-o,-a	*8th*	octavo,-a
4th	cuarto,-a	*9th*	noveno,-a
5th	quinto,-a	*10th*	décimo,-a

Ordinal numbers show agreement for both gender and number depending on the nouns they modify.

el quinto día	*the fifth day*
la segunda semana	*the second week*
los primeros meses	*the first months*

Primero and **tercero** also have short forms, **primer, tercer,** which occur before masculine singular nouns, whether modified or not.

Ganó el primer premio.	*He won the first prize.*
Es el tercer buen estudiante que se queja.	*He is the third good student who is complaining.*

Ordinal numbers are abbreviated in Spanish by adding the last syllable to the appropriate numeral; the ending varies according to the gender: **1ro. de enero; la 2da. fila, el 3er. capítulo, la 3ra. fila; el 4to. aniversario; la 7ma. semana,** etc.

Ordinals: 11th to 100th

These forms are presented as a useful reference. **Undécimo, duodécimo,** can also be expressed as **décimo primero, décimo segundo,** written as one or two words. **Décimo primero** also has a short form: **décimoprimer.** In Spanish

11th undécimo,-a	20th vigésimo,-a	+ primero, etc.:
12th duodécimo,-a	30th trigésimo,-a	
13th { décimotercio,-a / décimo tercero,-a	40th cuadragésimo,-a	21st vigésimo primero
	50th quincuagésimo,-a	
	60th sexagésimo,-a	65th sexagésimo
14th décimo cuarto,-a	70th septuagésimo,-a	quinto
15th décimo quinto,-a	80th octogésimo,-a	82nd octogésimo
16th décimo sexto,-a	90th nonagésimo,-a	segundo
17th décimo séptimo,-a	100th centésimo,-a	
18th décimo octavo,-a		
19th { décimo nono / décimo noveno,-a		

ordinal numbers are not used as frequently as they are in English. After "tenth" they are normally replaced by the cardinals:

el capítulo once	the eleventh chapter
el siglo veinte	the twentieth century
el Papa León XIII (trece)	Pope Leo the Thirteenth
Luis XVI (dieciséis)[1]	Louis the Sixteenth

Even ordinal numbers below "tenth" are sometimes replaced by the cardinals.

el capítulo quinto OR cinco	the fifth chapter
el siglo décimo OR diez	the tenth century
el siglo primero OR uno	the first century

BUT:

Carlos V (Quinto)	Charles the Fifth
Isabel II (Segunda)	Elizabeth the Second

Aniversario is one noun which always calls for an ordinal numeral.

En el tercer aniversario . . .	During the third aniversary . . .
Se celebra el vigésimo aniversario . . .	The twentieth aniversary is being celebrated . . .
Durante el sexagésimo quinto aniversario . . .	During the sixty-fifth aniversary . . .

POSITION OF NUMERALS

1. Cardinal numerals usually precede the noun, whether the noun is already modified or not. If the cardinals are used to substitute ordinals, they follow.

Trabajó quince días.	He worked fifteen days.
Vivieron aquí diez años.	They lived here for ten years.
Pasaron tres alegres semanas.	They spent three happy weeks.

---

[1] Spanish omits the definite article with these titles.

BUT:

Ocurrirá en el siglo veintiuno (vigésimo primero).	*It will take place during the twenty-first century.*

2. Ordinal numerals may precede or follow the noun they modify. Generally speaking, if the idea is to establish an order of priorities, the ordinals precede; if the intention is to specify or restrict that order within the priority, the ordinals follow.

Durante el segundo siglo de la invasión romana . . .	*During the second century of the the Roman invasion . . .*
Tuvo lugar en el siglo segundo.	*It took place during the second century.*
Fue el primer Carlos de España.	*He was the first Charles of Spain.*
Carlos Primero de España y Quinto de Alemania . . .	*Charles the First of Spain, the Fifth of Germany . . .*

3. Cardinal numerals may precede or follow ordinals.

Los tres primeros premios . . .	*The first three prizes . . .*
Las cinco primeras cifras . . .	*The first five digits . . .*
Las primeras cinco cifras . . .	

PARTITIVE NUMERALS

1/2	un medio			2/3	dos tercios
1/3	un tercio	1/11	un onzavo / un onceavo	2/4	dos cuartos
1/4	un cuarto			2/5	dos quintos
1/5	un quinto			3/10	tres décimos
1/6	un sexto	1/13	un trezavo / un treceavo	2/20	dos veinteavos
1/7	un séptimo				
1/8	un octavo	1/20	un veinteavo		
1/9	un noveno	1/45	un cuarenta y cincoavo		
1/10	un décimo	1/100	un centavo / un centésimo		
		1/1000	un milésimo		

Except for **un medio**[1] and **un tercio**, the other fractions up to 1/10 correspond to the ordinals. From 1/11 on, the fractions are expressed by adding the ending **-avo** to the cardinals, except for the special forms **centésimo** and **milésimo**.

---

[1] In mathematical terms **medio** means *a half*: **Paga ocho y medio por ciento**= *He pays eight and a half percent.* In other contexts **mitad** is used: **Le dio la mitad**= *He gave him half.* Other meanings of **medio** are "means", "middle": **Es el mejor medio de hacerlo**= *It is the best means to do it*; **Está en el medio**= *He is in the middle.* **Medio, -a** used as an adjective means "half": **Trabajó medio día**= *He worked half a day*; **media hora**= *half an hour.*
Medio and **mitad** can also function as adverbs, meaning "half": **Está medio dormida**= *She is half asleep*; **Es mitad hombre y mitad caballo**= *It is half man and half horse.*

With simple numerals **-avo** may form one word: **un onzavo** or **un onceavo**, etc. But with compounds it is hyphenated: **un treinta-y-tres-avo** = 1/33. If the numerator is larger, the denominator is pluralized: **dos cuartos** = 2/4.

Partitive numerals function as nouns, except when they modify the noun **parte**, in which case they are adjectives and as such show agreement in gender: **una media parte**, **una décima parte**, **una treceava parte**, **una milésima parte**, **dos veinteavas partes**, etc.

OTHER NUMERAL RELATED FORMS

Multiple numerals

Multiple numerals are adjectives or nouns which express a multiple series, i.e., *how many fold?*

Está escrito a **simple** espacio.	*It is written* single spaced.
Apostó el **doble**.	*He bet* twice *as much.*
Vimos un **doble** programa.	*We saw a* double *feature.*
Manda la solicitud por **duplicado**.	*Send the application in* duplicate.
Ganó el **triple**.	*He won* three times *as much.*
Mándala por **triplicado**.	*Send it in* triplicate.

Less frequent forms are: **cuádruplo** or **cuadruplicado** = *quadruple*; **quíntuplo** = *fivefold*; **séxtuplo** = *sixfold*; **décuplo** = *tenfold*; **céntuplo** = *a hundred*.

Collective numerals

Collective numerals are nouns which express a number considered as a unity.

Vinieron un **par** de personas.	*A couple of persons arrived.*
Compró un **par** de zapatos.	*He bought a* pair *of shoes.*
Una **decena** tiene diez unidades.	*A tenth totals ten units.*
Le trajo una **docena** de camisas.	*She brought him a* dozen *shirts.*
Recibió el pago de su **quincena**.	*He received his* by-weekly *check.*
Tiene una **veintena** de años.	*He is some* twenty *years old. (some*
(**treintena**, **cuarentena**)	*thirty . . ., some forty . . .)*
Ganó un **centenar** (una **centena**)	*He won a* hundred *dollars.*
de dólares.	
Ganó **cientos** de dólares.	*He won* hundreds *of dollars.*
Tiene un **millar** de dólares.	*He has a* thousand *dollars.*
Tiene **miles** de dólares.	*He has* thousands *of dollars.*
Gastaron un **millón** de dólares.	*They spent a* million *dollars.*
Gastaron **millones** de dólares.	*They spent* millions *of dollars.*

The pluralized forms **cientos** and **miles** are both used as collective numerals with the same meaning of **centenar**, **centena**, and **millar**, respectively. Nevertheless, only the singular **ciento** and **millar** can be used to express rate: **Pagó un dólar por el ciento** = *He paid one dollar per hundred*; **Cuesta cien dólares el millar** = *It costs a hundred dollars per thousand.*

NUMERALS AS ADVERBS

CARDINAL NUMBER + **vez**:

Lo hice **tres veces.**
I did it three times.   Expresses the number of times of an
La llamé **cinco veces.**   occurrence.
I called her five times.

ORDINAL NUMBER (FEMININE FORM) + **-mente**:

Primeramente . . .
Firstly . . .
Segundamente . . .   Expresses order of procedure.
Secondly . . .

Numerals may function as adverbs either to express the number of times of an occurrence or to express an order of procedure. Although **segundamente**, **terceramente**, etc., are possible, these numeral adverbs with **-mente** are not common in normal speech. The expressions **en segundo lugar**, **en tercer lugar**, *in the second place, in the third place*, respectively, are more widely used.

Multiple numerals **doble** and **triple** can also add **-mente** to function as adverbs: **Es doblemente importante** = *It is twice as important*, **Es triplemente difícil** = *It is three times more difficult.*

NOMINALIZATION OF NUMERALS

Cardinal and ordinal numerals nominalize by noun deletion:

Dame un dólar.   Dame uno.
Give me one dollar.   *Give me one.*

Cómprame cinco camisas.   Cómprame cinco.
Buy me five shirts.   *Buy me five.*

Es el primer estudiante de la clase.   Es el primero de la clase.
He is the first student in the class. *He is the first one in the class.*

Ordinal numerals may also nominalize by the addition of **lo** before the masculine form:

Es la primera cosa que dijo.   Es lo primero que dijo.
It is the first thing he said. *It is the first thing he said.*

Fue la tercera cosa que hizo.   Fue lo tercero que hizo.
It was the third thing he did. *It was the third thing he did.*

USEFUL EXPRESSIONS WITH NUMERALS

1. Arithmetical expressions:

5	+ **más**	12		17
9	− **menos**	4		5
5	× **por**	2	**es igual a**	10
20	÷ **dividido por**	5		4

2. Time of the day:

Spanish and English have similar patterns to express time, although there are some differences between the two languages:

Es la una.	*It is one o'clock.*
Son las tres de la madrugada.	*It is three o'clock in the morning.*
Son las siete de la mañana.	*It is seven o'clock in the morning.*
Son las doce del día.	*It is twelve noon.*
Es la una de la tarde.	*It is one o'clock in the afternoon.*
Son las siete de la noche.	*It is seven o'clock in the evening.*
Son las diez de la noche.	*It is ten o'clock at night.*
Son las doce de la noche.	*It is twelve o'clock at night.*
Son las dos en punto (de la tarde).	*It is two o'clock sharp* or *on the dot (in the afternoon).*
Son las nueve pasadas.	*It is past nine.*

Time is expressed with **ser** and the definite article precedes the numeral. In some Spanish-speaking countries the hours are expressed from one to twenty-four: **a las tres horas** (*3 a.m.*); **a las cinco horas** (*5 a.m.*); **a las trece horas** (*1 p.m.*); **a las quince horas** (*3 p.m.*), etc. With this system the word **horas** usually follows, especially after "12 noon" such as: **a las trece horas** (*1 p.m.*). Spanish has no other equivalent for the English "o'clock."

The expression **de la madrugada** (*at dawn*) refers to the period between 1 a.m. and 6 a.m. **De la mañana** is also used for this period and up to 11 a.m. **De la tarde** refers to the period between 1 p.m. and 6 p.m.; **de la noche** for 7 p.m. to midnight. Spanish does not distinguish between evening and night. **Mediodía** is noon; **medianoche** is midnight. *Twelve noon* can be expressed as **las doce del medio día, las doce del día**, or simply as **es medio día**. *Midnight* can be expressed as **las doce de la noche** or **es medianoche**.

MINUTES TO THE HOUR:

To express minutes to the hour Spanish uses several formulas with **ser** and **faltar**, as follows:

1.

faltar		
ser	+	Minutes **para las** Hour

faltan cinco (minutos)[1] para las ocho de la mañana
son cinco para las ocho

7:55 a.m. *it is five (minutes) til eight o'clock in the morning*

faltan quince (minutos) para las tres de la tarde
son quince para las tres

2:45 p.m. *it is fifteen (minutes) til three o'clock in the afternoon*

falta un cuarto para las tres de la tarde
es un cuarto para las tres

it is a quarter til three in the afternoon

2.

ser la(s) + Hour   **menos** Minutes

son las ocho menos cinco (minutos) de la mañana

7:55 a.m. *it is five of eight in the morning*

son las tres menos quince de la tarde

2:45 p.m. *it is fifteen (minutes) of three in the afternoon*

son las tres menos (un) cuarto[2]

it is a quarter of three

3.

ser + Hour   **y** Minutes

son las siete y cincuenta y cinco de la mañana

7:55 a.m. *it is seven fifty-five in the morning*

son las dos y cuarenta y cinco de la tarde

2:45 p.m. *it is two forty-five in the afternoon*

MINUTES AFTER THE HOUR:

To express minutes after the hour Spanish gives the hour first and uses the conjunction **y** to add the minutes. The word **minutos** is normally omitted, while in English *minutes* is used more often. An additional expression of time to add precision is optional.

Es la una y diez en punto.   *It is one o'clock sharp (on the dot).*
Son las doce y cinco del dia   *It is five minutes after (past) twelve*
  (mediodía).   *noon.*

---

[1] Literally, "five minutes are lacking for eight o'clock." The addition of the word **minutos** after the numeral is optional.
[2] Literally, "it is three o'clock less a quarter." **Cuarto** refers to *a quarter of an hour*, **un cuarto de hora.** **Un** may be omitted in this construction.

Son las dos y veinte de la tarde.	*It is twenty after (past) two o'clock in the afternoon.* *It is two twenty.*
Son las cuatro y quince de la madrugada.	*It is fifteen minutes after (past) four o'clock in the morning.* *It is four fifteen in the morning.*
Son las cuatro y cuarto.	*It is a quarter after (past) four.*
Son las seis y veinticinco de la tarde.	*It is twenty-five minutes after (past) six o'clock in the evening.* *It is six twenty five.*
Son las ocho y treinta de la noche.	*It is eight-thirty in the evening.*
Son las ocho y media.	*It is (a) half past eight.*

3. Dates:

When referring to dates of the month, Spanish uses the cardinal numbers, except for the first day which normally is expressed with the ordinal:

el primero de enero	*the first of January*

BUT:

el tres de febrero	*the third of February*
el veinticinco de marzo	*the twenty-fifth of March*

The word order in Spanish is fixed; there is no alternate as in English: *January the first* or *the first of January*; *February the third* or *the third of February*. In letter writing dates are expressed as follows: **15 de abril de 1978**. Note that in contrast with English, the name of the month is not capitalized and the days, months, and year are linked by the preposition **de**.

The English expressions *during the twenties, during the thirties*, etc., correspond in Spanish to **durante la década del año veinte** or **durante la segunda década de este siglo** (literally, *during the second decade of this century*).[1]

4. Age:

¿Cuántos años tiene Ud.? ¿Qué edad tiene Ud.?	*How old are you?*
¿Cuál es su edad?	*What is your age?*
Tengo veintiún años.	*I am twenty-one years old.*
Tiene cinco años y medio.	*He is five and a half years old.*

In Spanish, age is expressed by **tener** plus the cardinal number indicating the years. There is no equivalent for the English . . . *old*. The word **años** may be omitted if the context is clear: **Tengo veintiuno** = *I am twenty one*.

The nearest Spanish equivalent for the English expressions *He is in his*

---

[1] English has other expressions with *tens* that do not have a direct equivalent in Spanish: *His price is in the thirties* = **Su precio es alrededor de unos treinta y tanto** (literally, *around thirty some . . .*); *The temperature will be in the seventies* = **La temperatura subirá a unos setenta grados**.

teens, He is a teenager would be **Es un adolescente** (literally, *He is an adolescent*), **Está en los años de la adolescencia**. Other expressions of age are:

Está bien entrado en los cincuenta.	*He is well into his fifties.*
Esta mujer es una cuarentona.	*This woman is fortyish.*

Indefinites

Indefinites are a heterogeneous class of words which semantically refer to selection, quantity, or distribution in a general sense. Most of them function either as limiting adjectives (noun substitutes) or as pronominal indefinites (noun substitutes in subject and object position). A few function also as adverbials.[1]

Some indefinites have affirmative and negative counterparts. These are treated under Affirmative and Negative Words (page 380). Indefinites which have no corresponding negative forms are dealt with here. They are presented according to three main semantic categories: quantitative, distributive, and selective.

INDEFINITE QUANTIFIERS

These indefinites refer to quantity in a general sense. As limiting adjectives they normally precede the noun, which may be further modified by a descriptive adjective. As pronominal indefinites they have subject or object position. Not all indefinite quantifiers are inflected for gender and number, and not all of them may function as subjects and/or objects.

demasiado,-a	*too much, too*
demasiados,-as	*too many*

Hacía demasiado calor.	*It was too hot.*
Había demasiadas personas enfermas.	*There were too many sick persons.*
Hiciste demasiados.	*You did too many.*
Demasiados faltaron.	*Too many were absent.*

mucho,-a	*a great deal of* *a lot of, lots of*	**poco,-a**	*little*
muchos,-as	*a great many,* *many, lots of*	**pocos,-as**	*few, a few*

---

[1] See Chapter 19, Adverbs, page 349; also Affirmative and Negative Words, page 380.

Toma muchas bebidas frías.	*She drinks a lot of cold beverages.*
Tiene muchos enemigos.	*He has many enemies.*
Muchos fracasaron.	*A great many failed.*
Fracasaron a muchos.	*They flunked many.*
Hace pocas observaciones inteligentes.	*He makes few intelligent observations.*
Tiene pocos familiares íntimos.	*He has a few intimate relatives.*
Pocos lo apoyan.	*A few back him up.*
Vi a pocos.	*I saw a few.*

The plural forms **unos**, **unos cuantos**, and **unos pocos** are synonymous and may be used interchangeably to mean *a few, a small number of*:

Sólo unas personas se presentaron.	*Just a few people showed up.*
unas cuantas	
unas pocas	
Me quedan unos centavos.	*I have a few pennies left.*
unos cuantos.	
unos pocas.	
Se lo conté a unos.	*I told a few.*
unos cuantos.	
unos pocos.	

---

más	*more*
menos	*less, fewer*

Dame más azúcar.	*Give me more sugar.*
Consiguió más piezas antiguas.	*He found more antique pieces.*
Más llegarán mañana.	*More will arrive tomorrow.*
Dame menos azúcar.	*Give me less sugar.*
Consiguió menos piezas antiguas.	*He found fewer antique pieces.*
Menos llegarán mañana.	*Fewer will arrive tomorrow.*

Más and **menos** never vary their form. These indefinite quantifiers always refer to a plural or mass quantity. Thus, these forms can only modify plural count nouns (**más hombres, menos mujeres**) and singular mass nouns (**más café, menos sopa**). As pronominal indefinites in subject position they always occur with a plural verb form.

Menos se aplazaron esta vez.	*Fewer flunked this time.*
Más se interesan por los asuntos de la communidad.	*More (people) are interested in community affairs.*
Más se perdieron la última vez.	*More got lost the last time.*

Más and **menos** precede the noun when it is not modified by other quantifiers.

Surgen más problemas serios.	*More serious problems are coming up.*
Hay menos asuntos pendientes por resolver.	*There are less (fewer) pending matters to be resolved.*

When **más** and **menos** co-occur with other indefinites or modifiers, they follow the noun.

Había varias personas enfermas más.	*There were several more ill persons.*
Hay aún algunos otros asuntos pendientes más.	*There are still some more pending matters.*
Leí tres libros más.	*I read three more books.*

---

bastante,-s	*quite a few*	
	plenty of	
suficiente,-s	*enough*	

Tiene bastante dinero.	*He has plenty of money.*
Bastantes respondieron.	*Quite a few responded.*
No tiene suficiente paciencia.	*He doesn't have enough patience.*
Hay suficientes sobres blancos.	*There are enough white envelopes.*

Bastante and **suficiente** have no gender distinction but are inflected for number. **Bastante(-s)** may sometimes be synonymous with **mucho** in the sense of "abundance" (i.e., **tiene bastante [mucho] dinero**).

   Suficiente in the singular or plural functions occasionally as a pronominal indefinite.

Había suficientes como para comenzar la reunión.	*There were enough members to begin the meeting.*
Hay suficiente como para que se queden a comer.	*There is enough food so that you can stay for dinner.*
No tengo suficiente para pagarle.	*I don't have enough (money) to pay him.*

---

varios	*some*	
varias	*several* *various* *(= different)*	

Cometió varios errores graves.	*He made some (several) serious mistakes.*
Había varias personas esperando.	*There were several persons waiting.*
Varios se fueron.	*Several went away.*
Llamé a varios.	*I called several people.*

Varios has no singular form. It occurs only in the plural, but has inflection for gender. Besides its indefinite meaning of quantity, **varios**, depending upon the context, may also denote "difference" (in the sense of *different, sundry*).

Se encuentran allí varios (diferentes) tipos humanos.	*One can find there various (different) human types.*

The quantifier **todo**

As a noun modifier **todo** occurs in two constructions:

I.

todo **toda**	+	Noun	*every*

In the singular followed by an undetermined noun, **todo** has a generic value indicating the whole class of things represented by the noun.

Todo hombre tiene sus faltas.	*Every man has his faults.*
Toda ciudad tiene sus problemas.	*Every city has its problems.*

The masculine singular **todo** may occur as a neuter modifier.

Todo aquello es falso.	*All of that is false.*
Todo lo demás es mentira.	*Everything else is a lie.*
Todo lo otro . . .	
Todo lo suyo es caro.	*All of his is expensive.*
Todo lo cual era necesario . . .	*All of which was necessary . . .*
Todo lo bueno merece elogios.	*Everything good deserves praise.*

The plural forms seldom occur with undetermined nouns, except in some set phrases:

(a, por, en) todas partes todos lados	*everywhere*
en todas direcciones	*in all directions*
a todas horas	*at all times*
de todos colores	*of all colors*
de todos tamaños	*of all sizes*
de todas clases	*of all kinds*
de todos modos de todas maneras de todas formas	*at any rate, anyway*

or as a personal modifier:

ustedes todos	*you all*
todos ustedes	*all of you*
nosotros todos	*we all*
todos nosotros	*all of us*

2.

todo	+	{ Definite article Possessive Demonstrative }	+ Noun	*all (of), the whole, every*

Todo inflected for gender and number occurs before nouns determined by a definite article, a possessive, or a demonstrative, to indicate the entire whole or quantity of that noun.

Trabajé todo el día.	*I worked all day.*
Conocí a toda su familia.	*I met all of his family.*
Canceló todos los compromisos.	*He canceled all (of) his engagements.*
Todo el mundo lo sabe.	*Everyone (=everybody) knows it.*
Salieron todas esas noches.	*They went out all of those nights.*

$$\left.\begin{matrix} \textbf{todo} \\ \textbf{toda} \end{matrix}\right\} \; + \; \left\{\begin{matrix} \text{Indefinite} \\ \text{Article} \end{matrix}\right\} \; + \; \text{Noun} \qquad \textit{a whole, an entire}$$

Inflected for gender only, **todo** occurs before nouns determined by the indefinite article to express "wholeness," "completeness".

Pasamos allí todo un verano.	*We spent a whole summer there.*
(=un verano entero)	(=*an entire*)
Nos quedamos desamparados toda una noche.	*We were stranded a whole night.*
(=una noche entera)	
Es todo un señor.	*He is quite a gentleman.*

As a noun substitute the pronominal indefinite **todo** occurs in subject and object position.

Todo el asunto está resuelto.	Todo está resuelto.
The whole matter is resolved.	*Everything is resolved.*
	The whole thing . . .
Toda la fruta se pudrió.	Toda se pudrió.
All of the fruit got spoiled.	*All of it got spoiled.*
Todos sus funcionarios lo sabían.	Todos lo sabían.
All of his officials knew it.	*All of them knew it.*
	Everyone . . .
Todas las secretarias están de vacaciones.	Todas están de vacaciones.
All of the secretaries are on vacation.	*All of them are on vacation.*
Le conté todo el asunto.	Le conté todo.
I told her the whole thing.	*I told her everything (the whole thing).*
Vendieron toda la mercancía barata.	Vendieron toda la barata.
They sold all of the cheap merchandise.	*They sold all the cheap stuff.*

Todas esas personas que quieran ir
están invitadas.
*All of those persons who wish to go
are invited.*

Todas esas que quieran ir están
invitadas.
*All of those ones who wish to go are
invited.*

DISTRIBUTIVE INDEFINITES

Distributive indefinites relate one entity to another in several different ways.

1. **Ambos/Ambas**: expresses a relationship of one and the other.

Vinieron **ambos** hombres.
Vinieron **ambas** mujeres.

Both *men came.*
Both *women came.*

Ambos(-as) in everyday speech is often replaced by **los dos/las dos** = *the two*
or **uno y otro/una y otra** = *one and the other.*

2. **Sendos/Sendas**: expresses a relationship of one for each.

Les dio **sendos** regalos.
Les dio **sendas** corbatas.

He gave them each a gift.
He gave them each a tie.

3. **Cada**: expresses a relationship of one entity to others.

Viene **cada** tarde.
Hay un cuarto para **cada** tres
personas.
Le escribía **cada** tres semanas.
Cada uno de ellos será castigado.
Cada persona sabe lo que quiere.

He comes each (every) afternoon.
*There is a room for every three
persons.*
I used to write him every three weeks.
Each one of them will be punished.
Each person knows what he wants.

4. **Demás**: expresses a relationship of the remaining parts to its whole.

¿Dónde están **los demás** invitados?
Vino su hermano, pero sus **demás**
familiares se quedaron.

Where are the other guests?
*His brother came but her other
relatives stayed behind.*

Demás in this context may be substituted by **otros/otras** (i.e., **No he visto
a las demás chicas** or ... **a las otras chicas**).

The indefinites **ambos** and **sendos** can only occur with plural nouns. **Cada**
is invariable in form and occurs only with singular nouns, although it can
refer to plural nouns modified by a numerical expression (i.e., **Un cuarto
para cada tres personas**). **Demás** is invariable for gender and can only occur
with plural nouns preceded by the plural forms of the definite article or the
possessives. **Sendos** can only function as a noun modifier. **Ambos** and **los
demás** also function as noun substitutes, while **cada** requires the addition
of **uno(-a)** or **cual** to be used as a pronominal indefinite: **Cada uno dirá
algo** = *Each one will say something*; **Cada cual tiene su parte** = *Each one
has his own share.*

SELECTIVE INDEFINITES

Selective indefinites while implying quantity refer to choice or selection in a general sense. All of these forms function as limiting adjectives, preceding the nouns they modify.[1] Some are only used as adjectives, others function as pronominal indefinites in subject and object position. Not all of them are inflected in all forms according to gender and number.

cierto, a **ciertos,-as**	*certain*

Llamó **cierto** individuo sospechoso.	*A certain suspicious man called.*
Me dijo **ciertas** cosas.	*He told me certain things.*

As an indefinite **cierto** precedes the noun it modifies. The noun may occur with an indefinite article and occasionally a demonstrative.

Tenemos (un) **cierto** grado de confianza.	*We have a certain degree of confidence.*
No me gusta esa **cierta** falta de respeto que tiene hacia sus padres.	*I don't like that certain lack of respect that he shows towards his parents.*

When **cierto** follows the noun, it functions as a descriptive adjective, with the meaning of "true," "reliable," "sure."

Hemos recibido información **cierta**.	*We have received reliable information.*

tal	*such (a)*
tales	*such*

Renunció bajo **tal** presión.	*He resigned under such pressure.*
Nunca oí **tales** cosas.	*I never heard such things.*
Para vencer **tales** obstáculos . . .	*In order to overcome such obstacles . . .*

Tal has the same form for either gender and agrees only for number. It only functions as a limiting adjective. When preceded by the definite or the indefinite article, it may have pejorative connotations, indicating sarcasm, familiarity.

Vino una **tal** Cristina a buscarte.	*A certain girl called Cristina came by looking for you.*

---

[1] Some of these indefinites may be placed after the noun, in which case they are no longer limiting adjectives but descriptive and with a different semantic connotation (see Adjective Position and Meaning, page 235).

Te llamó un **tal** Fernández.	*A certain man Fernandez called you.*
Los **tales** amigos tuyos ni siquiera se presentaron.	*Your famous friends did not even show up.*
Parece que la **tal** condesa nos invitará a su fiesta.	*It looks as if that famous countess will invite us to her party.*

Semejante/semejantes when placed before a noun has the same meaning as **tal/tales**, but placed after a noun it is a descriptive adjective meaning similarity.

Nunca vi tales cosas (semejantes cosas).	*I never saw such things.*
BUT: Nunca vi cosas **semejantes** a estas.	*I new saw things like these.*

---

otro,-a	*another*
otros,-as	*other, other*

Atiende **otros** asuntos.	*Take care of other matters.*
Trajo **otras** consecuencias serias.	*It brought other serious consequences.*
Me ofrece **otra** ventaja.	*It offers me another advantage.*
Otros volverán más tarde.	*Others will return later on.*
Invita a **otros** que vengan.	*Invite others to come.*

Otro is used either as a limiting adjective or a pronominal indefinite and refers to either animate or inanimate nouns. For a less indefinite sense **otro** may occur with a noun preceded by the definite article, a possessive, or a demonstrative.

Las **otras** víctimas murieron.	*The other victims died.*
Mis **otros** hijos están en el extranjero.	*My other children are abroad.*
¿Viste ese **otro** muchacho?	*Did you see that other boy?*

A noun modified by **otro** never occurs with the indefinite article or the numeral *one*. The English *another* (*an + other*), *one other*, corresponds in Spanish simply to **otro**, i.e., *one other problem* = **otro problema**; *one other thing* = **otra cosa**. **Otro** can co-occur with other indefinites and with cardinal numbers.

1. With most indefinites **otro** normally follows:

Alguna **otra** solución mejor . . .	*Some other better solution . . .*
Ningún **otro** asunto importante . . .	*No other important matter . . .*
Ciertos **otros** individuos . . .	*Certain other individuals . . .*
Hay demasiadas **otras** cosas innecesarias.	*There are too many other unnecessary things.*
Tienen suficientes **otros** problemas.	*They have enough other problems.*
Cada **otra** tarde . . .	*Every other afternoon . . .*
Todas las **otras** alternativas . . .	*All the other alternatives . . .*

2. With the indefinites **mucho** and **tanto** and with cardinal numbers, **otro** may either precede or follow:

muchos **otros** buenos amigos⎫ **otros** muchos . . . ⎭	*many other good friends*
tantas **otras** alternativas sensatas⎫ **otras** tantas . . . ⎭	*so many other sensible alternatives*
tres **otros** productos nuevos⎫ **otros** tres . . . ⎭	*three other new products*

Idiomatic expressions with **otro**

Otro has combined with certain words to form idiomatic expressions.

De otro modo no se entiende.⎫ **De otra manera** . . . ⎭	Otherwise *one cannot understand it.*
Renunció el presidente y el gabinete hizo **otro tanto**.	*The president resigned and the cabinet did* likewise.
Han recibido **otras tantas** donaciones (como las que habían recibido).	*They received* as many more *donations (as they had received before).*

THE INDEFINITES CUALQUIER(A) AND QUIENQUIERA

cualquier	*just any(thing)* *any . . . at all* *any . . . whatever*
cualquiera	*(just) anyone*

Cualquier hombre sensato aceptaría.	*Any sensible man at all would accept.*
Tráeme **cualquier** cosa.	*Bring me just anything.*
Cualquiera podrá hacerlo.	*Anyone will be able to do it.*
Mandarán a **cualquiera**.	*They will send just anyone.*

Cualquier is invariable for gender and modifies singular nouns only. The plural **cualesquier(a)** is almost never used in the spoken language. The form **cualquiera** occurs as a pronominal indefinite in subject or object position and as a descriptive adjective in post-nominal position (i.e., **Es una mujer cualquiera** = *She is just an ordinary woman*). The nominalized form **un cualquiera/una cualquiera** means "a non-entity," "an ordinary, vulgar person": **Se ha casado con un cualquiera** = *She has married a non-entity.*

quienquiera	*whoever*

Quienquiera que sea las pagará.   *Whoever it might be will pay for it.*

Quienquiera is the only indefinite which **cannot** function as a noun modifier but only as a noun substitute. The plural **quienesquiera** is no longer used in the spoken language and even the singular **quienquiera** is rare. Instead, a relative construction or the indefinite **cualquiera** is preferred.

Sal con **quienquiera** te plazca. ⎫
Sal con **la que** te plazca.   ⎬   *Go out with whoever pleases you.*
Sal con **cualquiera que** te plazca. ⎭

Quienquiera desee venir será
  bienvenido.   ⎫
El que desee venir será bienvenido. ⎬   *Whoever wishes to come will be*
Cualquiera que desee venir será   ⎭   *welcome.*
  bienvenido.

Negatives

AFFIRMATIVE AND NEGATIVE WORDS

Both Spanish and English have a class of indefinite and negative forms which function syntactically as limiting adjectives, pronominal indefinites, or adverbials, but which are very much related semantically. Because of this correspondence in meaning they are simply referred to as affirmative and negative words.

The most important difference in the use of negative words is that in Spanish two or more negatives co-occur in one sentence to strengthen the negation. These could either be the negative **no** with a negative word (or words) or negative words only. This pattern of introducing a negative at several points in a sentence is not accepted in standard English where only one negative is possible, although it is sometimes done in substandard English.

No tenemos **nada**.
⎧ *We don't have anything.*
⎨ *We have nothing.*
⎩ (= *We don't have nothing.*)

No nos manda **nada nunca**.
⎧ *He never sends us anything.*
⎩ (= *He never sends us nothing.*)

USAGE OF FORMS

Some affirmative and negative words have different functions even though the forms remain unaltered. They are presented here according to their usage.

Usage: With animate and/or inanimate nouns as limiting
  adjectives and pronominal indefinites, subject and object[1]

alguno,-a **algún**	*someone* *any* *some (one of* *a group)* *either one* *(of two)*	**ninguno,-a** **ningún**	*no* *no one, none* *not anyone* *not any* *none (one of* *a group)* *neither one* *(of two)*
algunos,-as	*some* *several (of* *a group)*	**ningunos,-as**	*no* *none (of a* *group)*
alguien	*somebody* *someone*	**nadie**	*nobody* *no one* *not any one*
algo	*something*	**nada**	*nothing* *not anything*

Alguno and **ninguno** function either as limiting adjectives or pronominal
indefinites. They agree in gender and number with the nouns they modify or
substitute.

Que alguno (de ellos) se encargue
  hoy del correo.
—¡Pero nadie quiere!

Let someone (of them) take care of the
  mail today.
—*But no one wants to do it!*

Preséntame a alguna de tus dos
  primas.
—No te va a interesar ninguna.

Introduce me to one of your two cousins.
—*Neither will interest you.*

¿Has encontrado alguna casa que te
  guste?
—No, no he encontrado ninguna.

Have you found any house that you
  like?
—*No, I haven't found any.*

¿Es cierto que se han muerto algunos
  animales?
—No, no se ha muerto ninguno.

Is it true that some animals have died?
—*No, none has died.*

¿Has recibido algunos informes
  sobre su conducta?
—No, no he recibido ninguno.

Have you received any reports about
  his conduct?
—*No, I haven't received any.*

---

[1] As pronominal nouns in object position the indefinites **alguno, ninguno** (when referring to human
nouns) and **alguien, nadie**, require the personal **a**: **Mandaron a alguno (a alguien)** = *They sent
someone (somebody)*; **No mandaron a ninguno (a nadie)** = *They did not send anyone (anybody).*

A shortened form **algún/ningún** occurs as modifier before masculine singular nouns. This shortened form usually implies selection, i.e., it refers to the known subject of a group (animate or inanimate), or at least considered as known from the speaker's point of view.

No hay ningún estudiante (mío) aquí?	*Isn't there any student (of mine) here?*
—No, no hay ninguno.	*—No, there is none (no one).*

¿Por qué no llamas a algún pariente tuyo?	*Why don't you call some relative of yours?*
—Porque no tengo ninguno en la ciudad.	*—Because I have none in the city.*

The plural **ningunos (-as)** is rarely used, except with nouns of plural meaning, (such as, **pantalones**=*pants*; **tijeras**=*scissors*; etc.). Otherwise, the singular form is usually preferred.

¿Trajiste las revistas?	*Did you bring the magazines?*
—No traje ninguna.	*—I didn't bring any.*

¿No tienes ningunos pantalones más de vestir?	*Don't you have any dressier pants?*
—No, no tengo ningunos.	*—No, I don't have any.*

When **alguno** is placed immediately after a singular noun, it takes the negative meaning of **ninguno**, with emphatic connotations.

No tienen derecho alguno.	*They don't have any right.*
derecho ninguno	*(They have no right.)*
ningún derecho	

No toman precaución alguna.	*They don't take any precautions.*
precaución ninguna	*(They take no precautions.)*
ninguna precaución	

Alguien and **nadie** are used only in reference to human nouns and function as pronominal indefinites. These two forms do not imply selection or a definite reference; they do not refer to a known subject of a group as **alguno/ninguno**.

Alguno (de ellos) llamó por teléfono.	*Someone (of them) phoned.*
Ninguno (de Uds.) puede ir.	*Neither one (of you) can go.*
Alguien llamó, no sé quién.	*Someone phoned, I don't know who.*

BUT:

Nadie puede ir.	*No one (nobody, not anyone) can go.*

While a sentence with **alguno/ninguno** may be expanded by adding **de ellos, de ustedes**, etc., this is not possible with **alguien/nadie**.

   Algo and **nada** are used only in reference to inanimate beings and function here as pronominal indefinites. As **alguien/nadie**, these forms do not imply selection or a definite reference either. **Alguna cosa** is synonymous with **algo** in this context.

Necesito **algo** (**alguna cosa**) para abrir la puerta.
I need something (in order) to open the door.

No necesito **nada** para abrir la puerta.
I don't need anything to open the door.

Debe estar planeando **algo** (**alguna cosa**).
He must be planning something.

No debe estar planeando **nada**.
He must not be planning anything.

As a pronominal indefinite **algo** may be modified by an adjective, in which case it takes the masculine singular form **algo**.

Me dijo algo interesante.
She told me something interesting.

Me regaló algo muy práctico.
She gave me something very practical.

Usage: In reference to quantity of inanimate subjects, as adverbials of quantity

---

un poco de
algo de   +   Noun { a little / some / a few }

nada de   +   Noun { no / not any }

un poco   { a little / some }

nada   { nothing / not anything }

Un poco de and **algo de** are synonymous in this context. They are usually used as quantifiers with mass nouns (i.e., nouns that cannot occur with numerals), although they may also occur with count nouns. The negative counterpart is **nada de**.

Tráeme **un poco de** (**algo de**) azúcar.
Bring me some (a little) sugar.

No me traigas **nada de** azúcar.
Don't bring me any sugar.
Bring me no sugar.

Por favor, sírveme **un poco de** (**algo de**) papas.
Please serve me some (a few) potatoes.

Por favor, no me sirvas **nada de** papas.
Please don't serve me any potatoes.
Please serve me no potatoes.

Un poco does not have the partitive sense of **un poco de/algo de**. Its negative counterpart is **nada**.

Quiero **un poco**.
I want a little (some, a few).

No quiero **nada**.
{ *I don't want anything.*
{ *I want nothing.*

Usage: With reference to the degree of intensity, as adverbials of intensity

---

algo + Adjective $\begin{cases} somewhat \\ a\ bit\ (of) \\ rather \end{cases}$

nada $\begin{cases} not\ldots at\ all \\ anything\ at\ all \end{cases}$

Verb + **algo**   *a little*
    (something)

Algo is also used as an intensifier to describe the degree of intensity of a quality or the manner in which an action is carried out. The negative counterpart is **nada**.

Esta persona es algo interesante.
This person is somewhat (a bit, rather) interesting.

Esta persona no es nada interesante.
This person is not interesting at all.

Sus ojos son algo verdes.
Her eyes are somewhat green.

Sus ojos no son nada verdes.
Her eyes are not green at all.

Functioning here as adverbs, **algo** and **nada** modify the adjective, which in turn agrees with the noun.

Creo que entiende algo.
I think that he understands a little (something).

Creo que no entiende nada.
I think that he doesn't understand anything at all.

Bebe algo.
He drinks a little.

No bebe nada.
He doesn't drink at all.

Para nada may be used for more emphasis.

No bebe para nada.

He doesn't drink at all.

Usage: With reference to the action or quality of a subject which is extended to another

---

también   *also*

tampoco $\begin{cases} neither \\ not\ldots either \end{cases}$

También is used to express an action or a quality which is extended from one subject to another. The negative counterpart is **tampoco**.

Ustedes van y nosotros también (vamos).
You are going and we are also going. (and so do we)

Ustedes no van y nosotros tampoco (vamos).
You are not going, and we are not going either. (and neither do we)

Pedro es egoísta y también su
hermano. (es egoísta)
Pedro is selfish and his brother is also
selfish. (and so is his brother)

Pedro no es egoísta y su hermano
tampoco. (es egoísta)
Pedro is not selfish; neither is his brother.
(selfish)

Tampoco is sometimes used idiomatically instead of **no** in a sequence of negative
responses.

¿Sabes tú dónde están?
—No, no lo sé.

Do you know where they are?
—No, I don't know.

¿Y cuándo regresarán?
—Tampoco (sé).

And when will they come back?
—I don't know either.

Usage: In reference to place, as locative adverbs

Preposition +	**alguna parte** **algún lugar** sitio lado }	*somewhere*	**ninguna parte** *nowhere,* **ningún lugar** *not anywhere* etc.	

Iremos a alguna parte.
We will go somewhere.

No iremos a ninguna parte.
We won't go anywhere.
We'll go nowhere.

Pasaremos la noche en algún sitio.
We'll spend the night somewhere.

No pasaremos la noche en ningún
sitio.
We won't spend the night anywhere.

Lo encontré por algún lado.
I found it somewhere.

No lo encontré por ningún lado.
I couldn't find it anywhere.

The choice of preposition (**a, en, por**, etc.) will depend on the context. (See
Prepositions, page 315.)

Usage: In reference to time, as an adverbial of time

siempre	*always*		
alguna vez	*sometime*		
una vez	*once*	**nunca**	*never*
algún día	*someday*	**jamás**	*(not) ever,*
a veces	} *sometimes*		*never*
algunas veces			

Siempre sale los sábados.
He always goes out on Saturdays.

Algunas veces sale los sábados.
Sometimes he goes out on Saturdays.

Nunca (jamás) sale los sábados.
He never goes out on Saturday.

Una vez salió el sábado.
Once he went out on Saturday.

Nunca (jamás) salió el sábado.
He never did go out on Saturday.

A veces ha salido los sábados.
Sometimes he has gone out on Saturdays.

Nunca (jamás) ha salido los sábados.
He has never gone out on Saturdays.

Una vez normally refers to a completed action in the past; **algún día** normally refers to future time, while the other forms may be used in reference to any perspective of time depending on the context. The negative counterparts that correspond to all of these indefinites are either **nunca** or **jamás**. **Jamás** is usually a more emphatic negative than **nunca**. For a more emphatic negation:

1. **nunca jamás** may co-occur in this order:

Nunca jamás lo aceptaré bajo tales circunstancias.
Never ever will I accept it under these circumstances.

2. either **nunca** or **jamás** may co-occur with a phrase such as **en la vida**; **en mi vida**, etc.

Nunca en la vida diría tal cosa.
Never in my life would I say such a thing.

Jamás en su vida se lo imaginó.
Never in his life did he imagine such a thing.

¡Nunca jamás en tu vida lo vuelvas a hacer!
Don't you ever in your life do it again!

Nunca and **jamás** may correspond to the English *ever* if a negation is implied. **Nunca** is used if the negation is on the quality:

Está ahora más joven que nunca.
She looks now younger than ever.
(= She never looked younger than now.)

Jamás is used if the negation is on the action:

Se ve más joven ahora, como jamás se ha visto.
She looks younger now than she has ever looked.

Es la mejor escultura que el museo jamás ha adquirido.
It is the best sculpture that the museum has ever acquired.

Usage: With reference to the manner in which an action is done, as an adverbial of manner.

---

de algún modo	*somehow*	
de alguna manera	*(in) some way*	

de ningún modo	*in no way* / *by no means*
de ninguna manera	*not at all* / *not in any way*

Lo haré de algún modo.
       de alguna manera.
I will do it somehow.
       in some way.

No lo haré de ningún modo.
       de ninguna manera.
By no means will I do it.

In these expressions **modo** and **manera** are synonymous. In the negatives, the emphasis is on the negation, not just a mere denial of facts.

THE NEGATIVE CONNECTOR *NI*

ni $\begin{cases} not \ldots either \\ not\ even \end{cases}$

ni . . . ni $\begin{cases} neither \ldots nor \\ not \ldots either \ldots or \end{cases}$

Ni is used:

1. as a link word to connect negative statements the same way as **y** connects affirmative ones:

No la quiero ni la necesito.
El cambio de gobierno no produjo ni resultados positivos ni indicios de prosperidad.

I don't love her nor do I need her.
The change of government has brought about neither positive results nor indications of prosperity.

2. as a link word instead of **o** = *or* to connect two clauses embodying a negative or restrictive meaning:

Es muy difícil comprender toda su situación ni encontrar una solución adecuada.

It is very difficult to understand his whole situation or to find an adequate solution.

3. before a noun phrase corresponding to the English *not even*:

Ni su jefe tiene tanta influencia.

No tiene ni la más remota idea.
Ni por un momento lo dudes.
No me dijo ni una sola palabra.

¿Cuántos de ellos te visitaron?
—Ni uno.

Not even her boss has so much influence.
He doesn't even have the vaguest idea.
Don't you doubt it even for a moment.
She didn't even say one single word to me.
How many of them visited you?
—*Not (even) one.*

Ni + siquiera may be used for a more emphatic negation:

Ni siquiera me interesa.
Ni siquiera su jefe tiene tanta influencia.

I am not even interested.
Not even her boss has so much influence.

4. **ni que** + imperfect subjunctive is used as an exclamative of concession implying a negative conclusion:

¡Ni que fuera millonario!　　　　　　*As if I were a millionaire!*
　(¡y no lo soy!)　　　　　　　　　　*(and am not one!)*

Ni ... ni is used to negate two alternatives the same way as **o ... o** = *either ... or* would present them as an affirmative statement.

Estoy seguro que vendrán o su padre　　Estoy seguro que no vendrán ni su
　o su madre.　　　　　　　　　　　　padre ni su madre.
I am sure that either her father or　　*I'm sure that neither her father nor her*
mother will come.　　　　　　　　　*mother will come.*

(The tendency is for the verb to be in the plural, although the singular is also possible.)

WORD ORDER OF NEGATIVES OTHER THAN *NO*

The word order of negative words other than **no** is determined by the following restrictions:

1.

no + Verb +	Negative Word (except **no**)

No vino nadie (ninguno).　　　　　　*Nobody (no one) came.*
No espero que me dé nada.　　　　　*I don't expect her to give me anything.*
No necesito nada de café.　　　　　　*I don't need any coffee.*
No apruebo nada su conducta.　　　　*I don't approve of his behavior at all.*
No irás tampoco con ellos.　　　　　*You won't go with them either.*
No lo puedo encontrar nunca por　　　*I can never find it anywhere.*
　ningún lado.
No me han invitado a su casa nunca　　*They have never invited me to their*
　(jamás).　　　　　　　　　　　　*house.*
No trabaja ni deja que otros　　　　　*She neither works nor lets anyone else*
　trabajen.　　　　　　　　　　　　*work.*

The negative **no** must always precede the verb, if the other negatives follow it. The presence of **no** serves to emphasize more the negation.

2.

Negative Word (except **no**) + Verb

Nada necesito.　　　　　　　　　　*I don't need anything.*
Tampoco irás con ellos.　　　　　　*You will not go with them either.*

Por ningún lado lo pude encontrar.	*I couldn't find it anywhere.*
Nunca (jamás) me han invitado a su casa.	*They have never invited me to their house.*

This pattern of word order makes the negation less emphatic than the previous one. English may also make the same contrast by using either stress, intonation, or word order when permitted: **Nunca los llamo** = *I never call them* versus **No los llamo nunca** = *I* don't *call them* ever OR *I never call them.*

Several negative words may co-occur in one sentence, according to the following word order restrictions:

3.

Negative Word(s) (except **no**)	+	Verb	+	Negative Word(s) (except **no**)

Ninguno de ellos quiere ir tampoco.	*None of them wants to go either.*
Ninguno dijo nada.	*Nobody said anything.*
Tampoco nos escribe nunca.	*Neither does he ever write to us.*
Ni siquiera llamará a nadie.	*She won't even call anyone.*

Several negatives—except **no**—may follow the verb:

Nadie quiere ir tampoco a ningún lado.	*Nobody wants to go anywhere anyway.*
Ninguno opina nada nunca.	*No one gives any opinion ever.*

or may precede the verb:

Ni nadie tampoco me lo dijo nunca.	*No one ever said anything to me anyway.*
Ni ninguno de ellos jamás me habla de nada.	*No one of them talks to me about anything ever.*

NEGATIVE WORDS WITHOUT NEGATIVE MEANING

Certain negative words—**nadie, ninguno, nada, nunca, jamás**—are occasionally used without necessarily having a negative meaning.

1. In comparative constructions:

Habla más que nadie (ninguno).	*He talks more than anybody else.*
Es la persona más intrigante que jamás he conocido.	*He is the most intriguing person that I have ever met*

2. In exclamative expressions where a question is implied:

¡Habrá sido nadie tan ingenuo!	*Has anyone been so naive!*
¡Se ha hecho jamás tal cosa!	*Has anyone ever done such a thing!*
¡Hay nada más ridículo!	*Is there anything so ridiculous!*

3. In interrogative expressions where a negative answer is expected:

¿Se le ha ocurrido a Ud. nada igual?   *Has anything like it ever occurred to you?*

4. In affirmative statements where a negation is implied:

Es imposible conseguir a nadie.   *It is impossible to find anybody.*
Es inútil hacer nada.   *It is useless to do anything.*

5. After **sin, apenas, ni, antes de**:

Se fue sin despedirse de nadie.   *He left without saying good-bye to anyone.*

Apenas hizo nada.   *He scarcely did anything.*
Ni tú ni nadie aquí saben lo que   *Neither you nor anyone here knows what they are saying.*
dicen.
Ninguno entrará antes de que   *No one will enter before the police arrives.*
llegue la policía.

THE NEGATIVE *NO*

In Spanish, affirmative statements whether declarative or interrogative are trans-formed into negatives by simply adding the negative adverbial **no** before the entire verb phrase that the speaker wishes to deny.[1] Thus, **no** precedes **haber** or the auxiliary in compound verbal phrases. English uses one of the following three constructions depending on whether the verbal phrase is a simple tense, a compound tense, a **verb + INF**, or a **verb + -ndo** form. In the case of compound tenses English places the negative *not* between the auxiliary and the participle.

$$\textbf{no} + \begin{pmatrix} \text{Object} \\ \text{Pronoun(s)} \end{pmatrix} + \text{Verb Phrase} \qquad \text{Auxiliary} \quad \begin{matrix} do\ not/n't \\ not/n't \\ not \end{matrix} + \text{Verb Phrase} + \begin{pmatrix} \text{Object} \\ \text{Pronoun(s)} \end{pmatrix}$$

El profesor no quiere malos alumnos.   *The teacher does not want poor students.*
¿No preferías aquéllos?   *Didn't you prefer those?*
La función no ha comenzado.   *The performance has not begun.*
Cuando salimos no estaba nevando.   *When we left it was not snowing.*
Su propuesta no fue aceptada.   *His proposal was not accepted.*
¿No están aburridos aquí?   *Aren't you bored here?*
No deben llegar tarde.   *You must not arrive late.*
Comete un error en no responder a   *He is making a mistake by not responding to the accusations.*
las acusaciones.

---

[1] Note the difference in meaning between: **Comete un error en no responder a las acusaciones**= *He is making a mistake by not responding to the accusations* and **No comete un error en responder a las acusaciones**= *He is not making a mistake by responding to the accusations* or **No comete un error en no responder a las acusaciones**= *He is not making a mistake by not responding to the accusations.*

In Spanish the only items that can be placed between the negative and the verb phrase are object pronouns (direct, indirect, reflexive) when required.

No les dije que vinieran.	*I didn't tell them to come.*
Parecen iguales pero no lo son.	*They seem alike but they are not.*
¿No se la has dado aún?	*Haven't you given it to her yet?*
Aún no se ha dormido.	*He hasn't fallen asleep yet.*

Although a verb phrase previously expressed is omitted in a following clause, it is actually implicit, so the word order remains unaltered.

Han tratado a los prisioneros como animales, no (los han tratado) como seres humanos.	*They have treated the prisoners like animals, not like human beings.*
Me lo había enviado a mí, no (se lo había enviado) a ella.	*She had sent it to me, not to her.*

With some verb phrases formed by verb+infinitive in Spanish, **no** may sometimes precede the infinitive form, thus restricting the negation to a particular action.

Decidió no llamar.	*She decided not to call.*
Ha preferido no callarse.	*He has preferred not to remain silent.*
Logró no llegar demasiado tarde.	*He managed not to arrive too late.*

Occasionally the meaning may vary:

El anuncio puede no ser oficial.	*The announcement may not be official. (=it is possible that the announcement is not official, or the announcement does not need to be official)*

BUT:

El anuncio no puede ser oficial.	*The announcement cannot be official.*

English makes the same contrast in meaning either by rewording the statement or by stress and intonation. If the verb phrase is omitted but is implicit within the context, the negative **no** usually follows the concept it negates.

¿Harías el viaje con nosotros? —Sin suficiente dinero, no.	*Would you take the trip with us? —Not without enough money.*
¿Le digo que pase? —Sin antes averiguar qué quiere, no.	*Shall I tell him to come in? —Not without first finding out what he wants.*
El calor me abruma. —A mí, no.	*The heat overwhelms me. —Not me.*

The negative **no** may precede if the speaker wishes to take the emphasis away from the negation and wants to express some reservation.

¿Vendrán todos? —Las niñas no.	*Will they all come? —Not the girls. (=the girls definitely not)*

BUT: —No las niñas	—*Not the girls.* (=*all except the girls*)
El ruído me molesta. —A mí, no.	*The noise bothers me.* —*Not me.* (=*it doesn't bother me at all*)
BUT: —No a mí.	—*Not me.* (=*it really doesn't bother me.*)
¿Estudias mucho? —Para esta clase, no.	*Do you study a lot?* —*For this class hardly ever.*
BUT: —No para esta clase.	—*Hardly ever for this class.*

English also makes this contrast either by word-order, re-wording, or intonation. Since in Spanish the negative **no** always precedes a verb phrase, whether mentioned or implicit from the context, there is no equivalent for the English negative construction with *no* + nominal.

Make no promises. (=*Do not make any promises.*)	No hagas promesas.
He would offer me no other alternative. (=*He would not offer me . . .*)	No me ofrecía ninguna otra alternativa.
She is no younger than her husband. (=*She is not any younger than . . .*)	No es más joven que su marido.

Other uses of the negative **no**

Apart from its main function of transforming affirmative statements into negatives, **no** is also used as follows:

1. As a particle to introduce a negative response, just as **sí** would introduce an affirmative response:

¿Viven Uds. en San Antonio? —No, no vivimos en San Antonio.	*Do you live in San Antonio?* —*No, we don't live in San Antonio.*

2. In exclamations of interrogative form:

¡Qué no daría yo por ir a Europa este verano!	*What wouldn't I give to go to* *Europe this summer!*
¡Qué no diría tu mujer si lo supiera!	*What would your wife say if she* *ever found out!*

3. Redundantly after **hasta**, **a menos que**, **sin que**, to enforce the negation more:

No voy hasta que no me invite personalmente.	*I'm not going until he invites me* *personally.*
No llames al menos que no te pida perdón.	*Don't you call her unless she* *apologizes to you.*
No viajaré sin que no tenga todas mis reservaciones en orden.	*I will not travel without all my* *reservations in order.*

EMPHATIC NEGATIVE EXPRESSIONS

Spanish as English uses certain words and phrases which are not in themselves negatives but which function as such according to a given context. They usually occur with **no** for emphasis in the negation, instead of a negative word.

No había **un alma** (nadie) en el parque.	*There wasn't a soul (anybody) in the park.*
No pude entender **palabra** (nada) de lo que dijo.	*I couldn't understand a word (anything) of what he said.*
No me importa **un comino** (nada).	*I don't give a darn.*

In Spanish, furthermore, certain expressions (with no negative meaning) may be used without a negative marker to have an emphatic negative effect.

En mi vida he visto tal cosa.	*Never in my life have I seen such a thing.*
En el mundo hay otro igual.	*There is just no other one like it in the world.*
En toda la noche pude dormir.	*I couldn't sleep all night.*
En todo el invierno ha nevado tanto como hoy.	*During the whole winter it hasn't snowed so much as today.*
¿Le prestarás el dinero?	*Will you lend her the money?*
—**En absoluto**.	*—Absolutely not.*

In Spanish the occurrence of **no** or any other negative word with these expressions is optional, while in English it is obligatory.

INDEX